THE HISTORY OF THE NAZI PARTY: 1919–1933

THE *History* OF THE NAZI PARTY: 1919-1933

DIETRICH ORLOW

UNIVERSITY OF PITTSBURGH PRESS

SBN 8229–3183–4
Library of Congress Catalog Card Number: LC 69-20026
COPYRIGHT © 1969, UNIVERSITY OF PITTSBURGH PRESS
Manufactured in the United States of America

To Maria

Preface

This book deals with the organizational and administrative history of the German Nazi Party during the years of its rise to political power. It is both a contribution to the history of the Weimar Republic and, in a larger sense, an analysis of the internal development of a totalitarian political party in the context of a pluralistic society. I have attempted to avoid writing merely a history of the administration of the Nazi Party. Instead, the study represents a conscious attempt to interrelate the more visible, propagandistic activities of the NSDAP with the less conspicuous organizational and structural developments in the years 1919 to 1933. The basic reason for this approach is my belief, presented in more detail in the Introduction, that totalitarian parties, and particularly the Nazi Party, are unique political organisms whose organizational and programmatic developments alike are institutionalizations of certain unchanging assumptions about interpersonal relations in a mass society. The organizational history of the NSDAP from 1919 to 1933 is the story of an artificial society whose members had deliberately disengaged themselves from the values of the pluralist society in which they lived. Instead, the membership — in particular the leadership corps of the NSDAP — was united and animated primarily by a belief in the totalitarian myth of its leader and a hatred of the plural system it had set out to destroy. This monolithic concept of its role in history was the party's greatest political and organizational asset, but at times this very asset brought the party to the brink of disaster.

A few obvious omissions and commissions in the book may need explanation. The study concerns only the organizational history of the Nazi Party in Germany itself. It is true, of course, that in the late 1920's Hitler controlled the Austrian party as well, but developments outside of Germany played no major part in his and the NSDAP's politico-organizational conceptions throughout the *Kampfzeit* or "years of struggle," as the period 1919 to 1933 was called in the party. This book is based largely on unpublished sources, most of which are available to scholars both on microfilm and in the original. However, since the bulk of the original documents has been returned to Germany while the microfilms are readily available in the United States, I have usually cited the microfilm location of those documents that are readily accessible on microfilm. Finally, in the citations of newspaper articles, there are some deliberate inconsistencies. In general, I have followed the usual practice of not citing titles of newspaper articles, but on occasion I felt that the wording of a title was a significant piece of evidence in itself. In these cases, full citations are given.

Acknowledgments

This book could not have been written without the generous support and aid of a number of individuals and institutions. Both the College of William and Mary and the American Philosophical Society have provided generous financial support on a number of occasions. A year's stay as a Fellow in the Duke University–University of North Carolina Cooperative Program in the Humanities provided nine months' freedom from teaching duties to write and research.

In the course of doing research for this book I have used the resources of a number of libraries and archives in Germany and the United States and I would like to acknowledge the unfailing assistance of their various staffs. I would like to single out particularly Miss Lucille Petterson, until 1968 the director of the Berlin Document Center, Mr. Robert Wolfe at the National Archives, Professor Arnold H. Price at the Library of Congress, Dr. Werner Jochmann at the Forschungsstelle für die Geschichte des Nationalsozialismus in Hamburg, Dr. Weis at the Bayerisches Geheimes Staatsarchiv, and the staffs of the Bundesarchiv in Koblenz and the Institut für Zeitgeschichte in Munich. In addition, I would like to thank Dr. Albert Krebs, the Gauleiter of Hamburg from 1926–1928, for according me the privilege of interviewing him.

Portions of the manuscript also had the benefit of a critical reading by a distinguished scholar, Dean Reginald H. Phelps of Harvard University, and I would like to thank him for his criticism. My former teacher at the University of Michigan, Professor Gerhard Weinberg, has continued his unfailing kindness to me in a number of ways and this too I would like to acknowledge publicly. Needless to say, the responsibility for any shortcomings in the book is entirely mine.

Finally, my wife not only tolerated me during the writing of the book, but had the courage to read, criticize, and type the entire manuscript. It was a performance well beyond the call of duty.

D.O.

Syracuse, New York
September 1969

Contents

THE HISTORY OF THE NAZI PARTY: 1919–1933

Introduction

The National Socialist German Workers' Party (*Nationalsozialistische Deutsche Arbeiterpartei*, NSDAP) was a fascist,[1] totalitarian political party that was born and nurtured in the atmosphere of the "fascist epoch" that characterized Europe, and particularly Germany, after World War I.[2] There can be no doubt that this immense conflict represents a major crisis in recent European history. However it is expressed — in psychological, historical or political science terms — the First World War destroyed much of the societal foundation that had supported the various political systems in Europe more or less unchanged since 1815.[3] Specifically in Germany, the war caused not only the downfall of the royal and imperial dynasties, but also (temporarily at least) the eclipse of the stable, authoritarian, hierarchical society which the crowned figures had both epitomized and guaranteed. The war did not end sociopolitical life in Germany, of course; indeed, objectively, the democratic Weimar Republic was a far "better" political framework. But these were not times of objective appraisal. For some Germans (and later for many), the Weimar Republic was not an acceptable successor to Wilhelminian authoritarianism. To be sure, virtually all Germans had welcomed the Republic when it brought peace in 1918, but many began to despise it when the name of the Republic became associated with the concepts of defeat, infla-

1. For a summary of the fascist typology see Ernst Nolte, *Der Faschismus in seiner Epoche* (Munich, 1963), p. 48.
2. *Ibid.*, p. 34.
3. *Ibid.*, p. 26; and Eugen Weber, "Introduction," in Hans Rogger and Eugen Weber, eds., *The European Right: A Historical Profile* (Berkeley, Calif., 1965), pp. 7–9.

1

tion, and political dissension. The dissatisfied elements constituted a built-in Achilles' heel for the young Republic. As politically articulate individuals, they were a part of the "people" on whose authority a democracy must ultimately rest. Yet, by rejecting the democratic system in its entirety as a basis of political behavior norms, they lived as atomized individuals in a world of self-created political and social disengagement.[4] They lacked a real bond of cohesion with the pluralist society in which they lived.[5]

In the NSDAP many found an artificial substitute society. In joining the party, members (and even more, the leaders) of the NSDAP ceased to function emotionally in the real world. They lived in the Weimar framework only to destroy it; their positive emotional and social response was to a future society whose microcosmic prototype was the NSDAP.[6] Hitler himself, in the early days of the party, frequently compared the rise of the party to the growth of Christianity, and the most popular activity of party members was the celebration of the party's annual "German Christmas" parties. Here the synthetic society lived to the fullest its life of illusion; closed to outsiders, the "NSDAP family" celebrated its own feast day as a band of the righteous in the midst of alien customs and peoples.[7]

The organizational development of any political party is guided primarily by its corps of party workers and functionaries, that is, a group of party members to whom Maurice Duverger has applied the term "militants." [8] These members constitute the most committed and devoted followers in any party, but totalitarian parties demand much more of their militants than merely loyal service. In accepting a position in the Nazi party leadership corps, the militant entered the elite

4. Zevedei Barbu, *Democracy and Dictatorship* (New York, 1956), p. 123.

5. William Kornhauser, *The Politics of Mass Society* (Glencoe, Ill., 1959), p. 47; and Hannah Arendt, *The Origins of Totalitarianism* (Cleveland, 1958), p. 352.

6. Arendt, *Origins*, p. 371.

7. For Hitler's comparison of the party and the Christian church, see the reports on his speeches in Nü–Fü, "N/No. 54" and "N/No. 55," 4 Feb. and 21 March 1927, BGStA, M.A. 101251. For a good description of a Nazi Christmas party see Adalbert Gimbel, "So kam es," pp. 59–60 (MS, 1940), HA, roll 28, folder 534.

8. Maurice Duverger, *Political Parties*, tr. Barbara and Robert North (New York, 1954), pp. 110 ff.

group of an artificial, substitute society and accepted its code of behavioral norms. He submitted himself voluntarily to the new rules. There is little doubt that, at least until the Reichstag (German legislature) elections of 1930 (when bandwagon motives clearly drove many members and officials to the party), the primary reasons for joining the leadership corps of the NSDAP were sociopsychological ones: in the absence of police terror[9] and with the prospect of few (though not always negligible) material rewards, the NSDAP official voluntarily subjected himself to the social and emotional strait-jacket of the totalitarian mind-set.

What happens to the individual in the process of totalitarianization? Basically, he accepts a specific subjective view of political and social reality, a view that might be termed an extreme form of political myth. Political myths are not unique to totalitarianism, but this type, a totalizing and reflexive myth, is. Political myths are conscious or subconscious devices used to explain and give emotional meaning to social experience toward the conscious or subconscious end of justifying or rationalizing action toward political goals (in the case of an individual), or toward obtaining mass political support for a particular political party or movement (in the case of a group). Their political role is thus largely that of converters: they enable "political man" to personalize political abstractions and thus make them individually meaningful.[10] The nature of the prevailing myths in a well-functioning pluralistic or hierarchical political system is usually a milder form of oversimplification ("George Washington was the father of our country"; "We are fighting in South Vietnam to defend democracy there"). But a society in disequilibrium or psychosociological disengagement is a potential seedbed for the most radical form

---

9. Physical terror, one of the essential characteristics of totalitarianism discussed by Carl J. Friedrich and Zbigniew K. Brzezinski, *Totalitarian Dictatorship and Autocracy* (Cambridge, Mass., 1965), p. 10, is not a significant factor in the internal life of the Nazi party before 1933. The most severe sentence a party court could impose was expulsion from the party, i.e., exclusion of the member from the synthetic society of the NSDAP and forcible return to what was to him the chaotic void of the real world.

10. See, for example, Alfred McClung Lee, "The Concept of System," *Social Research*, XXXII (Autumn 1965), 229-31; and Kenneth Boulding, *The Meaning of the Twentieth Century* (New York, 1964), pp. 161–64.

of political myth, a type which might be termed a "totalizing and reflexive myth." This form of political distortion reduces all past, present, and future events to a binary division and simultaneously imparts a moral value to both of the factors in the set. Indeed, the moral values are reflexive; that is, they define each other. The myth knows only "them" and "us," and "we" are morally good, historically correct; "they" are morally evil, historically anachronistic. In the case of the Nazi Party the factors in the set were clearly Aryan (German) and Jew;[11] what ideology the party possessed quickly reduced itself to a definition of Aryan-German as total good and Jew as total evil.

In ascribing a moral judgment to all actions of the reflexive parts of the set, the myth also subjects to totalitarian controls all actions and beliefs on the part of those accepting the myth. It completely politicizes the individual, that is, totalizes his life. Once he has internalized the myth, the division between public and private actions disappears. The myth provides an interpretive framework for all past happenings and a guide for all future action.[12] With relentless logic, the totalizing and reflexive myth leads the individual or group that has internalized it to substitute a mythical reality for the empirically perceivable world around him.[13] Accepting the myth constitutes the "creeping rape *(schleichende Vergewaltigung)* of [a] human being through perversion of [his] thinking and social life" — which Hans Buchheim finds to be a "true characteristic" of a totalitarian regime.[14]

The myth itself is already a personalizing force in the political life of a mass society, but it receives even more fanatic adherents when it is crystallized in the will and the actions of a leader-figure with great personal magnetism. Adolf Hitler was clearly such a leader. He

---

11. Norman Cohn, "The Myth of the Jewish World Conspiracy," *Commentary*, XLI (June 1966), 35–37.

12. The similarity of the totalitarian's mind-set to that of the religious believer has been frequently noted. See Duverger, *Parties*, p. 122; Weber, "Introduction," p. 21; and, particularly, Ernst Niekisch, *Hitler—ein deutsches Verhängnis* (Berlin, 1931). Cf. also the section on pre-industrial religious sects in E. J. Hobsbawn, *Primitive Rebels* (New York, 1959), pp. 130 ff.

13. Hans Toch, *The Social Psychology of Social Movements* (New York, 1965), pp. 69–70.

14. Hans Buchheim, *Totale Herrschaft—Wesen und Merkmale* (Munich, 1962), pp. 14–15.

both believed the myth and identified himself with it. He regarded himself as an agent of history, the instrument of fate through whom "good" would triumph over "evil." In this role he was solely responsible to history and to history alone; his life was a service to fate.[15]

Hitler's unshakable certainty of his life mission complemented the rootlessness of many of the atomized, disengaged, and frustrated elements in Weimar Germany. World War I had forced each future Nazi Party functionary to live as a politically articulate individual in a democratic mass society. However, the politics of equilibrium of that society were unable to fulfill even a minimum of his politico-emotional needs. Consequently, in a decision often motivated by irrational fear of the real world around him, he voluntarily accepted the totalizing and reflexive myth extolled by the NSDAP and personified in the person of its leader as the basis of his political (and thereafter total)[16] behavior. He had now committed a revolutionary, political act: he joined a group living by its own norms that had pledged itself to impose its view of reality on the society[17] in whose midst it was still an insignificant, alienated minority.

The twin bases of the Nazis' political success were skillful propaganda and effective organization.[18] The two aspects of political activity were thoroughly complementary and interdependent; dynamically reinforcing each other, they eventually destroyed the political fabric of Weimar Germany. Propaganda reached the politically disengaged masses and reengaged some of them as party members and officials. The latter in turn became functioning units of the party's propaganda and organizing apparatus so that the cycle started all over again.[19]

15. The role that imagined superhuman laws of history play in the mind-set of the totalitarian leader is well described in Alex Inkeles, "The Totalitarian Mystique: Some Impressions of the Dynamics of the Totalitarian Society," in Carl J. Friedrich, ed., *Totalitarianism* (New York, 1964), pp. 87–108. See also Buchheim, *Herrschaft*, p. 53.

16. Sigmund Neumann, *Die Parteien der Weimarer Republik* (Stuttgart, 1965), p. 73.

17. Anton Lingg, *Die Verwaltung der Nationalsozialistischen Deutschen Arbeiterpartei* (2d ed.; Munich, 1940), p. 5.

18. Arendt, *Origins*, p. 361. See also Eugen Hadamovsky, *Propaganda und nationale Macht* (Oldenburg, 1933).

19. Adolf Hitler, *Mein Kampf* (Munich, 1938), I, p. 654; Arendt, *Origins*, p. 364.

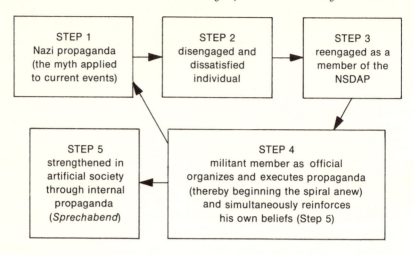

Diagrammatically this process might be sketched as shown above.[20]

The interconnection of the party's propaganda and the party's myth is fairly obvious and has often been studied. The mythical dichotomy of Jew and German was the basic point of every Nazi speech, and it is clear that this was not the result of tactical considerations. Rather, the myth became a very personal behavior guide. Even Hitler, by no means oblivious to the political usefulness of the myth, nevertheless was not its complete master: it was exceedingly difficult to tell at times who was slave and who was lord in the relationship.[21] Among the lower echelons the myth was clearly lord. The myth as interpreted by state and local party leaders was a crude and individual expression of personal hate and anger. Hitler might still rage against an evil system, but at the local level "evil" was simply a political caricature by the name of *Flaschenbiergustav*.[22]

The Nazis were not only effective propagandists, but also brilliant

20. It must be recognized, of course, that at least until 1930 very few of those reached by the party's propaganda actually joined the NSDAP but that is an irrelevant point here, since the organizational listing of a party concerns primarily only those who are actually members of the party or its affiliated front groups.

21. Weber, "Introduction," p. 27.

22. Hilgard Pleyer, "Politische Werbung in der Weimarer Republik" (Dissertation, Münster, 1959), pp. 172–77 gives an excellent analysis of the propagandistic interpretation of the Nazi myth in the utterings of various Nazi speakers from Hitler to local leaders. "Flaschenbiergustav" refers to the fact that the then foreign minister, Gustav Stresemann, had written his Ph.D. dissertation on the economics of the German brewery industry.

organizers.[23] And the totalizing and reflexive myth also played a major role in structuring the party's organizational framework and its administrative principles. The myth is Darwinian in its presupposition of long-term warfare between two set factors. Consequently, those engaged in the myth looked upon themselves as politician-soldiers who interpreted politics as struggle.[24] It was therefore natural that, like other totalitarian parties, the NSDAP's organization would be highly centralized and hierarchical.[25] Moreover, for the politician-soldiers, the masses were their field of battle. Since the German *Volk* (or masses) was the potential "good" of the two set factors that the Nazi Party set out to organize, the party had to adopt the most effective form of controlling and communicating within a mass society: they needed a highly bureaucratized administration.

Bureaucracies, ideally, are human computers. Their effectiveness lies precisely in their ability to systematize the work of the organization and to depersonalize the agent doing the work. The rules of procedure deliberately create a gap between the personal life and feelings of the bureaucrat and his official life as a cog in the bureaucratic machine.[26] The ideal, of course, is never attained. Numerous recent studies have shown that dictatorial control and bureaucracies usually become mutually contradictory concepts. Bureaucracies, even in political parties — that is, associations with an ideologically closely knit membership — have a way of developing their own interests and often become impregnable forces of self-concern.[27] This process of deterioration, so vividly demonstrated by the fate of the German Social Democratic Party (*Sozialdemokratische Partei Deutschlands,* SPD),[28] is usually the result of excessive personalization in the workings of the bureaucracy.

23. Neumann, *Parteien,* p. 83.

24. Karl-Dietrich Bracher, *Die Auflösung der Weimarer Republik* (3d ed., Villingen, Schwarzw., 1955), p. 112.

25. Friedrich and Brzezinski. *Totalitarian,* p. 19; Bracher, *Auflösung,* p. 120.

26. For a brief, but incisive study of bureautic functioning and rationale, see Victor A. Thompson, *Modern Organization* (New York, 1961).

27. See, for example, Peter Blau, *Dynamics of Bureaucracy* (Chicago, 1955), p. 9; and James G. March, "Some Recent Substantive and Methodological Developments in the Theory of Organizational Decision Making," in Austin Ramsey, ed., *Essays on the Behavioral Study of Politics* (Urbana, Ill., 1962), pp. 191–208.

28. This is studied in great detail in Robert Michels' classic work, *Political Parties,* tr. Eden and Cedar Paul (Glencoe, Ill., 1958).

The NSDAP successfully avoided the problem of bureaucratic ingrowth, but not by depersonalizing the relationship of bureaucratic superior and subordinate. The NSDAP combined personalization and bureaucratization in the party's organizational life. Hitler squared the circle, an achievement made possible by the operation of the myth within the organization of the party. The administrative system of "bureaucratized romanticism," as Theodor Heuss has aptly described it,[29] neither differentiated between the party functionary's role as private individual and as public person, nor did it seek to separate decision-makers from decision-administrators. Instead, as noted before, the myth created a bureaucratic functionary corps of extremely committed leader-executives who lived in their own synthetic society dominated by the totalizing and reflexive myth. In this atmosphere, an official's personal tastes in home furnishings might well have a decisive influence on his position within the hierarchy.[30] Similarly, such "normally" irrelevant factors as the physical deformities of a rival leader could become far more important in an evaluation of his status than his administrative ability.[31] As a result, while the party had a large corps of salaried employees, they were never civil servants as such: most of them were simultaneously "political leaders," active agitprops of the myth,[32] and even those who were merely clerks had internalized the myth to the extent that they were willing to make significant personal sacrifices for the propagation of the myth.[33]

In a "normal" bureaucracy this mixing of personal and bureaucratic factors should have led to endless intrigues resulting in administrative chaos and consequently a rapid loss of centralized control. In the Nazi Party, however, both the leader's personal power and the internal stability of the organization as a whole benefited in a variety of ways from the party's "bureaucratized romanticism." A Nazi official's

29. Theodor Heuss, *Hitler's Weg* (Stuttgart, 1932), p. 118.

30. Otto Dietrich, *The Hitler I Knew*, tr. Richard and Clare Winston (London, 1957), p. 189, reports that Hitler's estimation of Rudolf Hess sank perceptibly after he had inspected firsthand Hess's interior decorating.

31. A major controversy arose within the party in 1927 when Erich Koch, a provincial leader in the Ruhr, published an article in the Nazi press suggesting that Goebbels' club foot was a sign of racial impurity.

32. Lingg, *Verwaltung*, p. 77.

33. Joseph Goebbels, *Kampf um Berlin* (Munich, 1934), pp. 179–80.

usefulness was judged not merely on the basis of his day-to-day administration, but on the totality of his private and public life and of that of his ancestors and relatives. The total politicization of an NSDAP militant thus greatly multiplied the potential raw material for intrigues and innuendo campaigns among the party's subleaders. Hitler, in turn, was constantly called upon to referee these affairs.[34] Even more important (than this indirect by-product of the myth's importance for personal relations in the party's bureaucracy) was Hitler's direct, mythical status among the body of NSDAP functionaries. Clearly, comparing a man's whole life (as distinguished from his official life) with the myth ideal vastly increased the leader's possibility of direct control over his subordinates. Moreover, this possibility resulted in an increase of Hitler's absolute power, since there was no theoretical possibility of feedback.[35] Insofar as Hitler was the personification of the superhuman myth,[36] he was both changeable, individual person and unchanging absolute. In serving Hitler the myth, the Nazi official had to obey Hitler the person. This meant, in effect, that Hitler could apply his personal standards in judging his subordinates, but they could judge him in a similar manner only by questioning that he was the personification of the eternal myth. Thus his authority was abstract in theory (as a force of history), yet completely personal in practice.[37]

The personification was therefore a constant but ever-changing core of truth at the heart of the synthetic world of the Nazi militant. In this form Hitler gave the movement its reality of stability in the midst of apparent flux. Despite the constant intrigues among the subleaders and Hitler's own erratic decision-making patterns, no sizable portion of the functionary corps questioned his control of the party after 1921. The reason is again the paramount importance of the myth.

---

34. Arendt, *Origins*, p. 373, goes so far as to call the leader's referee functions the true basis of his power within the party.

35. Herbert Simon, "Notes on the Observation and Measurement of Political Power," *Journal of Politics*, XV (Nov. 1953), 506, defines "net power" as the strength of the original action minus the feedback from the subordinates affected by the action.

36. Goebbels, *Kampf*, p. 39.

37. Lingg, *Verwaltung*, pp. 55–56.

To question Hitler's authority in the NSDAP inevitably involved confronting the question of the validity of the myth itself. As the personification of the myth, Hitler's approval or disapproval of a militant's life and action was an absolute standard of myth-validity. The perverse logic of the myth allowed only the alternatives of subordination to the leader (again as personification of the myth) or leaving the movement. As long as Hitler and the myth were one concept, the Nazi militant really had no choice; rather than leave the ordered mind-set of the myth, he voluntarily submitted to an ironclad framework of personalized authority. His official and his private life found meaning only in serving Hitler as the personification of the myth.

In the final analysis, then, the totalizing and reflexive myth provided the NSDAP with an extremely high degree of both internal stability and centralization. It totally politicized the party militant and then submitted the politicized entity to the absolute approval or disapproval of Hitler's personal-impersonal will. With the leader of the party as the unchanging validity, the party militant had found both a haven of reengagement and an ever-present censoring office.[38]

38. This is illustrated by the almost total lack of success which the few dissident leaders had after they broke with the movement. Usually believing their own version of the totalizing and reflexive myth, they were unable to attract any significant following among the party militants when they presented them with the choice of "Hitler or me."

Growing Up in Bavaria*

At the beginning of 1919 a new party made its appearance on the already crowded and confused political scene in Munich, the capital city of the young Bavarian republic.[1] The establishment of the German Workers' Party (*Deutsche Arbeiterpartei,* DAP), as the new group called itself, went virtually unnoticed. The formation of new political groupings was hardly unusual in revolutionary Bavaria, and the DAP showed little promise of developing into more than yet another short-lived *Stammtisch*-creation (that is, the development of arm-chair politicians). Few contemporary observers would have predicted (even if they had noted the DAP's establishment) that this party, which lacked a program, an organizational structure, and financial resources, would in four years develop into a decisive political force among the Bavarian opponents of the Weimar Republic.

The DAP rose above its unprepossessing beginnings because Adolf Hitler chose to associate his propagandistic and organizational talents with the new party, but at the time of its establishment he had no connection with the fledgling DAP. The party was the joint creation of two men, a toolmaker, Anton Drexler, and a journalist, Karl Harrer. Since initially Harrer was the more dominant partner, the earliest political activity of the two men was organized along lines suggested by him.

*Portions of this chapter have appeared previously under the title "The Organizational History and Structure of the NSDAP, 1919–1923," in the *Journal of Modern History,* XXXVII (June 1965), 208-26.

1. For a description of the immediate postwar political scene in Munich see Georg Franz, "Munich: Birthplace and Center of the National Socialist German Workers' party," *Journal of Modern History,* XXIX (Dec. 1957), 319-34.

Harrer preferred a semi-conspiratorial discussion group to a public party as an organizational format. At his insistence membership in the group, the *Politischer Arbeiterzirkel* (Workers' Political Society), was restricted to seven.[2] The administrative structure was limited to a chairman (Harrer) and a secretary. The group met fairly frequently to discuss current political issues, with attendance restricted to the actual members, and, on occasion, their personally invited guests. The meetings followed an almost ritualistic pattern. Each time, Harrer opened the session with a lengthy lecture; afterwards the membership discussed the salient points of his talk.[3]

It soon became clear to Drexler that this type of activity and organization "did not serve much purpose."[4] Toward the end of 1918 (the Zirkel had been founded in the autumn), Drexler proposed that the Society should establish (alongside the Zirkel) a political party to publicize the group's political views, and win new members for its cause.[5] Harrer disagreed, but since most of the Zirkel's members were personal friends of Drexler, his views won the support of a majority of the membership. Harrer yielded to the wishes of the majority, and on January 5, 1919, the DAP was organized.

The formation of the DAP did not immediately establish the organizational structure of what was to become the Nazi Party. For some time the DAP existed largely on paper, while the Zirkel continued its regular meetings and thus remained the real focal point

2. Michael Lotter (in 1918, secretary of the *Zirkel*) to the Hauptarchiv of the NSDAP, 17 Oct. 1941, HA, roll 3, folder 78. (The surviving records of the Hauptarchiv have been microfilmed by the Hoover Institution. The films are organized into folders. Each folder may contain a number of documents and many of these documents are separately paginated. Unfortunately, however, the microfilms themselves are not divided into frame or flash numbers. Consequently, the citation of the roll and folder number, and, when available, a specific document page, is the most exact identification possible. For this reason any applicable page numbers will follow the document title rather than the folder number whenever HA materials are cited below.)

3. It is not clear how often the group met. Lotter speaks of meetings "once or twice a week" in his "Vortrag des Gründungsmitglieds der D.A.P. und 1. Schriftführers des politischen Arbeiterzirkels Michael Lotter am 19. Oktober 1935 vor der Sterneckergruppe im Leiberzimmer des 'Sterneckers,'" *ibid.*, p. 4, but the set of minutes in *ibid*, folder 76, documents fewer regular meetings.

4. Georg Franz-Willing, *Die Hitlerbewegung—der Ursprung, 1919–1922* (Hamburg, 1962), pp. 65–66.

5. "Vortrag des Gründungsmitglieds," p. 4, HA, roll 3, folder 78.

of early Nazi activities.[6] It was only during the spring and summer of 1919 that the party gradually eclipsed its parent organization. The DAP still had not found the courage to schedule public rallies, but Drexler and his friends invited ever-increasing numbers of potential sympathizers.[7] By August the party was already moderately well known among rightist groups in Munich. It was now able to attract as speakers at its meetings such prominent men as Gottfried Feder, the opponent of "interest slavery," and Dietrich Eckart, at that time publisher of the violently anti-semitic journal *Auf gut Deutsch.*

As the focal point of its political activities shifted increasingly from semi-secret discussions to quasi-public rallies, the DAP was also forced to expand the Zirkel's organizational structure. Consequently the party established a formal executive committee, headed by a first and second chairman (Drexler and Harrer, in that order). To write the increasing number of invitations (all requests to attend a DAP rally were handwritten and hand-carried at this time), the executive committee included two secretaries. Finally, the DAP elected two treasurers. Presumably one was responsible for collecting dues and hat-offerings at its rallies, the other in charge of paying bills. The significance of these various organizational changes must not be exaggerated, but it is nevertheless true that between January and September 1919 the DAP built an organizational framework and a membership base which were to prove an adequate foundation for the party's later rise under Hitler. Despite Hitler's later belittling comments,[8] the organizational history of the early DAP was by no means without significance. In the first eight months of 1919 Drexler had transformed the DAP from a neglected step-child of the "Harrer Society" into a political group that was "ready" for Hitler. Drexler's DAP was almost as ambitious to expand the horizons of its political activities as was Adolf Hitler.

---

6. See, for example, the minutes of "Sitzung 5. II. 19," *ibid.*, folder 76.

7. For a speech by Dietrich Eckart in August 1919, the DAP issued four hundred invitations (Drexler to Heimburg, 14 Aug. 1919, *ibid.*).

8. Adolf Hitler, *Mein Kampf* (Munich, 1938), I, p. 241. For an effective rebuttal to the Hitler-created myths about the DAP and his own role in its development, see Reginald H. Phelps, "Hitler and the Deutsche Arbeiterpartei," *American Historical Review*, LXVIII (1963), 976–86.

Both the DAP's political views and the party's decision to convey these views to a larger public were links in the chain of events that led Hitler to join the new party. The DAP's larger rallies attracted the attention of the Bavarian *Reichswehr* (Army) authorities, and since Hitler worked for the Reichswehr as a political indoctrination official, he was asked to report on the activities of the new party.

By his own account, Hitler was not impressed by the organizational acumen of the group, but he did appreciate the "good will" he found.[9] He undoubtedly referred to the anti-semitism which permeated the party's political message even then. In general, the DAP's political program was neither a unique nor a well-worked-out series of anti-capitalist, anti-democratic, and pro-nationalist sentiments.[10] In November Harrer still noted half apologetically that the DAP's political aims were "similar to those of the *Schutz- und Trutzbund*."[11] However, while much in the party's program remained ill-defined and unspecified, there was never any doubt about the party's anti-semitic views. Drexler had made the DAP's anti-Jewish attitude public almost as soon as the party was formally organized.[12]

Hitler joined the DAP in September 1919. With his extraordinary talents as a public speaker he rose quickly in the party's organizational hierarchy, and by the end of the year he was both chief of propaganda (*Werbeobmann*) and a member of the executive committee.[13] But Hitler was not content with his rapid promotion; on the contrary, he con-

9. Hitler described his first contact with the DAP in *Mein Kampf*, I, p. 241.

10. See the DAP's "Grundsatz," HA, roll 3, folder 77; and the discussion of this document in Reginald H. Phelps, "Anton Drexler, der Gründer der NSDAP," *Deutsche Rundschau*, LXXXVII (Dec. 1961), 1136–37.

11. See "Versammlung der Deutschen Arbeiterpartei am 13. November 1919 im Eberlbräukeller–P.N.D. M 35," in Ernst Deuerlein, "Hitlers Eintritt in die Politik und die Reichswehr," *Vierteljahrshefte für Zeitgeschichte*, VII (Apr. 1959), 206. The Schutz- und Trutzbund (literally the Protective and Offensive Association) was a large, amorphous rightist organization in Munich.

12. Werner Maser, *Die Frühgeschichte der NSDAP* (Frankfurt, 1965), pp. 151 and 155. Maser's study is a curiously uneven work. It provides a great deal of very useful factual information about events and people in the early NSDAP, but also contains within its pages an extraordinary amount of thoroughly superfluous trivia and some incredibly naive analytical judgments. A very perceptive review of the book is A.V.N. Van Woerden, "De jonge Hitler en de 'oude' NSDAP," *Tijdschrift voor Geschiedenes*, LXXIX (Dec. 1966), 439–45.

13. Franz-Willing, *Hitlerbewegung*, p. 67.

tinued to find a great deal to criticize in the DAP's organizational and administrative practices. He was appalled at the inefficient and unbureaucratic business procedures in the party. Hitler informed Harrer and the other members of the executive committee that it was unthinkable to administer the affairs of the party without such standard office equipment as rubber stamps, a safe, accounting books and well-kept membership rolls, and a mimeograph machine — all of which the DAP lacked. Harrer, with a realistic look toward the DAP's financial situation, thought Hitler was mad.[14]

The propaganda chief also criticized the system of intraparty democracy that characterized the internal administration of the DAP. Like most of the groups on the far right, the party took an ambiguous stand on the question of democracy and parliamentarism. While it vehemently opposed the national parliamentary system of the Weimar Republic, the DAP's internal decision-making processes were subject to very elaborate democratic rules. The party's entire membership elected the executive committee. Discussions within the committee were free and unrestrained; majority votes decided the DAP's basic policies. The party membership as a whole had the right of initiative: the executive committee was required to place on its agenda any item that one-tenth of the party's membership wanted to bring before the committee.[15]

In December Hitler proposed a thorough reform of the party's organization. At present, he claimed, the DAP resembled a "tea club" more than a political party.[16] As immediate measures to tighten the party's organizational structure, Hitler demanded the dissolution of the organizational bonds between the DAP and the Zirkel and an increase in the independent decision-making authority of the executive committee.[17]

---

14. Hitler, "Das Braune Haus," *VB*, 21 Feb. 1931. This is a commemorative article written on the occasion of formally occupying the Brown House. Hitler quotes Harrer as calling him *"grössenwahnsinnig."*

15. "Der Ausschuss der Ortsgruppe München" (ca. Autumn 1919), pp. 1–2, HA, roll 3, folder 77.

16. Report on Hitler's remarks to the special party congress on July 29, 1921, in *VB*, 4 Aug. 1921.

17. "Organisation des Ausschusses der Ortsgruppe München und seine Geschäftsordnung," HA, roll 3, folder 76. The document bears the marginalia in quotation marks: "Dezember 1919 Geschäftsordnung—Entwurf Hitlers zur Ausschaltung Harrers."

The DAP's old-line leadership rejected Hitler's ideas at this time,[18] but the proposals indicated a considerable level of political shrewdness on Hitler's part, even at this early date. Unlike his more timid partners in the leadership corps of the party, Hitler had recognized that the DAP as presently constituted had no real political future. Like so many other groups, the DAP understood the "evils" that had led to the collapse of the empire and the establishment of the Republic. The party had even gone one step further and decided to impart its newly acquired knowledge to the public at large, but neither of these activities in any way singled out the DAP from the dozens of extreme rightist groups. The present leadership was content with the status of one-among-many. When Hitler joined the party, the DAP's leadership regarded propaganda activities as ends in themselves. Only Hitler looked upon public rallies as the means to achieve a far greater end: the overthrow of the Republic and the seizure of power by the far right.[19] The differing concepts of the party's future were reflected in the divergent organizational plans of Hitler and the old leadership. An organizational structure administered along democratic lines would be able to plan impressive rallies but would be an ineffective conspiratorial instrument.

For the moment, however, the gulf that separated the political concepts of Hitler and the old guard was still bridged by their agreement that the party's immediate task was the improvement and expansion of its propaganda activities. Here Drexler and Hitler formed a united front against Harrer, who quickly recognized the futility of his opposition and resigned his party post in January. This was undoubtedly a victory for Hitler, but he was still far from controlling the DAP. Drexler became the new chairman, and while he supported Hitler's views on propaganda, he was by no means a puppet.[20] Drexler had opposed Hitler's proposals for cen-

---

18. This did not prevent Hitler from later recording that his efforts had been completely successful. See *Mein Kampf*, I, p. 401; Adolf Hitler, *Hitler's Secret Conversations, 1941–1944*, tr. N. Cameron and R. H. Stevens (New York, 1953), p. 267.

19. Hitler, "Der völkische Gedanke und die Partei," n.d., p. 2, in "Hitler Denkschriften," HA, roll 2, folder 46. An official stamp locating the party's business office in the Sterneckerbräu indicates that this memorandum was written before the end of 1921.

20. See Drexler to Gottfried Feder, 9 March 1921, HA, roll 3, folder 76.

tralizing the party's administrative apparatus as vigorously as Harrer had, and the shift in party leadership did not materially alter the intraparty parliamentarism. The executive committee was still composed of Drexler and his personal friends,[21] and they still met regularly to discuss all party affairs freely and openly.[22] Only the routine administration of the party's clerical matters had become more bureaucratized in line with Hitler's proposals. At the time of Harrer's resignation the DAP also obtained its first full-time staff official and a permanent central office. The new official received the title of business manager *(Geschäftsführer)*, and there can be little doubt that Hitler chose the first incumbent of the office: Rudolf Schüssler had not only served in the same regiment as Hitler, but the two had worked together in the political affairs department of the Bavarian Reichswehr after the war as well.[23]

Although the DAP was evolving into a more efficient and bureaucratized organization, the old leadership continued to reject Hitler's more basic organizational reform proposals (he had submitted his ideas again in April).[24] By late spring Hitler became convinced that the DAP would not become a centralized, bureaucratized political party while the old leadership retained its positions of power. If Hitler were to transform the party into a power-centered instrument of political activity, he would have to go outside the confines of the executive committee. Here, two courses of action were open to him. He could attempt to win the approval of the present membership for his ideas and thus force the committee to adopt his scheme. This approach, however, held little promise of success. The DAP's still relatively small membership was, socially and economically, a very homogeneous body. For the most part the members came from the same social milieu as Drexler and the old guard (indeed, many lived in Drexler's neighbor-

21. See the untitled and undated notes in Drexler's handwriting in *ibid.* The notes appear to have been written about August 1920. See also Maser, *Frühgeschichte,* p. 176, for a listing of the occupations of the executive committee members in January 1920.

22. See, for example, Karl Riedl, "Erstes Kassabuch der Partei—7.1.1920—[spring] 1921," p. 34, HA, roll 2A, folder 229.

23. Maser, *Frühgeschichte,* pp. 173 and 176.

24. See Riedl, "Kassabuch," p. 34. The minutes do not mention Hitler as the author of the proposal, but since the three-man *Aktionsausschuss* was the organizational form which Hitler imposed on the NSDAP in July 1921 (see below, p. 30), it is virtually certain that he was the father of the idea at this time as well.

hood), so that they could be expected to share the leader's views on party organization.[25] It was unlikely that they would desert the old leadership.

Hitler, however, had an alternative course of action. Since he was the DAP's only really effective public speaker, he could use his unrivaled talents at propaganda to dilute the present membership with an influx of new members. The old membership would obviously welcome the added stature that the increased membership would bring to the DAP. At the same time it was clear to Hitler, if not to Drexler and his friends, that a significant part of the newly won members would join the party primarily because of Hitler's association with it. Their first loyalty, in other words, would be to Hitler personally, not to the DAP as an institution.[26] Hitler was building a following that could in time be used to overthrow the old leadership, if Hitler chose. Beginning in early 1920, then, Hitler began to exercise his duties as the party's propaganda chief with new vigor.

Paradoxically, the old guard eagerly supported Hitler's efforts. Drexler and Hitler had already laid a foundation for the new drive by providing a more specific party program. In December he and Hitler had drafted the later-famous twenty-five points, a politically expedient mixture of extreme nationalism, violent anti-semitism, vast promises to all social classes, and Feder's ideas on the "breaking of interest slavery."[27] Armed with this set of party goals, Hitler began late in the winter to introduce what was really a new style of political propaganda. The DAP scheduled its first real public rally on February 24, and others followed quickly. From the beginning Hitler's appearances were deliberate, unique variations on the standard themes of rightist diatribes. Like all rightist speakers, Hitler deliberately exploited the Bavarian fear of Bolshevik revolutions.[28]

25. For the breakdown of the membership in 1920 according to social background, see Maser, *Frühgeschichte*, pp. 254–55.

26. It should be emphasized that Hitler's popularity at this time was a genuinely personal one. He was not yet a "superhuman" Führer-figure in the party. Thus, an early party member fondly recalled some years later that sometime in 1920 Hitler had danced with his wife—surely an unthinkable activity for the later Führer Hitler. See K. L. Liebenwerda to Gregor Strasser, 18 June 1932, HA, roll 29, folder 547.

27. For the party's program, see *Wesen, Grundsätze und Ziele der NSDAP*, ed. Alfred Rosenberg (Munich, 1930).

28. See Ernst Nolte, "Germany," in Hans Rogger and Eugen Weber, eds., *The European Right: A Historical Profile* (Berkeley, Calif., 1965), p. 297.

However, while other parties made blatant appeals for middle-class support, Hitler and the DAP emphasized their interest in the lower and especially the urban-worker classes. The reason was not so much a genuine interest in social questions as a far-sighted maneuver to convince the Bavarian Reichswehr and the post-revolutionary Bavarian government that the DAP's activities represented a significant contribution toward the effort to build a bulwark against further revolutionary attempts by the urban working classes.[29] The men who controlled the institutions of governmental power in Munich in 1919 and 1920 had no sympathy with the German Republic. The commandant of the Reichswehr, Franz von Epp, his chief of staff, Ernst Röhm, and the Munich chief of police, Ernst Pöhner, were eager to overthrow the Republic and openly encouraged and protected all effective ultranationalist movements in their jurisdictional areas.[30] Hitler's new style of propaganda soon attracted their attention to the party, which sometime in 1920 began to call itself the NSDAP *(Nationalsozialistische Deutsche Arbeiterpartei),* probably to give greater credibility to the "socialist" content of its propaganda line. In December of 1920, financial aid from the Reichswehr and Dietrich Eckart enabled the party to purchase the *Völkischer Beo-bachter (VB),* until then an independent völkisch newspaper; and Ernst Röhm, an early member of the DAP, persuaded many of his fellow soldiers to join the party.[31] As for Pöhner, Hitler noted proudly that "[he] never missed an opportunity to help and protect us."[32]

Still, the party was not a front organization of the Bavarian

29. See the letter from Rudolf Hess to Kahr, 17 May 1921, quoted in Maser, *Frühgeschichte,* p. 289. The letter also emphasized that Hitler was "a good Catholic."

30. Pöhner, for example, befriended Captain Ehrhardt when the latter was a fugitive from justice for his part in the Kapp Putsch ("Zeugenvernehmung vor dem Untersuchungsrichter des Staatsge. 2. Sch. d. R. . . . Walter Bruckner . . . ," 27 Nov. 1923, National Archives Microcopy No. T-253, roll 12, frame 1463523). Hereafter National Archives microfilm documents will be cited simply as "NA, T- . . ., roll no., frame no."

31. Ernst Röhm, *Die Geschichte eines Hochverräters* (2d ed.; Munich, 1928), p. 107; and Konrad Heiden, *Hitler* (New York, 1936), p. 71.

The word *völkisch* is one of those untranslatable terms in German politics. It refers essentially to those elements on the extreme right which rejected all of Western liberalism and sought to build a German political system on the basis of ill-defined racial, rather than legal, affinities among the German people. The term hereafter will be used in the German.

32. Hitler, *Conversations,* p. 306.

government; Hitler propelled the party to prominence with his own tactical inventiveness. The financial picture of the NSDAP improved rapidly. Hitler introduced the charging of entrance fees for his rallies, and as his popularity grew, individual supporters often contributed sizable sums to the party's war chest.[33] With Hitler as its untiring, driving force the party also ignored the traditional German political vacations. While other groups planned few activities during the summer months, the NSDAP was particularly active during this traditional lull.[34] By the end of the summer the party had gained a reputation for energy and activism in völkisch circles, while other parties appeared pale and listless by comparison.[35]

Although in a short year Hitler had succeeded in lifting the NSDAP above the obscure level in which he had found it in September 1919, his accomplishments must not be exaggerated. At the beginning of 1921 neither the NSDAP nor Hitler was well known outside the confines of Munich, and Hitler had not yet challenged the organizational control of the old guard. The party was still struggling to acquire a public image in Munich when other groups, with programs often little different from that of the NSDAP, had already established national organizational structures.[36] Under these circumstances the NSDAP was eager to cultivate the good will of the more established parties, and it laid considerable stress on the need for cooperation among all groups fighting the "common enemy."[37] Hitler's peripatetic nature and his lack of a steady job made him an ideal spokesman for the NSDAP at various rightist

33. Maser, *Frühgeschichte*, p. 171, and Wilhelm Hoegner, *Die verratene Republik* (Munich, 1958), p. 123. On the relative significance of the various sources, see Franz-Willing, *Hitlerbewegung*, pp. 177–78.

34. Deuerlein, "Hitlers Eintritt," pp. 188–89. For police or Reichswehr spies' reports on Hitler's early speeches, see Rosenberg, *Wesen*, pp. 207–21.

35. See the interesting article by Albrecht Ballrod, "Vom völkischen Parteileben," *VB*, 22 Aug. 1920. The *VB* was not an NSDAP organ at this time.

36. See, for example, the collection of material relating to the Deutsch-Sozialistische Partei (DSP), HA, roll 42, folder 839.

37. See the report on an early DAP meeting in the *Münchener Beobachter* (the earlier title of the *VB*), 22 Oct. 1919. It is also interesting to note that as late as 1921 Nazi members of the free corps in Silesia did not insist on separate organizations, but integrated themselves into the military formations. See Maser, *Frühgeschichte*, p. 311.

conferences outside of Munich. Since he had the leisure time to travel, his face and voice became familiar to the crowds at numerous meetings. Hitler and Eckart were in Berlin at the time of the Kapp Putsch.[38] Hitler, this time accompanied by Drexler, attended the congress of nationalist-socialist groups from Germany, Czechoslovakia, and Austria held in Salzburg in August 1920.[39] Later that autumn, Hitler (this time alone) went on a month-long speaking tour in Austria.[40]

Slowly, imperceptibly, Hitler's activities undermined the position of the old guard. There was no smooth and steady loss of power on the part of the old leadership,[41] but in retrospect it is nevertheless clear that Hitler increasingly gained control of the real power positions in the movement. Thus the purchase of what became the official party newspaper, the *Völkischer Beobachter,* was a very important milestone in the organizational history of the NSDAP. Since, within the party organizational structure, control of the paper's editorial content obviously fell to the propaganda chief,[42] Hitler had gained a significant addition to his power potential at the end of 1920. The *VB* became an indispensable ideological and organizational link between the party's central leadership and its local and, later, provincial membership. Hitler frequently used the pages of the *VB* to give ideological clarification and interpretation to current political issues, so that control of the newspaper was a major means of preventing uncontrolled discussion and disunity among the membership. And, perhaps even more significant, the *VB* became a major vehicle for transmission of orders and directives relating to the party's organizational developments.[43] Many of these developments lay in the future; however, the acquisition of the *VB* was of immediate significance as well. Through its pages Hitler could address the large group of sympathizers (and potential mem-

38. Hanns Hofmann, *Der Hitlerputsch* (Munich, 1961), p. 55.

39. *VB*, 12 Aug. 1920.

40. *VB*, 31 Oct. 1920.

41. Thus Hitler opposed a union of the Nazi parties in Austria, Germany, and Czechoslovakia in 1920, but the party's executive committee overruled him on this occasion. See Maser, *Frühgeschichte,* pp. 244–46.

42. "Ausschussitzung, 23. II. 21," in Riedl, "Kassabuch," p. 104.

43. This is particularly true of the *VB*'s column "Aus der Bewegung" (Notes about the Movement), first instituted in March 1922.

bers) who were repelled by the more theatrical atmosphere of the party's rallies. This group was quite large: the paper's circulation at the beginning of 1921 was considerably larger than the party's membership. Its initial circulation in January 1921 was 11,000, and while the monthly circulation figures varied during the year, they never dropped to less than 7,500 and even reached 17,500 in early 1922.[44]

Hitler's increasingly prominent role in the NSDAP led to yet another unobtrusive but significant development. Largely as a result of Hitler's propaganda activities, a new group of unofficial leaders, a sort of shadow leadership corps, collected around him. Dietrich Eckart became an intimate friend and admirer of Hitler.[45] Eckart in turn brought Alfred Rosenberg into the party. Hermann Esser, a man of rather shadowy and unsavory origins and habits,[46] became a member of the new group. Emil Gansser acted as liaison between Hitler and wealthy potential supporters.[47] None of these men shared either the values or the lower-middle-class origins of the old guard in the NSDAP. They were either upper-middle-class individuals, like Gansser, or, more frequently, asocial *demimonde* figures. Their mode of living did, however, resemble Hitler's in important respects. Like Hitler, Esser and Eckart had no regular jobs. The former apparently lived from the earnings of several mistresses,[48] while the latter was a poet and author. Several members of the new group (Esser is the outstanding example) also had considerable oratorical talents. And since, like Hitler, they had the time to make frequent public appearances, the new group quickly replaced the formal party leaders as representatives and spokesmen of the NSDAP in the public mind.[49]

44. See the untitled circulation figures and graphs in NA, T–84, roll 6, frame 5167.

45. Sam [sic] Knauss, "Erinnerungen meiner parteipolitischen Betätigungen in den Jahren 1888–1931" (ca. 1936), pp. 5 and 7, HA, roll 53, folder 1238; Eckart to Amann, 10 May 1923, *ibid.*, roll 54, folder 1317.

46. Alan Bullock, *Hitler: A Study in Tyranny* (New York, 1964), p. 74.

47. Hitler, *Conversations*, p. 179.

48. Bullock, *Hitler*, p.74.

49. In August 1920, the *VB* spoke of the DAP's "veteran founders [sic] and leaders A. Drexler and A. Hitler" (*VB*, 12 Aug. 1920). For police observers' reports on 1920 Nazi party rallies, see Reginald H. Phelps, ed., "Hitler als Parteiredner im Jahre 1920," *Vierteljahrshefte für Zeitgeschichte*, XI (July 1963), 289-330.

In effect, although only Hitler among the group held a party office before July 1921, the new men had a more concrete leader image than the members of the executive committee long before the organizational crisis of July.

Finally there is the most obvious and yet also most significant effect of Hitler's propaganda activities in 1920. By the end of the year the efforts of the Hitler group had vastly increased the party's membership, both in Munich and in the provincial areas, and thus substantially diluted the old-line membership. Within the city, the increase forced the NSDAP to expand its horizontal organization so that its previously unitary local *(Ortsgruppe)* was subdivided into four sections, corresponding to four of Munich's districts. The party also expanded its network of locals in the Bavarian countryside. The first local outside Munich was organized in Rosenheim in April 1920, and by the beginning of 1921 the party was organized in at least ten localities outside the Bavarian capital.[50] Somewhat later in the year, the party even established a local outside Bavaria, in Mannheim.[51]

The organizational expansion both increased and decreased Hitler's formal authority within the party's organization. In the autumn of 1920 the party acquired legal status by incorporating itself as the *National-sozialistischer Deutscher Arbeiterverein, eingetragener Verein (NSDAV e.V.).* To be a *Verein* (registered club), the NSDAV had to adopt a set of bylaws. As was the usual practice in German social and political clubs, the NSDAV's constitution vested control of the organization in a board of directors *(Vorstand),* consisting, in the case of the NSDAV, of two chairmen, two secretaries, and two treasurers. The propaganda chief was not a member of the board, so that on the surface, at least, Hitler was now excluded from the party's supreme policy-making body.[52] On the other hand, the establishment of the sections tremendously expanded Hitler's range of activity within the party. The primary activity of the new units was to conduct what were essentially agitation and propaganda sessions. Party members in the sections were

50. This rough estimate is based on the information on activities of the various locals provided in the *VB's* column "Aus der Bewegung" for the year 1920.

51. Maser, *Frühgeschichte,* pp. 314 ff.

52. "Satzungen des Nationalsozialistischen Deutschen Arbeitervereins (e.V.)," Oct. 1920, HA, roll 3, folder 79.

urged to attend weekly indoctrination sessions, so that "party comrades [would] . . . become familiar with and absolutely certain of the ideology of [the] movement."[53] The establishment of and original impulse for a primarily propagandistic utilization of the sections came from Hermann Esser, a leading member of Hitler's shadow leadership.[54] Hitler's control over the sections and their activities was considerable. As the party's propaganda chief, he probably selected the weekly discussion topics and supplied the sections with indoctrination material. It is also virtually certain that Hitler controlled the appointment of section leaders. There is no actual proof that he exercised such authority at this date, but the agitprop nature of the section leader's functions and some later statements by Hitler provide strong evidence that the flow of authority from Hitler to the section chiefs bypassed the executive committee.[55]

Similarly, the creation of new locals outside of Munich weakened the old guard and strengthened Hitler. The establishment of a new local usually followed a set pattern. A local organizer invited interested persons to hear a speech by one of the Munich leaders. The speaker explained the program of the party, and at the conclusion of his talk members of the audience were invited to become charter members of the new local.[56] The speaker from party headquarters was often one of Hitler's group.[57] After all, only Hitler and his friends had both the propagandistic talents to per-

53. *VB*, 2 April 1921.

54. [Hermann] Esser, "Nationalsozialistische Deutsche Arbeiterpartei — Satzungen der Ortsgruppe . . . [sic] e.V. (Entwurf!)," ca. early 1920, NA, T-84, roll 5, frame 4445.

55. Hitler later noted that the section leaders were something of a potential elite within the early party. It is also significant that on Mondays Hitler himself presided over an agitprop session. His audience was made up largely of section leaders, who, having been students on Monday, became teachers in their own sections on Tuesday and Wednesday. See "Besprechung des Führers mit General Reinicke am 7. Januar 1944 in der Wolfsschanze," n.d., (top secret), T-120, roll 2621, frame E381883. Reinicke had just been appointed head of the *NS-Führungsstab* (Staff of NS Leaders), and Hitler, in reminiscing about his early days, was suggesting "proper" methods of political indoctrination to him.

56. Wiegand (one of the DAP's secretaries) to a potential member in Augsburg, 7 June 1920, HA, roll 4, folder 111; *VB*, 2 Sept. 1920.

57. See, for example, *VB*, 2 Sept. 1920, 2, 18, and 22 Nov. 1920, and 3 Jan. 1921.

suade mass meetings and the leisure time for frequent travel. This also meant, however, that many of the members outside Munich joined the party largely because it was Hitler's or Esser's party. Moreover, these ties — to the man, thus the party — were not really affected by the actual establishment of the local, since the party's official leaders had little formal organizational control over the units outside Munich. The locals sent twenty percent of the money collected as regular dues and fifty percent of all voluntary contributions to Munich, and representatives of the locals could attend coordinating discussions held once a month in Munich,[58] but in all other respects the locals were virtually independent. They elected their own leaders, and local committees had the power to receive new members and to expel present ones.[59] It was even unnecessary to obtain formal permission from the party's executive committee before a new local could be established.[60] None of these provisions is surprising: a leadership that adhered firmly to the principle of intraparty democracy would hardly base relations between Munich and the party's horizontal organization on the leadership principle *(Führerprinzip)*.

The party that assembled in Munich for its first national congress on January 22, 1921, was a far different organization from the backroom discussion group Hitler had joined a little over a year before. It now had some 3,000 members;[61] it was a respected and influential part of the extreme right in Bavaria. The most significant factor in the membership and organizational growth of the NSDAP was the tireless work and magnetic personality of Adolf Hitler. The old membership had been nearly eclipsed by the influx of Hitler followers, and it might have seemed logical that Hitler would use the national congress to wrest control from the old leadership.

58. Franz-Willing, *Hitlerbewegung*, p. 183; NSDAP, Parteileitung, "Rundschreiben Nr. 3," 21 July 1921, HA, roll 3, folder 97.

59. "Satzungen des nationalsozialistischen deutschen Arbeitervereins e.V. Sitz München," Jan. 1921, HA, roll 3, folder 76. Prospective members whose applications had been rejected by the local committee had the right to appeal to Drexler, but expellees apparently had no right of appeal (*ibid.*).

60. See the appeal by G. Seifert, Head of the Ortsgruppe Hanover, in *VB*, 28 July 1921.

61. Wolfgang Schäfer, *NSDAP* (Hanover, 1956), p. 7.

By this time there was certainly no lack of friction between Hitler and the old guard. The old-line leaders and members were particularly critical of Hitler's personal living habits, but there were also fears that Hitler planned to become party dictator.[62] On the other hand, the quarrel was as yet muted and hidden, so that the rank-and-file membership was in no way prepared for a public power struggle at the congress. Then, too, only 411 members attended the congress, so that any attempt by Hitler or his entourage to oust the old leadership could have reached only a small minority of the membership. Hitler could have begun the battle for control at the congress, but given the intraparty democratic rules, it was impossible to win it before that forum.

The public display of unity at the congress could not hide for long the increasingly strained relations between Hitler and the party leadership. As Hitler continued his manner of living, criticism of his bohemian ways became more frequent.[63] In addition, the propaganda chief's ambition and independence seemed to grow along with the party's increasing membership. While the NSDAP's executive committee continued their efforts to cooperate with other kindred groups against the "common enemy," Hitler's enthusiasm for a united front of völkisch parties ebbed markedly as the NSDAP became more influential in its own right.[64] In July 1921 the smoldering fires finally erupted into open flames.

The issue of interparty cooperation triggered the outbreak of open warfare between Hitler and the old guard. The NSDAP's local in Augsburg, with the full knowledge and approval of the executive committee, negotiated an agreement of mutual cooperation with the German Socialist Party (*Deutsch-Sozialistische Partei,* DSP) organization in the city.[65] From the outset, both parties

62. The nature of Hitler's entourage was no secret in the party, and some party members did not hesitate to reproach him for his associations with the wealthy and with figures from the *demimonde* (Feder to Hitler, 10 Aug. 1923, in Oron J. Hale, ed., "Gottfried Feder calls Hitler to Order: an Unpublished Letter on Nazi Party Affairs," *Journal of Modern History,* XXX[1958], 360).

63. Heiden, *Hitler,* pp. 90–91; Franz-Willing, *Hitlerbewegung,* p. 107.

64. See the letter by a member of the Deutsch-Nationale Volkspartei to the *VB's* publisher, 26 Feb. 1921, HA, roll 50, folder 1172; Franz-Willing, *Hitlerbewegung,* p. 91.

65. For the history of the negotiations see Franz-Willing, *Hitlerbewegung,* pp. 109–10; and Maser, *Frühgeschichte,* pp. 231-32.

attached far more than local significance to the agreement. The DSP sent one of its leading figures, Otto Dickel, to the negotiations, and both sides regarded the contract as the first step on a path leading to the complete fusion of the NSDAP and the DSP. The two sides had even agreed that the national headquarters of the new party would be in Berlin, rather than Munich.[66]

On the surface, a union of the two parties seemed logical and natural. They had largely identical programs, and the DSP's leading Jew-baiter, Julius Streicher, could easily match the crudity of Esser's speeches. Nevertheless, the old leadership of the NSDAP was not primarily interested in creating a new and potentially stronger party. Its more immediate and overriding aim was to deprive Hitler of much of his political influence in the party. His political strength was concentrated in Munich and Bavaria, and his only hope for control of the party lay in mobilizing his mass followers in southern Germany. In July 1921 he had few followers in northern Germany, so that by transferring the headquarters of the new party into what was essentially DSP territory, the old guard clearly hoped to remove the new party's national office from the focal point of Hitler's popularity and influence. Hitler was fully aware of the real purpose of the merger plans and opposed the proposal from the beginning.[67] The old guard merely succeeded in concluding the agreement more quickly than he had anticipated. Ironically, Hitler was in Berlin on one of his periodic good-will and money-gathering trips at the time the agreement was concluded in Augsburg.[68] However, when Dietrich Eckart informed him of developments in Munich, Hitler immediately realized the gravity of the situation and hurried home.[69] His response was swift and decisive. Although he had often underscored the need for greater party discipline and tighter organizational structure, his actions now made it clear that he did not apply the bonds of party discipline to himself. Hitler neither accepted the decision of the

66. Heiden, *Hitler*, p. 108.
67. Maser, *Frühgeschichte*, p. 232.
68. Heiden, *Hitler*, p. 108. The Vorstand's actions were perfectly constitutional and legal. The decision to merge with another party was a decision of basic policy and as such well within the sphere of authority of the board, which did not include Hitler among its members.
69. *Ibid.*, p. 109.

executive committee to conclude the treaty with the DSP nor did
he attempt to convince the party leadership that its path of action
was wrong. Instead he simply resigned from the party. On July 12,
he was again an unaffiliated politician.

The first reaction of the executive committee — or at least of
some of its members — to this (apparently) completely unexpected
step was to issue an anonymous, politically inept broadside. Hitler
and some fifty other party members received copies in the mail.
The hastily written pamphlet accused Hitler of wishing to be party
dictator and severely criticized again his bohemian way of life, but
combined these basically true charges with other, manifestly absurd
accusations, so that the total impression created by the document
was that of charges invented on the spur of the moment by jealous
and vindictive political enemies. The accusations that Hitler was in the
pay of Jews and a supporter of the last emperor of Austria were
neither true nor credible.[70]

Actually, the executive committee's hasty, not to say panicky,
response to Hitler's resignation was unnecessary. It soon became
clear that Hitler had no intention of attempting to split the party.
Two days after he resigned, he wrote another letter setting down
his conditions for rejoining the NSDAP. He demanded that in the
future the party's organizational structure "must be . . . unlike those
of other nationalist movements." The party must be "structured and
led in a manner that will enable [it] to become the sharpest weapon
in the battle against the Jewish international rulers of our people."
As for his own role in the party, Hitler demanded his election as
first chairman with "dictatorial powers." He had not forgotten the
earlier organizational proposals. A three-man action committee
(*Aktionsausschuss*), named by himself, would replace the executive committee as the party's basic policy-making body. Members
who refused to accept his terms would be expelled from the party.
Finally, Hitler insisted that the old leadership call a special party
congress on July 20 to effect his election as chairman.[71]

70. *Adolf Hitler Verräter?*, HA, roll 2, folder 45. Maser has discovered that
the actual author of the pamphlet was an Ernst Ehrensperger. See Maser,
Frühgeschichte, p. 270.
71. Hitler to the NSDAP Parteileitung, 14 July 1921, HA, roll 3, folder 79.

One day later the executive committee capitulated. It agreed to accept all of Hitler's substantive demands, suggesting only a postponement of the special congress until July 29.[72] The total and unexpected collapse of the anti-Hitler front was due not to Hitler's convincing arguments, but to a split in the ranks of the old party leadership. Drexler, to judge from the respect which Hitler accorded him after the crisis, had personally decided to put the future of the NSDAP into Hitler's hands.

Anton Drexler was a very simple but fanatic man[73] who loathed intraparty strife and who was fully aware that the NSDAP owed its rapid growth largely to Hitler's propaganda activities. On the other hand, Drexler's personal friends were the leaders of the anti-Hitler faction, and, like them, he was fearful of Hitler's ambition. These latter considerations had led him to support the planned union of the NSDAP and the DSP. But when Hitler, instead of accepting his new subordinate role, dramatically resigned from the party, Drexler had second thoughts about his friends' schemes. On July 25 he made a last, halfhearted attempt to prevent Hitler's domination of the party. He went to the Munich police and altered the incorporation papers by declaring that Hitler was no longer a member of the NSDAP. In addition, the old guard had attempted to have at least a partial revenge by expelling Esser and Oskar Körner, the second chairman, from the party,[74] but these were petty gestures and did not affect the basic issue.

Drexler had always supported a vigorous program of mass appeals, and rather than risk losing the party's greatest propaganda asset, he urged the board to submit to Hitler's demands. Confronted with the unpleasant choice of either tying the NSDAP — without Hitler — to a party that by 1921 had passed the peak of its political influence, or safeguarding the NSDAP's continued growth — albeit under Hitler's dictatorship — Drexler chose to preserve the organizational life of his own creation. The rest of the executive com-

72. NSDAP Parteileitung to Hitler, 15 July 1921, in Franz-Willing, *Hitlerbewegung*, p. 113.

73. For a more detailed analysis of Drexler's personality and his role in the events of July, see also Phelps, "Anton Drexler," pp. 1140–41, 1143.

74. *Ibid.*, p. 1141; and "Rundschreiben Nr. 3," 21 July 1921, HA, roll 3, folder 97.

mittee members knew that no substantial portion of the membership would follow them against both Hitler and Drexler, and so they could do little but resign or yield. They yielded.

The special congress on July 29 was an anticlimax. Since the old guard had capitulated beforehand, there was not even a floor fight. The proceedings were orderly and disciplined. A member of the old executive committee moved the adoption of constitutional amendments that gave Hitler dictatorial control. They were adopted unanimously by the 554 members present. The board then resigned, and Hitler was elected chairman; the vote was 553 to one. The whole affair was over in two and a half hours.[75]

The new set of party bylaws approved by the July congress also formalized Hitler's future control of the party's entire organization and administration.[76] The board of directors remained a party institution, but only because as a registered club the NSDAP was legally obligated to elect a board of directors.[77] As the actual policy-making body in the new party Hitler established a three-man action-committee headed by himself. The old executive committee had rejected this organizational plan when Hitler first presented it in April 1920, but this time it had no choice; it paid the price of defeat in the July crisis. Hitler not only headed the action committee, but named its other two members as well. This group (that is, Hitler) formulated broad policy guidelines and then assigned the execution of these policies to six subcommittees: propaganda, finance,

75. "Protokoll über die ausserordentliche Mitgliederversammlung am Freitag, den 29. Juli 1921 im Hofbräu-Festsaal zu München," 30 July 1921, HA, roll 3, folder 79.

76. For the new bylaws, see "Satzungen des national-sozialistischen deutschen Arbeiter-Vereins," July 1921, *ibid.* It goes without saying that none of the old leadership's plans came to fruition. Under Hitler, the "Augsburg treaty" was repudiated and all negotiations between the NSDAP and the DSP were broken off.

77. The impotence of the board under the new leadership explains the absence from the board of leading members of the Hitler group (aside from Hitler and Körner). The new board even included one holdover from the previous leadership. The other members were respected, unambitious individuals who had played no prominent part in the power struggle. For the board's membership, see *VB,* 4 Aug. 1921.

youth organization,[78] sports and athletics, investigation, and mediation. Hitler personally appointed all but one of the subcommittee chairmen, and he named both the chairmen and the members of the subcommittee on investigation.

After the July crisis the members of Hitler's shadow leadership began to occupy important positions in the party's administrative hierarchy as chairmen of the various subcommittees. Esser headed the propaganda subcommittee, and Eckart became editor of the *VB*.[79] The chairman of the youth committee was undoubtedly Adolf Lenk, later the head of the NSDAP's youth organization. He was too young to be closely associated with either Hitler's group or the old guard, but he owed his position in the party hierarchy solely to Hitler.[80] The subcommittee on sports and athletics quickly transformed itself into the storm troopers (*Sturmabteilung,* SA) command, which was in turn clearly subordinate to the party's chairman. The head of the investigation subcommittee is not known, but, in view of this committee's supreme importance, it is likely that Hitler himself presided over its meetings. Hitler attached particular significance to his control of the subcommittee on investigation, since this group controlled the membership flow to and from the party. It decided the disposition of applications for party membership, and it could expel old members at will.[81] Hitler clearly intended this subcommittee to be a policing instrument, ready to reject prospective members or expel those of the present membership who threatened to become the core of an anti-Hitler group within the party.

Yet Hitler had no interest in a general purge of the party

78. This was the organizational forerunner of the Youth Association of the NSDAP (Jugendbund der NSDAP) which in turn was the predecessor of the Hitler Youth. In the years 1922-23 the Youth Association served primarily as a recruiting agency for the storm troopers (Adolf Lenk, "Das Werden der Nationalsozialistischen Jugendbewegung!" HA, roll 18, folder no. 333; "Satzungen des Jugendbundes der Nat.-Soz. Deutschen Arbeiterpartei," Mar. 1922, *ibid.,* folder 331).

79. Walter Görlitz and Herbert A. Quint, *Adolf Hitler* (Stuttgart, 1952), p. 160; *VB,* 28 July 1921.

80. Lenk, "Werden der NS-Jugendbewegung," p. 3, HA, roll 18, folder 333.

81. "Satzungen," HA, roll 3, folder 79.

membership. He knew that constitutional provisions alone were not sufficient to transform the NSDAP into his movement. Since the real basis of his power in the party was charisma, he could not effectively translate his paper authority into actual power until the party members willingly gave up their belief in intraparty democracy and became devoted followers of Hitler's dictatorial leadership in the NSDAP. Hitler used the person and name of Anton Drexler to establish an atmosphere of continuity between the old and new NSDAP and, more specifically, to reconcile some wavering elements to the organizational changes he had instituted. Hitler undoubtedly felt that Drexler, with his well-known dislike of intraparty strife, would use his position at the head of a subcommittee on mediation to ease the anger of the more passionately anti-Hitler elements. Consequently, Drexler was the only member of the old leadership group who was not relegated to a position of complete obscurity and impotence. He became chairman of the subcommittee on mediation. In addition, the new bylaws made him honorary chairman of the party for life and even left the former chairman with considerable residual powers. For example, Drexler had the right to call a special congress of the party if he felt the actions of the first chairman warranted such a step.[82] In addition, Drexler's title and the formal powers that came with it appear to have been Hitler's payment of his political debts to Drexler: the new chairman was fully aware that without Drexler's support his rise to the party chairmanship would have come far less easily and quickly.

Hitler moved swiftly to consolidate his formal organizational changes with a series of charismatic projections designed to transform the NSDAP's members into disciplined Hitler loyalists. At the July congress he had been elected chairman almost unanimously, but this represented a vote of confidence by only five hundred members. Would the rest of the membership, most of whom undoubtedly admired Hitler both as a propagandist and as a party leader, also be willing to accept him as party dictator? A curious lull occurred in the traceable activities of the party leadership between July and September. The new chairman issued no general orders; he made no attempt to impose tight discipline on the party. Instead, Hitler and his group were busy attempting to win the

82. *Ibid.*

voluntary support of the Munich party members. Articles in the *VB* began what was later to become the fully developed *Führer* cult.[83] The climax of the campaign to win the support of the Munich members focused on the meetings of the four Munich sections on August 16 and 17. These meetings were specifically called to discuss the recent organizational changes in the party,[84] and it is unfortunate that no detailed accounts of these important sessions have survived. Hitler himself did not appear at any of the meetings. Instead, Esser argued Hitler's case before two of the sections; Oskar Körner and Drexler prevailed at the other two.[85] The recently elected honorary chairman spoke in one of Munich's workers' districts, the locale and social milieu that was most familiar to him and where he was particularly respected.[86] Presumably, the guest speakers defended Hitler's actions and asked for the members' support of and loyalty to the new chairman. The first round of meetings was followed by another series a week later. Hitler himself spoke at two of these; in all probability, he appeared in the sections that had seemed least enthusiastic about the new regime the week before.[87] Apparently, he and his men were effective persuaders. By the end of August, Munich was secure; the membership was willing to accept Hitler as party dictator.

With the Munich membership as a solid block of support behind him, Hitler could turn his attention to the relations between central party headquarters and the locals outside the Bavarian capital. He and his group had never developed any enthusiasm for the loose ties between the central leadership and the locals which had been one of the characteristics of the old NSDAP. When Esser drafted his model bylaws for a local party organization in 1920, for example, he included a clearly worded clause that the locals should be "subordinate to [Munich]."[88]

Hitler began his effort to subordinate the locals to the direc-

---

83. See, for example, the article by Rudolf Hess, "Zum Flugblatt gegen Hitler," *VB*, 11 Aug. 1921.

84. *VB*, 14 Aug. 1921.

85. *Ibid.*

86. Drexler spoke in Neuhausen, which was apparently his home district (*ibid.*).

87. *VB*, 21 Aug. 1921.

88. Esser, "Nationalsozialistische," NA, T-84, roll 5, frame 4442.

tion of central party headquarters by significantly increasing the functions and authority of the party's national business manager. In the new organizational structure, the personality and position of the business manager were of considerable importance, since he, more than anyone else, was responsible for creating an atmosphere of discipline and organizational tightness within the party. In fact, the business manager was far more than his title indicated; actually he handled not only the day-to-day clerical routines, but headed the cadre administration as well.

The new party chairman found Schüssler unsuited to the expanded demands of the office and selected Max Amann as his successor. Amann was a completely new force in the party's administrative hierarchy. He was not even a member of the NSDAP when he became the party's business manager in July 1921; indeed, Hitler apparently happened to meet him in Munich and persuaded him to accept the job.[89] Like Schüssler, Amann had served in the same regiment as Hitler, although he had held a somewhat higher rank. His qualifications for the job included a complete lack of personal political ambitions, considerable managerial and organizational ability, utter incorruptibility, and, above all, complete loyalty to Hitler.[90]

Under Amann the party's permanent staff at central party headquarters expanded rapidly. In November 1921 the party moved into new and larger headquarters, and by April of the following year it already had thirteen full-time salaried employees. Simultaneously, the administration developed a system of reporting through channels, as well as a central archive and filing system.[91] Yet, while these are developments common to all mass parties with an expanding membership, the NSDAP's administrative principles sanctioned some very unbureaucratic practices. Thus the increasing bureaucratization was not accompanied by a corresponding increase in the depersonalization of jurisdictional grants. Even at this early date

89. Hitler, *Mein Kampf*, II, p. 665.
90. Albert Krebs, *Tendenzen und Gestalten der NSDAP* (Stuttgart, 1959), pp. 195–97.
91. NSDAP, Parteileitung (Hitler), "Rundschreiben Nr. 8," 8 Oct. 1921, "Rundschreiben Nr. 10," 22 Oct. 1921, "Rundschreiben Nr. 14," 3 Dec. 1921, HA, roll 4, folder 97.

Hitler did not restrict his role in the administrative hierarchy to issuing broad policy instructions, but concerned himself — in a completely irrational fashion — with whatever minute details of the party's organizational life he happened to find interesting.[92] The party's leader was just as likely to submerge himself in the routine bureaucratic life of the organization as to head and direct it; and only he knew when he would choose to do either.

During the summer months, while Hitler was still primarily concerned with strengthening his position in Munich, he left the provincial locals alone. Before the July crisis the former leadership had called a meeting of local representatives for August 21,[93] but Hitler ignored the date and the meeting was not held. During the summer the new regime did not establish formal contact with the locals outside Munich, but in mid-September Hitler issued his first circular letter *(Rundschreiben)*. He instructed the locals to acquire party flags and insignia, to submit to Munich copies of all resolutions passed at local meetings, and to inform the party leadership of the names of members serving on local committees.[94] This first circular letter of the new regime was a curious document, written in the heady atmosphere of Hitler's recent triumphs in Munich. It reads like a regimental order; Hitler commands, and he expects his commands to be obeyed instantly.

The locals, however, had as yet little liking for a parade ground atmosphere; they still functioned in the Drexler era of self-government, resolutions, and discussions. The new leader's efforts to institute intraparty bureaucratization by command met with considerable passive resistance. Some of the membership lists that Hitler ordered in September had not reached Munich by December.[95] Hitler quickly modified the tone, though not the substance of his epistles. After the first circular letter, the new leadership stressed the need for coordination and mutual information rather than subordination among the party units. As a result, the outlying locals remained largely autonomous units at the end of the year. The major change introduced by the new leadership was

92. Maser, *Frühgeschichte*, p. 279.
93. "Rundschreiben Nr. 2," 5 July 1921, HA, roll 4, folder 97.
94. "Rundschreiben Nr. 4," 10 Sept. 1921; "Rundschreiben Nr. 5," 17 Sept. 1921, *ibid.*
95. "Rundschreiben Nr. 14," 3 Dec. 1921, *ibid.*

to establish that the locals had very definite reportorial functions. The locals did send a stream of information to party headquarters: they now reported — albeit still slowly and erratically — membership statistics, changes in the local leadership, and the political activities of the organization. There was as yet no well-established line of authority along the vertical structure of the NSDAP, but at the end of 1921 the procedures to develop a regular flow of information had definitely been introduced.

The beginnings of an effectively coordinated party were a major step on the road to political prominence, but Hitler had little interest in coordination as an organizational end.[96] The party which he desired to create could not be established by circular letters alone. To achieve this goal he had to repeat his efforts in Munich: like the sections, the provincial locals (or at least their leaders) had to be personally confronted and persuaded to give up their status as leaders of largely independent units and to become instead disciplined party functionaries carrying out Hitler's personal will. He selected the 1922 national party congress to confront the provincial leaders with the living presence of his charisma.

The congress began on January 29 with a *Festabend*, a device the NSDAP had frequently used to combine propaganda (speeches and reading of patriotic poems) with entertainment (songs, satiric comic sketches, etc.). This put the local leaders in the proper frame of mind for the far more important session of the following day. On the afternoon of January 30 Hitler addressed the assembled leadership corps of the locals from outside Munich at party headquarters. In a speech lasting two and a half hours he stressed the need for a "tightly organized [party] leadership." In practice, Hitler specified, this would mean that, while the locals could remain financially autonomous, politically they would become

---

96. Hitler allowed the monthly discussion meetings of local representatives to fall into disuse. He scheduled a session for September, but for some reason it was not held. An October meeting was also scheduled, but it too does not seem to have taken place. The *Rundschreiben* do not indicate that a November meeting was even scheduled, and the one for December was officially canceled ("Rundschreiben Nr. 4," 10 Sept. 1921, "Rundschreiben Nr. 6," n.d., and "Rundschreiben Nr. 7," 5 Oct. 1921, HA, roll 4, folder 97).

subordinate to Munich.[97] At the conclusion of the speech, the local leaders expressed their complete confidence in Hitler and the party's new leadership.[98] By the end of the evening Hitler was able to institutionalize his charismatic triumph. The congress formally amended the party's bylaws to enable to first chairman to expel entire locals (not merely individual members) at will.[99]

The massive vote of confidence in January allowed Hitler and Amann to perfect the NSDAP's organizational structure. The entire vertical party organization became progressively more subordinate to the personal will of its leader, and the decision-making authority of the locals grew increasingly smaller. They could no longer negotiate local agreements with other völkisch groups. Material for local propaganda campaigns had to be obtained from Munich. Even the establishment of new locals became subject to Munich's approval; local initiative was not a *desideratum* in Hitler's NSDAP.[100]

The culmination of Hitler's campaign to impose centralized control of the provincial locals in the pre-Putsch party was the establishment of the office of delegate *(Delegierte)*. This system was created on paper in late 1922, but it was not effected until 1923. The delegates were appointed by Hitler and reported directly to him. They had the responsibility of overseeing the activities of the locals in specifically assigned geographic areas.[101] The scope of their authority was apparently very far-reaching; some did not hesitate to use their offices to install or dismiss local leaders.[102]

97. "Unsere Generalversammlung," *VB*, 4 Feb. 1922.

98. *Ibid.;* and *VB*, 1 Feb. 1922.

99. "Protokoll der ordentlichen Mitgliederversammlung des Nationalsozialistischen Deutschen Arbeitervereins e.V. (Nationalsozialistische Deutsche Arbeiterpartei) am 30. Januar 1922," p. 1, HA, roll 3, folder 79. The attendance figures reveal that the congress was staged primarily for the benefit of non-Munich locals; of 918 members present, 718 came from areas outside Munich, while only 200 represented city membership (*ibid.*).

100. NSDAP, Parteileitung (Hitler), "Mitteilungsblatt Nr. 14," 26 April 1922, pp. 2–3, HA, roll 4, folder 95.

101. Max Weber, "Bericht über den Stand der Bewegung in Württemberg, Ende Mai 1923," NA, T-84, roll 5, frames 4025–26.

102. First and second chairman of the Ortsgruppe, Stuttgart, "Denkschrift, bestimmt für 1. unseren Führer Adolf Hitler in München 2. den Delegierten für Württemberg, Herrn Max Weber, München," 9 Sept. 1923, *ibid.*, frame 3929.

All of these measures should not suggest that the NSDAP in 1922 or early 1923 was a fully developed microcosm of the stratified organizational giant of later years. Many of Hitler's centralizing measures met with determined opposition from the membership of the party,[103] and many directives issued in Munich had little immediate effect upon the day-to-day life of the party. Nevertheless, at least in retrospect, it is clear that the NSDAP was rapidly losing its character as a political party led by Hitler, and was developing instead into a group of disciplined followers willing to submit to Hitler's personal wishes and dictates.

The new atmosphere in the party was particularly apparent during the 1923 national congress. It was in large measure a personal victory for Hitler, and the entire atmosphere of the congress provided an eerie (if somewhat amateurish) foretaste of the later mammoth annual Nazi congresses (*Reichsparteitage*). As he would so often in later years, Hitler reviewed a parade of the SA, dedicated new flags, and outlined the party's future path to the assembled local leaders.[104] There were no discussions at this congress; Hitler spoke and the membership cheered. The party chairman had become "the honored leader."[105] The 1923 congress was a milestone in the organizational history of the NSDAP because it marked the beginning of Hitler's complete, personalized control of the party's functionary corps and organizational structure. Ever since the July crisis Hitler had progressively cast the members' and sub-leaders' submission to the spell of his personality into forms of institutionalized organizational hierarchy, centralization, and subordination. Hitler persuaded the membership to give up voluntarily the rights it had enjoyed under the democratic rules of the NSDAP and to accept instead a framework of discipline and obedience to himself. In turn he promised that his personalized control of the NSDAP would enable the party to play a more effective part in felling the Weimar Republic and replacing it with a Nazi–völkisch dictatorship.

There is no question that the transformation and control of the NSDAP was not an end in itself for Hitler. His political self-concept

103. Maser, *Frühgeschichte*, p. 369.
104. See "Die Fahnenweihe" and "Die Delegiertenversammlung," *VB*, 31 Jan. 1923.
105. "Die Fahnenweihe," *ibid.*

clearly included playing a major role in the German far right as a whole. Less clear is the precise nature and extent of his ambitions. Was he satisfied to let other leaders use his talents at propaganda to attain political power for themselves, as a recent analysis has suggested?[106] Or did he look beyond his role as drummer of the movement even before the November Putsch? Both his own actions and his directives to the party membership after he gained control of the NSDAP seem to indicate that Adolf Hitler regarded himself not merely as a propagandist; he wanted political power as well. As early as April 1922, he instructed the party's locals not merely to conduct propaganda campaigns, "but to secure political power for our movement (*die politische Macht in die Faust unserer Bewegung zu bringen*)."[107]

On the other hand, it would be misleading to suggest that the Putsch did not represent a significant dividing line in the political and organizational development of both Hitler and the entire far-right movement. The Bavarian rightist conspiracy before the Putsch was a far more cooperative, symbiotic movement than afterwards. There were few ideological or strategic differences among the various groups, although personality differences and the fetish for organizational independence abounded. Neither the NSDAP nor most of its kindred organizations had as yet discovered the political usefulness of exclusive dogmas and programs, and cross-memberships were very common among the rightist groups. In fact, some of the leading figures of the Nazi Party in later years were already active in the far-right movement, but not as members of the NSDAP.[108] This is not surprising, since the numerous groups really held not only a common ideology, but above all shared an emotional attitude toward political life in Germany. Without exception, the German far right was anti-semitic.[109] It was almost equally unanimous

106. Hofmann, *Hitlerputsch*, pp. 68, 148–49.

107. "Mitteilungsblatt Nr. 14," p. 3, HA, roll 4, folder 95.

108. Thus, Heinrich Himmler, though active on the far right, never joined the NSDAP before August 1923, and even then Hitler's name does not appear in his diary entries. See Werner T. Angress and Bradley F. Smith, "Diaries of Heinrich Himmler's Early Years," *Journal of Modern History*, XXXI (June 1959), 208–10.

109. Cf. Ernst von Salomon's statement "we were all anti-semites." Ernst von Salomon, *Der Fragebogen* (Hamburg, 1961), pp. 107–08.

in its endorsement of anti-Russian and anti-French policies. Moreover, by 1923 the movement was almost entirely a middle-class revolt;
the earlier emphasis on "nationalizing" the socialist aspirations of the
urban proletariat had disappeared. The new NSDAP shared all of
these sentiments. Its programmatic statements were saturated with
anti-Russian and anti-French sentiments,[110] and at least some locals,
following the example of the Italian Fascists, offered to provide physical protection for middle-class business establishments.[111]

The various groups also shared a basic belief that the Weimar
Republic would be overthrown by an armed insurrection of the
Bavarian groups. Hitler at one point considered participating in the
Bavarian elections,[112] but by the beginning of 1923 he had rejected
electoral activity for the NSDAP [113] and fully accepted the necessity
of a cooperative armed uprising.[114] In short, in the minds of the
leaders of its peer groups, at the beginning of 1923 the NSDAP
under Hitler was — ideologically, emotionally, and strategically — a
fully integrated unit in the multi-group conspiracy against the Republic. The NSDAP both regarded itself and was in turn regarded as one
of a number of political partners that would jointly overthrow the
legal government of Germany and establish a völkisch dictatorship in
its place.

Hitler's willingness to integrate the party into the overall conspiracy effort and, even more so, his acceptance of the need for
armed insurrection resulted in important changes of emphasis

110. This is based upon the articles published in the journal *Wirtschafts-
politische Aufbau-Korrespendenz über Ostfragen und ihre Bedeutung für
Deutschland* from January to October 1923. The editor of the magazine was
Max Scheubner-Richter, at this time Hitler's closest political advisor. Maser,
Frühgeschichte, pp. 405–06, gives a brief biographical sketch of Scheubner-
Richter.

111. See, for example, Ogrl. Geislingen to Executive Committee of the - - - - -
Guild [sic], 7 Aug. 1923, NA, T-84, roll 5, frames 3956–58.

112. At least Esser's 1920 draft constitution left the possibility open, and
Feder, in 1923, urged Hitler to allow NSDAP members to stand for election
(see Esser, "Nationalsozialistische," NA, T-84, roll 5, frame 4442; Feder to
Hitler, 10 Aug. 1923, in Hale, "Gottfried Feder," p. 362).

113. See Albrecht Hoffmann, *Der 9. November 1923 im Lichte der völkischen
Freiheitsbewegung* (Lorch, Württemberg, 1924), p. 5 and Hitler's testimony,
26 Feb. 1924, in *Hitler-Prozess,* NA, T-84, roll 1, frame 52.

114. This is clearly revealed through various references to Hitler in the paper
of General Epp, NA, T-84, roll 10, frames 9916 ff.

within the organizational structure of the NSDAP. These factors meant, in effect, that the party, like the other groups on the far right, would give primary status to its paramilitary forces, and simultaneously de-emphasize the routine organizational and propagandistic activities designed to increase the membership as a whole. The party's paramilitary unit, the SA, had been established as part of the reorganization of the party in July 1921.[115] A youth group, which was established a short time later, complemented the SA by recruiting and training younger party members, that is, those who had not seen military service in World War I.[116]

The SA's organizational structure paralleled that of the political administration, but Hitler did not allow the storm troopers to infiltrate and dominate the political structure of the party. The SA never had a completely separate organizational life; it was simply the "armed part of the movement."[117] Moreover, to preclude further the fragmentation of the movement into a political and a military wing, the organizational hierarchy of the party and the SA were completely intertwined. The SA was organized into regiments, corresponding to party locals, and, where necessary, into centuries (*Hundertschaften*), paralleling the sections in Munich. SA members trained with the centuries and regiments, but they also attended section meetings with regular party members.[118] Finally, although trained for eventual action in civil and guerilla warfare, the SA also served as guards and rowdies at Nazi propaganda meetings. Thus, at least in theory, they never lost contact with the day-to-day political activities of the party. Nevertheless, the SA quickly became not only the clearly recognized elite formation of the NSDAP,[119] but in fact the party's only significant power factor.

After the assassination of the German foreign minister, Walter

115. *VB*, 14 Aug. 1921.

116. See, "Satzungen," HA, roll 18, folder 331. See also Lenk, "Werden" *ibid.*, folder 333; and SA-Okdo. to Munich Regiment, "Befehl," 19 June 1923, NA, T-81, roll 90, frame 103037.

117. ST. [sic], "Verhältnis der S.A. zur Parteiorganisation," *Nachrichtenblatt* [of the SA], No. 2 (26 Oct. 1923), NA, T-81, roll 90, frame 102846.

118. SA Regiment Munich, "Regimentsbefehl Nr. 13 — Br. B. Nr. 31/5/23," 7 May 1923, *ibid.*, frame 102941.

119. See the report on Hitler's speech in Berlin on 8 Dec. 1921 in Johann K. von Engelbrechten and Hans Volz, eds., *Wir wandern durch das nationsozialistische Berlin* (Munich, 1937), p. 53.

Rathenau, in September 1922 the Weimar authorities sought ener-
getically to suppress the political activities of the extreme right.
The NSDAP was prohibited in virtually all German states except
Bavaria.[120] Here, however, Hitler and the NSDAP rose to increasing prominence. In December 1922 Hitler's foremost rival, the German Socialist Party, voluntarily dissolved itself and advised its members to join the NSDAP.[121] Simultaneously the SA devolped into
a formidable free corps type of unit which often participated in
joint military maneuvers with non-Nazi organizations.[122] This spirit
of cooperation also extended to the Reichswehr, and the Bavarian
command regarded the SA (along with other groups) as part of
the auxiliary force that could be readily mobilized to supplement
regular Reichswehr troops if the need arose.[123] All of these events
meant that, when the various conspiracy plans began to be formulated in earnest in the spring and summer of 1923, both Hitler as
a person and the NSDAP as an organization were political factors
that could not be overlooked. To be sure, Hitler did not always
play a very active role in the planning efforts, but it is nevertheless significant that he was consulted by such prominent conspirators as General von Seeckt and the industrialists around Hugo
Stinnes.[124]

The fitting climax of Hitler's and the NSDAP's political career
before the Putsch was Hitler's appointment as political leader of the
Kampfbund (Militant Association) in the spring of 1923. Sensing
that the complete disintegration of German political and social life
might be near, a number of militant far-right organizations formed a
loose union to coordinate their effort against the Republic. In addition
to the NSDAP, the association consisted of a number of Bavarian

120. Maser, *Frühgeschichte*, p. 345, lists the dates of the formal prohibitions
in the various states.
121. *Ibid.*, p. 233.
122. See SA Regiment Munich, "Rgt. Bef. Nr. 13," 7 May 1923, NA, T-81,
roll 90, frame 102942.
123. See Thilo Vogelsang, *Reichswehr, Staat und NSDAP* (Stuttgart, 1962),
p. 35; and the letter of a candidate for party membership to Hitler, 1 Oct. 1923,
NA, T-84, roll 4, frame 3039.
124. Maser, *Frühgeschichte*, pp. 385, 396; and George W. F. Hallgarten,
Hitler, Reichswehr und Industrie (Frankfurt, 1962), p. 89. Hallgarten's little
book is the most lucid guide through the maze of conflicting and interconnecting
putsch plans in 1923.

free corps, including Oberland, Reichskriegsflagge, and Bayern und Reich.[125] The Kampfbund had both a military commander, Colonel Kriebel, and a political leader. Hitler's functions were a curious amalgam of public relations duties and high-level policy formulation. Thus he helped to publicize the new confederation and was to some extent instrumental in associating additional organizations with it.[126] Yet he also represented the associated free corps organizations in the important negotiations with the Bavarian Reichswehr and governmental authorities.

Hitler's appointment to the Kampfbund was also an important event in the organizational history of the NSDAP itself. The party's chairman now began increasingly to neglect the political organization of the party and permitted the SA to become the focal point of virtually all party activity.[127] Hitler himself devoted his energies to the political preparations of the Putsch. As a result, the NSDAP was now formally a part of the overall rightist conspiracy, and Hitler no longer claimed an exclusive position for his party.[128] This was particularly true of the activities of the SA, which was no longer subject to Hitler's military orders but subordinate (along with the other free corps) to Kriebel's commands. In essence, Hitler now based his hopes for political power not on his own abilities and the organizational strength of the NSDAP but upon his effective political utilization of the free corps' bayonets.

The often nebulous Putsch plans assumed concrete form in August. The member organizations of the Kampfbund generally assumed that once a signal had been given by the Bavarian governmental authorities, a combined armed force consisting of the Bavarian units of the Reichswehr, the Kampfbund units, and other far-right groups would move northward from Bavaria to Berlin.[129] There was no doubt among

125. Kriebel (the military commander of the Kampfbund) to the members, 21 June 1923, NA, T-81, roll 90, frame 103027.

126. Hofmann, *Hitlerputsch,* p. 83; and Kurt Finker, "Die militaristischen Wehrverbände in der Weimarer Republik," *Zeitschrift für Geschichtswissenschaft,* XIV (1966, No. 3), 365.

127. SA Regiment Munich, "Rgt. Befehl Nr. 1" and "Rgt. Befehl Nr. 3," 9 April 1923, NA, T-81, roll 90, frames 102953 and 102956; see also SA-Okdo to Regiment Munich, 21 April 1923, *ibid.,* frame 103064.

128. See Röhm, *Geschichte,* p. 196; and Kriebel's oral testimony during the Hitler trial, in [Volksgerichtshof München] "Hauptverhandlung gegen Hitler und Gen. wegen Hochverrates" (Munich, 1924), NA, T-84, roll 1, frame 352.

129. ST., "Politische Lage," *Nachrichtenblatt* [der SA] No. 2, (26 Oct. 1923), NA, T-81, roll 90, frame 102846.

the leaders of the various conspiratorial groups that the Bavarian governmental authorities would lead the rebellion and cooperate with the far-right groups.[130]

At the end of October even some of the tactical details had been worked out. The SA was reorganized to function as a military battalion, and middle-echelon commanders were acquainted with the political goals of the insurrection.[131] The conspiracy became nationwide. The SA unit at Merseburg in Thuringia was placed under the command of Theodor Düsterberg, a special confidant of Ludendorff, who was, however, not a member of the NSDAP. Hitler himself acted in close cooperation with Albrecht von Graefe, one of the far-right leaders in the north.[132]

In early November all was ready. The paramilitary units stood poised; Hitler's (and the NSDAP's) political future rested upon the success of the Putsch. Only the signal from the Reichswehr and government authorities was needed to set the revolt in motion. The Kampf-bund leaders expected the sign shortly after, Hans von Seisser, the head of the Bavarian state police, returned from his talks in Berlin on November 4.[133] It did not come, and two days later Ritter von Kahr, the head of the Bavarian government, informed the Kampfbund leaders that the Putsch would not take place.[134] Hitler disagreed. As political leader of the Kampfbund he decided to proceed on his own. The paramilitary units received orders to mobilize on the evening of the eighth.[135] The "Hitler Putsch" was to run its course after all.

130. See Gregor Strasser's (at this time head of the SA in Landshut) testimony during the Hitler trial, NA, T-84, roll 1, frame 904. See also Göring's statement in a meeting of the Kampfbund leaders on 23 October in [Reichswehr], Wehrkreiskommando VII, 19. Inf. Rgt., "Der Putsch vom 8. November 1923 — Vorgeschichte und Verlauf" (Munich, 1924), NA, T-79, roll 57, frame 162. On the general problem of Reichswehr involvement see Francis L. Carsten, *Reichswehr und Politik* (Cologne, 1964), pp. 193–202. During his trial Hitler shrewdly forced Kahr and Lossow to all but admit that they had actively participated in the putsch plans. See NA, T-84, roll 2, frames 1346, 1425 ff. and 2027–28. The best recent account of the putsch and its preparations is Hofmann, *Hitlerputsch*.

131. See Gregor Strasser's testimony, NA, T-84, roll 1, frame 901.

132. SA-Okdo, "Befehl," 26 Oct. 1923, HA, roll 16, folder 299.

133. Hallgarten, *Hitler*, p. 77, n.79.

134. Wehrkreiskommando VII, "Putsch," NA, T-84, roll 4, frame 158.

135. SA, Rgt. Mü., "Regimentsbefehl Nr. 86 — Br. B. Nr. 266/XI/23," 7 Nov. 1923, NA, T-81, roll 90, frame 102831.

The Putsch failed, of course. Despite the efforts of Hitler and the hero of the entire far right, General Luderdorff, the independent action of the Kampfbund units could not bestir the Reichswehr from its "parade-rest" attitude. But precisely because it failed, it became a politically instructive experience for Hitler and an important lesson for the organizational development of the party. Hitler was forced to gamble his political future in November 1923 primarily because he had lost control of his options. He had allowed his actions to become dependent on the decisions of other power segments in the conspiracy to such an extent that he had no real choice but to move. He had already opted for a military solution when he accepted the political leadership of the Kampfbund. Although the membership of the NSDAP stood at 55,000 in November 1923 (of whom 287 had joined on November eighth and ninth)[136] Hitler could not really utilize this power factor since he had decided against a political solution. The party's future in November rested solely upon the shoulders of the SA and upon their non-Nazi allies; as a result, the party's leader himself had to ponder his political future as a prisoner in the fortress at Landsberg.

Hitler's failure in 1923 was the result of two fundamental organizational errors. He allowed the NSDAP to become a primarily military organization and he permitted the integration of its military force into an overall far-right command over which both Hitler as a person and the NSDAP as an institution had very little control. Hitler also trusted his fellow conspirators. There never was a "Hitler Putsch"; there was only a vast conspiracy of the entire Bavarian right, directed by the head of the Bavarian government and the commanding general of the Bavarian Reichswehr.[137] The "Hitler Putsch" was merely the last, desperate gamble of a man who had whipped up mass support for the Putsch and who now found himself deserted by his co-conspirators. The Putsch of 1923 was a lesson in political fickleness which Hitler neither forgot nor forgave.

136. Maser, *Frühgeschichte*, p. 463.

137. During Hitler's trial Kahr was forced to admit on the witness stand that he had previously deployed troops (Ehrhardt's brigade) in northern Bavaria in preparation for the putsch. See *Hitler-Prozess*, NA, T-84, roll 2, frame 1629.

Dissolution and Reconstruction*

The collapse of the Putsch, Hitler's imprisonment, and the swift, complete dissolution of the NSDAP were simultaneous developments.[1] The political organization of the party did not survive beyond the Putsch because it had never considered that the revolt might fail. On the contrary, Hitler had largely neglected the political and organizational aspects of the party's activities in the fall of 1923, so that the NSDAP had prepared no guidelines for underground activities or a clandestine organizational framework. Instead, most of the party's active members simply resumed their apolitical status in the wake of the Putsch. Their views on the Weimar Republic had not changed, and they would still cast their votes for völkisch parties, but most had left their physical activism, their élan, on the cobblestones of the Odeonsplatz.

Most, but not all. A small proportion remained militant and attempted to carry on some sort of organizational life. They were a numerically and politically insignificant group, particularly since they immediately split into a number of bitterly feuding factions. The successor organizations differed on a large number of issues, but considerations of organizational strategies and tactics occupied a prominent place among the controversies. Immediately after the

*Parts of this chapter have appeared earlier as an article entitled "The Conversion of Myth into Power: the NSDAP 1925–1926," *American Historical Review,* LXXII (April 1967), 906–24.

1. On the disintegration of the party see Bavaria, Generalstaatskommissar, "Lagebericht Nr. 3," 22 Jan. 1924 in Reichswehr, Wehrkreiskommando VII, 19. Inf. Rgt., "Der Putsch am 8. November 1923—Vorgeschichte und Verlauf" (cited hereafter as RW, "Putsch") (Munich, 1924), NA, T–79, roll 57, frames 261–64.

Putsch a more moderate wing of the former Reichsleitung[2] (led by Drexler and Feder) wanted to demilitarize the party by cutting all connections between the political organization and the SA. They were opposed by several of the recent SA leaders who hoped to continue in secret not only the activities of the storm troopers, but to reestablish ties with some of the free corps as well.[3] The split was by no means restricted to Bavaria. Sauckel in Thuringia sought to create an artificial community of militants whose entire social life was to be permeated by völkisch ideals. In the Upper Palatinate, on the other hand, it was considered much more important to revitalize the völkisch paramilitary groups.[4]

Actually these controversies were neither new nor representative of the essence of the division among the factions of the völkisch movement. Disagreements over the relative significance of political and military activities of the party had characterized the NSDAP long before the Putsch. Only the force of Hitler's personality had prevented their earlier emergence into public view. More important still, the conflict was far deeper than a mere disagreement over political tactics. Rather, it was a bitter struggle between two groups, dissimilar both socially and chronologically, over the very aims and organizational principles of the German völkisch movement. The older group, the "pioneers" as Joseph Goebbels later sarcastically dubbed them,[5] graduated to the postwar fellowship after an apprenticeship in the prewar anti-semitic movement. Born in the years 1860 to 1890, primarily of lower-middle-class origins, they saw their social status as shopkeepers or lower officials endangered even before the war, and turned desperately to

2. The term *Reichsleitung* will be used whenever reference is made to activities or decisions involving the party's administrative and political leadership at the national level. Such activities may have involved Hitler personally, but did not at all times. There are instances in which Hitler made a decision by not negating an order of a bureaucrat at the national office.

3. Reichswehr, Wehrkreiskommando VII, "Lagebericht vom 17.11.23," and "Geheime Richtlinien der K[ampf]-B[ünde]," 3 Dec. 1923, *ibid.*, frames 286–87 and 465.

4. Sauckel, "Vorschlag zur Organisation der NSDAP im Bezirk des Thüringerwaldes" (1924), NA, T-81, roll 116, frame 136962; and Bayr. Min. d. Inn., Referat 25, "Stellungnahme zu den aufgelösten Parteien und Organisationen," 31 July 1924, BAStA, M.A. 71536.

5. Joseph Goebbels, "Die Radikalisierung des Sozialismus," *NS-Briefe* (No. 6), 15 Dec. 1925.

the still ineffective anti-semitic, anti-urban, anti-industrial organizations with their club-like atmospheres and weekly beer evenings. For them the entire völkisch program could be reduced to the demand that the social status of the lower middle classes not be endangered by progressive industrialization and urbanization, evils which they in turn construed as Jewish manipulations. Their concept of the party's organization focused lovingly on the artificial society of believers who persevered and practiced völkisch ideals in the midst of an urbanized mass society.

The second group was recruited primarily from the "front-generation," that is, those born in the years between 1890 and 1900. They were quite often too young to have achieved a position of status in the prewar Reich, and for many of them standing in the trenches of World War I and experiencing there a sense of "front-line socialism" had been the most moving event of their lives. Consequently, for the second group the völkisch program was a form of social idealism or revolution rather than social reaction. Instead of attempting to mobilize the middle classes, they hoped to tap "the fermenting power that resides in the people." [6] Specifically, they would attempt to convert the proletarian masses from a belief in international socialism (Marxism) to faith in national socialism.[7] They self-consciously looked upon themselves as revolutionaries, countenancing the use of violence and ridiculing the futile efforts of those who "always remain decent and subdued, the savers [and] the social security recipients." [8] Nevertheless both groups enthusiastically accepted Hitler's leadership because in spite of their many differences they shared a belief in two important parts of the völkisch ideology: like the "pioneers," the "revolutionaries" believed the obstacle to realization of their aims to be the Jew; and, both groups rejected parliamentary democracy

6. *NS–Briefe* (No. 3), 1 Nov. 1925.

7. See, for example, the resolution of district leaders in the Cologne area, in GL Rheinland-Süd to RL, 2 March 1925, in BA, Schu. Slg. 203. This desire to establish contact with the laboring masses was at times carried to quite naïve extremes. G. Seifert, for example, became head of the Göttingen local because "he was a manual laborer." See Ludolf Haase, "Aufstand in Niedersachsen" (hereafter cited as "Aufstand") (handwritten MS, Göttingen [?], 1942), cited after the two-volume typescript copy in the possession of the Forschungsstelle für die Geschichte des Nationalsozialismus in Hamburg, I, p. 76.

8. Goebbels, "Radikalisierung."

and called for a personal dictatorship as the only suitable form of government in Germany.[9]

Before the Putsch the two groups suppressed their differences because each welcomed the overthrow of the Weimar Republic as the prerequisite for establishing its version of the völkisch millenium. However, when the crack of rifle shots ended the dream of an anti-semitic, national–military dictatorship, the artificial unity was at an end. The two wings now formed separate organizational entities which had little in common except a continuing veneration for the person of Adolf Hitler. The Greater German People's Community(*Grossdeutsche Volksgemeinschaft*, GDVG) became the most prominent haven for the militant pioneer elements; a majority of the revolutionaries joined the National Socialist Freedom Party (*Nationalsozialistische Freiheitspartei*, NSFP). The GDVG was numerically and politically the weaker group. Although it carried a number of prominent former NSDAP officials—such as Esser, Streicher, Schwarz, and Amann — on its membership rolls, it had no real organization outside of Bavaria, and even there its membership strength was concentrated almost exclusively in the three cities of Munich, Nuremberg, and Bamberg.[10] The only other significant pioneer organization was in Thuringia, where Artur Dinter and Fritz Sauckel were able to continue the party organization under the NSDAP label.[11]

By comparison, the NSFP was a far more viable political organization.[12] Although it was nominally a result of a merger between the old German Völkisch Freedom Party (*Deutschvölkische Freiheitspartei*,

9. The best overall discussion of the "revolutionary right" is in Otto-Ernst Schüddekopf, *Linke Leute von rechts* (Stuttgart, 1960). For the "pioneers" see Peter G. J. Pulzer, *The Rise of Political Anti-Semitism in Germany and Austria* (New York, 1964). The correlation between youth and revolutionary ideology is characteristic of revolutionary movements in general. See Harry Eckstein, "On the Etiology of Internal Wars," *History and Theory*, IV (1965, No. 2), 156.

10. GDVG, "Rundschreiben," 7 Aug. 1924, HA, roll 42, folder 857.

11. Dinter to Ogrl. Gössnitz and Schmöller, 12 Dec. 1924, HA, roll 7, folder 160. Thuringia was the only German state in which the NSDAP had not been forbidden after the putsch.

12. The political focal point of the entire movement during the interregnum was outside Bavaria. See Reichskommissar für die Überwachung der öffentlichen Ordnung, "Lagebericht Nr. 106," 22 Aug. 1924, BGStA, M.A. 101235. See also DVFP, Gau Frankfurt a.O./Grenzmark, "Sitzungsbericht über den Gauvertretertag in Frankfurt a. Oder am 22. Februar 1925," HA, roll 9, folder 198.

DVFP) and some of the northern NSDAP organizations, the DVFP remained the dominant influence in the new constellation. (Gregor Strasser was the only prominent NSDAP leader to join the northern group.) The pre-Putsch NSDAP in northern Germany had been very much of an organizational stepchild. Since Hitler expected the events in Bavaria to propel him to national prominence, he was not really seriously concerned with the party's organizational expansion outside of Bavaria. On the contrary, he welcomed the DVFP's presence in these areas. Late in the fall of 1923 he even agreed to the DVFP's proposal to assign geographic areas to one party or the other to prevent duplication of organizational efforts.[13] The DVFP, on the other hand, was relatively well organized in northern Germany and had already achieved considerable prominence in some areas, notably Thuringia and Mecklenburg.[14]

Both the NSFP and the GDVG pledged eternal loyalty to the imprisoned Hitler and simultaneously accused the rival group of betraying the erstwhile leader. A unity conference at Weimar in the summer of 1924 brought no solution: the northern group (with the general's permission) nominated Ludendorff as substitute hero, but Streicher and Esser refused to bow even before the name of the man modestly introduced as the "victor of Tannenberg." [15] In the meantime Hitler had gone into temporary retirement. Apparently he began his prison term with the hope that he could lead or at least arbitrate the various factions from his cell, but he soon found that this was impractical. While he became the dumping ground for innumerable complaints and counter-complaints, he was unable to exercise compensatory personnel and organizational control. In July he pronounced himself an unemployed politician again, and thereafter (until his

13. NSDAP [Esser] and DVFP [Graefe], "Abmachung," 24 Oct. 1923, HA, roll 69, folder 1508. The treaty was found in the offices of the *VB* when the Bavarian police raided the premises after the Putsch. See the marginalia on *ibid.*

14. Lewis Hertzman, *DNVP, Right-Wing Opposition in the Weimar Republic* (Lincoln, Neb., 1963), p. 162.

15. Hitler had originally appointed Alfred Rosenberg as organizational caretaker, but the party's chief pseudointellectual proved completely incapable of keeping the organization together. On Rosenberg's appointment see Haase, "Aufstand," I, p. 361. On the Weimar meeting see Reinhard Sunkel, "Nationalsozialistische Vertretertagung in Weimar vom 20. Juli 1924," Forschst. NS Hbg., folder "NSDAP–NSAG"; and Haase, "Aufstand," II, p. 500.

release) he categorically refused to intervene in the quarrels of his successors.[16]

Hitler's silence only encouraged his successors to continue their quarrels.[17] By the end of the year, the feud of the GDVG and the NSFP had created a number of potentially serious problems. In addition to an obvious north–south split in the movement, the interregnum brought up the Ludendorff problem. Hitler had always attempted to associate the party and himself with Ludendorff's respected position in völkisch circles, and the question of relative position, that is Ludendorff before Hitler or vice versa, had not arisen in the old party. But Ludendorff's clear option at Weimar for the NSFP and against the GDVG made a political identification of Hitler and Ludendorff considerably more difficult for many of the völkisch followers. This in turn rendered the organizational expansion of the party north of Bavaria a dubious political advantage for Hitler. The union with the DVFP had increased the number of Nazi-völkisch locals in the north, but many of the northern members had never met Hitler, and Ludendorff was a far more real and active leader-figure to them.

When Hitler emerged from his prison cell in December, he returned as a saint, eagerly awaited and welcomed by all of the völkisch groups.[18] The movement that unanimously greeted him was, however, a politically unimportant splinter group in the overall context of German politics. With the exception of some DVFP-dominated areas in the north, it had neither organizational cohesion or strength. All of this constituted a grave political setback for Hitler, but from an organizational standpoint it was not a completely unwelcome development. The failure of the Putsch had convinced Hitler that further attempts to overthrow the Republic by force would be futile. Consequently the pre-Putsch party with its image of a compact pseudo-military shock troop was not only anachronistic, but, in view of Hitler's probationary release from jail, politically dangerous. In the

16. GDVG, "Rundschreiben," 7 Aug. 1924, HA, roll 41, folder 857.

17. For a good description of the rivalries see Jeremy Noakes, "Conflict and Development in the NSDAP, 1924–1927," *Journal of Contemporary History,* I (Oct. 1966), 4 ff.

18. Haase, "Aufstand," I, pp. 368 ff.; and GDVG, "Rundschreiben," 7 Aug. 1924, p. 4, in HA, roll 42, folder 857. Each fully expected, of course, that its rivals would then be cast out of the new party.

new party he needed a mass political following, not an elite military one. While a putsch may be carried out by a few thousand well-organized men, winning power by means of other political pressures requires disciplined, well-organized mass support distributed over a wide geographic area. In November 1923 the NSDAP had not had this kind of support: it was not an all-German party, and its organizational distinction from the rest of the Bavarian völkisch movement was not always clear. To establish the new NSDAP on a basis of mass political following, Hitler had to adopt a complete change of organizational strategy. Specifically, he needed the support of both "pioneers" and "revolutionaries." [19] In view of their wide differences, this necessitated that both groups place loyalty to him above their programmatic aims; in essence he had to become the party's program. In other words, for the members and supporters of the new NSDAP, Adolf Hitler had to become the personalized fusion of their means and ends. His followers had to visualize his personal political successes and the realization of the völkisch program-myths as inseparable developments.

Hitler began his political comeback by establishing some much-needed priorities. Should he attempt to rebuild the party in the north or Bavaria first? His entire political background had been Bavarian, but the GDVG was certainly not an uncomplicated nucleus for a rebuilding program. The leaders of this three-city movement, Streicher and Esser, had considerable appeal in Bavaria but they were particularly unpopular among the Nazis in the north. Financially the GDVG was almost a liability. Its most active local, the Schwabing section of Munich, had managed to increase its debts from RM 56.00 in May 1924 to RM 124.00 at the end of June. As the year closed it had successfully reduced the figure to RM 40.00.[20]

Nonetheless, the GDVG had two assets that Hitler could not ignore: it controlled most of what remained of the Nazi membership in Munich and it administered the business affairs of the party newspaper, the *Völkischer Beobachter*. At the end of 1924 Max Amann, the executive secretary of the old NSDAP and now a leading member

19. Hess to Heinz Heim, 16 Aug. 1924, HA, roll 50, folder 1182.
20. See GDVG, Sektion Schwabing, "Sektionskasse-Tagebuch [März 1924–5.1.1927] (MS), HA, roll 2A, folder 227.

of the GDVG, headed the Eher publishing house. Although the firm employed only three persons at the end of the interregnum, it had preserved the house's legal and organizational continuity, so that it needed merely to be enlarged, not reestablished.[21] The GDVG's position in Munich was an equally important factor. Munich was the city of Hitlerian symbols: Bürgerbräukeller, Zirkus Krone, Feldhernhalle, Odeonsplatz. To build a political party personally loyal to himself, Hitler needed allegiance and support for a mythical super-person, and the process of creating that image could only begin in Munich. Only with well-organized, mass political support in Munich could Hitler begin to convert the image of the national martyr into the reality of politically useful charisma and power that would attract the völkisch masses all over Germany to his new NSDAP. He therefore decided "to create order in Bavaria first."[22]

During the first two months following his release Hitler remained silent. While he did nothing to discourage the waves of adulation that greeted the returning hero from all quarters of the völkisch camp, he refused either to speak publicly or to reveal his future plans to the numerous delegations that sought his advice and blessing. His only overtly political activities were behind-the-scenes conversations with his old collaborators Esser and Pöhner.[23]

His public silence did not, however, bespeak indecision about the future course of the NSDAP. This lull was primarily a tactical device: it assured that his first public appearance as party unifier would be a sensation, not merely another rally. It became precisely that. Though his first public speech was not scheduled to begin until 8 P.M. on February 27, the first visitors lined up in mid-afternoon. At six the police closed the hall; three thousand had found room inside,

---

21. See NSDAP, Hauptarchiv, *Die statistische und geschichtliche Entwicklung der NS-Presse 1926–1935;* Vol I: *NS-Gaupresse* (Munich, 1936), p. 212. On the history of the *VB* see Oron J. Hale, *The Captive Press in the Third Reich* (Princeton, N.J., 1964), chap. 1.

22. Hermann Fobke to Ludolf Haase, 21 Aug. 1924 in Werner Jochmann, ed., *Nationalsozialismus und Revolution* (Frankfurt, 1963), p. 134.

23. PD Nü-Fü, "Lagebericht N/No. 22," BGStA, M.A. 101249; and Friedrich Plümer, *Die Wahrheit über Hitler und seinen Kreis* (Munich, 1925), p. 55. Plümer was a member of the Drexler group who broke with Hitler later in 1925.

another two thousand had to be turned away.[24] When Hitler mounted
the podium, his speech was a masterful effort to connect the future
of the völkisch myths with specific events in his own past. He
spoke in the Bürgerbräukeller, the scene of his first public success
in 1920 and of the speech on November 8, 1923 that launched
the Putsch. He invoked the past unity of the movement; he spoke
as though 1924 had never happened. He had no differences with
Ludendorff, "the most loyal and selfless friend" of the movement.
Invoking the old pseudomilitary images, he appealed to those who
"in their hearts had remained old National Socialists" to rally again
under the unfurled swastika banner. The party's enemies had not
changed: as before, the NSDAP would fight Jewry (for the "pioneers") and Marxism (for the "revolutionaries").

The images of past unity and the assurance of renewed, vigorous leadership did their part. Then, at the end of the speech
Hitler asked that the movement accept him as its unconditional
leader for one year with the words, "I am not willing to accept
any conditions. Once again I take the responsibility for everything that happens in this movement." The stenographer noted
"enthusiastic applause and cries of Heil." At last, "overwhelmed
by the words of Hitler and the enthusiasm [of the crowd], the
rival Bavarian Nazi leaders rushed to the stage pledging loyal
cooperation to Hitler and to each other."[25]

Hitler's speech immediately catapulted him to new prominence
on the Munich political scene. But as yet his renewed popularity
was only the result of mutual emotional empathy between Hitler
and the völkisch masses of Munich: unstructured, unorganized political support. After the Bürgerbräukeller speech Hitler moved quickly
to convert emotional acceptance of his personification of the leader
myth in Munich into concrete, organizational control of those captured by his charismatic appeal. His method was simple. In effect,
he deliberately repeated his Bürgerbräukeller performance numer-

24. PD Mü, Abt VI to Bayr. Staatsmin. d. Inn., "Betreff: Öffentliche Versammlung der Nat. Sozial. Deutschen Arb. Partei am 27. Februar 1925," HA,
roll 87, folder 1835.
25. Adolf Hitler, "Die Rede Adolf Hitlers in der ersten grossen Massenver-
sammlung . . . 27. Februar 1925" (Munich, 1925); "Zum Wiedererstehen unserer
Bewegung," *VB*, 26 Feb. 1925.

ous times as throughout the spring and summer, as he tirelessly appeared at party section meetings in the city. Acting within the established organizational framework of the membership meetings, he was able to achieve man-to-man contact with almost all of the Munich membership. Through these meetings Hitler succeeded in solidifying and formalizing the effects of his charismatic control devices — oral communication, handshakes, eye-to-eye contact, and the like — into the members' personal subordination to his organizational leadership.

The rank-and-file membership in Munich enthusiastically accepted Hitler's claim that the future of the NSDAP depended upon his personal control of its organization. In March the GDVG voluntarily dissolved itself, and by the beginning of spring Hitler had complete organizational control of the party in Munich. Both the members of the executive committee and the various section leaders were his appointees and subordinates. The city executive committee met frequently during the spring and summer of 1925, but there is no evidence that it was more than a sounding board for Hitler's speeches.[26] A rival group, the National Socialist People's Association (*Nationalsozialistischer Volksbund*, NSVB), which refused to acknowledge the complete identification of Hitler's will and the future of the party, was unable to attract any significant support among the party membership. It was stillborn long before a pro-Hitler mob led by Esser and Streicher forcefully prevented a scheduled mass meeting and sealed its political oblivion.[27]

Paralleling Hitler's efforts in Munich, his two personal representatives, Esser and Streicher, utilized their own popularity in the Bavarian countryside. Tirelessly, they duplicated Hitler's tactics and persuaded the scattered outlying locals to rally behind the returned hero. By late March almost all Bavarian party locals had submitted a neo-feudal oath of subordination to Hitler's authority.[28]

---

26. A meeting in September 1925, for example, had no agenda; the minutes merely noted that "Mr. Hitler wanted to speak to the entire executive committee before he left on his lengthy trip." See BA, Schu. Slg. 373.

27. PD Nü-Fü., "Lagebericht N/No. 38," 9 Oct. 1925, BGStA, M.A. 101249. On the history of the Volksbund, see the earlier numbers of the police reports in *ibid.*; a pro-Volksbund account is in Plümer, *Wahrheit.*

28. "Lagebericht N/No. 26," 20 March 1925, *ibid.*

Throughout the Bavarian campaign, Hitler's, Esser's, and Streicher's speeches were singularly devoid of positive ideas, or even a discussion of issues. In Bavaria this was apparently not a serious handicap to political success. The Nazi membership there consisted primarily of "pioneers" for whom anti-semitism was the program of the party, and a handshake, a glance from the steel-grey eyes, and a vehement diatribe against "international Judah" (laced, in the case of Streicher, with pious pornography) was sufficient to send them to their knees in adoration.

Outside Bavaria this one-sided approach was less successful. While detailed statistical analyses of the Nazi Party membership in the formative years are still lacking, it is clear that significant differences existed between Hitler's supporters north and south of the Main River. The northerners were far younger; a large percentage of those joining the party in 1925 were under twenty-five years of age. It appears likely that some two-thirds of the membership in 1925 was not yet thirty.[29] Perhaps largely because of their youth, a far greater proportion of northern leaders and followers sympathized with the "revolutionary" wing of the völkisch movement. They continued to think of themselves as activist soldier-revolutionaries. Young, often declassed or displaced students and unemployable pseudo-intellectuals,[30] they rejected the norms of their elders as stagnant and reactionary. Immediately after the war their zeal for activity found an outlet in the various free corps. They defended the Reich against its external enemies in Silesia and Pomerania, and they battled what to them was German bourgeois cowardice and Jewish–Marxist democracy in the Kapp Putsch. They flocked to Bavaria in the fall of 1923 to participate in yet another national insurrection. Now that the era of violence was at least temporarily over, they prepared the way of the future by planning schemes to bridge the prewar dichotomy between the proletarian masses and the middle class.[31]

None of this meant, of course, that they rejected Hitler as their leader, but it did mean that their view of the party's leader and

29. Noakes, "Conflict," p. 11.

30. For example, Haase and Backe (in Göttingen) were students, Goebbels an unemployed writer, Pfeffer a former free corps leader, and Kaufmann the declassed son of a textile manufacturer.

31. Haase, "Aufstand," II, pp. 625–26 and 633–46.

his relation to his followers did not correspond to that of the Streicher's and Esser's.[32] For the revolutionaries, Hitler was one of them: he was the embodiment of the new type of courageous soldier-politician. They agreed with Hitler's anti-semitic outbursts,[33] but they admired even more the leader who braved police bayonets in November 1923, who made National Socialism a part of the NSDAP's name, and who had always acted in close comradeship with Ludendorff.

The initial response to Hitler's return to political life was no less favorable in the north than in the south. The NSFP dissolved itself in mid-March and urged its membership to join either the DVFP or the NSDAP.[34] In most locals and *Gaus* (party districts), the NSDAP won the ensuing popularity contest, since Hitler's northern lieutenants evoked the images of both Hitler and Ludendorff. In good conscience they assured the membership that Hitler and the general had no political or personal differences.[35] The immediate consequence of these tactics was a rapid growth of the network of NSDAP Gaus and locals in northern Germany. On the other hand, Hitler's unwillingness to be quite honest about either his political conceptions or his relationship with Ludendorff also led to the establishment of certain organizational practices and programmatic expectations that Hitler was later to find undesirable. Thus the identification of Ludendorff and Hitler encouraged northern leaders to continue their attacks on the southern pioneers,[36] thereby

32. This was sensed by contemporary observers as well. See R.Ko.In., "Lagebericht Nr. 7540/II," 16 Dec. 1925, BGStA, M.A. 101249; and Carlo Mierendorff, "Gesicht und Charakter der nationalsozialistischen Bewegung," *Gesellschaft,* VIII (June 1930), 503.

33. However, for the "revolutionaries" anti-semitism alone was not enough. The district leader of Lausitz (Silesia), for example, wrote that the NSDAP had to liberate the German worker from the "bonds of his Jewish and German seducers." See NSDAP, Bzl. Lausitz to Dinter, 25 Feb. 1925, in BA, Schu. Slg. 208 I.

34. See GL Schleswig-Holstein to Hitler, 6 March 1925, BA, Schu. Slg. 208.

35. "Bericht über die erste Gautagung der N.S.D.A.P. Gau Schleswig-Holstein in Neumünster am 1. März 1925," in *ibid.* "Honoring Ludendorff as of old, we move forward in loyal comradeship of arms with Adolf Hitler," read an early circular of the Silesian party leadership. See GL Silesia to the locals in Silesia, 20 March 1925, *ibid.*

36. See the report on a speech by Mutschmann (the GL of Saxony) to Dinter, 26 Feb. 1925, BA, Schu. Slg. 208 I.

deepening the cleavage between the two wings. In addition, Hitler's immediate interest in organizational growth per se resulted in the appointment of a large number of political entrepreneurs to leadership positions. Indeed, most local leaders were self-appointed in that they offered their services either to the Munich headquarters directly or through one of Hitler's personal acquaintances.[37] Hitler's northern legate, Gregor Strasser (who was well known in the north since he had opted for the NSFP during the interregnum) did provisionally appoint *Gauleiters* (Gau leaders) "as Adolf Hitler's plenipotentiary" (*mit Vollmacht Adolf Hitlers*), but the only criterion for appointment seems to have been the availability of a willing man. The Gauleiter of Hanover, for example, lost control over the district of Lüneburg and the city of Göttingen simply because there were two other energetic individuals who also wanted to be Gauleiter in Lower Saxony.[38]

The resultant leadership corps in the north was a group that strongly resembled the free corps activists, in both age and mentality. Four of the ten northern Gauleiters were under thirty-five years of age, and one was less than twenty-five. More than half (six) were under forty. Socially they represented the "solid" middle classes. Five had attended a university, eight listed themselves as civil servants or professionals, two as white-collar workers.[39]

After Hitler had "created order in Bavaria," he traveled extensively in the north reinforcing his leader image through personal appearances at closed party meetings. His deliberately schizophrenic leadership and his personal magnetism created strong personal, emotional bonds between leader and subleader in all parts of Germany, but this relationship was almost the antithesis of a bureaucratized mass party administration. Hitler himself was still not an able administrator; on the contrary, he was unable to work systematically or to

37. See, for example, Telschow (Gl Lüneburg-Stade) to RL, 3 March 1925; Paul Hacke (local leader in Potsdam) to Mrs. Bechstein, 18 March 1925, in BA, Schu. Slg. 202 I and 205; and Amann to G. Seifert, 17 Oct. 1925, HA, roll 6, folder 141.

38. For the terms of a GL appointment see GL Hannover-Nord to RL, 29 March 1925, BA, Schu. Slg. 202 I. On the problems in Lower Saxony see Rust (GL Hannover) to RL, 5 April 1925, *ibid.*

39. These statistics are based upon the biographical data available in the personnel records of the BDC.

delegate authority rationally.[40] On the other hand, he was acutely aware of the importance of establishing bureaucratic administrative patterns for the future growth of the NSDAP as a mass party,[41] and his abundance of charisma attracted the type of men who, having no magnetism of their own, needed the anonymity of the bureaucratic office to give them power and self-satisfaction. The early Nazi Party had the services of two efficient bureaucrat-administrators, the Executive Secretary, Philip Bouhler, and the Treasurer, Franz Xaver Schwarz. Both were notable for their lack of personal leadership qualities. Bouhler, an owlish-looking man whose personal authority vanished with the removal of his title and his rubber stamp, was aware of the extent of his dependence on Hitler. Even in later years he prefaced each sentence he addressed to Hitler with a slight bow.[42] Schwarz had spent his entire adult life in an accountant's office, first at the Munich city hall, and then at party headquarters. Together, Bouhler and Schwarz became complementary parts of a human computer. Bouhler delighted in issuing rules for office procedures that contained admonitions such as "Smoking during office hours is forbidden," and "The outgoing mail must be presented in the signature folder to the executive secretary at 5:30 each evening."[43] Schwarz watched with loving care over each incoming penny, and both men pounced upon any local that attempted to bypass the central administration in issuing local membership cards.

Despite its seeming innocuousness, the question of issuing membership cards was a very controversial one in the early years of the party's history, because it raised the issue of local and provincial administrative autonomy. The northern provincial party administrations, with their belief in a relationship of quasi-equality between

40. Hans Frank, *Im Angesicht des Galgens* (Munich, 1953), pp. 93–94.
41. Heinrich Hoffmann, *Hitler was my Friend*, tr. R. H. Stevens (London, 1955), p. 61, reports Hitler's remarks as he left Landsberg: "The first thing I need is office space."
42. Albert Krebs, *Tendenzen und Gestalten der NSDAP* (Stuttgart, 1959), pp. 142 and 197. On Schwarz's role in the overall administrative history of the NSDAP see Anton Lingg, *Die Verwaltung der Nationalsozialistischen Deutschen Arbeiterpartei* (2d ed.; Munich, 1940).
43. Bouhler, "Rundschreiben an das Personal," 21 March 1925, BA, Schu. Slg. 373.

Munich and the Gaus, were particularly anxious to retain control of the membership cards. Hitler, on the other hand, had no illusions about the dangerous implications of permitting provincial or local initiative in this area: it was only a short step from Gau control of the membership cards to provincial organizational autonomy and an essentially co-option type of party (not to speak of losing the initiation fee of one Reichsmark, which the national office desparately needed). Consequently, Hitler always remained adamant on the question of control of the membership lists. Munich consistently cited the need for greater discipline and alluded to the danger of recreating the chaos of the interregnum when opposing the provincial demands for decentralized administration of membership cards.[44] As a result, there were literally no exceptions to the rule that an applicant could not claim party membership until he was issued a card signed by Hitler and Schwarz.

The bureaucratized efficiency of Bouhler's and Schwarz's day-to-day administration of the party succeeded in progressively centralizing and depersonalizing the party's internal organization, enabling Hitler to concern himself with matters of long-range political strategy. Increasingly, institutional barriers separated Hitler from personal contact with the everyday life of the party. Therefore, the Reichsleitung created an organizational committee which settled local quarrels in Hitler's name, but without requiring Hitler's personal interference.[45] Hitler himself took a more active part in isolating the new NSDAP from the rest of the German völkisch movement. Many of the NSDAP's locals neither expected nor welcomed the self-isolation of the party. On the contrary, the former NSFP locals, for

44. For an exchange of letters on this issue see GL Mecklenburg to RL, 15 June 1925; and RL to GL Mecklenburg, 18 June 1925, in BA, Schu. Slg. 205. It may be of interest for the comparative study of totalitarian parties that the German Communist Party had to deal with the same pressure for local authorization of membership. See PD Nü-Fü, "Lagebericht Nr. 107/II," 3 May 1927, BGStA, M.A. 101251.

45. For the beginnings of the Organizational Committee, see the documents in HA, roll 8, folder 177. See also Hess to KL München, 31 July 1925, HA, roll 4, folder 86. Such local quarrels were everyday occurrences in the NSDAP during the rebuilding period. See, for example, the documents in NA, T–580, roll 20, folder 201; and HA, roll 4, folder 86 (for Halle); also BA, Schu. Slg. 205 (for Potsdam).

example, had fully anticipated that a spirit of friendly cooperation would continue between the members who opted for the NSDAP and those who joined the reestablished DVFP.[46] Hitler had other plans; his first opportunity to put them into practice came with the presidential election of 1925. While most of the other major völkisch groups had agreed to back Karl Jarres as the compromise candidate of the right, Hitler proclaimed Ludendorff as the choice of the NSDAP.[47] The other parties bitterly resented the Nazi break in the ranks, but the move served Hitler's purposes well. In nominating Ludendorff he underlined his respect for the field marshal's name, while at the same time Ludendorff's expected election defeat would document his political impotence. Above all, the Ludendorff-for-President movement forced every NSDAP member to choose between loyalty to the larger movement and loyalty and obedience to Hitler. That choice always involved a major dilemma: to choose Jarres meant disloyalty to Ludendorff and Hitler, and to choose Ludendorff meant a greater commitment to Hitler's organizational leadership than ever before. Many Nazi followers remained true to the larger völkisch movement[48] and refused to follow Hitler. Those who supported Hitler paid a heavy price: after the election[49] Hitler deliberately isolated the small band of his followers from the völkisch movement. A directive of May 1925 prohibited further organizational cooperation between NSDAP locals and their counterparts from other völkisch political units even though in the runoff elections Hitler had rejoined the völkisch movement and supported the victorious candidate, Field Marshal von Hindenburg. As reason Bouhler noted that the other parties had betrayed Ludendorff's cause in the

46. See, for example, "Protokolle des Völkisch-sozialen Blocks, Ortsgruppe Naumburg (Saale), 8.3.24–26.6.26," (MS); minutes of the membership meeting on 21 March 1925, HA, roll 6A, folder 872.

47. See Hitler's directive in *VB*, 21 March 1925. For the reaction in other völkisch groups, see "Turmwarts Tagebuch—Die Reichspräsidentenwahl," *Fridericus*, No. 13 (March 1925).

48. For an illustration of the effect of Hitler's decision on local party organizations, see Hermann Krüger, ed., *Wir waren dabei . . . Berichte über die national-sozialistische Bewegung und Entwicklung im ehemaligen Kreise Isenlage* (Wittingen, 1934), in BA, Schu. Slg. 202 I.

49. Ludendorff received less than 300,000 votes compared to 10.5 million for Jarres. For Hitler's decision in the runoff election, see *VB*, 10 April 1925.

presidential elections.[50] Thus, Ludendorff's very defeat increased Hitler's stature among the faithful. Despised by the rest of the völkisch movement, aware of Ludendorff's political incompetence, they had no choice but to look to Hitler for further leadership.

After the Ludendorff debacle only the DVFP remained as a serious, if rather unwilling, rival in the völkisch movement. The DVFP had no real programmatic differences with the NSDAP. It had also campaigned for Ludendorff,[51] and its leaders still hoped to resurrect the political alliance of the DNVP, the NSDAP, and the militant veterans' organizations (*Wehrverbände*).[52] Hitler promptly sabotaged that project. He forced the NSDAP's members to cut all formal ties to the paramilitary groups, in fact reversing his encouragement of such liaisons earlier in the year.[53] In addition, instead of the cooperation between the German Nationalist People's Party (DNVP) and the NSDAP that Graefe had envisioned, Bouhler set to work fashioning a deliberate and systematic personality-cult centered around Hitler that left no room for other völkisch heroes. Hitler's 1923 Putsch became the culmination of a series of events that had begun on August 1, 1914. Hitler was the personification of the German struggle against all enemies, foreign and domestic, from 1914 to 1923.[54] Hitler was not only the concrete leader of the future völkisch Germany, but his leadership had given meaning to the Reich's past struggles as well. He was *the* twentieth-century leader of the German people.

Hitler's image was looming ever larger over the right wing in southern Germany, but a crisis was developing in the north. There, initial enthusiasm turned to disappointment when, particularly after Ludendorff's defeat, the northern leaders realized that Munich looked upon the party not as a band of free-associating political soldiers,

50. PD Nü-Fü, "Lagebericht N/No. 32," 17 June 1925, BGStA, M.A. 101248. See also *F.Z.*, 12 June 1925.

51. DVFP, Ludendorff-Wahlausschuss für die Grenzmark, "Rundschreiben," HA, roll 9, folder 198.

52. "Protokoll über die Sitzung des Völkischen Führerringes Thüringen mit dem Führer der Deutsch-völkischen Freiheitspartei—Herrn von Graefe" [1925], NA, T–81, roll 116, frames 136980–83.

53. See Hess to Ogrl. Erfurt, 13 March 1926, HA, roll 18, folder 335; and Bouhler to GL Hannover, 23 May 1925, BA, Schu. Slg. 202 I.

54. RL "Rundschreiben," 4 Nov. 1925, BA, Schu. Slg. 373.

but as a group of bureaucratic subordinates largely subject to Bouhler's and Schwarz's control.[55] The sense of disappointment among the leaders was soon transferred to disinterest among the followers: of 138 members who had joined the Potsdam local after Hitler's release, only twenty or thirty remained at all active by August 1925.[56]

Hitler was fully aware of the growing differences within the party,[57] but for some months his primary concern had been simply to hide the Janus face of his leadership image. For this reason he pointedly refused to schedule an eagerly awaited national party congress.[58] Silence, however, was clearly not a long-term solution to Hitler's dilemma; in fact, silence was rapidly becoming a political and organizational liability. An obvious and ample source of both members and leaders needed for the party's future growth was the drifting and volatile elements in the northern areas who lamented the passing of the free corps era. As the free corps and paramilitary groups dissolved, their members searched for other suitable affiliations to continue their militant activities. At the beginning of the year these elements flocked to the NSDAP in sizable numbers, and soon became the most militant part of the membership in many northern areas.[59] The ambivalence of Hitler's programs and the party's increasing bureaucratization reversed the trend toward the end of the year, and many National Socialist sympathizers preferred instead affiliation with Ludendorff's Tannenberg Association.[60]

The last quarter of 1925 brought the disparate developments in the two wings of the party to a climax. Hitler still marked time, con-

55. The northern Gauleiters continued to object particularly vigorously to the centralized membership control system and accounting procedures. See GL Rheinland-Nord to RL, 22 Oct. 1925; and RL to GL Rheinland-Nord, 24 Oct. 1925, BA, Schu. Slg. 203.

56. Ogrl. Potsdam to RL, 22 Aug. 1925, BA, Schu. Slg. 205.

57. See the very revealing letter of Hess to the leader of the HJ group Cologne, 26 May 1925, HA, roll 18, folder 335.

58. For indications that such a congress was generally expected among the provincial leadership corps, see RL to GL Hannover, 28 May 1925, BA, Schu. Slg. 202 I.

59. See, for example, Johann K. von Engelbrechten, *Eine braune Armee entsteht* (Munich, 1937), pp. 36–37.

60. See the folder, PD Mü, Referat VId, "NS-Kameradschaftsbund Gross-Berlin," HA, roll 69, folder 1505.

tinuing the anti-semitic harangues which he knew were acceptable to both sides and increasing his standing in Munich.[61] The north, on the other hand, seemed determined to force some clear-cut decisions.[62] In essence, the north felt that the NSDAP's political future depended upon a programmatic and organizational strategy that would in later years be called an opening to the left; that is, the party should actively compete with the Social Democratic Party (SPD) and the Communist Party (KPD) for the support of the urban proletariat. For many northern leaders a specific endorsement of the opening to the left by the Reichsleitung would merely make official what was already common practice. After all, the largely proletarian membership of at least some northern locals[63] provided tangible evidence of the plan's practicality.

Hitler was considerably less eager to endorse this policy, not only because he had ideological reservations, but also because the opening to the left had far-reaching organizational implications. The ideological opening to the left and the organizational issue of party-affiliated unions were really inseparable concepts. The advocates of the plan clearly expected the establishment of Nazi labor unions. The expectation was by no means unreasonable. The idea of a völkisch union had been very much current during the interregnum. An association called Militant Völkisch Labor Unions (*Völkische Kampfgewerkschaften*, VKG) already existed (albeit largely on paper) and Gottfried Feder, one of the NSDAP's most prominent pseudo-intellectuals, had written a pamphlet in a series published by the VKG.[64] It is true that the VKG was never an official affiliate of any of the NSDAP successor groups during the interregnum, but since the qualifications for membership of the VKG and the NSDAP were

61. Plümer, *Wahrheit,* pp. 65–66.

62. ". . . We will proceed with our general offensive. The issue is [the future of] national socialism, nothing else . . ." noted Goebbels in his diary. Two months later the entry was, "We are really going places [now] (*wir radikal heran*)." See Goebbels, *Das Tagebuch von Joseph Goebbels, 1925–26,* ed. Helmut Heiber (Stuttgart, 1964), entries for 2 Oct. and 23 Nov. 1925, pp. 36 and 43.

63. Martin Broszat, ed., "Die Anfänge der Berliner NSDAP 1926/27," *Vierteljahrshefte für Zeitgeschichte,* VIII (Jan. 1960), 86–87. See also Noakes, "Conflict," pp. 17–18.

64. See Arno Chwatal, *Völkische Kampfgewerkschaften* (Berlin, 1924).

virtually identical, a formal affiliation of the two groups should have presented few difficulties.

Nevertheless, Hitler remained hesitant and kept his position ambiguous. In the spring he had refused to take a definite stand, though he let it be known that he "viewed the entire matter sympathetically."[65] Hitler was obviously concerned about the long-range ideological and organizational implications of the union concept. The emphasis on unions, particularly if the party took over the VKG, would dilute the anti-semitic stand of the party. To be sure, Arno Chwatal, the originator of the VKG, had called the Reichsbank a "Jewish stock company," but he also refused to draw a qualitative difference between Jewish and Christian capitalists, and he acknowledged that class warfare was necessary to overthrow capitalism.[66] Similarly, some northern party leaders emphasized that the NSDAP would liberate the workers from the oppression of both Jewish and German capital.[67] Hitler realized, of course, that such a shift of emphasis away from "pure" anti-semitism would annoy his pioneer followers in the south. There were signs late in the year that such a reaction had already set in. The party's Munich membership hovered around four hundred, and only one section, Schwabing, was at all active. The number of sympathizers was equally unsatisfactory: Hitler rallies that drew a crowd of four hundred instead of four thousand were not uncommon.[68] And there were other problems as well. The establishment of a National Socialist union as the party's main affiliate would mean a demotion in status for the militants who hoped to see the SA revitalized as the party's elite formation.[69] Above all, however, Hitler undoubtedly feared that the unions would prevent the progressive centralization of the party's administration. Since they would become the primary interest-group and the focal point of party

65. RL to GL Hamburg, 7 April 1925, NA, T–580, roll 20, folder 201.

66. Chwatal, *Völkische,* pp. 5, 9, and 13.

67. See NSDAP, Bezirksgeschäftsstelle Lausitz to Dinter, 25 Feb. 1925, BA, Schu. Slg. 208 I.

68. PD Nü-Fü, "Lagebericht," 19 Nov. 1925, BGStA, M.A. 101249; and PD Mü, "Öffentliche Versammlung der NSDAP am 9. Oktober 1925 . . . PND Nr. 517," HA, roll 87, folder 1835.

69. PD Mü, "Besprechung der SA der Sektion Schwabing am 7. November 1925, PND No. 521," HA, roll 73, folder 1551.

activities for the party's proletarian followers, their establishment could only lead to the creation of a parallel organizational hierarchy, at a time when the Reichsleitung was still combating struggles for autonomy among the Gaus and locals.

In August the northern Gauleiters began to fill what appeared to be a genuine leadership vacuum with some organizational moves of their own. They formed a National Socialist Working Association (*Nationalsozialistische Arbeitsgemeinschaft*, NSAG) and began publishing an internal party organ, the *National Socialist Letters (NS-Briefe)*.[70] The NSAG was in no sense a *fronde* against Hitler. It was an attempt to curb the growing power and influence of Bouhler, Esser, and Streicher. Indeed, the original impetus for its establishment was a secondary myth that explained Hitler's reluctance to endorse fully the "revolutionary" party line because of his constant association with unprogressive and bureaucratic advisors such as Bouhler, Esser, and Streicher. The north naïvely hoped to unfetter Hitler. Organized in the NSAG, the political power of the north would be sufficient to liberate Hitler from his "pioneer" associations and enable him to lead the way toward the "revolutionary" version of the völkisch millenium.[71] It does not seem to have occurred to any of the party leaders that there was something inconsistent about the parallel existence of the myth of the captive Hitler and the myth of the fearless, all-seeing revolutionary leader.

The NSAG waited until September to present a specific proposal, and even then the north challenged Munich directly only on a personality issue. After a meeting in Hagen the NSAG demanded Esser's dismissal and announced that the NSAG opposed the NSDAP's participation in election campaigns.[72] The first demand was clear enough, but the second involved a far more subtle tactic. Hitler had never

70. See Fobke to Dolle, 26 Jan. 1926, HA, roll 44, folder 900. The *NS-Briefe* were published with Hitler's approval, though Bouhler did issue a circular underlining the *VB*'s unique position as the party's only official press organ. See Gregor Strasser, "Geleitwort," *NS-Briefe* (No. 1), 1 Oct. 1925; RL, "Rundschreiben," 12 Sept. 1925, BA, Schu. Slg. 373.

71. Fobke (one of the local leaders in Göttingen and a fellow inmate of Hitler's at Landsberg), "Aus der nationalsozialistischen Bewegung," 11 Sept. 1925, Forschst. NS Hbg., folder "NSDAP–NSAG."

72. *Ibid.* See also Ludolf Haase, "Parlament und nationalsozialistische Bewegung," *NS-Briefe* (Nos. 2 and 3), 15 Oct. and 1 Nov. 1925.

announced that he favored electoral participation, so that the NSAG's statement could not represent an open disagreement. Instead, it was an attempt to remove a major ambiguity in the NSDAP's stand. If Hitler agreed with the Hagen statement, he would actually take a major step toward full adoption of the northern plan for an opening to the left. Without the ballot box, the party would have to achieve power through the use of what were essentially syndicalist tactics, that is, direct organization of the urban masses and subsequent ability to paralyze economic and social life in Germany through strikes, street terror, and other activist means. Hitler still maintained his silence, and the NSAG went one step further. They now decided to propose the amalgamation of the present three Gaus in the Rhine-Ruhr area into one massive super-Gau embracing all of Germany's industrial heartland.[73]

Simultaneously the northern leaders attempted to raise and clarify a number of other controversial issues. A series of articles in the *NS-Briefe* supported economic reforms closely akin to national bolshevism (including the expropriation of princely property).[74] Gregor Strasser privately circulated a detailed draft constitution for the future National Socialist Germany. Economically it was a combination of Mussolini-like syndicalist structures, National Socialist economic demands (51 percent of all stock in a vital industry to be publicly owned, 49 percent in all other businesses), pseudo-medieval guild romanticism, and naïve anti-capitalist sentiments. (For example, Strasser favored wages in kind whenever possible.) Politically, the program attempted to give expression to the vague völkisch ideals of Germanic democracy. The Reich's federal structure would have been abolished, but a national legislature, based on occupational representative bodies, would have been elected. This group in turn would elect a dictator-president for a term of seven years. The president, however, would have appointive power over national and provincial executive and administrative corps.[75] Strasser at no point challenged either Hitler's

73. Noakes, "Conflict," p. 28.
74. See, for example, Goebbels, "Mein Freund von der Linken," *NS-Briefe* (No. 2), 15 Oct. 1925; Ulrich v. Hutten (Pfeffer), "Gemeinnutz geht vor Eigennutz," *ibid.*, (No. 6), 15 Dec. 1925.
75. Strasser, "Dispositionsentwurf eines umfassenden Programms des nationalen Sozialismus," Dec. 1925, Forschst. NS Hbg., folder "NSDAP–NSAG."

leadership or his final program-making authority, though the very
circulation of his plan certainly implied that the provincial or regional
party organizations should participate in the formulation of major
party policy lines.[76] In addition, Strasser's views were at such clear
variance with the known "pioneer" views that the formal enumeration
of Strasser's proposals made it impossible to deny the existence of an
open rift between the two factions.[77]

When he did decide to act, Hitler met the challenge brilliantly.
First, he further isolated Nazi Party members from the general
völkisch movement. A new directive prohibited dual memberships in
the NSDAP and the Tannenberg Association. It speaks for the naïveté
of the northern leaders that they welcomed the new regulation: completely misinterpreting Hitler's intentions, they saw it as an attempt
to contrast the political and programmatic character of the NSDAP
with the ineffective veterans' reunion clubs organized in the Tannenberg Association.[78]

Next, for the first time since his release from prison, Hitler called
a meeting of top Nazi leaders from north and south. On February 4,
Bouhler sent invitations to about twenty Nazi leaders inviting them
to a secret party conference at Bamberg in northern Bavaria on February 14.[79] Everything about the meeting showed Hitler at his propagandistic best. Ostensibly, he chose Bamberg in order to reduce the
travel costs of the northern Gauleiters. To be sure, Bamberg was
geographically closer to northern Germany than Munich, but Bamberg was far more than that. It was part of Streicher's Nuremberg
Gau, solidly "pioneer" in sentiment. During the past year both Hitler
and Streicher had been particularly solicitous about the local party

76. Noakes, "Conflict," p. 3.

77. It would be misleading to describe Strasser's plan as representative of all
northern thinking. The plan was vigorously debated at a January meeting of the
NSAG and submitted to a committee for further revision. The point remains,
however, that the initiative at this time lay solely with the north. On the discussion of Strasser's plan see *ibid.*, pp. 26–27.

78. Strasser, "Wir und die vaterländischen Verbände," *NS-Briefe* (No. 6), 15
Dec. 1925.

79. See Bouhler to Rust, 4 Feb. 1926, Forschst. NS Hbg., folder "NSDAP–
NSAG." The northern leaders welcomed Hitler's decision. Goebbels felt that the
north could now play "the shy virgin and lure Hitler on our side," Goebbels,
Tagebuch, entry for 11 Feb. 1926, p. 59. See also Rust to Strasser, 4 Feb. 1926,
Forschst. NS Hbg., folder "NSDAP–NSAG."

organization. Hitler visited Bamberg twice during 1925, the second time to honor its Christmas party with his presence.[80] The invitation list for the meeting, though it included most of the leading Nazis from all sections of Germany, showed a preponderance of Streicher–Esser men.[81]

Bamberg offered an imposing spectacle to the visitors when they arrived on the thirteenth. Numerous placards announced public mass meetings for the evening of the fourteenth, listing several northern Gauleiters as speakers. The large Nazi local outdid itself in its enthusiastic welcome for Hitler and Streicher, and a reception on the evening of the thirteenth further mellowed the northern leaders. The overall impression on the northern leaders could have been only disheartening: while locals in their far more populous areas of the Ruhr and Rhineland had difficulty enlisting twenty or thirty members, the Bamberg city organization had obviously succeeded in enrolling a sizable percentage of the town's population.

The "revolutionaries" thus presented a rather uneasy group when they sat before Hitler on the afternoon of the fourteenth. Hitler spoke for five hours.[82] When he finished he had opposed most of the cherished ideals of the "revolutionaries" and most of the particulars of the Strasser program. He favored an alliance with England or Italy instead of an entente with Russia; he denounced the expropriation of the princes and he disagreed with the entire idea of the opening to the left.

Although substantively the speech was largely a defeat for the "revolutionaries," Hitler was careful to avoid the impression that he fully endorsed the "pioneer" position. He still paid lip service to the ideals of National Socialism and ironically he couched his attack on "revolutionary" ideals in "revolutionary" rhetoric. Forced to choose between two program approaches, Hitler chose a third alternative: he mythologized his own person into a program. The mistake of the "revolutionaries" was not only to have suggested a false program,

80. R.Ko.In., "Lagebericht Nr. 8160/II," 19 Dec. 1924 and "Lagebericht Nr. 900/II," 6 March 1926, BGStA, M.A. 101248.

81. For example, while Karl Kaufmann (Gauleiter of the Rheinland-Nord Gau) was not invited, Karl Holz (the deputy Gauleiter of Nuremberg) did attend. The Reichsleitung later claimed it was unaware that the former was a Gauleiter. See Noakes, "Conflict," p. 29.

82. R.Ko.In., "Lagebericht Nr. 900/II," 6 March 1926, BGStA, M.A. 101250.

but far worse, to have doubted the sufficiency of the inherited creed (which contained meaningless "pioneer" and "revolutionary" slogans) and its personification in Hitler. The program of 1920, said Hitler, in the key phrase of his speech, "was the foundation of our religion, our ideology. To tamper with it *(daran rütteln)* would [constitute] treason to those who died believing in our Idea." [83] And only Hitler, crucified at the Odeonsplatz, descended to Landsberg, but risen to lead the party, was the living link with and the embodiment of the primitive Nazi church.

The northern leaders were stunned. They had welcomed his call to Bamberg as an indication that he had freed himself from Streicher's and Esser's influence, and they confidently expected either Hitler's firm endorsement of their position or at least a genuine debate on the future course of the party. Hitler had done neither. Instead, he forced the Nazi leaders to choose between rejection of his leadership or acceptance of his self-deification. Hitler knew what their decision would be, because without him they had no place to go. They had already accepted him as the personification of the leader myth to the extent of alienating their party and themselves from the rest of the völkisch movement. To deny Hitler after his speech was not only to cast oneself adrift in a hostile and already alienated world, but to insult the martyrs of the Putsch as well; none of the northern leaders had the courage.

As if to demonstrate that there was really no practical alternative to his rule, a few days later Hitler supplemented his words at Bamberg with a remarkable demonstration of his continuing popular standing among the rank-and-file membership of the party. In late February a group of NSDAP members under the leadership of Streicher and Esser literally broke up a scheduled rally of the National Socialist People's Association in Munich. Hitler obviously approved of the performance; he was physically present in the hall and smilingly acknowledged the "Heil's" of his loyal followers.[84] The northern dissident movement (if indeed it ever deserved that name) collapsed.[85]

83. Hinrich Lohse, "Der Fall Strasser," p. 5, n.d., Forschst. NS Hbg., folder "NSDAP–NSAG."

84. P.D. Mü (Mair), "Betr.: Versammlung des nationalsozialen Volksbundes am 24.II. 1926 in Hofbräuhausfestsaal," 2 March 1926, HA, roll 69, folder 1508.

85. Although the NSAG was not dissolved until July 1926, it played no further part in the history of the NSDAP after Bamberg. See Noakes, "Conflict," p. 32.

It was now Hitler's turn to fill the vacuum with a series of decrees designed to tighten the line of organizational centralization in the party and to curtail the trends toward regional and local autonomy that had developed. The Gaus, which had been the focal point of autonomous activities in 1925, held congresses in the spring to acquaint their leadership corps with Hitler's Bamberg policy directives. The locals received instructions to enlarge their membership rosters — and thus indirectly to dilute the potential influence of the pre-Bamberg membership.[86] In addition, the party leadership moved quickly to integrate the new and older members more fully into the organizational life of the party. Throughout the spring the executive secretary poured forth directives increasing organizational centralization in the NSDAP. Locals were ordered to obtain prior approval from party headquarters for any local organizational changes. Munich ordered the establishment of local committees on propaganda. Once assembled, they received their instructions from and reported directly to Munich.[87] Bouhler was at the height of his derivative-power. Occasional complaints from local and provincial organizations received the laconic marginal comment "Hitler agrees [with me]."[88] Simultaneously Hitler conducted a review of his provincial and district subleaders;[89] most of the northern Gauleiters were rebaptized,[90] but a number of local and district leaders were found wanting.[91]

While Bouhler centralized the day-to-day operation of the party, Hitler used his personal charm to win over the only major northern figure not fully convinced by the performance at Bamberg, Joseph Goebbels.

86. *VB*, 5 March 1926. For the emphasis on organizational activities, see also Paul Schmitz, "Organisations-Fragen," *NS-Briefe* (No. 15), 1 May 1926.

87. Hitler to GL Rheinland-Süd, 17 May 1926; and RL, "Rundschreiben an alle Ortsgruppen" and the enclosure, "Organisationsplan zur Errichtung von Propagandazellen . . . ," 20 March 1926, BA, Schu. Slg. 202 I. It is symptomatic of the increasing importance of the party bureaucracy that in April the party leadership was making plans to enlarge the national headquarters by the purchase of two additional stories of office space. See RL, "Rundschreiben an alle GL," 7 April 1926, *Munich Institut für Zeitgeschichte*, "Akz. 2400/59 Fa 104."

88. See GL Hannover-Nord, Göttingen, Hessen-Nassau-Nord and Schleswig-Holstein to RL, 15 April 1925 and RL to GL Hannover-Nord, 20 April 1926, BA, Schu. Slg. 202 I.

89. After Bamberg, Strasser immediately withdrew his draft program.

90. NSAG, "[Rundschreiben]," 25 March 1926, Forschst. NS Hbg., folder "NSDAP–NSAG."

91. GL Rheinland-Nord to RL, 11 May 1926, BA, Schu. Slg. 203.

Goebbels, at this time executive secretary of the Ruhr Gau, had been the driving force behind the programmatic efforts of the National Socialist Working Association. He had not opposed Hitler publicly at the Bamberg meeting, but even his silence did not bode well for the future.[92] In late March, Hitler invited the doubting Thomas to Jerusalem to induct him into the inner circle of apostles. Goebbels came early in April to address a mass rally;[93] once he was in Munich, his conversion was rapid. His two and a half hour speech (with Hitler present), the cheering masses, his stay at one of the better hotels, Hitler's thoughtfulness in loaning him his car — all this was balm to Goebbels' acute sense of social and personal inferiority. And when Hitler gave him a personally conducted tour of party headquarters followed by a three-hour monologue repeating the Bamberg arguments, Goebbels was putty in Hitler's hands. "Hitler is a great man. He forgives us and shakes our hand. Let us forget the past,"[94] Goebbels wrote ecstatically in his diary.

Goebbels' conversion signaled the formal end of the Working Association affair. Hitler now graciously accepted the establishment of the Ruhr Gau and appointed Goebbels, Karl Kaufmann, and Franz von Pfeffer as a tripartite Gauleiter team to head the new Gau.[95] At the same time, Hitler was not willing to rest his organizational power on the present era of good feeling; he also insisted on concrete safeguards for the future. The culmination of Hitler's organizational reconsolidation in the party came at the national membership meeting in May. The membership meeting (which was not identical with the national congress) normally had been a purely perfunctory affair, scheduled only to satisfy the requirements of the German laws governing associations, but in 1926 the delegates approved sweeping changes in the bylaws of the party's legal corporation, the NSDAV

92. Hitler might have been more concerned if he had been able to read Goebbels' diary entries. His first comment was "reactionary?" and a week later he was still considering mobilizing the NSAG for a new programmatic effort. See Goebbels, *Tagebuch*, entries for 15 and 24 Feb. 1925, pp. 60 and 62.

93. See Bouhler to Goebbels, 27 March 1926, and Goebbels to Bouhler, 29 March 1926, BA, Schu. Slg. 203; and "Aus der Bewegung," *VB*, 2 April 1926.

94. Goebbels, *Tagebuch*, entry for 13 April 1926, pp. 71–72.

95. Hitler to Goebbels, Kaufmann, and Pfeffer, 9 April 1926, HA, roll 54, folder 1290.

e.V. (One of Hitler's more astute moves had been to make the party's legal corporation coextensive with the Munich party organization. As a result, constitutional changes were legally subject only to the approval of the Munich membership.) In general, the changes made Hitler superior to the executive committee and extended his right to expel individual and entire local organizations from the party.[96]

The party's improved financial situation also showed that the crisis was over. The NSDAP's national office registered an income of RM 55,000 for the period February 1925 to April 1926, and most of this sum was collected after the beginning of the year. During the spring the NSDAP was not only able to pay its regular salaried employees again, but had sufficient funds to hire additional personnel as well.[97]

In mid-1926 the party had fully weathered its first major crisis; it could now stage a national congress to publicly demonstrate the restored unity. In early July the first annual Nazi congress since the Putsch took place in Weimar. All of the major party leaders from north and south attended in order to document their loyalty to Hitler, and the meeting became an impressive demonstration of Hitler's standing among both the leadership corps and the rank-and-file membership. To be sure, the recent disagreements could not be entirely hidden. Goebbels still advocated making the urban areas the focal point of the party's organizational efforts, while Dinter put more faith in parliamentary maneuvers.[98] Hitler, too, was still living, in part, both versions of his image. On one hand, he sympathized in principle with the northern demand that the NSDAP refuse to participate in elections, yet he noted the practical difficulties in taking such a rigidly negative stand.[99]

Neither the continuing disagreements among the party's leaders

96. See Hitler and Schneider, "Niederschrift über die Generalmitgliederversammlung der Nationalsozialistischen Deutschen Arbeiterpartei . . . am 22. Mai 1926"; and "Satzung des Nationalsozialistischen Deutschen Arbeiter-Vereins e.V., Sitz München," BA, Schu. Slg. 374.

97. PD Nü-Fü, "[Lagebericht] N/No. 47," and "[Lagebericht] N/No. 49," 28 April and 22 June 1926, BGStA, M.A. 101250.

98. The various speeches at the congress are in HA, roll 21, folder 389, and NSDAP, Reichsparteitag 1926, "Reichsdelegierten-Kongress im Deutschen National-theater . . . 4. Juli 1926" (typescript, Munich, 1926?).

99. Hitler, "Betreff: Sondertagung über Wahlfragen," July 1926, HA, roll 44, folder 900.

nor his own ambiguous stand diminished Hitler's authority. At Weimar
all prominent figures in the NSDAP explicitly and implicitly acknowledged that only Hitler had the authority both to resolve his own
ambiguities and to accept or reject policies advocated by the subleaders. For this reason the atmosphere at the congress presented
a rudimentary foretaste of an all-pervasive *Führerprinzip*. In his instructions to the session chairmen at the congress, Hitler discouraged
initiative among the delegates and specifically reserved all final decisions on resolutions and reform proposals to himself.[100] Perhaps
as a result of such discouragement, the provincial and local party
organizations submitted only seventeen resolutions to the special
session on organizational matters. They covered a variety of subjects
ranging from timid attempts to salvage some of the northern programs to more typical pioneer proposals to Germanize the title of
the NSDAP. Hitler permitted referral of most of the proposals to
the party's Reich Organizational Department, but he was adamant
in his refusal to allow a resurrection of the northern programs. Thus
he rejected outright a proposal to favor blue-collar workers as candidates for Gauleiter positions whenever possible.[101]

Hitler's reactions to intraparty democracy and to the attempt to
bind his hands in the selection of Gauleiters epitomize the dominant
themes of the congress: the Reichsleitung (that is, Hitler) wanted
both control and flexibility to be made a part of the organizational
principles of the party. The public speeches of party leaders echoed
the theme. Schwarz admonished the organization to adhere to conservative financial practices, and Alfred Rosenberg (now Editor of
VB) emphasized the Reichsleitung's right to veto the establishment
of provincial papers, but Strasser encouraged the locals (but not the
Gaus) to show initiative and imagination in organizational not
programmatic, matters.[102]

Above all, the Weimar congress reestablished the party's image
as a unified, disciplined political organization with clearly established lines of authority. All final programmatic, administrative, and

100. Hitler, "Grundsätzliche Richtlinien für die Arbeit der Vorsitzenden und
Schriftführer der Sondertagungen am Reichsparteitag," n.d., HA, roll 21, folder 389.
   101. The texts, authors, and dispositions of the resolutions are in *ibid.*
   102. See the text of the speeches in "Reichsdelegierten-Kongress."

organizational decision-making power rested in the person of Adolf Hitler, who delegated portions of his omnipotence to derivative agents as he saw fit.[103] This in itself was an important element of political strength, not in the overall context of German politics, but in the more immediate sphere of völkisch rivalries. The first fruits of the new image were already evident in Weimar as some völkisch groups, impressed by the unity and physical power of the NSDAP, decided to give up their independent organizational status and merge their organizations into the party.[104] In a small way at least, Hitler had succeeded in extending his political influence so that not only his person but his organization as well were again becoming the focal point of the German extreme right.

103. See GL Schlesien, "Richtlinien für Ortsgruppen und Stützpunkte," 1 Aug. 1928, BA, Schu. Slg. 208.

104. See Bouhler to Kasche, 1 Oct. 1926, HA, roll 9, folder 199. Siegfried Kasche headed a small völkisch group in Sorau (near Frankfurt a.O.) which until now had attempted to mediate between the NSDAP and the DVFP. Kasche later became a leading SA official and German ambassador to Croatia (1941–1945).

The Failure of the Urban Plan

As Hitler left the rostrum in the Weimar *Nationaltheater* at the conclusion of his major address on the last day of the congress, he heard the loud and prolonged cheers of the delegates behind him. He had reason to be proud. In just eighteen months he had healed the party's schisms and united its feuding members into a devoted band of personal followers. The party's membership was not large, but it contained a very high proportion of militants; of 35,000 members in July 1926, some 3,600, or better than one in ten, had traveled to Weimar.[1] And they had come to see and hear Adolf Hitler. In fact as well as in name the NSDAP was again the Hitler movement.

Yet the scenes in Weimar documented failure as much as success. To be sure, the delegates' radiant faces in the *Nationaltheater* documented the power of Hitler's charisma, but they were also evidence of the NSDAP's political insignificance in Germany as a whole. Thirty-five thousand is not an impressive figure when measured against the 15.6 million politically articulate Germans at the time.[2] In addition, the political horizon in mid-1926 did not look hopeful for a party which had always fed primarily on resentment and whose only program was total negation of the present.[3]

1. The figure 35,000 for July 1926 is an estimate. The NSDAP claimed 27,117 members at the end of 1925 and 49,573 a year later. See Hans Volz, *Daten der Geschichte der NSDAP* (10th ed.; Berlin, 1939), p. 21.

2. In June 1926, 15.6 million Germans voted in the national referendum on the question of expropriating the princes. See *Statistisches Jahrbuch des Deutschen Reiches* (cited hereafter as *Stat. Jahrb., 1926*) (45th ed.; Berlin, 1926), p. 453. The *VB's* circulation in 1926 was 10,700.

3. Karl-Dietrich Bracher, *Die Auflösung der Weimarer Republik* (3d. ed.; Villingen, Schwarzw., 1955), p. 106; Walter Görlitz and Herbert A. Quint, *Adolf Hitler* (Stuttgart, 1952), p. 269.

Unemployment was declining, real wages and salaries increasing, and the stabilized Republic now had a president who was a nationally respected war hero, Field Marshal von Hindenburg. With the Weimar congress "tranquility had been restored"[4] within the party, but it remained to be seen whether Hitler could convert the personal loyalty of a small number of followers into a significant power factor in German politics.

The pre-Putsch NSDAP had relied primarily on the pseudo-military SA to achieve political power, but the failure of November had closed that road to success for the foreseeable future. The new party had to achieve power by gaining and organizing mass support. But which masses? The industrial workers? The farmers? The lower middle classes? And how should the support be organized to seize power? Through elections and legislative pressure, economic means such as strikes and boycotts, or paralysis of sociopolitical life by means of physical terror?

These were not new issues, of course. The year between Hitler's first speech after his release from prison and the Bamberg conference was filled with ideological debates among the party's subleaders over the answers to precisely these questions. The issue was not merely that of programmatic emphasis; there were also profound organizational implications. Winning the industrial workers required the establishment of National Socialist unions. The support of the lower middle classes, on the other hand, could be most effectively channeled into quasi-Fascist organizations and pseudoguilds. Moreover, each of the ideological directions also represented frameworks for discussing ever more involved plans for the party's role in all aspects of human life: the discussion of Strasser's plans had quickly evolved into debates over proposals for racial breeding institutes, universal military training plans, and proposals to keep actors out of the party.[5] Hitler had cut the Gordian knot at Bamberg by pro-

---

4. Gregor Strasser in "Öffentliche Versammlung der NSDAP München am 7. Oktober 1926 . . . ," PND No. 552, HA, roll 87, folder 1835.

5. See [Haase and Fobke], "Der Nationalsozialismus—Göttinger Antwort auf die Denkschrift von Herrn Strasser," and "Zucht—Eine Forderung zum Programm von Frederik [i.e., Pfeffer], Weihnachten 1925." The latter memorandum bears the handwritten marginalia, "Osaf v. Pfeffer—Antwort auf den Entwurf Strassers der eingestampft werden musste . . . vorgelegt bei der Bamberger Tagung." HA, roll 44, folder 895.

claiming his own person as sufficient answer to all of the questions raised. The Gauleiters had agreed to this solution, so that the conference firmly established the "romantic" part of the Hitler–subleader relationship in the NSDAP. The Weimar congress reinforced and bureaucratized the charismatic image of the leader. Both meetings, however, postponed substantive decisions on the propagandistic direction and the long-range organizational format of the party. Hitler's immediate task ahead, then, was to convert even more securely the spell of Weimar into bureaucratic control of the party cadres and to decide on the programmatic emphases and organizational forms that would obtain a mass following for the NSDAP and expand its political power.

Hitler knew that both the membership expansion program of the party and the transformation of members into reliable party workers were, to a large extent, dependent upon an efficient administrative apparatus and bureaucratic forms of administration.[6] Although he himself was thoroughly disorganized in his personal habits and work patterns, he was extremely proud of the party's triple membership registration system, and he grew positively lyrical when he discussed the acquisition of new filing cabinets and safes for the national offices in the Schellingstrasse.[7]

He began the process of thoroughly bureaucratizing the party by instituting some organizational changes that could be effected without raising any programmatic issues. During these formative years, bureaucratization and centralization in the NSDAP always proceeded from the center outward. Hitler's position of personal and organizational authority in the party found its most immediate expression in his image and his control functions in the party's Munich local, so that virtually every measure adopted by the Reichsleitung to increase its control over the party was first instituted in Munich and subsequently extended to the outlying Gaus.[8] In a

6. It is significant that the Reichsleitung canceled all agreements giving certain Gaus special rights or privileges almost as soon as the Weimar meeting had adjourned. See RL to GL Danzig, 18 Aug. 1926, NA, T-580, roll 20, folder 200 (Gau Danzig).

7. See Hitler's speech in "Mitgliederversammlung der Sektion Süd der NSDAP am 22. April 1926," PND No. 536, HA, roll 88, folder 1838.

8. Hitler, "Betreff: Sondertagung für Organisationsfragen: zu Antrag 18," n.d., HA, roll 21, folder 390.

sense this was only natural. Munich had been accorded the singular honor of having the myth-person as head of the city organization. Hitler was the Gauleiter of Munich; Hermann Esser became head of the NSDAP in Upper Bavaria and Swabia in September 1926, but the city of Munich was specifically excluded from his jurisdiction.[9] The city received other preferential treatment as well. The party's members there were consistently awarded the lowest membership numbers,[10] and Hitler spoke more frequently in Munich than in any other German city.

Hitler's relationship to Munich was governed by more than sentimental preference for the city and its inhabitants. Quite literally, the continuing bureaucratization of the national party could not be carried out without the active support of the Munich membership. Apart from the legal coextension of the local Munich membership and the national legal corporation of the party, the NSDAP in Munich had to bear the primary burden of financing the party's central bureaucratic apparatus, a financial liability that was constantly growing. The personnel and physical expansion at the party headquarters was very rapid during 1926; the office space at party headquarters was expanded three times during the year.[11]

The additional space was justified less by spectacular membership increases than by the growth of the party's executive superstructure. Hitler realized that the confrontation of Bamberg had become necessary only because the ad hoc cooperation of the northern Gauleiters had been allowed to assume forms that made them potentially autonomous. The party lacked an institutionalized instrument of day-to-day control over the activities and personnel of the lower echelons. To prevent renewed organizational floundering in the party, Hitler revitalized the national investigation committee shortly after the Weimar party congress. The *Untersuchungs- und Schlichtungsausschuss* (or Uschla), had always been one of Hitler's preferred means for controlling the organizational orthodoxy of the

9. *VB*, 18 Sept. 1926.

10. Karl Wahl, *Es ist das deutsche Herz—Erlebnisse und Erkenntnisse eines ehemaligen Gauleiters* (Augsburg, 1954), p. 50. This practice continued a custom common in the GDVG. See Friedrich Plümer, *Die Wahrheit über Hitler und seinen Kreis* (Munich, 1925), p. 55n.

11. See Hitler's New Year's Proclamation in the *VB*, 1/2/3/ Jan. 1927.

party's subleaders. Subject to his appointment and dismissal, the members of the party court served to translate his personal will into depersonalized decrees governing party behavior. It will be recalled that in July 1921, after his intraparty coup, Hitler had personally headed the investigation committee. He resurrected the Uschla in late 1925, but it proved ineffective in halting the northern disorders and fell into disuse. Now, however, there remained no further obstacles to its effective functioning. The events of 1926 had clearly established the principle of Hitler's personal will as the epitome of the party's political and organizational norms, and the institutionalization of that changing will into specific party rules could follow. The Uschla served Hitler well in the process of instituting "bureaucratized romanticism" throughout the party. As Hitler had intended, it translated his whims into binding party policy.[12] At the same time its decisions, as the product of an institution that stood above individual persons,[13] did not blacken Hitler's personal image. The committee effectively protected Hitler's standing as living myth by drawing any possible dissatisfaction with its decisions to itself, not to the leader-figure whose creature and instrument it was.[14] Finally, Hitler had found an almost perfect chairman: Bruno Heinemann, a retired army general (he was sixty-eight in 1926) and long-time Munich party member, became chairman of the national Uschla when it began its work on October 1, 1926.[15]

The establishment of control and coordination organs in Munich was only the first step in the process of in-depth bureaucratization and centralization of the party. Decisions at the center could only

12. Cf. the tone of the Uschla's letter to Fobke, one of the more active leaders in Göttingen: "Mr. Hitler has ordered that Hermann Esser should be used again [as party functionary and speaker] in a limited way. With this decision all criticism [must] cease." Heinemann to Fobke, 9 Nov. 1926, HA, roll 44, folder 900.

13. Hitler underlined this image of the Uschla when, in April 1928, he specifically subordinated himself to the committee's jurisdiction. In concrete terms, of course, his declaration had little meaning, not only because of his charismatic standing in the party, but also because he appointed and removed the Uschla's chairman at will.

14. Dr. Albert Krebs, the Gauleiter of Hamburg from 1926 to 1928, confirmed that the average party member did not include Hitler himself in any criticism he might direct at the Reichsleitung, in a conversation with the author on 3 Sept. 1965. This conversation will hereafter be cited as "Krebs Interview."

15. *VB*, 4 Sept. 1926

be enforced throughout the party if a highly reliable state organization could execute the decisions of the Reichsleitung at the local level. The NSDAP clearly could not center its organizational decision-making power in Munich *and* in the local organizations. A political party whose seat of power is the local party organization will, in all likelihood, develop into a decentralized, co-option type of party. The key personnel and organizational element in the NSDAP's drive for centralization throughout the structure was, therefore, the Gau and its Gauleiter.

The position of a Gauleiter in the party in 1926 was not yet fully clarified. He was appointed by Hitler, and he served at the party leader's pleasure, subject to instant dismissal. He could not be removed without Hitler's consent, and while in office, he was Hitler's personal executive agent for that particular district of administration,[16] though even then his authority was frequently superseded by ad hoc roving ambassadors appointed by Munich to handle specific crises in his district.[17] All of the Gauleiters were personally loyal to Hitler in mid-1926; not all however were also bureaucratized executive agents. Most of them were still native to their district and consequently were ambitious to have the NSDAP in their Gau grow and prosper even at the expense of other Gaus. Above all, they valued their derivative status as Hitler's agents. They followed a myth-person, but they had not yet fully identified that myth-person with the impersonal bureaucratic apparatus known as the Reichsleitung. To a large extent they were still retainers of a knight, not organization men.

Hitler and the central office instituted a variety of measures to effect their transformation. Perhaps the most important of these was the clear establishment of financial control in the offices of the Reichsleitung. Money and money management became very important bases of evaluating the performance and success of a particu-

---

16. Reichsleitung, "Rundschreiben an die Untergaue und Ortsgruppen des Gaues Halle-Merseburg," 20 July 1926, IfZ., Akz. 2400/59 Fa. 104; Hitler to Ortsgruppe Halle, 30 July 1926, HA, roll 6, folder 138; and Hitler to Albert Krebs, 24 Feb. 1927, HA, roll 54, folder 1290.

17. See, for example, Hitler's "Vollmacht" for Heinemann and Gregor Strasser, 22 July 1926 and 29 March 1927, HA, roll 54, folder 1290.

lar Gau.[18] Each Gau was expected to adopt businesslike accounting procedures and much of the day-to-day administration of the Gau was put into the hands of a salaried business manager[19] (who often held the position of deputy Gauleiter as well) accountable for the performance of his duties less to the Gauleiter than to Bouhler's and Schwarz's offices in Munich.[20] His position hardly fit the party's image as an anti-materialist association, but it became increasingly vital. In money matters the NSDAP's idealism had no place; its accounting principles were cold, hard,[21] and did not tolerate interference by the political leader.[22]

The central leadership also reserved the administration of SA supplies and later the SA insurance scheme to its sole jurisdiction.[23] This, too, was an important means of financial control and centralization. Since the appeal of the party depended in large part upon its uniformed propaganda bands roaming the countryside or marching through city streets, no Gauleiter would hesitate to promote the growth of the SA organization in his Gau. At the same time, the specific prohibition of Gau equipment outlets and Gau SA groups

18. For example, Bruno Scherwitz was appointed Gauleiter of East Prussia in early 1926 largely because his predecessor had been unable to solve the financial problems of the Gau. See Scherwitz to RL, 2 Feb. 1926, NA, T-580, roll 24, folder 207 (Ostpreussen).

19. See Kaufmann's (Gauleiter of the Ruhr and later of Hamburg) oral testimony at Nuremberg, 30 July 1946, *IMT*, XX, 65. Himmler received RM 120.00 per month as deputy Gauleiter of Lower Bavaria at this time (see Roger Manwell and Heinrich Fraenkel, *Himmler* [New York, 1965], p. 16), and the business manager of the Berlin Gau was paid RM 180.00. The starting salary of a comparable civil servant at the Reich level in April 1927 was RM 266.00. See Germany, Statistisches Reichsamt, *Deutsche Wirtschaftskunde* (Berlin, 1933), p. 292.

20. *VB*, 1 Sept. 1926.

21. In January 1926, the Gauleiter of Halle wrote that he felt it was more important to spend money for the good of the movement as a whole than to support destitute individual party members, no matter how much they had done for the movement in the past. Schwarz commented in a marginalia: "very right." Ernst to RL, 10 Jan. 1926, HA, roll 6, folder 138.

22. Heinemann to Lutze (then business manager of the Ruhr Gau), 30 Jan. 1927, BDC, OPG, "Gliemann g. Terboven."

23. The national insurance plan was mentioned as early as November 1926 and a central quartermaster agency began its work in February 1927. See Pfeffer, "SABE 5," 5 Nov. 1926, HA, roll 16, folder 302, and "Bekanntmachung," *VB*, 16 Feb. 1927.

before a centralized leadership had been set up prevented the establishment of regional centers of financial or organizational power.

The Reichsleitung often controlled the Gauleiter's personal financial affairs as well. At least some of them drew an outright salary from the central office,[24] while others supported themselves by combining the positions of Gauleiter and Gau business manager.[25] Still other subleaders received compensation as legislative deputies in the Reichstag or the state legislatures. Here again, the financial rewards were under the complete control of the Reichsleitung and Hitler personally. Hitler determined whether a party official should be a candidate, for what office he should run, and in what order the candidates for the Reichstag or state legislatures would appear on the ballot.[26] Increasingly, he named the Gauleiters as candidates so that they, quite literally owed their personal incomes to the central office in Munich.

More important than these "material" control and centralization measures was Hitler's ability to withdraw the favor of his leader-myth approval from a Gauleiter who failed to bureaucratize himself or the administration of his Gau. The man who regarded himself as a personal derivative agent could perform this role only by successfully becoming an impersonal administrative organ of a centralized bureaucracy. It is obvious that the Gaus of a party that identified itself as the "Hitler movement" and that demonstrated its unity with Hitler by identical commemorative services for the dead of the Hitler Putsch each November[27] found the climax of their political activity in the presence of their leader in their particular area. A Hitler speech was the most wished-for event in the life of any NSDAP organization. Hitler's decision to speak or not to speak in particular localities was a powerful element of control, because his presence in a Gau or local organization confirmed the subleaders in their derivative-agent status. The leader's stay in a locality involved not only the speech

24. Goebbels is an outstanding example. See below, p. 93.

25. Robert Wagner (Gauleiter of Baden) to RL, 14 Aug. 1926, NA, T-580, roll 19, folder 199 (Baden).

26. Bouhler to Lohse, 28 March 1928, NA, T-580, roll 25, folder 208 I (Schleswig-Holstein). See also Wahl, *Herz*, p. 53; and Hans Fabricius, *Geschichte der Nationalsozialistischen Bewegung* (Berlin, 1937), p. 38.

27. See *VB*, 27 Oct. 1926.

itself, but a series of attendant ceremonies of perhaps even greater import for the relationship of leader and subordinate. The local and state subleaders as well as the "active party comrades" were introduced to Hitler and rewarded with the famous handshake and steady look from the steely eyes.[28]

A Hitler speech was a gracious gift bestowed as a reward for a well-functioning Gau or local. Throughout most of 1926 and 1927 (in Prussia until September 1928), Hitler was prohibited from speaking in public rallies in virtually all of the German states.[29] He was therefore restricted to addressing closed party membership meetings, and his appearance acquired even more the character of an intraparty reward for the Gau. Hitler's personal appearance in a Gau was granted only after the state party administration had fulfilled certain conditions. After Weimar, these involved to an increasing degree satisfactory progress in provincial and local administrative bureaucratization. The personal contact with the myth-person was granted only after the myth had been converted into a functioning, impersonal administration. Fervent pleas from the Gaus had no effect on Hitler's travel plans; his stops were centrally determined at the Reich level.[30] The Reichsleitung left the Gauleiters under no illusions as to what factors would favorably influence Hitler's final decision: he positively refused to speak in any Gau that was overdue on its financial obligations to Munich, but Gaus that showed an ability to pay their dues and to launch impressive propaganda efforts with local funds as well could be sure of a high rating at national headquarters.[31]

Hitler's appearances were the incomparable propagandistic highlights in the history of a lower party organization, and Hitler always used the opportunity to provide guidelines for the future work of the Gau. But the Reichsleitung also instituted less spectacular, day-

28. "Adolf Hitler im Rheinland," *VB*, 3 Dec. 1926.

29. The exceptions were Brunswick, Mecklenburg, and Thuringia. Most of Hitler's major public speeches were read for him by Adolf Wagner, later Gauleiter of Munich, because his Bavarian accent and voice quality was very similar to Hitler's own. See Max Domarus, ed., *Hitler, Reden und Proklamationen 1932–1945* (Munich, 1965), I, p. 48.

30. See *VB*, 22 March 1927 and 20 Jan. 1928.

31. See Hess to Ortsgruppe Nürnberg, 26 July 1926, NA, T-580, roll 20, folder 200; RL to GL Lüneburg-Stade, 19 Aug. 1926, BA, Schu. Slg. 202 I; and the reports on the various Gau party congresses in the *VB* throughout 1926 and 1927.

to-day controls of the myth's application at the lower echelons. Hitler did not forget that much of the impetus leading to the Bamberg crisis had been the result of the articles that appeared in the *NS-Briefe* in the latter half of 1925,[32] and the Reichsleitung's national propaganda committee moved quickly to cast Hitler's image into press control decrees. The Munich *Völkischer Beobachter,* Hitler's propaganda organ, obtained a status as "Reich newspaper," though it continued to be edited primarily from the perspective of Munich and Bavaria.[33] All local organizations had to carry at least one subscription to the *VB*,[34] and the publication of new Gau organs was consistently discouraged, largely because such papers might compete with the *VB*.[35] In addition, the central leadership placed severe restrictions on the relatively few official papers that were not published by the Eher publishing house. They were obligated to print all official party pronouncements and had rigid instructions to follow the editorial line indicated by articles in the *VB*.[36]

The Gauleiter-administrator as Hitler's provincial agent supervised a number of local leaders, but despite the emotional acceptance of the *Führerprinzip* throughout the vertical structure of the party,[37] his relationship to his subordinates was far from clear. In general, a Gauleiter's control over the local leaders and the local party organization in this period increased proportionally as he himself became increasingly subject to centralized control measures issued in Munich. In effect, Hitler allowed the Gauleiters to continue the process of bureaucratization and centralization only after they had placed themselves in the proper relationship to the Reichsleitung.

32. The *NS-Briefe* continued to be published, but they were closely watched and occasionally publicly reprimanded. See *VB*, 23 April 1927.

33. Otto Strasser, "Die nationalsozialistische Presse," *NS-Briefe,* No. 17 (1 Jan. 1926).

34. Reichsleitung, "Rundschreiben," 6 May 1927, BA, Schu. Slg. 373.

35. Kaufmann to Terboven (district leader of Essen), 14 Sept. 1927, BDC, OPG, "Gliemann g. Terboven"; and Bodo Uhse, *Söldner und Soldat* (Paris, 1935), p. 176.

36. For a discussion of the NSDAP's press setup in the years 1926 to 1928, see Oron J. Hale, *The Captive Press in the Third Reich* (Princeton, N.J., 1964), pp. 40–44.

37. Note the proud report that the Gau party congress in Baden had "completely eliminated parliamentary discussion methods." *VB*, 12 Oct. 1926.

In the immediate aftermath of Bamberg, Hitler strengthened the local organizations' autonomy by instituting the election of local leaders, instead of allowing the Gauleiters to appoint them.[38] As a result, at least some local organizations developed feelings of excessive grandeur. They withheld monies due the Gau organization for considerable time,[39] and on at least one memorable occasion the united local leaders of Halle-Merseburg dismissed the Gauleiter by a majority vote.[40] This last episode, however, was both the climax of the autonomy developments among the locals and the beginning of the new era. Apparently genuinely surprised by the events in Halle, Hitler limited the independence of local leaders: he amended his earlier decree ordering the election of the local leader by the members under his jurisdiction with a provision that the election was valid only after it had been certified, that is, approved by the Gauleiter. In addition, he empowered the Gauleiters to appoint sub-Gauleiters and district leaders as additional control agents over the activities of locals.[41]

The revised rules for the election of local leaders did not remove all elements of ambiguity from the relationship of Gauleiter and local leader, but it certainly pointed the way toward a further strengthening of the Gauleiter's position. In terms of the *Führerprinzip,* the party's organizational centralization and bureaucratization were about halfway complete at the end of 1926. No doubt the Reichsleitung would have preferred to continue transforming the party, but further changes were dependent upon, or had to be paralleled by a solution to the programmatic questions that had been raised at Bamberg. The powers, functions, and personal qualities of the Gauleiters and local leaders would depend on whether the party decided to organize National Socialist unions or to concentrate its efforts instead on organizing the rural population and small-town lower middle classes with their farmers' unions and guild associations. It was clear that Hitler refused to develop the NSDAP solely

---

38. NSDAP, KL Lübeck, *Der NSDAP Kreis Lübeck: Werden und Wachsen* (Lübeck, 1933), p. 15; and Wahl, *Herz,* p. 52.

39. Ogrl. Erfurt-Blücher to KL Erfurt-Stadt, Jan. 1937, HA, roll 7, folder 160.

40. Reichsleitung, "Rundschreiben an die Untergaue und Ortsgruppen des Gaues Halle-Merseburg," 20 July 1926, IfZ., Akz. 2400/59 Fa. 104.

41. *VB,* 24 Oct. 1926.

into a workers' party or middle-class party, but it was equally apparent that the Reich leadership would have to determine program and propaganda emphases and priorities to end the ambiguities in the movement. But with his myth-image brighter than ever, Hitler could turn his attention to experimenting with assigning politically effective priorities to the "socialist" and "nationalist" appeals of the party.

For much of 1926 and 1927 it appeared as though Hitler had decided on the Strasser plan after all. An uninitiated observer listening to the speeches at the NSDAP's provincial congress in Stuttgart in May 1927 might well have wondered if he had strolled into the wrong meeting. While Hitler thundered "we reject the political aims of the industrialists," Goebbels, in a phrase that the Communist leader, Ernst Thälmann, could not have bettered, described the Berlin police as "the pimp *(Zuhälterin)* of capitalism."[42] Only the attacks on Jews and Jewish Marxism gave the rally an aura of *déjà vu*.

The Württemberg meeting was by no means atypical. On other occasions Goebbels had discussed the "money pigs of capitalist democracy" and the central propaganda committee (headed by Gregor Strasser) had demanded Reich-wide protest meetings against "police terror in the capitalist state."[43] In fact, all over Germany the party seemed to pour propagandistic venom on the capitalists and decadent bourgeoisie. Its focal points were the major cities, and its basic aim was seemingly to wrench the industrial workers of Germany from their allegiance to the two Marxist parties.[44] To be sure, the party's appeal was never crudely one-sided;[45] it still hoped to win adherents

42. The quotations are taken from [Landespolizei Württemberg?], "Ausschnitt aus W[ochenbericht] Nr. 157," 18 May 1927, HA, roll 70, folder 1516.

43. Goebbels, "Nationalsozialisten aus Berlin und aus dem Reich," and Strasser, "Anordnung VIII der Propagandaabteilung," *VB,* 4 Feb. and 10 May 1927.

44. The largest concentration of prominent speaker personnel took place in the area of the Ruhr, Saxony-Thuringia, and Berlin. The whereabouts of the party's leaders and the general tenor of their utterances in public rallies can be gathered from a perusal of the *VB*'s columns "Aus der Bewegung," and "Unser Vormarsch." For the corroborating judgments of contemporary police reporters see R.Ko.In., "Nr. 120," 3 Nov. 1926; "Nr. 121," 28 March 1927 and PD Nü-Fü, "N/No. 56," 6 May 1927, BGStA, M.A. 101250, 101251, and 101251a.

45. As an example of "anti-socialist" writing see Alfred Rosenberg's article, "Nationaler Sozialismus," *VB,* 1 Feb. 1927.

from all social strata in Germany, and its propaganda emphases varied from region to region, but Hitler did seem to be convinced that with radically anti-capitalist and nationalist slogans, and with effective organizations in the large, industrial cities, the NSDAP would achieve political power more readily than by emphasizing its pioneer image. Consequently, much of the party's organizational history in 1927 was made in the Ruhr, in Berlin, in Hamburg, and in Thuringia-Saxony.

Hitler thought he had good political reasons for his "socialistic" emphasis. In 1927 the NSDAP needed members, effective organizers, and a clear-cut image in the völkisch movement, all of which were potentially available in the cities under the general heading of National Socialism. The front-line socialist myth permeated most of the nationalist, anti-parliamentary right in Weimar Germany. It had particularly strong currency among the members of the strongest veterans' organization, the *Stahlhelm*, which maintained its national headquarters in Thuringia. Also, the workers' appeals established the NSDAP as a revolutionary and radical völkisch party, differentiating it from its chief rival, the DVFP, which had always explicitly refused to direct its appeal to the industrial workers as a class.[46] NSDAP writers could thus draw a sharp distinction between the völkisch bourgeoisie (DVFP) and völkisch social revolutionaries.[47] Moreover, aside from Munich and perhaps Nuremberg, the NSDAP had no really strong organization in southern Germany, while despite all organizational shortcomings some quite dynamic elements had joined the party in the Ruhr, in Thuringia, and even in Berlin.[48]

Thus, on the whole, "revolutionary National Socialism," carried forward from a geographic base of northern big-city organizations (and Munich), seemed to provide more promise of success than organizing the pioneer sentiments of the lower middle classes in

46. See Graefe to Siegfried Kasche (at this time still head of a local political group attempting to mediate between DVFP and NSDAP and later NSDAP district leader of Sorau), 17 June 1925, HA, roll 9, folder 199. On the differences between the two parties see also Martin Broszat, "Die Anfänge der Berliner NSDAP 1926/27," *Vierteljahrshefte für Zeitgeschichte*, VIII (Jan. 1960), 88–89.

47. See, for example, Gregor Strasser, "Deutsch-Völkische Freiheitspartei und wir," *NS-Briefe*, No. 22 (15 Aug. 1926); Strasser, "Die Gründe des Austritts aus der V.A.G.," *VB*, 9 March 1927, pp. 1–2.

48. Joseph Goebbels, *Kampf um Berlin* (Munich, 1934), pp. 17–18.

the south. This does not mean that a specific decision was embodied in a formal decree. Rather, the organizational emphasis was indicated by such qualitative factors as the tone of speeches by party leaders, the social composition of areas that Hitler chose to reward by his presence, major personnel appointments in the party, and Hitler's own negotiations with other völkisch groups. All of this gave the party a preponderant image and a political strategy. It now needed suitable tactics and appropriate functionary personnel to translate the strategy into political significance.

Ostensibly, the "how" of achieving political power is a simple matter for a totalitarian and revolutionary party: by any means possible. For the NSDAP in 1927, however, the answer was neither simple nor obvious. Like the German Communist Party in 1919,[49] the Nazis were confronted with the historical fact that a previous attempt to seize political power by revolutionary, military, illegal means had failed. On the other hand, the obvious alternative — electoral victories — seemed to many NSDAP leaders a distasteful compromise with parliamentarism,[50] not to mention the bitter memories of Ludendorff's dismal showing in 1925 it recalled. Hitler himself seems to have been undecided and consequently issued no directives on the issue of electoral participation. Indeed, the Weimar congress had seen something like an officially sponsored debate on the matter. The Reichsleitung specifically asked one of the most radical opponents of electoral participation to air his views at the congress.[51] The net result was again a state of uncertainty: while the NSDAP was represented in the Reichstag (as a result of the national elections of December 1924) and in a number of state legislatures, as late as September 1926 some Gaus refused to endorse electoral activities.[52] Hitler's own equivocation, some indirect

49. See Ossip K. Flechtheim, *Die Kommunistische Partei Deutschlands in der Weimarer Republik* (Offenbach a.M., 1948), pp. 40 and 46, for the debate on parliamentary participation in the early KPD. The comparison with the German Communists is also made by Weigand von Miltenberg [Herbert Blank], *Adolf Hitler–Wilhelm III* (Berlin, 1931), p. 53.

50. See, for example, Goebbels, "Parlamentarismus," *NS-Briefe*, No. 33 (1 Feb. 1927).

51. See Hess to Fobke, 29 June 1926, Forschst. NS Hbg. "NSDAP–NSAG." See also Hitler's speech in Munich, 15 June 1927, in PD Mü., "PND No. 577," HA, roll 88, folder 1839.

52. *VB*, 21 Sept. 1926.

evidence suggests, was not finally resolved until November 1927,[53] i.e., a time when the possible alternatives to electoral victories had been tried and exhausted.

If neither putsch nor elections, what then? The weight of the party's mass support. This road to power was less well defined, but it is reasonably clear what Hitler had in mind. He was always impressed by two pseudorevolutionary seizures of power: the German revolution of 1918 and Mussolini's successes in 1922.[54] In both cases, the revolutionaries, in Hitler's view, used no military force per se. Instead, the weight of their mass support and the effectiveness of their organization simply paralyzed the economic and political life of the country and therefore forced the government to yield power into their hands. It appears that Hitler hoped the NSDAP could succeed in gaining power with similar methods. Like the Marxists in 1918, the NSDAP would seize power "[by developing] two dozen cities into unshakable foundations of our movement."[55] This method required neither military prowess nor election victories. It did, however, necessitate the existence of effective organizations in urban areas to win the support of the industrial proletariat and the establishment of a militant force to control the streets. The first requirement could be met by effective urban party organizations and the creation of National Socialist unions; the second, by reviving the SA.

There were some obvious geographic centers of organizational activity under this urban plan. At the very least, the NSDAP would have to create strong bases in Thuringia-Saxony, in the Ruhr, and in Germany's largest cities, Berlin and Hamburg — all of which in 1926 and 1927 voted substantially or even overwhelmingly SPD and KPD. Nevertheless, the party had already achieved some organizational successes in these areas; it was relatively well established in Thuringia and Saxony. The Thuringian Gauleiter, Arthur Dinter,

53. The RL wrote the GL of Pomerania in late Nov. 1927 that Hitler wanted to discuss the question of elections at a leadership conference in Weimar. An agenda for the meeting or the text of Hitler's remarks is not available. See Bouhler to Corswant, 24 Nov. 1927, NA, T-580, roll 24, folder 207 (Gau Pommern).

54. For Hitler's views on the Revolution of 1918 at this time see Werner Jochmann, ed., *Im Kampf um die Macht–Hitlers Rede vor dem Hamburger Nationalklub von 1919* (Frankfurt, 1960), pp. 78–85.

55. Goebbels, "Neue Methoden der Propaganda," *NS-Briefe*, No. 22 (15 Aug. 1926).

was hardly sympathetic to the "socialist" wing of the party, but as a long-time party member, intimate friend of Julius Streicher, and member of the state legislature (*Landtag*), he had apparently created a quite sizable NSDAP organization.[56] Saxony was under the leadership of Martin Mutschmann, an industrialist of questionable repute, but as in neighboring Thuringia, the fear of renewed Bolshevik terror[57] strengthened the NSDAP's overall political appeal. In the Ruhr, too, the party could point to the beginning of success. While it was not a major political force in the industrial hub of Germany, there were indications that its hopes for growth were not completely groundless. The party in the Rhineland-Westphalia area had some extremely effective propagandists and administrators: Pfeffer, Kaufmann, and Goebbels were all able, devoted to Hitler, and eager to achieve leadership positions. The troika system of leadership established in the summer of 1926 had not worked out,[58] but the Nazis could nevertheless point to some very significant organizational triumphs in the Ruhr. The party had achieved its greatest success in the city of Hattingen, an industrial town of about ten thousand not far from Essen and Bochum, which they apparently made into something of a pilot project. By concentrating its most effective speakers (Hitler spoke there three times between December 1926 and April 1927) and organizers in the town, the party had won the allegiance of at least a substantial number of workers and physically terrorized the Marxist parties into submission.[59]

Berlin and Hamburg presented the party with its most immediate organizational problems. In both cities the party organization was in a state of disarray bordering on chaos, and the two Gauleiters were completely unable to control the feuds that permeated their

56. For an example of Dinter's "Du" see Dinter to Esser and Streicher, 20 Jan. 1925, BDC, Parteikanzlei Correspondenz (hereafter cited as PKC), "Akte Dinter."

57. In 1919 and 1922–23, both states had been governed by an SPD–KPD coalition. See Werner T. Angress, *Abortive Revolution* (Princeton, N.J., 1963), pp. 380–82, 386–87, 426 ff.

58. For specific accusations and counter-accusations of the three Gau leaders see BDC, OPG, "Akte Franz v. Pfeffer"; Bouhler to Kaufmann, 1 June 1927; and Pfeffer to Hitler, 5 Oct. 1927, HA, roll 4, folder 86.

59. Goebbels, *Kampf*, p. 16; and Albert Krebs, *Tendenzen und Gestalten der NSDAP* (Stuttgart, 1959), p. 187.

organizations.[60] To secure the "flank position"[61] of the party's political thrust in Berlin, Hitler selected Joseph Goebbels as the new Gauleiter. With this appointment of one of the party's best-known speakers and organizers, Hitler underscored the party's commitment to the urban plan. In late 1926 Goebbels was in many ways an ideal choice for Berlin. He combined to a great degree the qualities of administrator-agitprop type of Gauleiter. As Strasser's private secretary and as business manager of the Ruhr Gau, he had gained ample administrative experience. At the same time he had acquired a reputation as one of the party's most effective propagandists among industrial workers,[62] so he would not find it difficult to establish rapport with a Berlin membership saturated with extremely radical, anti-bourgeois elements.[63] In addition, Goebbels had demonstrated that his belief in Hitler as the myth-person superseded all other political or even personal emotions. His desertion of the Strasser cause between February and April 1926 established him as a man whose faith and trust in the Hitler myth had no limits.[64]

Goebbels was less certain that Berlin was ideal for him. When the Reichsleitung first approached him in June, his reaction was almost completely negative.[65] Not until October had he convinced

60. The documents contained in folder 205 of the BA, Schu. Slg. provide the best firsthand impression of the chaotic Berlin Gau organization in 1926. For an analysis see also Broszat, "Anfänge," p. 90, and Reinhold Muchow, "Situationsbericht Nr. 5," Oct. 1926, *ibid.*, pp. 102–03.

61. "Nationalsozialismus in Grossberlin," *VB*, 20 Nov. 1926.

62. Goebbels himself later claimed that he had been responsible for the party's worker appeal. See Rudolf Semmler, *Goebbels—the Man Next to Hitler* (London, 1947), pp. 56–57. On Goebbels' "Socialist" reputation, see also Johann K. von Engelbrechten, *Eine braune Armee entsteht* (Munich, 1937), p. 47.

63. Cf. Reinhold Muchow's (at this time propaganda chairman of the Sektion Neukölln) statement "[the Berlin NSDAP] has had it up to here *(die Nase voll)* with all variations *(Schattierungen)* of the bourgeoisie" in his "Situationsbericht Nr. 3" (Aug. 1926), in Broszat, "Anfänge," p. 97.

64. It is significant in this connection that the Reichsleitung did not consider Goebbels for the Berlin position until his conversion in April. Schlange, the previous Berlin Gauleiter, submitted his resignation on 18 Feb. 1926, and Heinemann merely noted in his marginalia that a successor would have to be found. See Schlange to Hitler, 18 Feb. 1926, NA, T-580, roll 19, folder 199a (Gau Gross-Berlin).

65. His diary entry was a laconic, "thanks a lot for the stone desert." Joseph Goebbels, *Das Tagebuch von Joseph Goebbels, 1925–26,* ed. Helmut Heiber (Stuttgart, 1964), entry for 10 June 1926, p. 82.

himself that Berlin was worth his efforts: "Berlin is after all the center. For us as well. Cosmopolitan city (*Weltstadt*)."[66] The reasons for Goebbels' change of mind can only be surmised. They almost certainly involved some crass material considerations. He needed money, and the Reichsleitung was willing to pay him an adequate salary as Gauleiter.[67] He was ambitious, and the reorganization of the Ruhr Gau had virtually precluded a prominent leadership position for him there. The decisive factor, no doubt, was Hitler's personal request that he go to Berlin. It appears likely that Hitler sought Goebbels out at the Weimar congress and simply and earnestly asked that he become Hitler's representative in the Reich capital.[68] The true believer mentally clicked his heels, raised his right arm, and went to Berlin.

Goebbels was a new type of Gauleiter in practice as well as in theory. In return for the absolute trust which Hitler could place in him, he received special organizational powers which gave him complete control of the vertical and horizontal party organization in Berlin. Like Hitler in Munich, Goebbels in Berlin appointed the section chiefs (that is, local leaders) and controlled the SA, two rights no other Gauleiter except Hitler possessed.[69] Simultaneously, he bureaucratized the Gau and put the "urban plan" into action. When he arrived in Berlin, Goebbels found the NSDAP permeated with a clubby atmosphere and an "opium den" for a business office.[70] Goebbels quickly changed this. Within two months he had found a new site for the party headquarters, established regular office hours, and regulated his conferences by strict adherence to an appointment calendar. The Gau treasurer, in the meantime, removed the business and financial operations of the party from political or personal considerations and established a rigidly centralized accounting system under the control of the

66. *Ibid.*, entry for 18 Oct. 1926, p. 108. See also Semmler, *Goebbels,* p. 57.

67. Schmiedecke (of the Berlin party organization) to Goebbels, 16 and 29 Oct. 1926, IfZ., Akz. 2437/59 Fa. 114.

68. There is only indirect evidence for this statement (Goebbels, *Kampf,* pp. 21–22), but since Hitler liked to confer with party leaders against the background of the militant myth marching forward, it appears very likely that Goebbels agreed in principle to his appointment in early July.

69. Goebbels, "Rundschreiben Nr. 1," 9 Nov. 1926, IfZ., Akz. 2437/59 Fa. 114. See also Goebbels, *Kampf,* p. 38. For the organizational relationship of the SA to the party see below, pp. 99–101.

70. Goebbels, *Kampf,* p. 24.

Gauleiter.[71] The rewards were not long in coming: by February 1927 the Berlin Gau had paid its debts, owned some RM 8-10,000 worth of office equipment, and proudly held title to a used Benz four-seater.[72]

A Gau-owned car was the greatest status symbol in the early NSDAP. Aside from that, it enabled an urban Gau to conduct its propaganda far more effectively. The car could transport the Gauleiter to rallies far more quickly, it could be mounted with a loudspeaker system, and it made it possible for party poster-crews to cover a great deal more territory than by streetcar or bus. Goebbels was tireless, both personally as an agitprop and as an organizer of propaganda in the Gau as a whole. The content of Goebbels' propaganda in Berlin was, by and large, a repetition of the anti-capitalist, pseudosocialist, violently anti-communist and anti-semitic themes he had used in the Ruhr.[73] Goebbels organized his Gau propaganda effort efficiently and bureaucratically. He established a school to train public speakers in order to enable the Gau to blanket Berlin with Nazi Party rallies. One Sunday afternoon per month was reserved for a Gau party conference to organize the entire propaganda effort for the coming month. The conference determined speaker assignments, evaluated feedback reports for the previous month, and made necessary organizational changes.[74]

The second largest city in Germany, Hamburg, also received a new Gauleiter in 1926. The Hamburg party organization had been headed by Josef Klant, a long-time member and typical pioneer. The membership itself was composed almost entirely of lower-middle-class individuals, and the party had made no significant effort under Klant to attract worker support. By mid-1926, the membership had stagnated, the organization was faction-ridden, and the Gauleiter was increasingly isolated and unable to control his sub-

71. Goebbels, "Rundschreiben Nr. 1;" Goebbels, *Kampf*, pp. 26 and 52; and Gau Berlin-Brandenburg, Gaukassenwart to all local groups and sections, 19 Nov. 1926, HA, roll 9, folder 198.

72. Muchow, "Situations-Bericht Nr. 9," Feb. 1927, in Broszat, "Anfänge," p. 112.

73. The *Standarte*, the literary and intellectual organ of the Stahlhelm organization, termed Goebbels' approach an appeal "to the envious instincts of skid row *(lumpenproletarisch)* thinking." See the quotation in *VB*, 3 June 1927.

74. Goebbels, *Kampf*, p. 43.

ordinates.[75] As a result he offered to resign, in the apparent expectation that his resignation would be refused. Instead, the Reichsleitung
at first did nothing, and then dispatched Strasser to settle the feuds
in Hamburg. Strasser in turn dismissed Klant[76] and proceeded to
supervise the election of a new Gauleiter. This proved to be far
more difficult than retiring the old one, but in the end the various
factions compromised on an outsider, Albert Krebs.[77] At the same
time, the Hamburg Gau was reduced to the status of an autonomous
local.[78] Like his colleague Goebbels, Krebs was an enthusiastic supporter of the urban plan. Though not proletarian himself, he combined his Gauleiter position with a full-time job as a white-collar
union functionary, and he made energetic moves to attract proletarian
members into the NSDAP. He also drew upon his own administrative experience to introduce greater control measures over the section leaders, thus centralizing and bureaucratizing the administration of his local.[79]

With adoption of the urban plan, the NSDAP in effect set itself
up as the competitor of the SPD and KPD. There is no doubt that
it could register some local successes in the Ruhr and in Berlin, but
it was also apparent that an effective party organization even in
certain pivotal areas could not by itself become a serious political
threat to the Marxist parties. The NSDAP still lacked a sufficiently
large leadership corps to expand the urban plan horizontally all
over the Reich. Above all it lacked a counterpart to the KPD's
militant street-fighting organization, the *Rotfrontkämpferbund* (RFB),
and a union organization that could provide real material benefits
for the workers the party was attempting to win over.

Hitler was well aware of all these deficiencies, but he was espe-

75. Krebs, *Tendenzen*, pp. 40–42.
76. Klant promptly protested his dismissal and appealed to other Gauleiters
for support against Strasser. See Hohnfeldt (GL of Danzig) to Klant, 27 Dec.
1926, in Werner Jochmann, ed., *Nationalsozialismus und Revolution* (Frankfurt, 1963), p. 264. On the other hand, Klant abruptly cut off his campaign
when he realized that Hitler stood behind Strasser. See Klant to Uschla, 24 Jan.
1927, *ibid.*, p. 265.
77. Klant to Hitler, 6 Nov. 1926, *ibid.*, pp. 243–44, and Krebs, *Tendenzen*,
pp. 42–44.
78. Strasser to the district leaders of the NSDAP in Hamburg, 2 Nov. 1926,
BDC, OPG, "Akte Josef Klant."
79. Krebs, *Tendenzen*. pp. 44–53.

cially concerned about the party's lack of able subleaders, particularly at the Gauleiter level.[80] Many of the old pioneer types were
simply not suitable for an urban-oriented, bureaucratized party. For
example, even so pivotal a Gauleiter as Dinter in Thuringia left a
great deal to be desired. He was loyal to Hitler in a manner of
speaking, but his primary goal was to establish himself as the leader
of a new Germanic religion, and he never accepted Hitler as myth-
person.[81] There were more able men, of course, but by and large
Konrad Heiden's description of the Gauleiter corps in 1926 and 1927
as "semi-madmen" is not completely inaccurate.[82] Hitler hoped to
augment the party's functionary corps from two sources: the DVFP
(German Völkisch Freedom Party) and the paramilitary organizations. The persistent Nazi barrages against the DVFP throughout
1926 and 1927[83] led to progressive self-isolation and an increasing
"we-alone feeling" in the NSDAP,[84] but it also decimated the DVFP's
socialist wing. It is no exaggeration to say that the NSDAP's urban
approach won over the most effective DVFP agitators.[85] The most
prominent among these was Count Reventlow, the editor of the
semi-official DVFP organ, *Reichswart,* who joined the NSDAP early
in February because the DVFP refused to endorse his demand for
fifty per cent managerial control by the workers in any enterprise.

80. Hitler, "Betreff: Sondertagung für Organisationsfragen [at the party
congress 1927]," HA, roll 21, folder 390; and "Niederschrift über die Generalversammlung der Nationalsozialistischen Deutschen Arbeiterpartei und des
Nationalsozialistischen Deutschen Arbeitervereins am 30. Juli 1927 . . . in
München," p. 8, HA, roll 3, folder 81/82 [sic].

81. In May 1927 Dinter attributed an unfavorable decision on Hitler's part
to the "great demands which have been placed on your nerves recently." See
Dinter to Hitler, 19 May 1927, HA, roll 4, folder 86.

82. Konrad Heiden, *Der Führer* (Boston, 1944), p. 262.

83. See, for example, Gregor Strasser, "Deutsch-Völkische Freiheitspartei und
wir," *NS-Briefe,* No. 22 (15 Aug. 1926); and Alfred Rosenberg, "Der Abgesang
der Soz. [sic] Deutschvölkischen-Freiheitspartei," *VB,* 3 March 1927.

84. For the progressive self-isolation of the NSDAP see "Zur Thüringer Landtags-
wahl" *VB,* 23 Sept. 1926, and Bouhler, "Rundschreiben an die Gauleitungen
und selbstständigen Ortsgruppen der NSDAP," 5 Feb. 1927, HA, roll 9, folder
187.

85. By May 1927 the DVFP was no longer a significant factor in German
politics. See Dillinger (Regierungsrat in the office of the R.Ko.In.), "Die
Entwicklung der rechtsradikalen Bewegung seit Anfang 1926" (cited hereafter
as Dillinger, "Entwicklung"), p. 15, 20 May 1927, BAStA, No. 71490.

The NSDAP at this time supported such a demand. The DVFP state leaders in Brandenburg and Württemberg, Wilhelm Kube and Christian Mergenthaler, joined Reventlow in deserting the DVFP. They were welcomed with open arms. Hitler and Goebbels traveled to Stuttgart to receive Mergenthaler personally, and Kube was appointed Gauleiter of the Ostmark very shortly after he became a party member.[86]

Less successful, though potentially more spectacular, was Hitler's attempt to realign the militant veterans' organizations *(Wehrverbände)* with the movement. The large number of paramilitary and patriotic associations in Germany led an increasingly frustrated and futile existence after 1923. They opposed the Weimar Republic and pluralistic politics in general, but they also realized the hopelessness of destroying the Republic by further putsch attempts. Yet, they prided themselves in their "apolitical," supra-party status, and distrusted all political movements and politicians, including Hitler and the NSDAP. In late 1926, however, Hitler saw indications of a potential alliance with the Wehrverbände. His relationship to the free corps movements in Bavaria before the Putsch had been excellent: united in the Militant Association *(Kampfbund)*, they had accepted his political leadership,[87] while he in turn did not interfere in their day-to-day military activities. In the fall of 1926 Hitler felt he recognized an opportunity not only to augment his leadership corps, but also to magnify the power status of the NSDAP by indirectly subordinating the vast membership of the patriotic associations to his political leadership.

The scene was Thuringia. Here a number of circumstances seemed to prepare the way for a successful realignment of the party and the Wehrverbände. Two of the most important of these associations, the *Stahlhelm* and the *Wehrwolf*, had their national headquarters

86. *VB*, 11 Feb. 1927. For a description of the ceremonies in Stuttgart, see *VB*, 24/25 April 1927. The party's desperate need for leadership material at this time is apparent from Kube's previous relationship to the party. As recently as September 1926, NSDAP gangs attempted to break up Berlin rallies of Kube's "Völkisch-Socialist Working Association in Greater Berlin." See Kube to PD Berlin, 13 Sept. 1926, HA, roll 56, folder 1357.

87. Cf. Kriebel's testimony during the Hitler trial in 1923. *Hitler-Prozess*, 3. Verhandlungstag, NA, T-84, roll 1, frame 352.

in Thuringia. At first glance both seemed disposed to cooperate with the NSDAP. The Stahlhelm, under the influence of its newly elected second president, was anxious to use the political potential of its vast membership as a power factor in German politics.[88] The Wehrwolf had a far smaller membership, but the relatively large percentage of working-class members in its ranks[89] and the determination of its leader Ernst Kloppe (like Düsterberg from Halle) to "become political" presumably disposed it toward cooperation with the NSDAP and its urban plan. Even more important, the Thuringian Wehrverbände, in anticipation of the state elections in January 1927, had already joined to form a political action committee, the "Völkisch Leadership Ring of Thuringia" (*Völkischer Führerring Thüringen*, VFTh).[90]

In October 1926 Hitler traveled to Weimar to argue his case for union of the far right under his political leadership before the members of the VFTh. A great deal was at stake. Agreement by the VFTh would have meant a sudden multiplication of Hitler's power potential: instead of speaking with the weight of thirty thousand NSDAP members behind him, he could point to over a million who followed his political instructions. The party could have tapped the pool of potential leadership personnel that held membership in the Wehrverbände, many of whom had already demonstrated their leadership abilities as free corps officers. And, perhaps from Hitler's point of view at this time, an election agreement between the party and the VFTh might have resulted in NSDAP–Wehrverbände control of a German state government. Hitler argued his case long and eloquently. He pointed to the rampant Marxist danger in Germany, a threat that could be halted only by drawing the workers away from the Marxist allegiance and uniting all patriotic Germans under his leadership. He tried to assure his listeners that, as in the fall of 1923, his political direction strengthened the far-right cause rather than controlled or stifled it. Hitler failed. The VFTh agreed to an electoral pact of sorts, but the Stahlhelm, by far the largest of the Thuringian associations, refused to issue specific recommendations

88. Bracher, *Auflösung*, p. 137.
89. Karl O. Paetel, *Versuchung oder Chance* (Göttingen, 1965), p. 31.
90. Count von Görtz-Wrisberg (head of the VFTh) to RL of the DVFP, Sept. 1926, HA, roll 7, folder 160.

to its membership to vote NSDAP in the election.[91] During the actual campaign the NSDAP received little cooperation from the associations, and the outcome of the election was an overall loss of National Socialist votes.[92]

In retrospect, it is not difficult to grasp what had happened at Weimar.[93] In effect, the leaders of the far-right associations refused to accept Hitler's claim to myth-person status. Hitler, on the other hand, could not give up his claim, both because he believed in it, and because to do so would irreparably damage his image within the NSDAP. Instead he had no choice but to turn to the party and isolate it even more from the overall völkisch movement. Seeing only his own historic mission, he accused the VFTh of sabotaging the unity of the völkisch movement and issued a new decree to the party membership prohibiting any further double membership or even fraternization between NSDAP members and adherents of other nationalist groups.[94] Despite these acts of revenge the NSDAP had suffered a major setback in its drive for political power. The failure to reach an agreement with the Wehrverbände meant that for the party there would be no easy solutions to its organizational problems: no militarily trained battalions to control the streets, no sudden influx of needed subleaders, and no easy access to a vastly increased number of political followers.

The party's alternative to the Stahlhelm battalions was a revitalized SA. The storm troopers, of course, had been the heart of

91. Hitler's remarks and the subsequent discussion of his aims among the VFTh are in NA, T-81, roll 116, frames 136453–62.

92. See, "Protokoll über die Sitzung des [VFTh] am 7.11.26," NA, T-81, roll 116, frames 136448–51.

93. Hitler may well have had some doubts about the Thuringian experiment from the very beginning. It is interesting to note that while Hitler was in Weimar, the Baden party leadership issued a statement pointedly denying that it had concluded a working agreement with the provincial nationalistic organizations. See *VB*, 15 Oct. 1926. Other party leaders were also dubious about the scheme, but put their loyalty to Hitler before their pragmatic skepticism. See Kaufmann to Bouhler, 18 Jan. 1927, NA, T-580, roll 20, folder 203 (Gau Rheinland-Nord).

94. Hitler to Count Görtz-Wrisberg, 23 Feb. 1927, HA, roll 7, folder 160; and Hitler, "Rundschreiben an die Gauleitungen und selbstständigen Ortsgruppen der NSDAP," 5 Feb. 1927, BA, Schu. Slg. 373. See also *VB*, 29 Jan. 1927, and 9 Feb. 1927.

the old NSDAP, and many locals were eager to reorganize SA units as soon as the party had been reestablished.[95] Propagandistically and physically the SA was indispensable to the success of the urban plan, but the Reichsleitung also wanted to be certain that the new SA would be a completely reliable political (and not military) organization. Consequently, while it did not prohibit the establishment of local SA units, it did refuse to allow the formation of Gau groups and centralized Gau administrations until a suitable national SA leader could be appointed.[96] Hitler realized that the rebuilding of the SA presented some difficult problems for the party. To begin with, many of its members had not forgotten their military heritage, and when whole companies of Röhm's *Frontbann* joined the new SA in a body (as was the case in Berlin), the primacy of political control was at least potentially endangered.[97] Also, since the SA leaders were often the most dynamic and experienced elements among the party membership, they made natural leaders for a variety of political posts and thus permeated Gau and local party organizations with an "SA spirit." [98] That "spirit" in the large cities — and these, after all, were the focal points of the party's activity at this time — was dynamic, ruthless, aggressive, strongly anti-bourgeois, and extremely eager for action of any sort. These characteristics, if well disciplined and ably led, could provide immense assets for the party's campaign of terror, counter-terror, and propaganda in the cities, but without firm leadership SA activities could easily get out of hand and lead to the prohibition of the party as a whole — a possibility that Hitler feared constantly in these years.

By the end of July 1926 Hitler had found a new *Osaf* (*Oberster SA-Führer*, the highest SA-leader). He was Franz von Pfeffer, a member of the Gauleiter triumvirate in the Ruhr.[99] Pfeffer was in many ways a strange and yet also a logical choice. He had been an

95. Heinrich Bennecke, *Hitler und die SA* (Munich, 1962), p. 125.

96. GL Danzig to RL, 21 July 1926 and RL to GL Danzig, 29 July 1926, NA, T-580, roll 20, folder 200 (Gau Danzig).

97. Engelbrechten, *Braune Armee*, pp. 45–46. See also Goebbels, *Kampf*, pp. 29–30.

98. Cf. the group photograph of the Berlin Gau leadership corps in *ibid.*, p. 193.

99. Goebbels, *Tagebuch*, entry for 30 July 1926, p. 95; and Hess to Fobke, 18 Aug. 1926, HA, roll 44, folder 900.

able free corps leader, and he was a stern disciplinarian with a passion for military order, hierarchy, and above all, abbreviations.[100] These characteristics would obviously be helpful in controlling the most activist and dynamic party members. More dubious assets were Pfeffer's avowed monarchist leanings (the party itself had no firm stand on this issue at the time) and his basic opposition to the socialist emphases in the party.[101] These difficulties had to be settled in negotiations between Pfeffer and Hitler, with the result that Pfeffer's formal appointment was held up until November 1.

In the end Pfeffer yielded on most points. The new SA became a strictly legal, non-military body, whose only training consisted of marching exercises and physical fitness programs. The new SA would not be a small group of conspirators, but "one hundred thousand fanatic fighters for our *Weltanschauung*. Its activities will be tremendous mass demonstrations, not secret cabals." [102] On the other hand, Pfeffer did impose pseudomilitary salutes, rigid discipline, and military superior–subordinate relationships into the SA. In fact, the SA and Pfeffer had a relationship to the party that was not unlike that which Hitler had offered to the Wehrverbände in Thuringia: the SA was organizationally tied to the myth-person, all SA members had to be members of the party, and each one swore an oath of personal loyalty to Hitler. The SA carried out tasks determined solely by the party's political leadership, but the political leaders did not interfere in the day-to-day administration of the SA.[103]

If one hundred thousand members of the new SA were to be the

100. Pfeffer's penchant for abbreviations soon resulted in a veritable flood of SABE's *(SA-BEfehl)*, GRUSA's *(GRUndSätzliche Anordnungen)*, GRUF's *(GRUppenFührer)*, etc.

101. See the exchange of letters between the RL and Pfeffer in October 1925, in BDC, PKC, "Akte Pfeffer." He had also played a leading part in the NSAG (Bennecke, *Hitler*, pp. 128–29), but so had Goebbels and Strasser.

102. Hitler to Pfeffer, 1 Nov. 1926. Hitler's letter set down basic guidelines for the SA, and Pfeffer in turn incorporated the entire document in his "SABE 1" of 1 Nov. 1926. See Bennecke, *Hitler*, pp. 237–38.

103. Osaf, "GRUSA III," 3 June 1927, Jochmann, *Nationalsozialismus*, pp. 266–67. It has not been the purpose of this section to discuss in detail the organization and activities of the SA, but merely to indicate the SA's place in the overall organizational history of the party during these years. The SA itself is covered in considerable detail in Bennecke's book.

"backbone"[104] (significantly not the head) of the NSDAP's thrust to power, its membership at the end of 1926 had only begun to jell. As yet it had little mass support, even in the urban areas. On the other hand, there existed an obvious source for members, a source long ago tapped by the SPD and the KPD: the NSDAP was well aware that the RFB and the *Reichsbanner Schwarz-Rot-Gold* (the SPD's paramilitary wing) gained a large number of their members through the labor unions in the case of the *Reichsbanner* and the association of unemployed in the case of the RFB.[105] That the NSDAP would have to travel the same road seemed to many party members so obvious as to require no formal statement or authorization. Consequently as early as 1925, local groups, particularly those with strong SA contingents, began to form either labor unions or associations of unemployed linked to the SA and party organizations. Since Arno Chwatal's Militant Völkisch Labor Unions (VKG), whose membership qualifications and program corresponded almost exactly to those of the NSDAP in 1926,[106] had made little organizational headway, it would have presented no difficulty to annex this fledgling union to the party, particularly since Gregor Strasser was in charge of "union affairs" at the Reichsleitung.[107]

Hitler, however, refused to place the keystone on the urban plan: he would not move on the question of unions. Although the lower echelons continued to discuss and even to expect the founding of National Socialist unions,[108] the party neither established its own unions nor did it negotiate an associate status for the VKG. But it also placed no restrictions on membership in non-NSDAP unions for party members.[109] In the end, the Reichsleitung said "yes" in

104. Goebbels, *Kampf*, p. 89.
105. "Zusammenkunft der SA Schwabing der NSDAP am 4. November 1925—PND Nr. 521," HA, roll 73, folder 1548; and Muchow, "Situationsbericht Nr. 3," Aug. 1926, in Broszat, "Anfänge," p. 97.
106. See above, p. 65.
107. RL to Ortsgruppe Danzig, 15 Jan. 1926, NA, T-580, roll 20, folder 200 (Gau Danzig).
108. The Munich police reports on party section meetings show how lively the union issue was for the average party member in 1926 and 1927. See HA, roll 88, folder 1838.
109. Hans-Gerd Schumann, *Nationalsozialismus und Gewerkschaftsbewegung* (Hanover, 1958), p. 33.

theory, and "no" in practice. The *Völkischer Beobachter* supported the idea of party-affiliated unions, but added immediately that the time for their establishment had not yet come.[110] In practice this meant that, while the Reichsleitung did not issue a specific prohibition of union activities in the Gaus and locals, it sharply discouraged such enterprises whenever a specific case came to its attention.[111]

Hitler's refusal to establish unions had far-reaching consequences. It is by no means certain that any sizable number of industrial workers would have followed the call of the party to join National Socialist unions, but there is no doubt whatever that the lack of such unions severely reduced the party's urban appeal. It is also unlikely that Hitler, as an astute politician and student of Marxist party tactics, did not appreciate the connection between party-affiliated unions and the success of the urban plan. In other words, significant considerations must have persuaded the Reichsleitung to jeopardize the entire urban plan before its political success could really be evaluated. In part, the decision was motivated by a fear that the fledgling unions might fall under Marxist influence.[112] There also seems to have been some disagreement between Hitler and Strasser over the issue of how "political" the unions should be.[113] But far more decisive than either of these factors was Hitler's very real fear that the unions might lead to a process of "myth-disintegration." In the same way in which the SPD-associated labor unions had become increasingly pragmatic and less ideological, Hitler feared that national socialist unions would become mere bread-and-butter organizations, thus weakening the totalized aspect of the movement as a whole.[114] For political reasons Hitler could not allow this: the Hitler myth and the Hitler party were indivisible. Material benefits, if any, for a party member would have to be the result of a belief in Hitler the

110. Dr. B[uttmann], "Adolf Hitler und die Gewerkschaftsfrage," *VB*, 24 Dec. 1926.

111. See, for example, RL to GL Danzig, 16 Dec. 1926, NA, T-580, roll 20, folder 200 (Gau Danzig). Goebbels, again the prototype of the new Gauleiters, had prohibited NSDAP unions or associations of unemployed in his first Gau circular.

112. Buttman, "Adolf Hitler," *VB*, 24 Dec. 1926.

113. Schumann, *Nationalsozialismus*, p. 32.

114. This thesis cannot be proven, but some indirect evidence supporting it is in RL to GL Danzig, 16 Dec. 1926, NA, T-580, roll 20, folder 200 (Gau Danzig).

myth-person, not the consequence of pragmatic collective-bargaining sessions. And in this sense Hitler's decision was undoubtedly correct: it sabotaged the urban plan and condemned him to a few more years of political impotence, but it also removed a serious political danger to the image of the myth-person.

The "postponement" of NSDAP-sponsored unions condemned the urban plan to a slow death, forced the party militant to become a political schizophrenic,[115] and threatened to reopen the schisms of 1925. Hitler's characteristic refusal to issue clear orders to the party's organizational and propaganda offices resulted in a political entity in which a variety of centrifugal forces were again coming to the surface. In Berlin extreme activism repelled all middle-class elements, while in other regions local "clubbiness" threatened to end the messianic drive of the party.

"Clubbiness" *(Vereinsmeierei)* was a condition of progressive ingrowth that began to characterize many of the party's rural and even some urban locals during the era of the urban plan.[116] Despite constant admonitions to go outside and win converts,[117] locals often preferred the close company of the few militants that made up the synthetic society in their village or town. One obvious factor in the tendency toward localization in "pioneer" areas was the propagandistic neglect of these areas during the period of the urban plan. Feeling little kinship with the industrial workers, they remained loyal to Hitler, but did little to publicize the party outside their own localities. In part, too, the Reichsleitung itself had raised the problem. The efforts after Bamberg to encourage local autonomy as a counterweight to the Gauleiters strengthened the feelings of local camaraderie. The Reichsleitung recognized the problem, but attempted only halfhearted remedies. Instead of furthering centrality

115. Thus the SA in Schwabing solved the problem by preparing two leaflets on various issues: one for the workers and one for the "fat bourgeoisie" *(Spiessbürger)."* See PD Mü, "Appell der SA Schwabing am 9. Juni 1927, PND No. 576," HA, roll 73, folder 1552.

116. For a good description of the condition see Krebs, *Tendenzen,* p. 54. For intraparty recognition of increase in socializing see G.R. [Gregor Strasser?], "Vertiefung," *NS-Briefe,* No. 31 (1 Jan. 1927); and Mücke to RL, 25 May 1927, BDC, OPG, "Akte Fritz Tittmann."

117. PD Mü, "Zentralsprechabend der Ortsgruppe München der NSDAP am 4. April 1927, PND No. 568," HA, roll 88, folder 1839.

and hierarchy directly by increasing the power of the Gaus, Hitler attempted to solve the problem indirectly by issuing new bylaws for all local organizations and by curtailing their power to subdivide themselves. And even these directives were not issued until late March 1927.[118]

What some rural locals lacked in proselytizing, a number of urban organizations possessed in overabundance of activist enthusiasm. This was particularly true of party organizations with strong SA units, and since a close correlation existed between the SA strength and the urban emphasis of the party, the strongest and best organized SA groups in 1927 and 1928 were consistently the units in urban industrial areas.[119] By and large these elements wanted the NSDAP's push to power to begin with a terroristic take-over of Goebbels' "dozen cities." Consequently, they demanded, in addition to political indoctrination, party-sponsored military training to prepare themselves for at least the possibility of another putsch. Hitler knew the hopelessness of such an undertaking, but his refusal to "unleash" the SA presented a sizable dilemma. He had reestablished the SA to use it as the backbone of the party's urban demonstration and terrorist activities. With the progressive curtailment of the "urban plan," the SA felt increasingly frustrated and useless (particularly since Hitler had not yet finally decided to channel its fervor into election campaigns as he did later). For the moment, the Reichsleitung's indecision led to two major organizational crises: in the spring of 1927 in Munich, the SA openly challenged the authority of the Osaf, and in Berlin the SA's campaign of street terror gave the police an opportunity to prohibit the party itself.

The Munich party membership was basically a pioneer group, but the SA unit was composed largely of extreme activist elements who were proud of their violent heritage of 1923 and who took the

118. *VB*, 25 and 31 March 1927. Moreover, the subdivision order applied to the Gaus as well as locals.

119. The Reichsleitung used as a test of organizational strength the number of SA members enrolled in the SA's national insurance plan (*VB*, 23 Nov. 1927). The Reich areas that stood consistently at the top of the list were: Franconia (presumably as a result of the special situation in Nuremberg), Ruhr, Saxony, Munich, and Berlin-Brandenburg. See the comparative listings in *VB*, 23 Nov. 1927, 25 Jan., 13 April, and 8 May 1928.

party's admonition to convert members of the KPD to National Socialism seriously.[120] Like their comrades in other cities, they demanded military training. When Pfeffer refused, two of the more outspoken Munich SA leaders began to complain openly that the party was being taken over by "bosses *(Bonzen)* and cowards." [121] As always when open insubordination threatened the authority of a sub-leader appointed by him, Hitler fully covered Pfeffer and expelled the pair from the party. Nevertheless, it was too late to prevent the outbreak of a real crisis of confidence in the leadership of the SA in Munich and some other areas.[122] Absenteeism grew in the Munich SA, and Hitler had to present the myth-person, "live," to bolster the authority of his SA chief. In May 1927 he confronted "his" SA in Munich personally. He used the familiar rhetorical and charismatic tactics that had been successful so often before. He assured his listeners that he understood their desire to "start attacking," but that circumstances rendered such an attempt futile. He also noted that he would much prefer serving as a simple SA man to being party chairman — but this too was impossible. At the conclusion of the speech Hitler came down from the rostrum, shook hands with each member, and received a renewed pledge of personal loyalty and a promise to serve as disciplined party soldiers.[123]

The Berlin SA had dominated the party organization both before Goebbels arrived and, to a lesser extent, after he became Gauleiter. Its membership was largely proletarian and lumpenproletarian; its political work, an unending series of street brawls.[124] Even within the party, observers did not agree on the success of these antics. On one hand, Goebbels had unquestionably put the NSDAP on the

120. PD Mü, "Appell der 2. Kompagnie der SA. Schwabing . . . am 9. September 1926 . . . PND No. 550," HA, roll 73, folder 1551.

121. PD Mü, "Komp.-Appell der S.A. Schwabing der NSDAP am 13.V. 1927–PND No. 573," *ibid.*, folder 1552.

122. *VB*, 2 June 1927. The crisis was not restricted to Munich. See the reports on SA and SS activities in Bavaria (other than Munich) in HA, roll 16, folder 303; and SA Schwerin, "SABE Nr. 3," 19 Sept. 1927, HA, roll 16, folder 303.

123. PD Mü, "Generalappell der SA München . . . am 18. Mai 1927," and ". . . am 25. Mai 1927," PND 574 and 575, HA, roll 73, folder 1552.

124. The best account (precisely because it is a biased description of the SA activities in Berlin) is in Muchow's "Situation Reports," in Broszat, "Anfänge," pp. 92–118.

political map in Berlin and the street battles created a strong sense of *esprit de corps* among a rank-and-file membership composed almost solely of extreme activists. On the other hand, the element of physical danger also repelled many adherents to the National Socialist myth who might have become card-carrying members in a less active setting. Basically, as Karl Kaufmann noted, Berlin made "a great deal of noise, but [there was] little substance."[125]

How successful the Berlin strategy could have been in offsetting, after a time, the loss of lower-middle-class members with corresponding gains from the Communists (as the Berlin party leadership clearly intended) will never be known, since the SA activities led to an earlier and unexpected result. By April 1927 the Berlin NSDAP had already become a byword for disturbers of the peace, and Hitler's presence in their midst aggravated their enthusiasm. On May 1, the traditional socialist labor day, Hitler appeared in the capital to speak in a closed party meeting. (He was still forbidden to speak publicly in Prussia.) His remarks were, for him, surprisingly mild and free of demagogic outbursts. If this was intended to dampen the ardor of the Berlin militants, it failed. On the contrary, the audience was visibly disappointed to hear a less radical Hitler,[126] and four days later another massive disturbance rocked a Nazi rally. For the Berlin police, this was the last straw: a few days later the Berlin party organization was declared illegal.[127]

The dissolution order was a severe setback for the expansion plans of the party, and it no doubt demonstrated again to Hitler the difficulties inherent in the urban plan. The Berlin party organization had failed to heed the most important organizational rule in the new NSDAP: to avoid governmental prohibition of party activities. Not even Goebbels' clever slogans (*Trotz Verbot, nicht tot;* despite prohibition, not dead) could prevent a general sense of depression and frustration, the "sour-pickle-days," among the Berlin members in the summer of 1927.[128]

125. Kaufmann to Homann (Gau Hannover), 26 March 1927, HA, roll 5, folder 136.
126. See the reports on his Berlin speech, May 1927, in *VB*, 3 May 1927; and *Vorwärts*, 2 May 1927. See also Goebbels, *Kampf*, pp. 145–46.
127. The dissolution order and the party's futile efforts to appeal the order are in NA, T-580, roll 19, folder 199a.
128. Goebbels, *Kampf*, pp. 203 and 207.

For the various Gauleiters concerned, widespread *Vereinsmeierei* and legal prohibitions were personal crises, since these problems meant delays in fulfilling their roles as derivative agents in history, but the internal difficulties that had permeated the party by mid-1927 did not result in action until the malaise had become crystallized into factors that Bouhler and Schwarz could understand. These terms were almost wholly statistical: increasing lack of funds, sluggish membership growth charts, and a growing absenteeism among the members of the Munich local.

Since the Munich local largely supported the day-to-day operations of the Reichsleitung, a perceptible decrease of enthusiasm among its members was of the most immediate concern to the central office executives. Some northern leaders had written the south off as early as August 1926,[129] and while this reflected more regional prejudice than political realism, there is no doubt that the adoption of the urban plan involved a certain neglect of Munich's prima-donna status in the party. The consequences were not encouraging. The Munich membership as a whole was aging rapidly,[130] an indication that the party was unable to attract a sufficient number from the younger element. In addition, those who remained loyal were rather sluggish in fulfilling their propagandist and financial obligations to the party.[131] Throughout 1926 and until 1928 Schwabing was the most active among the Munich sections. It was headed by Karl Fiehler, then an NSDAP member of the Munich city council and after 1933 lord mayor of Munich. The section had 526 members at the end of 1927, and the rolls showed 45 new members and 78 resignations, making the average for the year 509.[132] Since the monthly dues per

129. Haase, "Parteigenossen," Aug. 1926, HA, roll 44, folder 900.
130. See the report on a National Socialist rally in May 1927, in Franz Hofstetter (a police reporter), "Bericht," 13 May 1927, HA, roll 88, folder 1839.
131. Analyses of the party's financial situation must of necessity remain sketchy, since according to Franz X. Schwarz the party's official receipt book and accounting records were burned shortly before the end of the war. See George W. F. Hallgarten, *Hitler, Reichswehr und Industrie* (Frankfurt, 1962), p. 120 n34. The conclusion on the lack of enthusiasm among the members is based upon the extensive collection of police reports on the mood and attendance at Hitler's rallies in 1926 and the first half of 1927, in HA, roll 88, folder 1839 and 1940.
132. These figures are based on Fiehler's reports to the section as quoted in PD Mü, "PND No. 601 v. 19.1.28," *ibid.*, folder 1838.

member were 50 Pfennige at the beginning of the year and 80 Pfennige at the end (they were raised in late May), the section's income from dues for the period January 5–December 1, 1927, should have been around RM 3,500. The receipt book, however, indicates membership dues of only RM 403.60 for the period.[133] Even allowing for some belated entries and the prevailing custom of allowing members up to three months' grace before instituting expulsion proceedings, it is not surprising that no Munich rally was complete without an earnest appeal to the audience to remember the collection box on the way out.

Schwarz and Hitler would no doubt have been less concerned if receipts from the regions of propagandistic emphasis had compensated for the sluggishness of Munich, but the Reichsleitung was to be disappointed again. Receipts from the rest of the Reich also seem to have been considerably below expectations. The party had an average of 35,000 members in 1926; using the same basis of calculation as for the section Schwabing, total dues receipts for 1927 should have been at least RM 210,000. But even Hitler claimed membership dues receipts of only RM 84,000 for all of 1926.[134] And such developments as the party's prohibition in Berlin augured ill for dues collection in 1927.

The second traditional major source of party income, the voluntary and often secret contributions of sympathetic, but not yet totally indoctrinated businessmen, was also declining rapidly. It is no doubt true, as the party claimed, that the bulk of its day-to-day operations was financed by receipts from membership dues, the income from rallies, the sale of the *VB*, etc., but it is equally apparent that much of its propaganda effort, the first segment of the totalization spiral, was financed by these voluntary gifts. Some individuals, notably the Bechstein family and the publisher Bruckmann, continued to give significant sums to the party or to Hitler personally,[135] but in general

133. Sektion Schwabing, "Hauptkassabuch für Beiträge [1924–1933]," HA, roll 2A, folder 226. January 5–December 1, 1927, are the dates covered in the "Kassabuch." The financial difficulties are also reflected in the large number of expulsion proceedings (150 in Munich alone) which were pending at the end of 1926. See PD Nü-Fü, "Lagebericht N/No. 52," 15.11.1926, BGStA, M.A. 101250a.

134. Police spies estimated the receipts as RM 13,000, but this was no doubt wishful thinking. See PD Nü-Fü, "[Bericht] N/No. 54," 4 Feb. 1927, pp. 18–19, BGStA, M.A. 101251.

135. PD Nü-Fü, "N/No. 54," 4 Feb. 1927, p. 18, BGStA, M.A. 101251.

the return of prosperity and the prevailing leftist orientation of the NSDAP under the urban plan repelled many of the party's erstwhile business friends.[136]

Hitler tirelessly attempted to convince the industrial barons of the Ruhr that the party's urban plan represented an advantage rather than a threat for business:[137] since the NSDAP denied the existence of class conflict, a worker immersed in the party would actually feel a sense of community with his employer through their joint loyalty to a higher ideal, the German nation.[138] Hitler's reasoning, however, met with little positive response,[139] so that by the summer of 1927 the party faced serious, if not yet insurmountable, financial difficulties. The central leadership clearly had no effective solution to the problem. Various devices, such as proclaiming May as "sacrifice month" or selling delegate cards to the 1927 party congress at RM 3 apiece,[140] were in reality self-defeating since they constituted renewed appeals to the already committed militants whose listlessness or disappointment was at the heart of the problem in the first place. The only real solution seemed to be either a massive infusion of funds from sources outside the party or a rapid growth of membership. Actually, the two were closely interconnected; in the past, the former had always been the result of the latter development.

The Reichsleitung, therefore, looked anxiously at its only other meaningful gauge of "success," the membership figures (that is, the quantitative measurement of the party's ability to draw more politically articulate Germans into its synthetic society). It is almost as difficult to obtain meaningful data in this area as it is to surmise the party's financial situation. The NSDAP did not issue detailed member-

136. Even Hitler claimed only a total of RM 12,000 "voluntary contributions" for 1926—a far cry from the RM 100,000 made available in the fall of 1923. Cf. R.Ko.In., "[Bericht] Nr. 123," 15 Oct. 1927, BGStA, M.A. 101251a.

137. Between December 1926 and April 1927, he had spoken to business leaders three times in Hattingen (these speeches were in addition to the mass rallies mentioned earlier), twice in Essen, and once in Königswinter. The speaking engagements were announced in the *VB.*

138. This theme is best developed in the Hitler speech before the Nationalklub von 1919 in Hamburg on 27 Feb. 1926.

139. Schumann, *Nationalsozialismus,* p. 44.

140. [PD Nü-Fü?], "Betreff: Finanzierung der NSDAP (streng vertraulich)," Aug. 1927, HA, roll 90, folder 1869; and "N/No. 61," 24 Nov. 1927, HA, roll 69, folder 1507.

ship reports, and while the end-of-the-year figures always showed a sizable increase, these statistics must be viewed with considerable caution. Schwarz's office issued membership cards in strict numerical order without adjusting the gross numbers issued for resignations and expulsions. There do exist, however, concrete figures for a very few geographically scattered locals and some election results. Together, these statistics may support at least some tentative conclusions for the Reich as a whole. Concrete membership figures by locals are available in the following table.

TABLE 1

Local	Gau	1925	April 1926	Dec. 1926	Jan. 1927	Dec. 1927
Göppingen[a]	Württemberg					20
Eggenstein[b]	Baden			6		
Münster[c]	Westphalia	66		87		61
Greifenhagen[d]	Saxony		6	12		6
Lübeck[e]	Mecklenburg	60				90
Nürnberg	Bavaria	✿	✿	✿	✿	✿
Frankfurt a.M.	Hessen	†	†	†	†	†

[a] *Kreiskongress der NSDAP am 3. und 4. November 1934* (Göppingen, 1934).

[b] Ludwig Griesinger, *Chronik der NSDAP Ortsgruppe Eggenstein* (Eggenstein, 1933).

[c] *15 Jahre NSDAP Münster* (Münster, 1937).

[d] *10 Jahre NSDAP—Ortsgruppe Greifenhagen* (Greifenhagen, 1936).

[e] *Der NSDAP Kreis Lübeck—Werden und Wachsen* (Lübeck, 1933).

✿ "Considerable increase," Reichskommissar für die Überwachung der öffentlichen Ordnung, "[Bericht] Nr. 8080/II," 23 Dec. 1926, Bayerisches Geheimes Staatsarchiv, M.A., 101250a.

† "Very little increase," Maria Regina Rumpf, "Die lebensalterliche Verteilung des Mitgliederzuganges der NSDAP vor 1933 aufgezeigt an einer Grossstadt und einem Landkreise" (Dissertation, Heidelberg, 1951), p. 13.

Since for many party members the issue of electoral participation was by no means positively decided, election results are, if anything, even less reliable for analyzing the party's true membership statistics. Nevertheless, the results of the few provincial elections in which the NSDAP nominated its own list of candidates show little evidence of massive growth. For example, in the October 31,

1926, election in Thuringia, 27,946 (or 3.5 percent) NSDAP votes were cast; and in Mecklenberg on May 22, 1927, 5,611 (or 1.8 percent) NSDAP votes were cast.[141] Finally, some qualitative judgments tend to support the general impression of a movement that was moving forward at a very slow pace. The *VB*'s announcement that as of August 7, 1927, some thirty (of perhaps two hundred) locals had not ordered the required posters announcing the party congress scheduled to begin August 18 and the party's inability to fill its meeting halls, even in some areas of propagandistic emphasis,[142] were certainly outward manifestations of an internal crisis.

All of these factors combined to permeate the official annual membership meeting in late July (that is, the meeting of the Munich local) with an atmosphere of somber realism. Schwarz gave the meeting an extremely frank report. He noted that while the party had made great strides in 1926, its rate of growth was restricted by lack of funds,[143] which was another way of saying that there were too few members to pay the costs of propaganda campaigns and that money from other sources was not forthcoming. Similar confessions of disappointment are available for specific Gaus as well.[144] In general, then, the party on the eve of its 1927 congress was horizontally extended to all parts of the Reich, but it lacked organizational depth in many areas, and its membership had not grown significantly as a result of the urban plan.[145] At least in its truncated form, the urban plan was a failure.

141. *Stat. Jahrb. 1928*, pp. 582–83. However, there was still a fairly strong völkisch sentiment in Mecklenburg: the combined vote of the NSDAP and the DVFP was 7.5%.

142. *VB*, 10 Aug. 1927, p. 3. Albert Hellweg, *Vom Kampf and Sieg des Nationalsozialismus im Kreise Lübeck* (Lübeck, 1934), p. 20, reports that a public rally in Tengen (Westphalia) drew a crowd of 10 persons.

143. "Niederschrift über die Generalversammlung der Nationalsozialistischen Deutschen Arbeiterpartei und des Nationalsozialistischen Deutschen Arbeitervereins am 30. Juli 1927 . . . in München," HA, roll 3, folder 81/82 [sic].

144. Goebbels, "Rundschreiben," 22 May 1927, HA, roll 9, folder 200. See also Ogrl. Erfurt-Blücher to KL Erfurt-Stadt, Jan. 1927, HA, roll 7, folder 160.

145. In August 1927, the following SA-Gaustürme (i.e., at least 30 members) were organized: Bavaria, Brandenburg (Berlin), Thuringia, Saxony, Hamburg-Holstein, Hessen, Ruhr, Austria, Pomerania-Mecklenburg, Baden, Saar, Silesia, Württemberg, and Franconia. SABE Nürnberg, 15 Aug. 1927, HA, roll 16, folder 303. On the other hand, nationally prominent speakers totally avoided certain Gaus like Schleswig-Holstein and Mecklenburg, because the membership there was too small. See *VB*, 29 Dec. 1926 and 30 Jan. 1927.

Unlike other totalitarian parties, the NSDAP seldom introduced significant organizational or programmatic changes abruptly. On the contrary, moves toward greater organizational centralism might well coexist for some time with a variety of centrifugal factors, and two diametrically opposed propagandistic emphases could receive official sanction until one gradually superseded the other. Thus, while the urban plan really lost its momentum at the beginning of the year, and every speech at the July membership meeting documented its quantitative and qualitative failure, the plan was never really canceled (of course it had never really been announced either); it just faded away. Characteristically, no immediate replacement came into view. The party merely subsisted on a steady diet of organizational routine and propagandistic negativism. The July membership meeting was, in a sense, dead center. Hitler's speech to the meeting represented a low point in forward thrust during this period of the party's history: he did not present one positive emphasis, but merely reiterated ad nauseam the tried and uncontroversial anti-semitic harangues.[146]

The visible beginning of a new chapter in the NSDAP's organizational and propagandistic history came at the 1927 national congress. The formal announcement of the congress appeared very soon after the prohibition of the Berlin party organization,[147] and it may have been intended partly as a gesture of defiance against the governmental authorities in Berlin. The meeting was staged in Nuremberg, an ideal location for a gathering of the militant members of the synthetic society. Nuremberg was one of the party's genuine growth areas, a town that had not only a well-organized local party, but also a large body of sympathizers who found Julius Streicher's pornographic, anti-semitic harangues peculiarly appealing. The cheering crowds of Nuremberg provided the party militants assembling in the city an illusion of success and popularity that could not be found in any other city in the Reich. Hitler used the atmosphere of Nuremberg well: the concrete resolutions and decisions of the congress again demonstrated the unique interdependence in the NSDAP

146. "Niederschrift . . . ," p. 8, HA, roll 3, folder 81/82 [sic].
147. *VB,* 11 May 1927. The announcement was dated 7 May. The first planning session for the congress took place in Munich on May 17 with Hitler presiding. A day later "transport chiefs" had been appointed for all areas of Germany. *VB,* 18 May 1927.

between externally induced mass atmosphere or mood and voluntarily adopted rules that converted the mood into regulations. The
external picture of the congress was the familiar succession of well-
planned parades, mass rallies, and torchlight demonstrations.[148]

The delegates who marched past Hitler to the strains of stirring
military airs carried their closed-rank discipline into the working
sessions as well. It is as though the exhilarating experience of parad-
ing past the stern face of their Führer lifted them to a higher sphere
of emotion, one that transformed the mundane tasks of discussing
organizational problems, into yet another opportunity to serve and
obey Hitler.[149] A special session on organizational matters was held
on the afternoon of August 19, a Friday.[150] On the agenda were a
series of petitions submitted to the Reichsleitung prior to the congress, requesting organizational changes or clarifications. Hitler had
expressed his opinion on each petition to the chairman of the session
(Heinemann) and also admonished him that he represented the
Reichsleitung, not the petitioners.[151] The admonition was really unnecessary, for, as Goebbels said, "there was no debate on the matters
to be debated." [152] In fact, if the petitions are an accurate reflection
of the membership's feelings, the party militants were anxious to
lose their individuality and become more than ever a functioning
part of the synthetic, unique, centralized, and hierarchial society.
In all, twenty one petitions had been submitted. Of these, four demanded name and title changes (for example, from "party" to
"movement"), thirteen requested more centralization, particularly an

148. Attendance estimates ranged from 100,000 (*VB*, 23 Aug. 1927) to 15,000–
20,000 (R.Ko.In., "Lagebericht Nr. 123," 15 Oct. 1927, BGStA, M.A. 101251a),
but Krebs, *Tendenzen*, p. 58, writes that he definitely counted 15,000 SA.

149. Cf. the statement in the official party report on the congress, "all sessions
[were dominated by] the intellectual shadow of Adolf Hitler." Alfred Rosenberg
und Wilhelm Weiss, eds., *Der Reichsparteitag der Nationalsozialistischen Deutschen
Arbeiterpartei, Nürnberg, 19./21. August 1927* (cited hereafter as *Reichsparteitag
1927*) (Munich, 1927), p. 6.

150. *Ibid.* The time is not without interest, since it indicates that many
Gauleiters were by this time salaried employees of the party. Otherwise they
would have had considerable difficulties getting off work.

151. Hitler, "Grundsätzliche Richtlinien für die Arbeit der Vorsitzenden und
Schriftführer der Sondertagungen am Reichsparteitag 1927," n.d., HA, roll 21,
folder 390.

152. Goebbels, *Kampf*, p. 230.

increase in the authority and power of the Gauleiters, three concerned what the petitioners saw as a potentially dangerous parallelism of the SA and the newly established protection squads (Schutzstaffeln, SS) for Hitler and other leaders, and one demanded even more isolation of the NSDAP from other völkisch groups. Hitler was sympathetic to some of these suggestions. For reasons of practicality and tradition he refused to change the party name. He agreed in principle that the Gauleiters should receive additional powers, but for the present, practical reasons precluded this step. The party simply lacked a sufficient number of "able" men to institute a thorough and rigid centralization. Hitler absolutely refused to modify the relationship of SA and SS. He saw no conflict of interest and established a rather forced division of labor: the SA was the guarantee of unity within the movement, the SS a special elite corps.[153]

Hitler's stand on the SA and SS violated the basic developments toward centralization but it was symptomatic of the new era that the congress inaugurated. To be sure, as always the indications of change were subtle and almost hidden beneath the bombast of speeches emphasizing the unchangeability of the movement. But the indications were nevertheless there. In addition to de-emphasizing the SA's reign as an elite association of activists in the party, the congress all but buried the union question. A special session on union affairs was held, but "it was clear from the outset, that the party [that is, the Reichsleitung] had not the slightest interest in unions." [154] Characteristically, the congress voted to hold a special conference on the union question some time in the future,[155] but it resolved to establish a National Socialist Scientific Association to attract middle-class and intellectual support without calling a prior conference to discuss the project.[156]

153. The petitions and their fates are in "[Akte] Organisation" and Hitler's comments in Hitler, "Betreff: Sondertagung für Organisationsfragen," HA, roll 21, folder 390.
154. Anton Rothenanger to RL, 16 April 1929, HA, roll 21, folder 391.
155. Rosenberg and Weiss, *Reichsparteitag 1927*, p. 53.
156. R.Ko.In., "Lagebericht Nr. 123," 15 Oct. 1927, BGStA, M.A. 101251a; and *VB*, 21/22 Aug. 1927. The organizational realization of the latter project was the *Kampfbund für Deutsche Kultur* (Militant Association for German Culture). See *VB*, 26 Oct. 1927.

The immediate importance of the congress was a renewed demonstration to Hitler that the magic of the myth-person was more
effective than ever before. In spite of the indications of major propaganda, perhaps even ideological changes, the party militants as a
whole did not abandon or even question their faith in the Hitler
myth. The trend toward centralization and bureaucratization became
synonymous with subordination to Hitler's person, regardless of what
propagandistic zigzags the Reichsleitung might decree. The major
difference between 1926 and 1927 lay in this intensification of mood.
In 1926, Hitler as a person could still be emotionally separated
from Hitler as the Reichsleitung; in 1927, the delegates clamored
to lose themselves in the bureaucratization that had begun a year
earlier. They had no desire to assert their own personalities — even
within the bounds of the myth. Heinemann reported that the loudest
applause at the special meeting on organization greeted a spontaneously introduced resolution not even to discuss "inappropriate
questions [that is, some of those before the meeting] so as not to
lower the standards of the congress."[157] Significantly, this change
was not the result of a massive personnel turnover in the top cadres
of the party. The "Lenin-tomb" type of photographic evidence (in
this case a group photograph of the party leaders at the congress)
reveals virtually no unfamiliar faces.[158]

The mood of the congress indicated to Hitler that the party's
functionary corps would enthusiastically accept abandonment of the
urban plan as well as a further increase in the centralization and
bureaucratization of the party. Hitler both anticipated and utilized
the congress' endorsement of his plans. Even before Nuremberg the
Munich office personnel had been substantially increased,[159] and
steps toward more centralization had already begun in late 1926,
in what seemed at first to be an isolated development. In December,
the Reichsleitung abolished the right of the Munich local sections to
elect their own chairmen. These officials were now appointed by

157. Heinemann to Wagner, 21 Aug. 1927, HA, roll 21, folder 390.
158. Rosenberg and Weiss, *Reichsparteitag 1927*, plate 1.
159. "Niederschrift . . . ," p. 19, HA, roll 3, folder 81/82 [sic]. By the spring
of 1928, the central offices had 25 full-time executives and 3 cars. "Korreferat des
Regierungsrates Bernreuther der Polizeidirektion München gehalten auf der Nach-
richtenkonferenz des R.Ko.In. 28. April 1928 in Dresden," BAStA, No. 71490.

the Munich Gauleiter, at this time Hitler himself.[160] In a sense the change was a paradox. On the one hand, the appointment by Hitler raised the Munich section leaders to the same direct derivative status as the Gauleiters, who were also appointed by Hitler directly. Yet, the move also initiated the rapid elimination of *Vereinsmeierei*. By increasing the ties between Hitler and the lower party officials at the time of appointment, Hitler had effectively undermined the feelings of local camaraderie that often centered around the person of an elected local leader. The new local leader identified vertically with his bureaucratic superior, not horizontally with his local membership. Six months after the local leaders began to be appointed from above, the character of the local organizations had fundamentally changed from neighborhood clubs to propaganda distribution units.[161]

The counterpart in the rest of Germany to Hitler's powers in Munich was the appointment of local leaders by the respective Gauleiters, a power that Hitler had been reluctant to entrust to the Gauleiters before. He was far less hesitant to take this step after the 1927 congress, primarily because another massive dose of personal contact had reaffirmed most of the Gauleiters in their self-image as derivative political agents and effectively neutralized whatever desires for organizational autonomy remained. In addition, the simultaneously introduced propaganda changes promised to dilute the concentration of old subleaders at the provincial and particularly the local level by attracting men from the middle class into the party cadres. The party spared no effort to revise its propaganda line to give it a more middle-class image. It largely abandoned socialism and substituted apolitical super-patriotism. Gustav Stresemann and the government's foreign policy replaced capitalism as the party's primary whipping boy. In 1927 and 1928 Hitler and other leaders made a seemingly endless series of speeches against the Reich's

160. PD Nü-Fü, "N/Nr. 53," 21 Dec. 1926, BGStA, M.A. 101250a.

161. See PD Mü, "Ausserordentliche General-Mitgliederversammlung der Sektion Westend der NSDAP am 1.6.1927 im Hackerkeller, PND No. 575," HA, roll 88, folder 1838. It should be noted that such centralizing measures were often counterproductive in their immediate consequences: in October 1927, the RL dissolved 3 Munich sections because of persistent lack of interest among the members in party activities. See "PND No. 60 v. 8.10.27," *ibid.*

rapprochement with France and the folly of opposing Mussolini's Italianization measures in Tyrol.[162] Simultaneously, the party began to cater to the traditional concern of middle-class Germans with culture. In October, the Militant Association for German Culture (*Kampfbund für Deutsche Kultur*, KDV) was founded, and in January staged its first public rally. The speaker was Rosenberg, who addressed an audience of only one hundred persons (mostly students), but these few included such party luminaries as Frick and Hitler.[163]

The shift became equally noticeable in the economic emphasis of the party's propaganda and in its sociological direction. Hitler spoke far more frequently in Munich and Bavaria in late 1927 and 1928, another indication that the Ruhr orientation of the party was a thing of the past. The NSDAP now concentrated its attacks on the traditional enemies of the small town lower-middle-class Germans — the chain stores and largely apolitical agricultural associations that enrolled primarily well-to-do farmers.[164] The shift culminated in the dramatic reinterpretation of Point 17 in the party's program in April 1928, when the party suddenly announced that its advocation of expropriating agricultural estate lands had never been meant to include anyone but Jewish owners.[165]

The bulk of the new propaganda emphasis was directed at the middle classes in general, but the party singled out university students and Wehrverbände leaders as the new priority groups in Germany.[166] After the 1927 congress adjourned, the Reichsleitung began to decrease its vehement denunciations of the Wehrverbände and their leaders. The propaganda committee issued a special pamphlet designed to demonstrate the similarity of the party's and the Wehrver-

162. The foreign-policy emphasis was apparently conceived as a long-range campaign project. Both Rosenberg and Hitler wrote books on foreign-policy questions during the period, though Hitler's manuscript was not published during his lifetime. See Alfred Rosenberg, *Der Zukunftsweg der deutschen Aussenpolitik* (Munich, 1927); and Adolf Hitler, *Hitlers Zweites Buch*, ed. Gerhard L. Weinberg (Stuttgart, 1961).

163. PD Mü, "PND Nr. 600," 17 Jan. 1928, HA, roll 88, folder 1839.

164. *VB*, 7 Jan., 2 March, and 29 March 1928.

165. *VB*, 19 April 1928.

166. It is noteworthy that while the *VB* reprinted in full a Hitler speech to some students in Munich it provided very little coverage of his addresses at the same time in Hamburg and Ludwigslust (Mecklenburg). See *VB*, 23 Nov. 1927.

bände's goals and organizational forms. At the same time the *Völkischer Beobachter* commented sympathetically on remarks of various leaders among the Wehrverbände and began to feature stories of conversions among its former leaders.[167]

The various changes of emphasis resulted in both quantitative and qualitative changes in the NSDAP. The actual membership of the party increased somewhat after it shifted its propaganda emphasis,[168] but this growth was as yet hardly spectacular. More significant were qualitative changes. The party did succeed in recruiting more members of the middle classes and even the former elite of German society[169] to its leadership corps. There was no need for a massive turnover of Gauleiters after the congress, but the few new state leaders that were appointed do suggest that the party's functionary corps was undergoing significant changes, particularly if it is assumed that changes at the top reflected even greater changes among the lower ranks.[170] None of the new Gauleiters, that is, those who had not been in office in July 1926, was from a lower-class background. Albert Krebs (Hamburg) had been a white-collar union official, Wilhelm Loeper (Anhalt) was a retired army captain, and Walther von Corswant (Pomerania), a Junker landlord. On the other hand, Hitler dropped a number of Gauleiters who were either too actively committed to the urban plan or who lacked the qualifications of bureaucratized technicians of power. Thus, Bruno Scherwitz in East Prussia was expelled from the party, while Theodor Vahlen in Pomerania, Hans Hohnfeldt in Danzig, and Paul Schulz in Hesse

167. For the announcement of the pamphlet see *VB*, 17 Sept. 1927. On the "capture" of a Wehrverbände leader see "Übertritt eines Wehrwolfführers zur NSDAP," *VB*, 21 Sept. 1927. The *VB* commented on a speech by the Stahlhelm leader Franz Seldte in *VB*, 10 Dec. 1927, "Beiblatt Münchener Beobachter."

168. For Nazi estimates see PD Mü, "Bericht über die Überwachung der Volksversammlung der [NSDAP] am 9. Nov. 1927," 10 Nov. 1927, HA, roll 88, folder 1839; and Kube (Gauleiter of the Ostmark, i.e., Eastern Brandenburg), "[Rundschreiben], Tgb. Nr. 2363/28," 27 April 1928, HA, roll 9, folder 200.

169. A particular triumph was the conversion of the hero of the Bavarian counterrevolution, General von Epp, to the National Socialist cause. See Epp, "Warum ich Nationalsozialist geworden bin," *VB*, 10 May 1928.

170. There is some concrete evidence to justify this assumption. See, for example, the occupational listing of district leaders in the Anhalt Gau just before the congress. The group included a lawyer, 2 engineers, a white-collar worker, and a high school teacher *(Studienrat)*. *VB*, 21 July 1927.

all took leaves of absence from which they never returned to their posts.[171] Indeed, so obviously successful was the campaign for new leaders that some of the older, proletarian-oriented Gauleiters, privately expressed their concern about "the elements that this year [1927] has brought to the surface [in the NSDAP],"[172] though none, of course, blamed Hitler for this development.

Indeed, the old group suppressed whatever preference they might have had for activist revolutionary behavior and joined the new officials in becoming legal, bureaucratized revolutionaries. By the fall of 1927, Hitler had apparently given up all hope of becoming the German Mussolini. Failure to capture the workers coupled with the relative success of the new line among the middle classes apparently convinced him that power would never be his unless he could capture and integrate the despised German bourgeois *(Spiessbürger)*. To do this the party needed able administrators of election campaigns and membership activities, not organizers of terror. This is not to say that the party committed no further acts of violence, but merely that physical activism ceased to be the main component of the party's thrust for power.

In the new era the party concentrated on election victories as the fundamental demonstration of its growing political power. Although the potential disadvantages of participating in elections still existed — the possibility of disastrous losses, legislative dilution of revolutionary fervor, etc. — the significant propaganda revisions since the beginning of 1927 gave considerably greater promise of electoral success. To begin with, the middle-class sympathizers might vote NSDAP, but would seldom fight or march in a demonstration. Then, too, a Reichstag election was coming up. As a national political experience, the campaign for the Reichstag would stir and unify all party militants and at the same time lend itself to centralized propagandistic direction. Moreover, the organization of electoral activities provided a constitutional loophole for illegal party organization.

171. Scherwitz's expulsion notice is in *VB,* 5 Oct. 1927. Few of the "retired" Gauleiters broke with Hitler or the movement. On the contrary, most were heartbroken that for whatever reason they could not continue their service to the myth-person and offered their services to Hitler to use in whatever capacity he saw fit.

172. Kaufmann to Himmler, 7 June 1927, BDC, PKC, "Akte Kaufmann."

The prohibited Berlin Gau administration continued to function under the legal cover of an "Office of the Deputies [of the Prussian state legislature]" *(Büro der Abgeordneten)*.[173] And, in the last analysis, the Reichsleitung made a virtue out of necessity. The urban plan had clearly failed and putsch actions were still futile; election victories alone remained. It was of course more than a happy coincidence that the new men who entered the ranks of the NSDAP's administrative corps were ideally suited to conduct campaigns. Few of them were activists in the old sense; most were men with a civilian skill (white-collar worker, teacher, etc.) that could be easily utilized in the new party bureaucracy, oriented to paper work.

Hitler was aware that shifting the focus of party activities to elections required some massive organizational and top-level personnel changes. At the beginning of 1928, the venerable General Heinemann, apparently too old and unsuited for the new paper-and-pencil party, resigned both as head of the Uschla and of the Reich organizational committee. His successor in the latter position was Gregor Strasser, the most effective and dynamic organizer in the party and since Bamberg an undeviating follower of Hitler. The Uschla's new chairman was Walter Buch, like Heinemann a retired army officer, but far younger and a long-time believer in the Hitler myth.[174] Next came the break-up of at least some of the urban Gau complexes. Under the urban plan, massive Gau complexes extending over several Reichstag election districts had been created around such urban concentrations as Berlin and the Ruhr. This made sense if the focal point of party activity was the urban complex, but it was administratively cumbersome if the basic goal of the party was an election victory in each Reichstag voting district. Consequently, the party changed the geographic boundaries of some Gaus. This did not yet involve the Ruhr Gau, but at the beginning of 1928 a new Ostmark Gau was created out of the Berlin concentration. It was

---

173. Goebbels, *Kampf*, p. 264.

174. Buch had been a party member since 1921 and an SA leader at the time of the Putsch. Since then "[his] inner relationship to Hitler had never changed." Buch to DVO (Deutscher Vaterländischer Orden), 13 May 1927. See also his undated, handwritten essay, "Der Mensch Adolf Hitler," HA, roll 56, frame 1375; and Krebs, *Tendenzen*, pp. 198–99.

headed by Wilhelm Kube and had the same boundaries as the Reichstag election district Frankfurt/Oder.[175]

The geographic relocation of Gau boundaries and the personnel changes within the Reich and state administrative offices signaled important changes in the relationship of Gauleiters and the Reichsleitung. The Gauleiters were rapidly becoming, in fact as well as in theory, division managers of a highly centralized party-corporation. The central office used election campaigns and legislative efforts both to redesign the image of the party executive and to tie him even closer to the Reichsleitung. As political soldier and street terrorist, the party official had no positive status in the society in which he lived. He might be admired for his brute strength and ruthlessness, but he was not socially respectable. In an election-oriented party, physical prowess counted for little; abilities to organize poster campaigns, to distribute speakers, to foresee concentrations of potential voters, and to utilize money effectively were qualities that counted. In short, the party official needed an ability to translate paper directives from Munich into paper directives at his particular level. Whether or not he marched in the street was really immaterial. The rewards for a successful campaign were perhaps less immediately satisfying than the sight of a dozen political enemies moaning on a beer hall floor, but they were socially far more acceptable. If elected, the party official became a member of the Reichstag or the Landtag, positions of considerable prestige in Germany. In addition, there were very tangible material benefits: a successful Reichstag candidate received a salary for each legislative session he attended and a free railroad pass to travel throughout Germany. (Landtag members obtained a salary and a pass good within the boundaries of the state). He thus became more mobile, though financially more dependent upon the Reichsleitung.[176] Hitler personally selected all can-

175. For the announcement of the personnel and administrative changes see *VB*, 4 Jan. 1928. While Heinemann, according to the *VB*, asked to be relieved of his duties, it appears that serious differences with Hitler over the handling of the Pfeffer–Kaufmann controversy were the real cause of his dismissal. See Miltenberg, *Adolf Hitler*, p. 81.

176. Kube, one of the least mythologized among the Gauleiters, cautioned his personal friend and district leader in the Ostmark Gau, Kasche, against accepting a salaried position from the party: "otherwise your independence of will is gone." Kube to Kasche, HA, roll 9, folder 200. Munich also showed little interest in placing

didates on the Reich list and at least the first two on each district list, and he did not hestitate to use the lists for rewarding or punishing individual party officials.[177]

In other respects, too, the Gauleiters became more passive figures. While previously the Gauleiter had offered his services to Munich and Hitler had then carved out a Gau for him, the Reichsleitung now had a sufficiently large store of potential leaders in most areas[178] to enable it to proceed more rationally and create a district first, then find a man to head it.[179] Once appointed the Gauleiter was now entrusted with a far more formidable arsenal of control functions over the sub-organizations of his Gau. He had the power, by using his Gau-Uschla, to dissolve sub-Gaus and districts,[180] and in financial matters, the Gau now became the only official intermediary agency between the Reichsleitung and the locals.[181]

All of these measures also affected both the party officials' relationships to each other and their attitudes toward the membership. The camaraderie at the local level was clearly at an end. The locals following the example of Munich, became propaganda organizations and executive organs. Each local created its own organization committee, thereby beginning a division of labor at the lowest echelon that paralleled the horizontal division at the top. The duties of a local organization committee were clearly defined by a Munich directive.[182] Like any unit in a bureaucracy, the locals reported as well as executed. They sent detailed monthly reports on their agitprop activity (separated by category) through channels to Munich to serve as the basis for planning

---

officials who already received a salary from the party, such as Gau business managers, on the candidate lists. See Himmler to Corswant, 31 March 1928, NA, T-580, roll 24, folder 207 (Gau Pommern).

177. Cf. the correspondence between Corswant, Kube, and Frick from March to May, 1928, NA, T-580, roll 24, folder 207.

178. The lack of suitable Gauleiters in the Ruhr area seems to have been the major reason for not dividing this area into 3 or 4 new Gaus.

179. Gau Brandenburg to Kasche *et al.*, 19 Feb. 1928, HA, roll 9, folder 200. Goebbels to Kasche, 16 Jan. 1928, HA, roll 10, folder 209.

180. *VB*, 23 Sept. 1927; 4/5 and 23 March 1928. The establishment of Gau Uschlas became mandatory after Hitler's "Bekanntmachung," *VB*, 28 Apr. 1928.

181. Schwarz excluded the districts from the accounting procedures on Sept. 1, 1927. See Schwarz to Kube, 1 March 1928, HA, roll 53, folder 1240.

182. "Prozesssache Gogo & Gen. g. im Wege & Gen. 30328/27," 26 April 1928, HA, roll 5, folder 136.

new regional and national propaganda campaigns.[183] The complete
loss of real decision-making power at the local level did not, however,
enable the Gauleiter to increase his power at the expense of the Reichsleitung. Administratively as well as emotionally he identified with
Munich. In October 1927 the Reichsleitung announced the formation
of a separate Reichsleitung local, an organizational entity whose members consisted solely of Gauleiters, Reich and state legislators of the
party, high SA leaders, and the permanent executives of the Reichsleitung. Hitler did not, however, permit the creation of analogous
Gauleitung sections.[184]

The deliberate transformation of the "mood" within the party did
not go unnoticed by those elements in the party to whom political activity meant violence and activism and for whom political leadership
was the opposite of the pencil-pushing Gauleiter-administrator. Understandably, the opposition to the new course was concentrated in the
SA, an organization destined to be less important in an election-cen-
tered party than in an activist group dealing in civil disobedience and
terror.[185] The SA complaints were particularly vehement in Munich,
no doubt because the SA organization there was aware that the most
enthusiastic advocates of the new course were the executives at the
Schellingstrasse. The complaints centered on two issues: money and
propaganda tactics. Actually, the two were closely related. There is

183. RL, "An die Gauleitungen und selbständigen Ortsgruppen der NSDAP,"
13 Feb. 1928, HA, roll 3, folder 81/82 [sic]. Such a listing might look as follows:
27 Discussion Groups (*Sprechabende*), 3 German Evenings, 1 General Membership
Conference, 1 Excursion, 1 Christmas Party, 1 Variety Show (*Unterhaltungsabend*).
See "Auszug aus dem Mitteilungsblatt der Sektion Westend [München] . . . ,"
24 Jan. 1928, HA, roll 88, folder 1838. It is significant that all of the activities of
the section for 1927 involved only the members or invited guests. The absence of
any public rallies clearly indicates the growing *Vereinsmeierei*.

184. *VB*, 1 Oct. 1927; and RL to GL Magdeburg-Anhalt, 14 Feb. 1928, NA,
T-580, roll 22, folder 204. The Gauleitung is the Gau equivalent of the Reichsleitung, i.e., the totality of the party's bureaucratic institutions at the Gau level.
A decision or activity of the Gauleitung thus may or may not mean personal
intervention by the Gauleiter.

185. As part of the party's reorientation, the Reichsleitung forced all SA leaders
to resign from any political leadership position they might have had. (A number
of Gau SA leaders were also deputy Gauleiters.) The decree created a division
between SA leaders and political chiefs such as the party had previously established
between political and financial administrators. See *VB*, 2/3 Oct. 1927.

no doubt that faithful SA service involved considerable financial burdens for the individual SA man. At this time (actually until 1929),
the individual member still had to pay for his own uniform and transportation to rallies.[186] The least he expected in return was the right to
march, demonstrate, and actively terrorize. Hitler, speaking through
the Osaf, refused. As they had in the spring, the SA men began to grum-
ble about "the mess of red tape *(Paragraphen-Wirtschaft)*," that is,
the bureaucratization in the party. There is also some evidence of a
slowdown in their performance of rally duty.[187] But, again, the pseudo-
revolts were directed not against Hitler, but against his bureaucratized
institutionalization in the Reichsleitung. Indeed, the revolt was not
against Hitler but for him, which made it considerably easier to deal
with. In addition, the dissatisfactions were concentrated among rank-
and-file members and some lower echelon leaders. Pfeffer agreed fully
with Hitler's tactics (which earned him the description "coward" from
the grumbling opposition),[188] and Hitler could trust the SA leader in
Bavaria, Buch, so completely as to make him head of the Uschla in
January 1928. In the end, the opposition collapsed before the reality of
Hitler's myth-person. In early January Hitler, as he had earlier in May,
explained personally to the Munich SA that the activist tactics simply
would not work; they would merely send him back to prison. As for
the SA's more material demands, the Reichsleitung could not provide
a subsidy for uniform purchase, etc., but Hitler would be willing to
devote one evening a month to SA affairs.[189]

With the disintegration of the internal opposition there still remained the external danger of a very poor showing at the polls. This
would not disengage the already committed militants in the party, but
it might reopen the debate over the best means to achieve power and
certainly would not encourage the flow of financial contributions from
business sources. For these reasons, the Reichsleitung organized its

186. Bennecke, *Hitler*, p. 141.
187. PD Nü-Fü, "N/No. 61," 24 Nov. 1927, HA, roll 74, folder 1553; and PD
Mü, "Führersitzung der Standarte I der SA am 8. November 1927, PND No. 592,"
ibid., folder 1552.
188. "PND No. 592," *ibid.*
189. "Führerbesprechung des Sturmes I der SA Müchen am 15.XI.1927, PND
No. 594," and "Generalappell der SA Standarte I (München) am 9. Januar 1928,
PND No. 599," *ibid.*

1928 Reichstag election campaign carefully and far in advance. The first planning sessions on election procedures were held shortly before the 1927 congress, almost a year before the election actually took place.[190] By the end of 1927, the Reichsleitung had established centralized planning and control procedures,[191] and some Gaus were well on their way toward instituting their own regional campaign plans.[192] With the return of milder weather in the spring (poster glue had a tendency to freeze in the winter), the party devoted all of its agitprop activities and virtually all of its financial resources to the election campaign. Hitler and other nationally prominent speakers concentrated their efforts on the areas of Germany in which the party expected its most significant successes: Bavaria, Saxony-Thuringia, and the Ruhr. The north (Hamburg and Schleswig-Holstein) and the east were left largely to local and provincial speakers.[193]

The lists of NSDAP candidates were issued in early April. It was a very interesting assembly of names, clearly revealing both the extra- and intraparty significance of electoral participation. Of the thirty-six candidates on the Reich List, twelve were Gauleiters and another seven prominent national leaders (Epp headed the list) or central office executives. Several prominent officials had their chances of election increased through a multiplicity of candidacies. Thus, Strasser was a candidate for the Reichstag in the following election districts: East Prussia, Pomerania, Magdeburg, Schleswig-Holstein, Westphalia-North, Westphalia-South (both of these were in the Ruhr), Hessen-Nassau, Düsseldorf-East, Düsseldorf-West, Lower Bavaria, and the Palatinate. Goebbels could boast an almost equally large number of

---

190. See Hess to Strasser, 8 Aug. 1927, HA, roll 44, folder 900.

191. *VB*, 14 Dec. 1927. The actual "Reich election leaders," Frick for the Reichstag and Kube for the Prussian Landtag, were not announced until early April. See *VB*, 3 Apr. 1928.

192. Gau Brandenburg to Kasche, 7 Dec. 1927; and Goebbels, "Rundschreiben Nr. 8," 6 Jan. 1928, HA, roll 9, folder 200. For the organization of the party's campaign in a Gau see Gau Ruhr, "Rundschreiben Nr. 76," 24 April 1928; and "Rundschreiben Nr. 77," 7 May 1928, HA, roll 5, folder 136.

193. The judgment on the geographic focal points in the campaign is based on the speaking engagements of prominent leaders announced in the *VB*. The campaign was financed at the Reich level at least in part by the simple device of subordinating new locals directly to Munich, thereby collecting all of their dues. See the *VB* announcements of new locals in April and May of 1928.

candidacies. The members of the party functionary corps who failed to find a place on the Reich list did not need to feel neglected. Most of the other Gauleiters, SA leaders, and central office executives occupied prominent positions on the lists for state legislators or on the regional Reichstag lists. In fact, if all of the NSDAP candidates had been elected, its legislative delegations would have consisted almost entirely of full-time party functionaries.[194]

194. *VB*, 3, 15/16, and 21 Apr. 1928.

"Socialism! That is really an unfortunate word."*

On Sunday, May 20 (German elections were always held on Sundays to encourage a large turnout), 30.7 million Germans, 74.6 percent of those eligible, went to the polls to elect a new Reichstag. The NSDAP was very hopeful of achieving a major political breakthrough: it ran candidates in all thirty-five German election districts, it was well organized in the most populous areas of the Reich, it had waged a vigorous campaign,[1] and its list of candidates was headed by a major nationalist hero. There were, therefore, some sound political reasons for feelings of optimism and anticipatory excitement among the party faithful who gathered at the national headquarters on Sunday evening. A rudimentary election central had been set up for the several hundred who came to cheer the incoming returns. SA messengers on bicycles brought in tabulations from the polling places around the city, and telegrams reached Munich from the more distant parts of Germany. Hermann Esser announced favorable results to the accompaniment of loud cheers. Towards the end of the evening, after it was clear that he had been elected, General Epp made a triumphal entrance. Hitler appeared about midnight and delivered a curiously negative speech. His remarks dealt almost entirely with the evident electoral gains

---

* Hitler in Bodo Uhse, *Söldner und Soldat* (Paris, 1935), p. 202.

1. In terms of raw statistics, the party had used 118 speakers and held 10,000 rallies. See PD Nü-Fü, "N/No. 67" and "N/No. 68," 13 June and 13 July 1928, HA, roll 69, folder 1509.

of the two working-class parties, and he seemed to derive an almost perverse satisfaction from the defeat of the German moderate middle and rightist parties.[2]

Hitler's address transformed an obvious Nazi defeat at the polls into a triumph of political prediction and omniscience. His decision is understandable, for the election of 1928 was a significant step on the road to power only in retrospect. The first impression on Monday morning could hardly be anything but that the NSDAP had failed in its attempt to achieve major political status in Weimar Germany. Altogether the party polled 100,000 fewer votes than in December 1924. It lost heavily in the urban areas and in the districts east of the Elbe; it won 16,478 votes (1.4%) in Berlin; 8,105 votes (0.8%) in all of East Prussia; 17,768 votes (2.6%) in Hamburg; and 31,839 votes (1.3%) in the Ruhr area.[3] The figures were not an impressive showing for a party whose organizational strength at this time lay in the urban areas.[4] The NSDAP did score some impressive gains, but they had no relation to the major organizational efforts of the party in the last two years. The NSDAP achieved genuine political upsets in the *Geest* areas (the less fertile inland farm regions) of western Schleswig-Holstein, in parts of Hanover, and the rural areas of Upper Franconia around Nuremberg. In Schleswig-Holstein the party received 18.1%, 17.7%, 10.4% and 8.6% of the vote, respectively, in the counties of Norderdithmarschen, Süderdithmarschen, Steinburg, and Rendsburg.[5] The party was also relatively successful in the rural areas of Hanover and Bavaria, especially Franconia. (See Table 2.) With the exception of Nuremberg and Schleswig-Holstein after January,[6] the Reichsleitung had treated

---

2. *VB*, 22 May 1928.

3. The figures are from Wilhelm Dittmann, *Das politische Deutschland vor Hitler* (Zurich, 1945). See also Heinrich Striefler, *Deutsche Wahlen in Bildern und Zahlen* (Düsseldorf, 1946), pp. 23 and 46. The NSDAP vote in Berlin was so insignificant that the police lifted its ban on party activities shortly after the election. See Konrad Heiden, *Geschichte des Nationalsozialismus* (Berlin, 1932), p. 241.

4. R.Ko.In., "Lagebericht Nr. 126," 20 July 1928, HA, roll 24A, folder 1758; and Rudolf Heberle, *Landbevölkerung und Nationalsozialismus* (Stuttgart, 1963), p. 160.

5. Heberle, *Landbevölkerung*, p. 42.

6. Gerhard Stoltenberg, *Politische Strömungen im Schleswig-holsteinischen Landvolk* (Düsseldorf, 1962), p. 145.

TABLE 2

Election District	NSDAP Vote	Percent
Schleswig-Holstein	31,814	4.0
Weser-Ems	36,388	5.2
Südhannover-Braunschweig	46,361	4.4
Oberbayern-Schwaben	72,127	6.2
Franken	100,761	8.1

SOURCE: Figures from Wilhelm Dittman, *Das politische Deutschland vor Hitler* (Zurich, 1945).

all of these districts as organizational backwaters in the past, and in some areas no prominent party leader had ever spoken.

Under the intricate proportional representation system of the Weimar Republic the NSDAP won twelve seats in the Reichstag. Of these, six received a sufficient number of votes in individual election districts; the other six moved into the legislature via the Reich list. The group was both typical and unusual in several respects. (See Table 3.)

The party's Reichstag delegation was relatively old; half of the twelve members were over forty (that is, twenty-six at the beginning of World War I), 25 percent were in their thirties, and only one member was still in his twenties. Significantly, the older group contained a large number of professional soldiers who were unable to continue their careers after 1918; the occupation "author" is probably a face-saving circumvention of their inability to find a slot in civilian life. It is noteworthy, however, that while this group was probably typical of many party members from the prewar generation at this time, it was not representative of the party's functionary corps. All but one (Buch) of the new Reichstag deputies who might be described as party functionaries were considerably younger than the retired soldier group. Finally, the delegation included a high proportion of members with charismatic appeal in their own right: despite the number of candidates who held Gauleiter positions, all but one (Strasser) of the four personally most popular candidates (as measured by votes cast for the individual in single districts) — Epp,

TABLE 3

Name	Year of Birth	Occupation	Party Function
Buch	1883	Army major (retired)	Chairman, Reich Uschla
Dreher	1892	Mechanic	Local leader in Ulm and Stuttgart
Epp	1868	Army general (retired)	—
Feder	1883	Engineer	—
Frick	1877	Civil servant (Oberamtmann)	—
Goebbels	1897	Author	Gauleiter of Berlin
Göring	1893	Air Force captain (retired) and author	—
Reventlow	1869	Navy lieutenant (retired) and author	—
Stöhr	1879	Union official and author	—
Strasser	1892	Pharmacist	Reich Organization Leader
Wagner	1899	Elementary school teacher	Gauleiter of Westphalia
Willikens	1893	Army officer (retired) and farmer	—

SOURCE: Bureau des Reichstags, ed., *Reichstags-Handbuch IV. Wahlperiode 1928* (Berlin, 1928).

Strasser, Feder, and Stöhr — had been politically prominent long before they joined the NSDAP.

The outcome of the election was a distinct surprise to the Reichsleitung. In a very real sense, the electoral results and the party's organizational efforts showed a very high degree of negative correlation. Basically, the party had been unable to disengage any significant number of politically articulate Germans in the urban areas (other than its own membership) from the pluralistic values of Weimar. On the other hand, it made significant inroads into some specific rural areas, that is, areas of small-scale, marginal farming and in the small towns that depended on such farming for their economic life. In western Schleswig-Holstein, in Hanover, and in Franconia, the NSDAP politically spoke for the young, small-scale farmer and the small-town shopkeeper who feared an agricultural depression. The party was the unanticipated beneficiary of economic fear and frustration among parts of Germany's rural population.[7] Moreover, the NSDAP's propaganda shift away from the urban plan in 1927 enabled rural voters to articulate their economic fears in the form of a patriotic pledge. A vote for the NSDAP was a vote for Hitler, the man who preached chauvinistic love of *Volk;* for Epp, the general who destroyed Bolshevism in Bavaria; for Göring, the dashing flyer of World War I, who wore the *Pour-le-Mérite* around his neck. In casting their ballots for the NSDAP the rural voters took a significant step toward full engagement in the totalitarian myth, but the vast majority was neither conscious of this factor nor had it traveled far beyond that first step. Organizationally the rural voters were as yet only a virgin — though potentially very fertile — field.

At first the Reichsleitung seemed as bewildered by the election results as the rural voters had been by the signs of the agricultural depression. The first reactions in the *VB* followed Hitler's election-night speech with a banner headline "Down with International Marxism." This was followed by gleeful satisfaction that Epp had been elected in Bavaria while Stresemann failed to get the required number of district votes and a morbid fascination with the political death throes of the German Völkisch Freedom Party in Bavaria.[8] It was over a week before the Reichsleitung made public an overall interpretation of the election statistics.[9] At the end of May the Reichsleitung coupled a frank admission that "certain districts did less well than we expected," with a hopeful but realistic interpretation of the rural vote. Simultaneously the party leadership accepted the organizational and propagandistic implications of the election

7. Heberle, *Landbevölkerung*, pp. 32, 48–52, and 130; Charles P. Loomis and J. Allan Beegle, "The Spread of German Nazism in Rural Areas," *American Sociological Review*, II (Dec. 1946), 726–27; and *Central-Verein* [deutscher Staatsbürger jüdischen Glaubens] *Zeitung*, 25 May 1928.

8. *VB*, 22 May 1928.

9. During this time the *VB* filled its pages with reports on individual triumphs in isolated towns and counties. Some party members seem to have been very discouraged over the election results. See PD Mü, "Mitgliederversammlung der NSDAP Sektion Schwabing am 6. VI. 1928 . . . PND Nr. 618," HA, roll 88, folder 1838; and PD Nü-Fü, "N/No. 68," 13 July 1928, HA, roll 69, folder 1509. Despair over the elections of 1928, which marked the highpoint of Republican popularity in Germany, was widespread among the extreme right. See Ernst von Salomon, *Der Fragebogen* (Hamburg, 1961), p. 94.

results: the NSDAP needed to follow up its rural triumphs with a propaganda saturation campaign in the rural areas; and, less obviously, it needed to redraw Gau boundaries to facilitate the incorporation of the rural population.[10]

What the party leadership proposed was nothing less than an organizational revolution. It represented a departure in strategy fully as important as Hitler's programmatic decisions at Bamberg. And, like Bamberg, it necessitated another personal confrontation of the leadership corps and the Hitler myth-person to prevent a possible crisis of faith among the urban-oriented Gauleiters. A logical setting for such a personal meeting of living myth and its agents would have been the 1928 national party congress. But after months of indecision[11] Hitler decided against a congress in 1928. The reasons were primarily financial; the Reichsleitung, already burdened by unpaid election debts, feared the additional expense. In addition, Hitler also hesitated to burden the congress' image with discussions about a potentially divisive issue. He preferred to settle the difficult problems in a less public atmosphere and reserve the national rallies for mass demonstrations and set speeches. On the other hand, canceling the congress created a momentary decision vacuum. While the Reichsleitung had already proclaimed the need for organizational reform, it had not yet cast the new principles into the form of concrete organizational directives. In the meantime, the state and local organizations had no positive instruction for their future work, so that Munich had to move quickly to prevent the reemergence of autonomous organizational forms at the Gau level. With separate directives issued in late May and early August, Hitler first required prior permission from the center to organize a Gau congress and then flatly prohibited such rallies.[12] The Reichsleitung also intervened when the long-debated National Socialist unions seemed to

10. *VB*, 31 May 1928. For a reaction to the election results at the Gau level see Adalbert Gimbel, "So kam es" (typewritten MS, 1940), p. 67, HA, roll 28, folder 534.

11. *VB*, 25/26 Mar. and 19 Apr. 1928; and Bouhler to GL Sachsen, 6 July 1928, NA, T-580, roll 25, folder 208 I (Sachsen).

12. *VB*, 26 May and 3 Aug. 1928. The latter order was apparently unexpected. Both Berlin and Ruhr had already scheduled a meeting for August 25 and 26, but altered their plans in view of the new directive. See *VB*, 15/16 Aug. 1928, and GL Ruhr to *VB*, 24 July 1928, NA, T-580, roll 20, folder 203 (Gau Rheinland-Nord).

become organizational reality. While Munich still tolerated the establishment of a "Secretariat for Labor Affairs" in Berlin,[13] it prohibited
party affiliation for unions of any kind after a group of party members founded a thoroughly innocuous Greater German Union (*Grossdeutsche Gewerkschaft*, Grodege).[14] On the positive side, Hitler
made some key personnel changes. In Bavaria, Fritz Reinhardt, a
close associate of Heinrich Himmler and a reputed expert in rural
agitprop methods, became head of the sub-Gau of Upper Bavaria.
In the Ruhr, Karl Kaufmann was dismissed in the wake of the
election and replaced by Josef Wagner.[15]

These personnel changes were both preludes to the major work
of organizational reform and indications of the directions in which
Hitler wanted the party to move. Hitler became considerably more
specific about the future of the party at a leadership conference
in August. The Reichsleitung decided to combine the annual membership meeting with a full-scale conference of the entire leadership
corps, that is, executives of the Reichsleitung, Gauleiters, SA-leaders,
Reichstag and Landtag delegates, the Hitler Youth leader, and the
head of the National Socialist Women's Association — some seventy
individuals in all.[16] As always, Hitler selected the setting for a
major milestone in the party's organizational history with great care.
The site of the meeting was Munich, the mecca of the movement,
and, more recently, the site of at least a minor Nazi election
triumph. In the Reichstag elections the NSDAP had captured third
place among the parties running in Munich, though, to be sure,
it was a very poor third. The membership meeting itself provided
Hitler with a very cordial atmosphere. Since only the Munich members of the party constituted the legal corporation under the party's
bylaws, Hitler could be certain of a very enthusiastic and utterly
loyal audience.

The meeting began on Friday morning (August 2) with an address

13. Goebbels appointed Johannes Engel to head the new office. See Johann K.
von Engelbrechten, *Eine braune Armee entsteht* (Munich, 1937), p. 79.

14. The Grodege was founded on Aug. 12; the *VB* announcement came 2 days
later. See Grodege, "Rundschreiben Nr. 1," Aug. 1928, HA, roll 70, folder 1519
and *VB*, 14 Aug. 1928.

15. *VB*, 1 June 1928; and Wagner to "Parteigenossen des Gaues Ruhr," late July
1928 [sic], HA, roll 5, folder 136.

16. The first announcement of the leadership conference appeared in the *VB*,
15/16 July 1928.

by Hitler to a plenary session of all delegates, followed by a discussion of "all organizational questions of general interest." [17] In the afternoon the party's chief counsel, Hans Frank, discussed the always delicate subject of legal activities in a revolutionary party, and in the evening the entire conference adjourned to attend the membership meeting in the tradition-laden Bürgerbräukeller. Hitler's speech here on the "State of the Party" set the mood for the working sessions of the leadership conference scheduled to begin the following morning. Aside from the high praise he bestowed on Franz Schwarz, his remarks were noteworthy for their serious, almost somber tone. Although Hitler pointed to some major election victories for the NSDAP (for example, he singled out Stresemann's defeat in Bavaria again), he also admitted that the party had only reached a plateau, and not a very lofty one at that. In terms of its organizational effectiveness, the NSDAP had forged a framework of organizational strength, but the detailed picture within the framework needed thorough reexamination.[18]

Following Hitler's speech a minor sensation occurred as a member introduced a resolution from the floor. (As noted earlier, under the German laws of associations even the membership meetings of anti-democratic groups had to be run along democratic lines.) Artur Dinter, until recently Gauleiter of Thuringia, but now a sharp critic of the party's administration, called for a formal consultative assembly (Senate) to be appointed by Hitler, but empowered to advise the party leader on all major issues — whether he asked for the advice or not. This was a revolutionary proposal, not so much for what it said as for what it implied. It could only be put into effect if the party members abandoned the Hitler myth-person as the center of the NSDAP's organizational and programmatic life. Dinter, who had become disengaged from the Hitlerian totalitarianism and reengaged in his own religio-mystical ideas, wanted to achieve precisely this. Hitler had anticipated the resolution[19]

17. While it is no doubt true that "[the] possibility of discussion in a Führer conference existed without restriction up to the resignation of Strasser in 1932 . . . ," as Karl Kaufmann claimed (oral evidence on 30 July 1946, *IMT*, XX, 28), the Bamberg conference had shown that there was very little to discuss after a major Hitler speech.

18. PD Mü, "Betreff: Generalmitgliederversammlung der NSDAP am 31.8.28 PND Nr. 626," 31 Aug. 1928, HA, roll 70, folder 1516.

19. Hitler to Dinter, 25 July 1928 in Dinter, "Der Kampf um die Vollendung der Reformation—Mein Ausschluss aus der Nationalsozialistischen Deutschen Arbeiterpartei," *Geistchristentum*, I (Sept.–Oct. 1928), 353–56.

and accepted the challenge. He told the meeting that his style of administration had no need for a collective body of advisors. It was far more efficient simply to consult the specific subleader *(Unterführer)* who was in charge of a particular administrative competency. In effect, Hitler admitted that he alone had the authority to originate decisions. He was the decision-making apparatus of the party; his executive-administrators might be consulted on specific issues, but their primary function was to convert Hitler's decisions into administrative practice. The members left no doubt about the sanctity of the Hitler myth-person: to the accompaniment of "boo"-calls, Dinter's resolution was unanimously (that is, only Dinter voted for it) defeated.[20]

The working sessions of the leadership conference provided a graphic and immediate illustration of Hitler's administrative principles. Subleaders were divided according to their bureaucratic roles, so that Hitler could consult with them on the specific issues that fell into their administrative spheres of competence. From 9 o'clock in the morning until 6 o'clock in the evening on Saturday, Hitler and the executives of the Reichsleitung scheduled individual consultations with various Gauleiters to discuss the problems of their specific areas. Like division managers of a corporation, the subleaders of the party came to Munich to give an account of themselves, to be judged, to give advice (if asked), and finally to carry out the new directives in their Gaus or legislative positions. Also like division chiefs of a corporation, each Gauleiter arrived with the statistical abstracts of his success or failure: financial statements, membership rolls, activity reports, and requests for speakers. On the final day of the meeting the delegates assembled again in plenary session, but only to hear two major speeches: in the morning Pfeffer on the relationship of party and SA, and as the closing address in the afternoon Hitler's remarks on "The Future Work of the Movement." [21]

Unfortunately, the speeches and the content of the discussions at the conference are no longer available, since minutes or notes made at the time have either been destroyed or lost, and police spies were unable to infiltrate the closed meetings. Nevertheless, it is possible to de-

20. "PND Nr. 626." The *VB's* account of the meeting (2/3 Sept. 1928) did not mention Dinter's resolution.
21. *VB,* 27 and 30 July 1928.

lineate the basic propagandistic and organizational changes that the Reichsleitung proposed to the delegates. Hitler demanded a complete abandonment of the urban plan and a shift of tactical emphasis to electoral victories as the primary means of winning political power. This required in turn a far greater organizational penetration of the rural areas, and, as a prerequisite, the development of propaganda lines that appealed to the rural population. It was not difficult to find persuasive financial and political reasons for abandoning the urban plan. The financial picture of the party was not good after the election. At the end of August, the party had debts of RM 14,000, and party organizations around the country had similar financial problems. Schwarz had been able to balance the books only by such dubious devices as listing on the credit side of the ledger dues of an expected membership increase and subtracting RM 40 per month from the salary of each NSDAP legislator.[22] The Reichsleitung hoped to obtain additional revenue from a source that had helped the party at times in the past, the German business community, with a series of "begging trips" by Hitler and other party leaders. Since their basic approach was to emphasize the party's role as protector of property and bulwark against international socialist influences among the workers,[23] all vestiges of a strong anti-capitalist line in the NSDAP propaganda had to be eliminated.

Perhaps equally important, many of the urban areas had reached political dead ends. In terms of membership, the fastest growing area in the Berlin-Brandenburg Gau was the province of Brandenburg,[24] an area that Goebbels had treated as an organizational stepchild. In Hamburg, the NSDAP vote had been dismal, but neighboring Schleswig-Holstein had provided the Reichsleitung with its most pleasant surprise. And if additional negative correlation were needed, the Ruhr Gau provided instructive figures. Here the piecemeal de-emphasis of the urban plan in 1927 and the following spring

22. "PND Nr. 626." For indications of financial difficulties in the Gaus and locals see Hilble, "Kassabericht der Sektion Schwabing der NSDAP pro 1928," 31 Dec. 1928, HA, roll 2A, folder 224; and Kube to Kasche, HA, roll 9, folder 200.

23. For an example of the approach to business leaders see the description of Hess' presentation in Hamburg in Albert Krebs, *Tendenzen und Gestalten der NSDAP* (Stuttgart, 1959), pp. 174–75. For the success of the solicitations see [PD Mü?], "Notiz," 31 July 1928, HA, roll 24A, folder 1758; and PD Mü, "Abt. VI/ N Nr. 975/28—Vormerkung," 29 Sept. 1928, HA, roll 90, folder 1869.

24. *VB*, 14 Nov. 1928.

had led to an organizational laxity that bordered on passive resistance. In June some twenty-seven locals were from two to four months behind in their financial obligations to the Gau, and lack of interest in the Reichstag campaign was so prevalent that twelve days before the election only five or six locals had ordered the requisite campaign materials from the Gau office.[25] Hitler's immediate dismissal of Kaufmann was therefore not unjustified.

To be sure, abandoning the cities as organizational focal points raised a number of corollary problems. With the possible exception of Bavaria, Schleswig-Holstein, and Thuringia, the NSDAP's state organizations in the fall of 1928 still had urban-oriented leaders and boundaries. It was thus indispensable that these leaders accept the programmatic bases of what may be termed the "rural-nationalist" plan. This was not an easy choice, for it inevitably involved giving up the last vestiges of the revolutionary program of 1925. The rural-nationalist plan essentially restricted the party to the ballot box as a means of achieving national prominence and power. No matter how quantitatively impressive the total rural membership, it could never be amassed as effectively in physical demonstrations as the combined membership of a metropolitan center. Thus in abandoning the urban plan the party also gave up whatever lingering hopes it may have had of achieving power through a Mussolini-like paralysis of Germany's economic and political lifelines. In addition, the rural population of Germany sociologically belonged to the lower-middle and middle classes. These were societal groups which had been elite hangers-on in the Wilhelminian era, and for many such matters as the party's stand on the "monarchy *vs.* Germanic Republic" issue or the NSDAP's relation to the churches were not irrelevant or dead questions, but concerned integral parts of their inherited value system. Hitler knew this and the Munich conference had provided Hitler an opportunity to deal with these issues as well. The catalyst was again Dinter. During the conference, presumably after Hitler's Friday morning speech, Dinter demanded the right to proselytize his neo-Germanic religious ideas in the party and accused Hitler of being a tool of the Roman Catholic Church.

Hitler was prepared because he knew the potential explosiveness of the religious issue. It not only raised the specter of a new north-south

25. GL Ruhr, "Nachtrag zu Rundschreiben Nr. 77," 8 May 1928, HA, roll 5, folder 136.

split among Catholics and Protestants in the party, but simply to reopen the discussion of programmatic issues would negate the results of Bamberg. He had therefore taken the precaution of instructing the Reich Uschla to poll the Gauleiters' views on Dinter's resolution before the meeting. As expected, all but one (who was not named) opposed Dinter. Hitler therefore not only rejected Dinter's request, but carried his objections to the public forum of the membership meeting itself. He quite literally begged the members not to engage in religious discussions (there were cries of "very true" from the audience at this point), and, perhaps encouraged by the approbation from the audience, also included debates on the future form of the German government among the proscribed topics in the party.[26]

This left only the question of National Socialist unions as a major unsettled programmatic issue. Although the Reichsleitung had prohibited party-affiliation for independently formed National Socialist unions, even its August directive favored the establishment of such organizations in principle. Albert Krebs, the Gauleiter of Hamburg from late 1926 to October 1928 and a prominent white-collar union official, took advantage of this ambivalence to urge the establishment of National Socialist unions or the party's formal affiliation with one of the established right-wing unions. This time Hitler's reaction was to remain silent, but his very silence doomed the proposal to failure. His obvious lack of interest in the whole question effectively discouraged any support or even discussion of Krebs' proposals.[27]

After laying, at least negatively, the programmatic base of the rural-nationalist plan, Hitler could turn to the reorganization of the party's Gau structure. Basically, he proposed to redraw the boundaries of the Gaus to correspond to the boundaries of the Reichstag electoral districts. This meant, in effect, that the Gau would become a year-round tactical campaign unit, and the Gauleiter a permanent regional campaign manager. The reorganization would be uni-

---

26. *VB*, 2/3 Sept. 1928. For Dinter's side see Dinter, "Religion und Nationalsozialismus," *Geistchristentum*, I (July–Aug., 1928), 274 ff.; and "Stahlhelm, Hitlerpartei und sittlichreligiöse Erneuerung," *ibid.*, II (1929), 333; and Reich-Uschla (Buch), "Vorgang," 12 July 1928, in Dinter, "Kampf," p. 356. General Epp, whom Dinter accused of being the Church's agent in the NSDAP formally denied the charge in *VB*, 28/29 Oct. 1928.

27. Krebs, *Tendenzen*, p. 132. Krebs erroneously gives the date of the meeting as October 1928.

form throughout the entire Reich with two exceptions: the territory of
the state of Bavaria — Hitler's "home Gau"—remained one Gau, divided
into 9 sub-Gaus directly subordinate to Munich; and the Reichsleitung
also took direct charge of two districts in the old Ruhr Gau.[28] It appears
likely that Hitler outlined his reorganization plans on Friday morning
and then used the individual conferences on Saturday to discuss details
with the individual Gauleiters. There is no evidence that any of the subleaders raised objections to this revolution in the political strategy of
the NSDAP.

In practice the reorganization affected primarily four geographic
areas of Germany: Berlin, Hanover, the Ruhr, and Bavaria.[29] Each
of these regions either contained promising rural areas previously
neglected by urban-oriented Gau organizations or had proved too
large for propagandistic and organizational saturation. Thus the old
Ruhr Gau had simply proved too large for effective administration.[30] On the other hand, Hanover and the Franconia area of
Bavaria, the districts in which the NSDAP had made its best showings after Schleswig-Holstein, underwent deliberate restructuring to
enable in-depth penetration of their rural areas. In both cases larger
Gaus became multiple units. Hanover was divided into three Gaus
— Weser-Ems, South Hanover/Brunswick, and East Hanover; Franconia was subdivided into Upper, Middle, and Lower Franconia.
The Reichsleitung hoped in these cases that the overall reduction
in the size of the Gaus would permit organizational saturation of
the rural areas of Germany, in spite of the often rudimentary transportation and communication facilities.[31]

28. The two districts were Bergisch Land/Niederrhein (Electoral District
Düsseldorf-Ost) and Essen (Electoral District Düsseldorf-West). A listing of the
new Gaus, their Gauleiters, and the corresponding electoral districts is in R.Ko.In.,
"Lagebericht Nr. 127," 31 Oct. 1928, HA, roll 24A, folder 1758.

29. Some Gaus, like East Prussia and Schleswig-Holstein, were already coextensive with electoral districts.

30. Walter Görlitz and Herbert A. Quint, *Adolf Hitler* (Stuttgart, 1952), p.
271, regards the breakup of the Ruhr Gau as a defeat for the Strasser forces, but
this appears to miss the point that a Gau that functioned as ineffectively as the
Ruhr Gau did in 1928 could hardly be regarded as a power base. In addition, there
is no evidence that Strasser was in even latent opposition to Hitler at this time.

31. GL Südhannover-Braunschweig, *Führer zum Gautag am 21. und 22. Februar
1931* (Brunswick, 1931), p. 15, NA, T-580, roll 21, folder 202 I (Gau Südhannover-
Braunschweig). The Reichsleitung had redrawn the boundaries of two Gaus
(Oberbayern-Schwaben and Hessen-Nassau-Süd) at the beginning of the summer.
Perhaps these served as pilot projects. See *VB,* 1 June and 4 July 1928.

Some major personnel changes, or rather additions, in the Gauleiter corps complemented the structural reorganization. In the new Gaus yet another generation of party functionaries emerged in the front ranks of the leadership corps. They were generally younger than the "pioneers," but had little in common with the intellectualized soldier-revolutionaries in the north. Rather, they were the product of the more recent disengagement among the lower middle classes in the small towns and rural areas. Before September 1928 they occupied an ill-defined place between the "Old Fighters" of pre-1923 days and the soldier-revolutionaries, but now their administrative gifts became very useful. The party more than ever had need of able bureaucrats who would be content with a purely managerial role, and the new group of Gauleiters met these requirements. (See Table 4.)

Precisely because the new and old Gauleiters accepted the introduction of the rural-nationalist plan without even mild dissent, Hitler was able to include a significant strengthening of the Gauleiters' position as part of his general reorganization in 1928. In return for their accepting a role as bureaucratized campaign managers, Hitler established the Gauleiters' unquestioned superiority over the local and district party organization in his region.[32] In fact, the straight vertical line of authority and control was now complete for all but one of the party-affiliated entities.

In the SA the urban-rural rivalries smoldered on. With few exceptions the strongest SA units continued to be those in urban areas,[33] and since the SA leadership did not reorganize its own structure to correspond to the new Gau boundaries, numerous rivalries developed between the political and SA leaders.[34] Hitler made no effort to force a structural realignment of the SA. Indeed, the SA became financially more independent of the party when it established its own quartermas-

---

32. See *VB*, 4 July 1928.

33. Acording to Osaf's own gauge of organizational effectiveness—the number of paid subscribers to the SA insurance plan—the following areas ranked highest in September 1928: Saxony, Austria, Franconia, Ruhr, Berlin-Brandenburg, Munich. See *VB*, 13 Sept. 1928.

34. See, for example, Kube to Schwarz, 14 March 1929, HA, roll 53, folder 1240; Hildebrandt to Bouhler, Osaf, Uschla of the Reichsleitung, and the editor of the *VB*, 12 Apr. 1929, NA, T-580, roll 23, folder 205 (Mecklenburg); and Bezirk Bergisch-Land/Niederrhein to Osaf, 1 March and 14 March 1929, NA, T-580, roll 19, folder 199b.

TABLE 4

Gauleiter	Gau	Year of Birth	Occupation	Education
Grimm, Wilhelm	Mittelfranken	1889	Civil servant	Grade 12
Hellmuth, Otto	Unterfranken	1896	Dentist	University
Holz, Erich	Brandenburg		High school teacher	University
Koch, Erich	Ostpreussen	1896	Railroad official	Business college
Murr, Wilhelm	Württemberg	1888	White-collar worker	Grade 8
Reinhardt, Fritz	Oberbayern	1895	Business college teacher	Business college
Ringshausen, Friedrich	Hessen-Darmstadt		Teacher	University
Röver, Karl	Weser-Ems	1889	White-collar worker	Grade 12
Schemm, Hans	Oberfranken	1891	Teacher	University
Sprenger, Jakob	Hessen-Nassau-Süd	1884	Civil servant (post office)	Grade 8 [?]
Terboven, Josef	Essen	1896	Bank teller	Grade 8
Wagner, Adolf	Oberpfalz	1890	Business executive	University
Wagner, Josef	Westfalen	1899	Teacher	University
Wahl, Karl	Schwaben	1892	Law office clerk	Grade 8 [?]
Weinrich, Karl	Hessen-Nassau-Nord	1887	Civil servant (tax official)	Grade 12

SOURCE: Birth and occupation statistics are taken primarily from *Reichstags-Handbuch*, ed. Bureau des Reichstags (Berlin, 1936 and 1938). The educational data was compiled by the author.

ter and accident insurance services at the beginning of 1929.[35] The reasons for permitting the parallel structures were no doubt both political
and financial. The arrangement constituted a system of mutual checks,
and the SA-owned quartermaster service, once established, turned over
considerable profits to the party leadership.[36]

It was symptomatic of Hitler's confirmed status as myth-person in
the party that the Gauleiters and Reichsleitung executives immediately
proceeded on their own to put the far-reaching organizational changes
into effect at the district and local levels. The derivative-agent machinery functioned so smoothly that Hitler could devote his full attention to
the aftermath of the Dinter affair. As in the case of Gregor Strasser, Hitler was apparently willing to tolerate Dinter in the party if the latter
would abandon his effort to challenge Hitler's sole decision-making authority in the NSDAP.[37] Dinter, however, refused to accept such a role
for himself. After a series of sharp letters between the two men and a
fruitless mediation effort by Hans Frank, Dinter was expelled in early
October.[38] Hitler utilized the opportunity to confirm again his status
as myth-person among the party's leadership corps. The Reichsleitung
asked all Gauleiters to sign, stamp, and return a printed statement ex-
pressly rejecting all of Dinter's reform ideas. All Gauleiters returned the
required statement.[39]

After the Dinter affair had been settled, Hitler could withdraw
from active involvement in party affairs in November and December to spend several weeks with the Bruckmanns at Berchtesgaden.[40]
In the meantime Schwarz and Strasser supervised the administra-

35. See PD Nü-Fü, "N/No. 72," 17 Dec. 1928, HA, roll 69, folder 1509; and
VB, 27 Nov. 1928; and [Bormann] (head of the accident insurance system),
"Entwurf," 7 April 1931, HA, roll 31, folder 595.

36. Walter Oehme und Kurt Caro, *Kommt "Das Drittle Reich"* (Berlin, 1930),
p. 92.

37. PD Mü, "Notiz," 18 Oct. 1928, HA, roll 24A, folder 1758.

38. Dinter published the exchange of letters between Hitler and himself, as well
as other documents in Dinter, "Kampf," pp. 352–86.

39. Strasser, "Rundschreiben," 8 Oct. 1928, in Dinter, "Kampf," p. 376; see also
GL Sachsen to Strasser, 10 Oct. 1928, HA, roll 88, folder 1838. Dinter's exit had no
appreciable adverse effect on the Gau organization in Thuringia. See GL Thüringen,
"Bericht der Gauleitung Thüringen . . . an die Reichsleitung über das 1. Vierteljahr
1929," 2 April 1929, NA, T-580, roll 26, folder 209 (Gau Thüringen).

40. [PD Mü], "Auszug aus Lagebericht München No. 73," 31 Jan. 1929, HA,
roll 70, folder 1510.

tive reorganization of the party. On September 15, the Reichsleitung announced new and "damn stiff" accounting procedures for the Gauleiters.[41] The Gauleiters in turn tightened up their financial regulations and began to rearrange their geographic jurisdictions to correspond to the Munich decisions.[42] This process often involved considerable administrative work, since, at the very least, membership lists and financial records of locals which changed Gau-affiliation had to be exchanged. At times more serious problems arose. As a result of the very uneven organizational penetration of many of the old Gaus, some areas lost the center of their organizational strength to another Gau.[43] Not all of the Gauleiters found the outlook of their rearranged fiefs encouraging,[44] but all bravely set out to please Hitler and carry his decisions to the last local. Once installed the Gauleiter could survey his new subordinates at a Gau congress. Between mid-September and the end of the year each Gauleiter confronted his local leaders as Hitler had confronted him. Only now it was the locals' turn to be judged on the basis of their membership statistics and financial records.[45]

In late January the Reichsleitung called a second leadership conference to assess the success of the reorganization. As if to demonstrate the party's continued strength in Dinter's home base of Thuringia, the site of the conference was Weimar. The atmosphere was far more businesslike than it had been in Munich. Indeed, Hitler did not take any overt part in the sessions, since no major policy decisions were to be made. Instead, the executive heads of the Reichsleitung divisions — Schwarz, Strasser, and Himmler — chaired the various meetings. Schwarz gave some glowing and rather inflated

41. *VB*, 3 Dec. 1928. GL Ostmark (Kube) described the NSDAP as *"saugrob"* when it came to finances. See "Rundschreiben des Gaus 'Ostmark' der NSDAP, Tgb. Nr. 3350," 24 Oct. 1928, HA, roll 9, folder 200.

42. Kube, "Rundschreiben," 22 Oct. 1928.

43. Cf. Sauckel's comment "I simply cannot give up additional areas in Erfurt county." Sauckel to Strasser, 3 Jan. 1929, NA, T-580, roll 26, folder 209. This document also gives a good example of a division of locals among three Gaus as a result of the reorganization.

44. Himmler wrote his friend Koch encouragingly that potentially East Prussia was as promising as Schleswig-Holstein. Himmler to Koch, 11 Nov. 1928, NA, T-580, roll 24, folder 207 (Gau Ostpreussen).

45. This account of the various Gau congresses is based upon GL Westfalen, "Rundschreiben," 11 Sept. 1928, HA, roll 5, folder 136.

statistics on the NSDAP's membership increase (65 percent over 1928)[46] while Himmler in his role as propaganda chairman no doubt delineated the propagandistic details of the rural-national plan. The Reichsleitung also demonstrated its satisfaction with the numerical and organizational progress of the party by publicly scheduling its national congress for August 1–4. Finally, Strasser ascertained the near-completion of the Gau reorganization and issued permission to the Gauleiters to subdivide their Gaus into districts if the organizational strength of the Gau justified such a step.[47]

The Weimar conference marked the end of a period of major reorganization for the NSDAP. In several important respects the party was a far different organizational entity in the spring of 1929 than it had been a year earlier. Perhaps the most significant development was the simultaneous clarification of both the functions of the Gauleiters and their relationship to Hitler. In part the definition was negative. It was now clearly established that a Gauleiter could not function as a semi-autonomous condottieri on a momentary and special mission. Rather, he had to accept a dual role as bureaucratized executive serving simultaneously as the romantic agent of history in the person of Hitler and as the subordinate of a thoroughly unromantic bureaucratic superior, the Reichsleitung. He was primarily responsible for the propagandistic and organizational penetration of a clearly defined geographic area, and the success of his efforts had to be easily quantifiable in rising membership figures and increased votes for the party.[48] It was of decisive importance for

46. PD Mü, "Auszug aus Lagebericht München," 23 Feb. 1929, HA, roll 70, folder 1510; and Staatspolizei Württemberg, "W 3," 6 Feb. 1929, HA, roll 58, folder 1402. The *VB* reported the following percentage increases as "examples": for the Saar an 88% increase in members, and for Schleswig-Holstein and East Prussia 300% each. *VB*, 23 Jan. 1929.

47. No detailed report on the Weimar meeting is available. PD Mü, "PND Lagebericht No. 79," 31 Jan. 1929, HA, roll 70, folder 1510, merely gives a brief resumé of the conference decisions. The PND report does not specifically mention permission for the Gauleiters to subdivide their Gaus, but the large number of announcements of subdivisions in a number of Gaus published in the *VB* in the weeks following the meeting is indirect evidence that such a step was authorized at the Weimar conference. The district boundaries were generally coextensive with those of the governmental county units.

48. Cf. the *VB*'s comment that "elections are always a measuring stick for the activism of individual leaders and [of the effectiveness] of their work." *VB*, 11 Jan. 1929.

his status as myth agent that the Gauleiter look upon himself as a functionary appointed by the Reichsleitung and responsible only to the central leadership, not to the party members in his Gau.[49] It was also vitally important for the success of the Gauleiter's self-image as an agent of Hitler that Hitler the person and Hitler the Reichsleitung be fused into one entity in his mind, even though overwhelmingly his relations would be with the executives of the central leadership and his meetings with Hitler the person few, hurried, and usually in a mass context. It is true, of course, that the Gauleiters constantly sought to supersede their formalized relationship to the Reichsleitung by approaching Hitler personally.[50] But for the most part a Gauleiter had to be content to deal directly with Hitler only in his institutional form, particularly since Hitler often left written communications addressed personally to him unanswered for several weeks.[51] In practice, then, a Gauleiter after January had to be satisfied with the assurance that the tabulation of votes in his district and his own obedience to the centralized directives of the Reichsleitung assured the victory of the totalizing and reflexive myth and thus guaranteed his own status as that myth's agent in his Gau.

Several of the newly appointed Gauleiters delighted in their role as chief of a bureaucratic branch office. Perhaps the best example of a thoroughly "executivized" Gauleiter was Fritz Reinhardt, the new Gauleiter of the sub-Gau Upper Bavaria/Swabia.[52] Immediately after his appoint-

49. In the "Krebs Interview," Albert Krebs noted that after 1928 Hitler routinely appointed Gauleiters without prior consultation with the local leadership. On the Gauleiter's place "in front of the troop [members] not among them" see Buch to Robert Wagner (Baden), 11 June 1929, HA, roll 56, folder 1375.

50. Thus Bouhler was still reviewing a request for permission to publish a Gau newspaper from the Gau Schleswig-Holstein apparently unaware that Hitler had already given oral permission to Lohse to begin publication. See Bouhler to Lohse, 24 Oct. 1928; and Lohse to Bouhler, 20 Nov. 1928, NA, T-580, roll 25, folder 208 I. The Gauleiters usually attempted to restore personal contact when Hitler spoke in their Gaus. See Lohse to Hitler, 5 Feb. 1929, in Werner Jochmann, ed., *Nationalsozialismus und Revolution* (Frankfurt, 1963), p. 277.

51. See, for example, Kaufmann to Hitler, 24 June 1929, in Jochmann, *ibid.*, p. 280.

52. Reinhardt was obviously a particular favorite of the Reichsleitung at this time. The *VB*, 19 July 1928, accorded Reinhardt the singular honor of devoting a two-column report to a rally organized by his local organization in Herrsching.

ment a veritable flood of form letters, circulars, questionnaires, surveys, etc., issued from his office.[53] Among the older Gauleiter group, too, some found the new priority assigned to "just organizing" very much to their liking.[54] And even for those who were not "natural" bureaucrats, the new role had certain undeniable advantages. For one thing it brought sizable financial rewards, not an inconsiderable lure for many of the new subleaders who had failed in their postwar civilian occupations. While as yet few of the Gauleiters actually received a salary, the parliamentarization of the party held out the promise of a legislative seat, and the honoraria that went with speaking engagements often yielded tidy sums for the division chiefs.[55] In addition, many of the Gauleiters were not slow to appreciate the value of material status symbols in the new NSDAP and began actively to compete with each other for such symbols.[56]

An additional incentive to accepting the Gauleiters' role was the greatly increased and much more clearly defined scope of their authority in dealing with the local organizations in the Gau.[57] The 1928–1929 reorganization firmly established the principle of rigid pyramidization throughout the vertical structure of the party and clearly established the locals' place at the bottom of the pyramid. Immediately after the Munich conference had adjourned, the Reichsleitung formalized the relationship of Munich, the Gaus, and locals by issuing a new set of directives on the functions and powers of

53. HA, roll 9, folder 188, contains vivid examples of Reinhardt's organizational activism.

54. Lohse, in Schleswig-Holstein, for example, was among these. See Krebs, *Tendenzen*, p. 211.

55. Kaufmann received up to RM 50 per speech, Kube RM 25. See Kube to Kempner (local leader in Mannheim), 12 Sept. 1929, HA, roll 53, folder 1240; and Bodo Uhse, *Söldner und Soldat* (Paris, 1935), p. 159. See also Weigand von Miltenberg, *Adolf Hitler–Wilhelm III* (Berlin, 1931), pp. 79–80.

56. Koch wrote Himmler that the Reichsleitung had given Lutze, the business manager in Westphalia, the funds to buy a Gau car, and he asked Himmler to talk to "the chief and Hess" to obtain similar benefits for East Prussia. Koch to Himmler, 15 Feb. 1929, NA, T-580, roll 24, folder 207 (Gau Ostpreussen). Helmut Klotz, *Seht Euch Eure Führer an* (Berlin, 1932), NA, T-580, roll 34, folder 232, while highly polemical, is still a good resumé of the type of moral and financial failings common among high and middle echelon Nazi leaders.

57. For a Gauleiter's use of his authority see Staatspolizei Württemberg, "W 2," 23 Jan. 1929, HA, roll 58, folder 1402.

the various organizational levels throughout the NSDAP's structure. The party had three organizational levels: the Reichsleitung, the Gaus, and the locals; and each level was clearly subordinate to the one above. Communications and orders throughout the system moved through channels at all times, that is, the Reichsleitung corresponded only with individual Gaus, and the Gaus handled communication to the locals. (The new regulations specifically prohibited working associations involving several Gaus.) The Gauleiter was responsible for all political activity in his Gau and sent a monthly summary of that activity on printed forms to Munich. The local leaders in turn supplied the data for these monthly reports.[58] Many locals resented their loss of autonomy,[59] but the Reichsleitung remained adamant and firmly supported the Gauleiters.[60] The organization had thus established an unbroken vertical chain of command and information from the Reichsleitung to the locals. The only links in the chain that occupied a somewhat special position were the various treasurers. Although subordinate to their political superiors (that is, the Gau treasurer to the Gauleiter, etc.), they were also responsible to the Reich treasurer, who could supersede the political leaders in financial matters at all times.[61]

The reorganization of 1928–1929 involved primarily the stratification of the vertical structure of the NSDAP, but the party was also expanding its horizontal structure through the creation of new affiliates and front organizations. The penetration of rural and small-town areas and the intended engagement of the lower middle classes in these areas required the establishment of specific organizations which would visibly demonstrate the party's concern with maintaining the societal status and values of these classes. Moreover, such front organizations would serve as organizational steps on the way toward full militant membership in the party for social groups that were traditionally proud of their apolitical but patriotic stand.

58. RL, "Richtlinien für die Untergliederungen der Nationalsozialistischen Deutschen Arbeiterpartei," 15 Sept. 1928, HA, roll 69, folder 1509.
59. PD Mü, "Auszug aus dem N.-Bericht Nr. 68 am 13. Juli 1928," 1 May 1930 [sic], HA, roll 70, folder 1516.
60. Wilhelm Loeper, "Notiz," *VB*, 5 July 1929.
61. RL, "Richtlinien . . . ," p. 4, HA, roll 69, folder 1509.

In the spring of 1929 the Reichsleitung established a number of new party affiliates and redefined the status of some already existing ones. Since the May elections had revealed the NSDAP's popularity among younger voters, the party paid particular attention to its youth groups. In July 1928, Kurt Tempel, the leader of the National Socialist Student Association (*Nationalsozialistischer Deutscher Studentenbund,* NSDStB), resigned. His successor, Baldur von Schirach, immediately began to change the propagandistic approach of the group. Under Tempel the NSDStB had been something of a revolutionary organization, deliberately opposing the snob-appeal of the traditional German student associations. Schirach immediately abandoned the pseudosocialist emphasis and cooperated far more with the traditional fraternities in emphasizing militant nationalism and anti-semitism in the universities.[62] Similarly, the Hitler Youth (*Hitler-Jugend;* HJ) changed in character. Under the urban plan, the HJ had been primarily a recruiting organization for the SA. Now, however, its role was redefined as that of a youth group with its own organizational status and life.[63] Clearly, the party intended to make the HJ attractive to lower-middle-class parents as a counterforce for their children to the "moral decay" of Weimar Germany. The NSDAP was equally concerned about the SA veterans who were too old to serve in the regular units. A newly created SA Reserve made it possible to retain the camaraderie for the older members.[64] The National Socialist Women's Order (*NS Frauenbund*) also achieved a greater "in-group" status; after the beginning of the year only party members could join the association.[65] Finally, the party began its establishment of occupation-oriented front groups with the founding of specific party-affiliated associations for lawyers and teachers.[66]

Inevitably, the far-flung geographic and functional expansion of party activities and the internal stratification led to the establishment of a formidable bureaucratic apparatus, but the party had not developed effective means of counteracting the tendencies toward

62. *VB*, 11 July 1928; and Heiden, *Geschichte*, pp. 246–47.

63. Gruber (head of the HJ) and Pfeffer (for the RL), "Richtlinien zwischen Hitler Jugend und Partei," 23 April 1929, HA, roll 89, folder 1849.

64. SABE, 28 March 1929, HA, roll 16, folder 304.

65. PD Mü, "Auszug aus Lagebericht München," 31 Jan. 1929, *ibid.*

66. R.Ko.In., "Lagebericht No. 128," 20 Feb. 1929, HA, roll 70, folder 1510.

increasingly cumbersome decision-making processes that just as inevitably accompanied bureaucratic growth. The NSDAP's administration was well designed to prevent negative decisions from being
put into effect, but the apparatus was correspondingly ill equipped
to rapidly translate information from the bottom into directives at
the top. The administrative system was excessively top-heavy. Its
most obvious characteristic was a concentration of all but strictly
routine decisions in the person of Adolf Hitler.

A large number of officials in theory reported directly to Hitler.
These involved not only the Gauleiters, but also the heads of the
auxiliaries and the various legislative representatives of the party.
In addition, Hitler was obviously in direct control of such semi-
official activities as the negotiations and maneuverings of Hermann
Göring, who, while he had no official party status, nevertheless quickly
became a major National Socialist leader.[67] It is true, of course, that
the top executives of the Reichsleitung functioned as an institutional Hitler, but even they could only make routine administrative
decisions. Hitler's own dislike of day-to-day desk administration had
not changed. He preferred to let some matters take care of themselves by simply not answering correspondence,[68] but with the growing complexity of the administrative structure this device became
increasingly unsatisfactory. The party therefore needed a conscien-
tious decision-making instrument that could speak in the name of
Hitler and give unquestioned orders to the Reichsleitung without
endangering Hitler's own status in the party. With the 1928–29
reorganization Rudolf Hess, Hitler's personal secretary, informally
assumed this position, and became, next to Hitler, the most important
decision-maker in the NSDAP. In the latter 1920's the man who would
later serve as a case study for ineffective administration of the
Third Reich[69] was a figure of great respect and decisive power in
the party. He was the "chancellery" that gave orders to the division chiefs of the Reichsleitung, he opened and apparently answered
Hitler's personal mail, and on occasion he even finalized Gauleiter

67. See Hitler's comments on Göring in PD Mü, "PND Nr. 634," 29 Oct. 1928,
HA, roll 88, folder 1841.

68. "Sitzungsprotokoll der Böckenhauer Opposition . . . 27. 10.29," in Jochmann,
Nationalsozialismus, pp. 289–90.

69. Louis Schmier, "Martin Bormann and the NSDAP, 1941–1945" (unpublished
Ph.D. dissertation, University of North Carolina, 1968), chapters I and II.

appointments.[70] None of this real exercise of power, however, diminished Hitler's mythical status within the party, since Hess had a religious faith in Hitler's personification of the positive set factor in the National Socialist totalizing and reflexive myth, and quite consciously regarded himself as Hitler's "tool." His own exercise of power was for him merely an opportunity to relieve Hitler of some of his more onerous administrative duties to free him for the greater task of awakening the German people.[71]

With the introduction of the 1928–29 organizational changes the division of actual decision-making power in the NSDAP may be summarized as follows: Hitler made all major political decisions (and he defined what these were),[72] Hess made the routine political decisions, while the division chiefs of the Reichsleitung made routine administrative decisions.[73] The Gauleiters carried these out for their geographic regions, but also attempted to supersede the Reichsleitung and deal directly with Hitler. Finally, local leaders carried out the orders of their Gauleitungs. The auxiliaries operated according to broad guidelines worked out in consultation with Hitler or Hess. The two service organizations, the Women's Order and the SA, occupied special positions, insofar as they accepted only full party members, and in the case of the SA, possessed an autonomous structure that negated much of the theoretical subordination to the Gauleiters.

In the spring of 1929 the NSDAP was administratively and structurally ready to put its new propaganda strategy, the rural-nationalist plan, into effect. Like its predecessor, the new plan was a device to achieve the party's constant goal: to fulfill its program by giving absolute power to a "man who has been selected by destiny to

70. See Heinemann's marginalia on GL Danzig to RL, 5 Aug. 1927, NA, T-580, roll 20, folder 200 (Gau Danzig); Dinter's secretary to Hess, 30 Aug. 1928, in Dinter, "Kampf," p. 372; and Lohse to Hitler, 21 Feb. 1929, in Jochmann, *Nationalsozialismus*, p. 278.

71. This assessment of Hess' relationship to Hitler is based on Krebs, *Tendenzen*, pp. 26 and 170–71.

72. The power of definition was not unimportant, since Hitler routinely reserved such matters as uniform changes in the SA for his personal decision. See *ibid.*, p. 142.

73. The Gauleiters complained that these decisions were at times made too routinely—i.e., without regard to the geographic and sociological differences between the various Gaus. See Kube's complaint to Himmler, 10 May 1929, NA, T-580, roll 23, folder 205 (Gau Ostmark).

lead [and who] will never allow that his actions be limited by the ridiculous . . . provisions of a constitution."[74] The new propaganda strategy did, however, involve far-reaching changes in the mood and the content of National Socialist propaganda. To begin with, the Reichsleitung ordered the Gaus and locals to minimize physical contact with opposing forces in their agitprop work[75] and prohibited any joint action with Communist groups against bourgeois targets.[76] At the same time the SA was ordered not to engage in military games of any kind.[77] In order not to tarnish the image of an unchanging party line, Hitler did not specifically denounce the radical or urban elements in the NSDAP,[78] but he did take great care to disassociate his own myth-person from the more radical and socialist elements in the party. He was conspicuously absent from the spring Gau congress in the Ruhr, although such prominent speakers as Goebbels, Ley, Kube, and Stöhr did appear.[79] Hitler also

74. Hitler to Bundesleitung des Stahlhelm, May 1929, NA, T-81, roll 116, frame 136565. In this letter Hitler explained his reasons for refusing to support a Stahlhelm plan to use the initiative provisions of the Weimar constitution to force through a constitutional amendment giving the Reich President more authority over the Reichstag. He does not mention Germany's new leader by name, but the implication is obvious.

75. PD Mü, "Auszug aus Lagebericht München v. 23. II. 29," HA, roll 70, folder 1510. The order was in the form of a confidential circular signed by Strasser, but the SPD newspaper *Münchener Post* gleefully published the document on 14 Feb. 1929.

76. R.Ko.In., "Lagebericht Nr. 127," 30 Oct. 1928, p. 127, HA, roll 24A, folder 1758. This was directed primarily against SA groups in Berlin and perhaps the Ruhr. Engelbrechten, *Braune Armee*, p. 40, notes the SA in Berlin consisted of up to "80% of proletarians [who] lived radical socialism."

77. *VB*, 30 Nov. 1928. The *VB* reprinted this notice on 19/20 May 1929. The official reason for this absolute prohibition was the party's fear of official reprisals, particularly after the Bavarian government had dissolved the Rotfrontkämpferbund in the spring of 1929. See Hitler, "Bauern, hütet Euch vor Provokateuren," *VB*, 23/24 Dec. 1928; and Uhse, *Söldner*, p. 166.

78. Privately he was far less hesitant to denounce the party's socialist image. See Uhse, *Söldner*, p. 202. Hitler's arguments in discussing the party's tactics with Uhse sometime in early 1929 are virtually the same as the ones he advanced in the famous confrontation with Otto Strasser. See Otto Strasser, *Aufbau des deutschen Sozialismus* (2d ed.; Prague, 1936), p. 122; and Krebs, *Tendenzen*, p. 143.

79. *VB*, 21/22 April 1929. His absence was particularly noteworthy since the party organization in this area had fought side by side with the workers during wage disputes in the fall of 1928. See Staastpolizei Württemberg, "W. Nr. 41," 12 Dec. 1928, HA, roll 58, folder 1401.

avoided many traditionally radical areas in his travels,[80] and when he did speak in these areas, he deliberately emphasized the nationalist image of the party.[81]

This was part of a massive remolding of the party's propaganda image which accompanied the organizational changes. The NSDAP deliberately set out to become the political party that gave the most blatant expression to the fears and prejudices of the middle and particularly the lower middle classes in the rural and small town regions of Germany. At the same time the party portrayed itself as the only effective organizational remedy for the problems of these elements in German society.

A list of the numerical distribution of prominent National Socialist speakers in late 1928 and the topics they chose (Table 5) illustrates the party's new image.

TABLE 5

Topics	Number of prominent "Speaker-experts"
Agriculture	10
Civil Servants	2
Railroad Affairs (Dawes Plan)	3
Disabled Veterans	2
Banks, Money, and the Economy	4
Free Masons and Bolshevism	1

SOURCE: NSDAP, Propaganda-Abteilung, *Propaganda* (Munich, 1928), p. 18.

As the large number of "speaker-experts" (45.45 percent) on agriculture indicates, the main object of the party's propaganda was the farmer. Hitler quickly exploited the party's surprising popularity in Schleswig-Holstein by making a major speech in the heart of the Dithmarschen country.[82] The NSDAP soon realized, however, that Schleswig-Holstein was a double-edged sword. The economic

80. HA, roll 9, folders 200 and 201 (Ostmark), provide a good illustration of a Gau working very much on its own at this time.

81. When Hitler spoke publicly in Berlin for the first time, Epp conspicuously sat next to the rostrum. See *VB*, 24 Nov. 1928.

82. "Adolf Hitler vor den Dithmarschen Bauern," *VB*, 19 Oct. 1928.

problems of the *Geest* farmer were similar to those of his counterparts in Hanover and Franconia, but his reaction was somewhat
different. In Schleswig-Holstein the anti-Weimar sentiments took the
form of direct action and violence against governmental buildings
and tax collectors,[83] and the farmers' support of the NSDAP was
based at least in part upon the party's image as a revolutionary
political group.[84] After the election the NSDAP faced a dilemma.
It clearly did not wish to lose the support of either the dissatisfied
farmers in Schleswig-Holstein or of those further south. On the
other hand, supporting the radical elements in Schleswig-Holstein
could disaffect farmers in other regions and also expose the NSDAP to
the charge of "me-tooism" since the rebellion in the north had already
been well organized under right-wing social revolutionaries before the
party discovered the farmers' plight.[85]

Hitler chose not to support the economic radicalism of the *Landvolk* movement, but decided instead to discourage violent acts among
his followers and, when this proved impractical, to interpret violence in Schleswig-Holstein as evidence of intense nationalist con-
sciousness, rather than economic desperation. In March 1929, a political death provided Hitler with a welcome opportunity to interpret
the events in Schleswig-Holstein. An SA man in Albersdorf, a village
near Heide, had been killed after a clash with police and political
opponents. Hitler rushed to the funeral, accompanied by Buch,
Pfeffer, and his photographer Heinrich Hoffmann. Lohse met them
in Hamburg. Together the group traveled to the villages of St. Anna
and Albersdorf and Hitler later reported on the funeral in one of the
few humanly moving articles he ever wrote. He had high praise
for the farmers of Schleswig-Holstein, the "nobility" of the German
people. He described his emotions after hearing Lohse's funeral
address: "And now I am supposed to speak. But what can one say
on such an occasion?" Nevertheless, he was able to bring out a few

83. The best accounts of the "mood" of the farmers' rebellion are Uhse, *Söldner;* and Salomon, *Fragebogen,* pp. 220 ff.

84. Heberle, *Landbevölkerung,* pp. 160–61. Lohse had written an article for the
NS *Jahrbuch 1927* seemingly supporting radical measures. See Stoltenberg, *Politische Strömungen,* pp. 144–45.

85. For the history of the Landvolk movement, see *ibid.,* p. 144 ff.; Otto-Ernst
Schüddekopf, *Linke Leute von Rechts* (Stuttgart, 1960), pp. 306–09; and Karl
O. Paetel, *Versuchung oder Chance* (Göttingen, 1965), pp. 108–29.

words in which he emphasized the national import of the tragedy. The dead SA man, as a follower of Hitler and a member of the NSDAP, epitomized Germany's national rebellion against Weimar and Versailles. The SA man's sole crime had been "to love his people and his Fatherland." Hitler also noted that he was not alone in this interpretation of the tragedy; the Stahlhelm, too, acknowledged the nationalist implications of the events by sending a delegation to honor the dead hero.[86]

The nationalist mantle which Hitler bestowed upon the farmers' violence in Schleswig-Holstein also provided the link that united the party's propaganda effort among the lower middle classes in general and its more specialized rural campaigns. The NSDAP did not concentrate its new strategy exclusively on the farmers, but attempted to include other segments of the lower-middle-class population as well. This is well illustrated by the 1928 list of "speaker-experts" (Table 5); 45 percent of the speakers devoted their energies to the farmers, but almost as many (40.91 percent) attempted to engage non-farming audiences. It is also noteworthy that several of these groups were not experiencing acute economic hardship at this time. These groups did, however, share with the farmers a sense of continuing national frustration which led them to disengage themselves increasingly from the values of Weimar. In addition, they feared socioeconomic difficulties in spite of the present economic prosperity. The NSDAP attempted to exploit both of these feelings. Thus the party continued its attacks on department stores and in the late fall launched a veritable saturation campaign to reinforce the party's image as political protector of the small business enterprise.[87] Similarly, it directed attention to civil servants and ordered the Gaus to design propaganda material appealing particularly to women.[88]

86. A.H. [sic], "Das todbringende heutige Verbrechen: Sein Volk und Vaterland zu lieben," *VB*, 16 and 17/18 Mar. 1929. The funeral in turn touched off a new clash, "the bloody night of Wöhrden." See Stoltenberg, *Politische Strömungen*, pp. 147–48 and Appendix III.

87. See *VB*, 30 Nov. 1928. The campaign in some instances paid off handsomely in increased advertising revenue for the party press from small shopkeepers. See Ernest K. Bramsted, *Goebbels and National Socialist Propaganda 1925–1945* (East Lansing, Mich., 1965), p. 44.

88. *VB*, 13 and 23/24 Sept. 1928, and GL Ostmark to district leaders, 10 June 1929, HA, roll 10, folder 203.

The NSDAP combined its economic scare propaganda with a very heavy emphasis upon its championship of traditional German middle-class political and social prejudices. To make its picture of an impending Marxist take-over credible, the party deliberately exploited the identification in the average German middle-class mind of the SPD and KPD as "Marxists." Actually, of course, the SPD (unlike the KPD) had no revolutionary ambitions, and its election victories in 1928 were indications of legislative and democratic stability in Germany. Similarly, the NSDAP suddenly became a champion of states' rights, another value dear to most middle-class Germans. Although in the past Hitler himself had often called for a strictly centralized state, he now publicly recognized the viability of the federal system and the sovereignty (*Eigenstaatlichkeit*) of the states.[89] From here it was only a step to participation in legislative coalitions. The party that had long debated whether or not to field candidates began in 1929 to deal in backroom compromises in Saxony just like any other interest group. No wonder that to a dedicated revolutionary the NSDAP had become "to put it bluntly, a pig stye!"[90]

The NSDAP even began to provide ostensibly apolitical services as part of its new image. The NSPK (National Socialist Press Correspondence) was organized in mid-1929 to provide free of charge newspaper copy about the NSDAP and its aims to the "neutral" — that is, rightist but not party-owned — provincial press.[91] The party even activated its "save-our-culture" organization. Though established at the party congress of 1927 to preserve the "Germanness" of the German cultural heritage, the KDV did not schedule a full series of public functions until early 1929,[92] when this organization

89. PD Nü-Fü, "N/No. 72," 17 Dec. 1928, HA, roll 69, folder 1509.

90. The Saxony negotiations produced a minor crisis in the party insofar as Hitler publicly disavowed his representative in Saxony, v. Mücke, who in turn resigned in protest from the party. For the NSDAP version of the affair, see *VB*, 9 July 1929; for Mücke's story, his letter to the *Fränkische Tagespost*, 1 Aug. 1929, and his letter to Friedrich, 29 Aug. 1929, HA, roll 56, folder 1355.

91. *VB*, 19 June 1929. See also Oron J. Hale, *The Captive Press in the Third Reich* (Princeton, N.J., 1964) pp. 40 ff. (The leadership conference of 1928 is given erroneously as having taken place in Weimar.) With few exceptions the Reichsleitung actually discouraged Gau-owned newspapers at this time, since it expected greater political return from subtle infiltrations of the traditional press organs. See Schemm (Gauleiter of Upper Franconia) to RL, 16 Nov. 1928; and RL to Schemm, 5 Dec. 1928, NA, T-580, roll 19, folder 199.

92. *Weltkampf*, VI (Jan. 1929), 23.

(which had no official connection with the party)[93] became useful as yet another device to demonstrate the NSDAP's support for middle-class values.

Finally, the party continued its less belligerent attitude toward the nationalist paramilitary and patriotic organizations as part of its effort to make the sponsorship of middle-class ideals credible. In the summer and fall of 1928 the NSDAP proclaimed what amounted to a national emergency. At the time of the Munich conference, Alfred Rosenberg published an article in the *VB* noting that diplomatically Germany had never been more isolated (and hence more powerless) than at this time,[94] and the paper thereafter continued masochistically to wallow in every real or imagined setback suffered by the Weimar government in international affairs. In a sense, of course, this was nothing new, but the political conclusions which the party drew from this state of affairs were novel. The Reichsleitung utilized its emphasis on national degradation under the new rural-nationalist plan to stage a limited comeback to the far-right fold in German politics. Instead of attempting to isolate itself further, the party now felt strong enough to associate itself with other far-right groups in specific "patriotic" causes and thus demonstrate its championship of nationalist, "apolitical" middle-class values. The party never gave up its organizational independence nor its political goals, but it no longer insisted upon organizational subordination of other groups as the price for cooperation by the NSDAP in joint projects.

In particular, the NSDAP's relationship to the Stahlhelm and the Wehrwolf became considerably less strained. Hitler conferred several times with Düsterberg during the fall and winter,[95] and while no concrete agreements were concluded, the new spirit of cooperation accomplished in part what Hitler's threats in Thuringia in 1926 had failed to do. The Wehrwolf organization in Saxony, for example, specifically instructed its members to vote for the NSDAP list in

93. Its office, however, was only a few houses down from the party's central office, and the *NS-Jahrbuch 1929* (Munich, 1928), p. 139, listed the association as a party organization. The latter "error" was corrected by a *VB* announcement on 4/5 Nov. 1928.

94. *VB*, 1 Sept. 1928.

95. Nü-Fü, "N/No. 72," 17 Dec. 1928, HA, roll 69, folder 1509. Propagandistically the new line was inaugurated immediately after the elections. See Alfred Rosenberg, "Abkehr des Stahlhelms von bürgerlicher Unfähigkeit," *VB*, 6 June 1928. For a sympathetic *VB* description of a Stahlhelm rally see *VB*, 4 June 1929.

the state elections of June 1929.[96] On an even grander scale was the joint action of the NSDAP and other far-right groups in the *Fememörder* affair.[97] These self-appointed vigilantes enjoyed a good deal of popularity among middle-class Germans, and their punishment as common criminals was widely criticized. Hitler personally fanned the criticism,[98] and the party officially took part in staging a mass intergroup protest rally in July 1929. It was almost like 1923: side by side the flags of the Stahlhelm, the NSDAP, and other black-white-red outfits were carried into the hall.[99]

The task of translating the new propaganda mood of the rural-nationalist plan into saturation campaigns that reached even the remotest hamlets[100] fell to the party's functionaries in the provinces. They were responsible for converting the overall atmosphere of appeals to middle-class values and the image of cooperation with other nationalist groups into rallies that led specifically to increased numbers of NSDAP members and voters. In carrying out their task, the party workers introduced two major innovations into the style of political campaigning in Germany: 1) their agitprop work continued unabated even in the absence of specific election campaigns, and 2) they went to the villages rather than wait for the farmers to make their infrequent trips to the county seat. This meant in turn that the party's propaganda effort needed a maximum of organization and coordination and that the NSDAP had to produce a supply of public speakers that could blanket the German countryside with National Socialist rallies.

The latter problem was perhaps the most acute. Despite the outstanding oratorical magnetism of some of its top leaders, the party had few effective speakers in 1929, and it could obviously not exhaust these in a series of village rallies. On the other hand,

96. *VB*, 11 May 1929.

97. The Fememörder were several rightist extremists who took it into their own hands to punish those "traitors" who had reported German violations of the disarmament clauses of the Versailles treaty to either the German government or Allied authorities. See Emil Gumbel, *Verräter verfallen der Feme* (Berlin, 1929).

98. Buch to Weiss, 8 June 1929, HA, roll 56, folder 1374.

99. *VB*, 6 July 1929. A similar all-rightist rally took place in Augsburg.

100. In many instances the party gained immediate political advantages from these efforts, since the social homogeneity of the hamlets often resulted in unanimous votes for the NSDAP. See Heberle, *Landbevölkerung*, p. 44.

a village speaker did not need to be a Goebbels; the mere fact that he could stand up and address a group of shy, sullen farmers coherently could make him an effective propagandist. The party therefore set out to train public speakers en masse through a correspondence school. In 1928 Fritz Reinhardt had set up such a school as a training institute for local speakers,[101] and when the elections revealed the party's extraordinary appeal in rural areas, Hitler — no doubt on the advice of Himmler — made Reinhardt's school into the official School for Orators of the NSDAP (*Rednerschule der NSDAP*).[102] Reinhardt's method of instruction was designed for the already totalized NSDAP member; it was primitive, single-minded, but highly effective. After some theoretical instruction, the student in effect memorized a simple speech written by Reinhardt and did some mirror-practice with it. At the same time, he wrote a speech of his own and sent it to Reinhardt for corrections. Along with the corrected version, Reinhardt sent questions to prepare the student for the next month's topic. (For example: "A factory worker complains about low wages. What would you answer?") Thus the training institute had very limited objectives. It offered no political education in any broad sense, but it did provide a large number of speakers with some knowledge of the rudiments of public-speaking techniques, a store of set speeches, and some memorized answers for typical questions from the audience.[103]

The series of mass-produced Reinhardt speakers were the foot soldiers of the NSDAP's army of agitators. The party did not expect them to persuade any large number of disengaged Germans to vote for or join the NSDAP, but, hopefully, they would demonstrate the party's interest in the village audience and stir at least some of the

101. See PD Mü, "PND Nr. 68," 13 July 1928, HA, roll 70, folder 1529.

102. Himmler to Reinhardt, 18 April 1929, NA, T-580, roll 24, folder 206 (Obb.-Schwaben); and RL to all Gauleiters, Representatives, and Speakers, 5 May 1929, HA, roll 10, folder 203.

103. By May 1930 Reinhardt claimed a total of 2300 students, of whom 600 had actually spoken in public and 1500 were ready to give their first public address. Fritz Reinhardt, *Rednerschule der NSDAP* (Herrsching a. Ammersee, 1930). Some urban party organizations looked upon Reinhardt's efforts as unsuitable for their areas, but Himmler supported Reinhardt's claim to universal usefulness. See Himmler to the editor of *Angriff*, 22 June 1929, NA, T-580, roll 46, folder 260 (Presse vor 1930).

hearers to undertake a more or less inconvenient journey to a nearby town to hear a rhetorically far more effective Gau or Reich speaker.[104] Gau speakers (they carried a certificate from the Gauleiter permitting them to use this title) were party agitators skillful enough to handle a major rally, but either unwilling to travel outside their Gau, or not sufficiently prominent to attract any sizable audience outside their own Gau.[105] The highest level of agitator, the Reich speaker, was apparently an invention of Heinrich Himmler. These agitators were men of considerable prominence and demonstrated speaking ability who could attract an audience of at least one hundred to one thousand.[106] They spoke only in major towns and cities.

Before a disengaged German would bestir himself to attend even a local rally, he had to be aware of the party's existence and its attempt to capture his attention. This was the function of the party's posters and leaflets. Like the training of speakers, the preparation of printed materials was a highly centralized process. The Gaus sent a steady stream of suggestions to Munich, but they did not determine the final content. Many designs and ideas originated with Himmler, but he was not the decisive voice either. He usually sent all proposals (including his own) to Reinhardt or another expert for editorial revision.[107] The new version then went to Hitler's office, and the final, official version of a major pamphlet or poster always had the personal approval of Hitler or Hess.[108]

Despite the reactionary content of its propaganda, the NSDAP was quick to incorporate new technical devices into its arsenal of propaganda methods. In November 1928 the party established a National Socialist Film Service to distribute "patriotic" and party movies and coordinate the use of party-owned projectors. Here, again, the propagandistic impact would be most clearly felt in the more remote rural areas, where a movie would be a sufficient sensation in itself to draw an audi-

104. RL to GL Ostpreussen, 7 Sept. 1929, NA, T-580, roll 24, folder 207 (Ostpreussen).

105. The Gau's business manager, for example, was usually a prominent Gau speaker.

106. On the qualifications of a Reich speaker see NSDAP, Propaganda-Abteilung, *Propaganda* (Munich, 1928), p. 19.

107. For the process of leaflet and poster creation see HA, roll 3, folder 81/82 [sic].

108. Himmler to Hildebrandt, 18 June 1929, NA, T-580, roll 23, folder 205.

ence. Within a year the Film Service had proved so successful that all
locals were ordered to add film projectors to their store of propaganda
materials.[109] The party also expanded its use of other "cool" media.
After October 1, 1928, the *Illustrierter Beobachter* appeared as a weekly
(instead of biweekly), and, as if to embellish its now more frequently
appearing photographic images, the Reichsleitung spent a great deal
of time and effort to perfect uniforms and insignia of party and SA
leaders.[110]

The political climax of all these devices came in "propaganda concentrations," a type of political-saturation advertising in which the
party scheduled between seventy and two hundred rallies in the
space of seven to ten days in one Gau. The Reichsleitung, in particular Himmler, planned these concentrations under Hitler's personal supervision. Drawing up the plans involved what can only be
called highly sophisticated and almost scientific campaigning. A concentration was usually planned to coincide with a state election in
a Gau or the staging of a major party event, such as an upcoming
national congress.[111] Basically, the object of the planning was to
use the relatively few prominent National Socialist speakers and
especially Hitler himself in Gaus where their presence would yield
a maximum return in measurable terms, such as membership and
voter increases. In practice this meant avoiding concentrations in
areas where the NSDAP was already making rapid progress (and
hence Hitler's presence would be superfluous) or belaboring regions
where the party still had so little support as to make even a Hitler
speech a waste of effort. Instead, Himmler, Hess, and Hitler carefully selected localities in regions where the correlation of population and membership figures had reached a point at which a concentration might result in a genuine breakthrough for the party.[112]
The bases for reaching the decision were the monthly Gauleiter re-

109. PD Nü-Fü, "N/No. 72," 17 Dec. 1928, HA, roll 70, folder 1529; and *VB*,
24 Nov. 1929.

110. For a criticism of this enterprise see GL Ostmark (Kube), "Rundschreiben
. . . an die Bezirksführer, Gruppenführer und Funktionäre der politischen Organisation," 9 Oct. 1928, HA, roll 9, folder 200.

111. Himmler to Hildebrandt, 17 May 1929, NA, T-580, roll 23, folder 205
(Mecklenburg).

112. Himmler to Kube, 7 Nov. 1928, *ibid.*

ports which Himmler received. From these reports he established
relationships between population and membership figures and when
he felt that the area was ripe for a concentration he noted the proposal on his master list.[113] The actual scheduling of a Hitler speech
in turn had to be correlated with a number of other factors, such as
proximity to an already well-organized Gau, the effect of a travel
schedule on Hitler's health,[114] and the availability of other Reich
speakers. About once a month Hitler, Himmler, and Hess met to
draft final plans for the party's concentrations during the following
month,[115] using Himmler's statistical analyses as the basis for the
schedule.

The system of planning concentrations worked out quite well in
practice. Though some Gauleiters complained of undue neglect,[116]
the campaigns accomplished their purpose. The concentration in
Saxony before the state election of June 1929 may serve as an example.
The NSDAP used its Bavarian stronghold of Hof, close to the Saxon
border, as a base for its move into Saxony. Next came Plauen, which
had a strong National Socialist local and which at this time was the
national seat of the Hitler Youth. From both Hof and Plauen party
agitators then fanned out into all areas of Saxony, though they concentrated on the marginal farmers and outworkers of the Erzgebirge.
More than half of the thirteen hundred rallies staged during the
election campaign were held in this region. By election day the
party had literally missed no locality in the Erzgebirge; the area had
experienced a massive propaganda campaign.[117]

An integral part of each concentration was a systematic follow-up
of *Sprechabende* in the Gau. Here less prominent speakers went over
the principal themes of the concentration rallies again and again, but
the audience had changed. These were smaller, more intimate meetings of already committed militants who were joined by those who

113. Himmler's handwritten planning materials are in HA, roll 3, folder 80/81
[sic].

114. In November 1928 Himmler noted that it was physically impossible for
Hitler to speak more often than once every five days. Himmler to Kube, 7 Nov.
1928, NA, T-580, roll 23, folder 205 (Mecklenburg).

115. *Ibid.*

116. See Kube's sharp letter to Bouhler, 16 Sept. 1929, HA, roll 53, folder 1240.

117. Central Verein-Zeitung (No. 20; 1929), quoted in *VB*, 26/27 May 1929.

had been partially won over by the larger rally and wanted to know more about the party.[118]

The results of detailed staff planning and the general impact of the rural-nationalist propaganda line were encouraging for the NSDAP. Despite the extremely unfavorable weather conditions in the winter of 1928/29 (on several days the temperature dropped to —14° F), the party filled its meeting halls with larger and more enthusiastic audiences than had been the case under the urban plan.[119] There are also indications that the membership grew more rapidly. To be sure, the rate of growth in some high priority areas like Schleswig-Holstein was far greater than in other regions,[120] but there was disquieting evidence that the NSDAP all over Germany was beginning to undermine the societal structure of the Republic. Notably, the bandwagon effect became increasingly evident; the "neutral" provincial press took note of party activities and reported "objectively" (that is, favorably) on them.[121] In the summer of 1929 the NSDAP, to use Ludwig Erhard's famous phrase, "was somebody" again.

The party could well be pleased with the quantitative success of the rural-nationalist plan, but there were elements in the organization that regarded it as an unmitigated qualitative failure. For them the price of numerical success, the courting of the bourgeoisie *(Spiesser)* and the cooperation with bourgeois and feudal nationalists, had been too high. Not all of the dissatisfied elements were committed socialists; some were merely disgruntled office-seekers who had been passed over or individuals who disliked a particular Gauleiter.[122] For the most part they consisted of isolated groups who were of no real danger to the cohesiveness of the party, and who, like earlier dissident groups, would either reintegrate themselves or pass into political oblivion. One group of intellectuals, however, posed a poten-

118. NSDAP, *Propaganda*, p. 24.

119. For the overall mood of National Socialist rallies in the winter 1928–1929, see the collection of PND reports in HA, roll 88, folders 1840 and 1841.

120. Lohse to Hitler, 21 Feb. 1929, Jochmann, *Nationalsozialismus*, p. 278.

121. This is indicated by the *VB's* increasingly frequent reprints of "objective" reports from "neutral" press organs in late 1928 and 1929.

122. See the Berlin police report on the party rivalries in Pomerania, HA, roll 56, folder 1370; and "Sitzungsprotokoll der Böckenhauer-Opposition . . . 27.10.29," Jochmann, *Nationalsozialismus*, p. 290.

tially more serious threat to the NSDAP's cohesiveness, not because of their numerical strength, but because of their strategic location and their connections. Several of the group were prominent in the Schleswig-Holstein *Landvolk* movement[123] and thus represented an important liaison between the party and this movement. However, they and the party leadership differed widely on the nature of their liaison function. While the Reichsleitung demanded that the *Landvolk* movement follow the NSDAP's lead, the left-wing revolutionaries wanted the party to integrate itself into the overall front of conservative revolutionaries in Germany.[124]

The left-wing fringe also voiced some of the same complaints as the SA leadership and the SA's membership in Schleswig-Holstein was growing very rapidly.[125] From the viewpoint of the Reichsleitung this was not an unmixed blessing. Despite the Munich and Weimar conferences, the relationship between the political and the paramilitary wings of the party remained strained. In theory a clear division of labor existed,[126] but in practice numerous points of friction remained. The SA demanded a status of organizational autonomy that could not be reconciled with the preponderance of power now assigned to the Gauleiters, and Pfeffer's creation of a staff structure that transcended Gau boundaries only antagonized the political leaders further.[127] In addition, the influx of rural members attracted by the rural-nationalist plan threatened the SA's control of certain Gaus where the political and SA leadership had been largely identical

123. Bruno v. Salomon to Heinz, 22 Feb. 1929, HA, roll 13A, folder 1349; Paetel, *Versuchung*, pp. 29–31 and 108; and Uhse, *Söldner*, p. 157.

124. Heinz to B. v. Salomon, 19 July 1929, HA, roll 13A, folder 1349.

125. Of the 24 new SA *Stürme* recognized at the party congress in 1929, 4 were in the Schleswig-Holstein Gau; see *VB*, 27 July 1929.

126. In his "GRUSA III," 3 June 1927, Jochmann, *Nationalsozialismus*, p. 266, Pfeffer had stated that the political leadership determined how the SA was to be used, while the SA controlled its own actions once the service had begun.

127. Heinrich Bennecke, *Hitler und die SA* (Munich, 1962), p. 140. For indications of severe frictions between SA and party organizations at the Gau level and complaints by political leaders about the expansion and autonomy of the SA staffs see Loeper to Schwarz, 3 and 10 Jan. 1929, NA, T-580, roll 23, folder 204 (Elbe-Havelgau); and Fritz Sauckel, "Bericht der Gauleitung Thüringen der NSDAP an die Reichsleitung über das 1. Vierteljahr 1929," 2 April 1929, NA, T-580, roll 26, folder 209 (Gau Thüringen).

up to now.[128] As a result of these various factors the relations between Pfeffer and Hitler–Hess in the summer of 1929 continued to be marred by mistrust and mutual accusations.[129]

It was thus at least conceivable that the opponents of the rural-nationalist line could unite with Pfeffer to put pressure on the Reichs-leitung. For a brief moment the left-wing in Schleswig-Holstein might have had the illusion that it could reverse the decisions of 1928–29. But the hopes of the intellectuals, too, collapsed before the reality of the living myth-person. The correspondence between two of the more radical party leaders in Schleswig-Holstein in 1929, Friedrich Wilhelm Heinz and Bruno von Salomon, reveals the progressive dissatisfaction of the northern intellectual groups with the direction of the party.[130] Heinz came to the NSDAP from the Stahlhelm and served as local leader in Hanover and editor of the National Socialist paper there in 1928–29; Salomon was a friend of Gregor Strasser and had joined the party in 1925. Both supported the violent actions of the extreme wing of the *Landvolk* movement and deplored Hitler's stand against revolutionary activity. Within the party leadership corps, they claimed the sympathy of a number of prominent leaders, notably Count Reventlow, Adolf Wagner (Bavaria), Helmuth Brückner (Silesia), and Otto Strasser, Gregor's controversial brother.[131] In the final analysis, the proto-opposition group achieved no practical results. None of the prominent sympathizers were willing to oppose Hitler himself, and such lame proposals as removing Hitler from his evil advisors in Munich were as impractical as they had been in the weeks before Bamberg. The handful that did find the courage to oppose Hitler soon found that their opposition had to be continued outside the party. The NSDAP had no room for members who refused to equate Hitler and the programmatic concepts of National Socialism. For a time at least dedicated revolutionary totalitarians, like Heinz and Salomon, found a more hospitable home in the Com-

128. Cf. the *VB* report that in the Ostmark Gau, SA and party organization were often identical. *VB*, 26 Jan. 1929.

129. Pfeffer to Hitler, 12 June 1929; Hess to Pfeffer, 15 May 1929; and Pfeffer to Hess, 11 June 1929, HA, roll 4, folder 86.

130. The correspondence is in HA, roll 13A, folder 1349.

131. Heinz to B. v. Salomon, 19 July 1929, *ibid.* See also Krebs, *Tendenzen*, p. 206. Heinz mentioned only the name "Strasser," but it is unlikely that he meant Gregor.

munist camp.[132] On the eve of the 1929 national congress in August, the NSDAP as a whole was united in its support of Hitler and the rural-nationalist plan, and eagerly awaited what promised to be the greatest demonstration of National Socialist strength and unity to date.

As the first national party congress in two years, the 1929 rally was an important milestone in the history of the party. Since it would provide foe and "objective observer" alike with an opportunity to judge the public image of the party and compare it with its status in 1927, Hitler and the Reichsleitung executives approached the planning of the congress as though it were a climactic propaganda concentration,[133] which in a sense it was. The site and date had been announced in late January, and by mid-February Hitler was already at work on names for the new SA standards which he planned to award in August.[134] Throughout the spring, Reichsleitung executives held a series of planning sessions with local leaders in Nuremberg. The SA leadership, for its part, appointed transportation officers for each Gau to organize and supervise the departure of special trains to Nuremberg and secured marching routes, mass sleeping quarters, feeding schedules, etc., in Nuremberg itself.[135]

In addition to organization, the party was most concerned about finances. The public image impact of the rally was directly proportional to the number of marching feet shaking the medieval streets of Nuremberg, which in practical terms meant granting massive subsidies to party and SA members to enable them to travel to Nuremberg.[136] This involved a great deal of money, and the party still remembered its sizable debt after the 1927 congress. This time the Reichsleitung attempted to accumulate a war chest before the

132. On the later political activities of Heinz and Salomon see the police reports in HA, roll 13A, folder 1349. On Salomon, see also the autobiography of his brother Ernst v. Salomon (who remained on the far right), *Fragebogen*, pp. 221–23.

133. Hitler wrote that "in strictly organizational terms the rally will be a masterpiece." Hitler, "Grundsätzliche Richtlinien für die Arbeit der Vorsitzenden und Schriftführer der Sondertagungen am Reichsparteitag 1929," n.d., HA, roll 21, folder 391. To generate enthusiasm for the congress, the Reichsleitung actually scheduled a propaganda concentration in Franconia for late June. See RL, Propaganda-Abt. to GL Mittelfranken, 22 April and 11 June 1929, NA, T-580, roll 19, folder 199b (Gau Franken).

134. *VB*, 29/30 March 1929.

135. The planning papers for the 1929 congress are in HA, roll 21, folder 391.

136. Staatspolizei Württemberg, "W.7," 3 April 1929, HA, roll 58, folder 1402.

rally began, rather than pay off its debts afterwards. Begging agents made the rounds among the German business community, and each official delegate to the congress (that is, all party functionaries from the local leader on up) had to pay RM 10.00 for his pass.[137]

The 1929 congress, like its predecessor, consisted of both working sessions and public demonstration marches, but for Hitler the rally's essential purpose was to demonstrate the numerical strength, the discipline, the unanimity of the movement under his leadership. The NSDAP was to stand forth as "the young popular movement [*Volksbewegung*] that would one day destroy that which today was bringing destruction to Germany." [138] The congress was therefore divided into two quite distinct phases. During Friday and on Saturday morning (August 2 and 3) the party functionaries held closed meetings to which rank-and-file party members were not admitted. Their functions did not begin until Saturday as special trains arrived from all over Germany bringing the troopers to Nuremberg for the demonstration marches on Saturday afternoon and on Sunday.[139]

The special session on organizational questions was held on Saturday morning from 8 to 10 A.M., hardly a time designed to attract much public attention. In general it was an even more listless and "rubber-stamp" session than the one in 1927; neither the party membership nor the leadership had any real desire to initiate changes in the organizational pattern of the party from below. The Reichsleitung had received only twelve petitions (despite significant organizational growth, fewer than in 1927). Only one had been submitted by a Gauleitung (Schleswig-Holstein requested a "scientific" analysis of the weaknesses of Marxism); all others were proposals of private members or lower echelon officials. Taken together the petitions were either expressions of a nostalgic wish to recreate the camaraderie of the early days of the party or of an impatient desire to centralize the party even more. Thus of the twelve, one demanded mandatory *duzen* (to use the familiar pronoun *du* rather than the

137. See Friedrich Bucher to Hitler, "Betr.: Besuchsergebnis und Lagebericht über Gau Hamburg," 20 July 1929, in Jochmann, *Nationalsozialismus*, p. 283; and GL Ostmark to delegates to party congress, 15 June 1929, HA, roll 10, folder 203. The RM 10.00 fee included the cost of giving an "artfully executed" medal to each delegate in commemoration of his attendance.

138. Hitler "Grundsätzliche Richtlinien . . .," HA, roll 21, folder 391.

139. *VB*, 3 July 1929.

formal *Sie*) in the party and three others proposed formal prohibitions on coalitions with other parties, on multiple office-holding within the NSDAP, and on purchases in Jewish stores by party members. Hitler rejected all of these as impractical. He had praise for only one of the petitions: a party member from Brandenburg suggested that all of the Gau business offices should be reduced to the status of branches of the central office. Hitler commented that this was the "eventual goal of the Reichsleitung." [140] The session produced no protests against the rural-nationalist plan, no disagreement with the increasing bureaucratization in the party. In fact, there was neither debate nor real discussion.[141] The special session on organization was only one of fifteen such meetings, but the mood of the delegates was typical of the rest. In each case, the delegates listened to the views of the Reichsleitung executive handling their particular areas of interest (press, youth groups, etc.) and then enthusiastically endorsed whatever recommendations he (that is, Hitler through him) proposed. Hitler did not expect major policy discussion at these sessions. In fact, he did not attend any of them.

Only the session on union matters produced a minor crisis. This was the belated realization of the special session promised at the 1927 congress. Hitler, repeating the tactic which had been so effective at Munich a year earlier, showed no interest in the meeting beyond noting that National Socialist unions were not an acute issue at this time. Apart from this statement, he had no instructions. "We'll just let them talk. [*Sie sollen sich ruhig aussprechen*]." [142] Not many delegates attended the session, but those who did were enthusiastic supporters of at least some sort of party-affiliated union activity. The Reichsleitung had prohibited National Socialist unions earlier, and attempts to form working agreements with established far-right, white-collar unions were equally fruitless.[143] There remained the

140. The list of petitions and Hitler's comments are in HA, roll 21, folder 391.
141. Needless to say, the Reichsleitung discussed organizational problems in specific Gaus directly and privately with the political leader involved. Strasser to Murr, 24 July 1929, NA, T-580, roll 26, folder 209 (Gau Württemberg-Hohenzollern).
142. See Hitler's comments on the petitions submitted to the special session in HA, roll 21, folder 391.
143. Krebs, *Tendenzen,* pp. 16–17.

Organization of National Socialist Industrial Cells (*Nationalsoziali-stische Betriebszellenorganisation* NSBO), an association of white collar party members founded in Berlin and organized on a factory-by-factory basis for the purpose of conducting agitation among the workers. The NSBO was in no sense a union, but with some finan-cial backing it could have developed into one. It was an officially approved party affiliate in the Berlin Gau. The sub-Gauleiter of Upper Bavaria, Adolf Wagner, had even worked out an elaborate scheme to raise RM 96,000 per year for the NSBO to expand its work and functions.[144] In addition, the now disaffected left-wing had circulated a clandestine fourteen-point program among the delegates, incor-porating many of Gregor Strasser's old ideas.[145] Partly because of the potentially exciting future of the NSBO, and also because the chairman of the session, Johannes Engel, was head of the NSBO in Berlin, the discussion quickly turned to the subject of expanding the NSBO concept into full-fledged unions. Some heated arguments developed and Engel was powerless to control the delegates. At this point Hitler intervened. Robert Ley, the gruff Gauleiter of the Rhineland, was dispatched to restore order. He delivered some very blunt remarks: "I don't know why [all of you] wish to speak, com-rades. After all, we are not in a parliamentary gossip hut [*Schwatz-bude*] here, with discussion, votes, and agendas. You know you can't make decisions here. You came here to hear the opinion of the Führer; [and] I have told you that. Now act accordingly." [146] The delegates, confronted again with the reality of the myth-person, acted accordingly. There is no indication that any walked out or continued their critical discussion.

Hitler's lack of interest in the working sessions contrasted visibly with his enthusiasm for the propagandistic phase of the congress. This was indeed impressive. The party presented a picture of a uniformed, disciplined force united under the direction of a super-leader. Hitler was literally untiring as the brown armies streamed into Nurem-

144. Adolf Wagner, "[Gewerkschaftsantrag Nr. 8]," n.d., HA, roll 21, folder 391.
145. Heiden, *Geschichte*, pp. 263–64; and Paetel, *Versuchung*, p. 51.
146. Uhse, *Söldner*, p. 230. On the early activities of the NSBO see also Engel-brechten, *Braune Armee*, pp. 32–33 and 66.

berg.[147] He spoke, he greeted special incoming trains, he laid a wreath in memory of the World War I dead, and, when all others were exhausted, he made nighttime visits to the SA bivouacs.[148]

Hitler's unequal division of interest was reflected in the formal and informal results of the congress. The fifteen special sessions resolved very little, except to continue, improve, and intensify the work the party was already doing. In the area of organization, the party abolished the last vestiges of local autonomy and empowered the Gauleiters to appoint local leaders.[149] The Gauleiters' (as well as Hitler's own) position was also strengthened by the mandatory establishment of Uschlas throughout the vertical structure of the party. Each of the three vertical party levels now had an Uschla, whose members were appointed by the political leader. Since the Gauleiter had full control over the local leaders, this meant that he directly or indirectly appointed the judicial review boards throughout his area of administration. At the same time, Hitler's own personal control potential remained unabated. Appeals from lower Uschlas to higher ones moved through the Uschla channels and culminated in the authority of the Reich Uschla headed by the thoroughly indoctrinated Buch. Yet, Hitler's personal control remained bureaucratically institutionalized, since Buch's tribunal specifically had the right to give "higher party reasons," as its sole justification for refusing to accept a decision of a lower Uschla.[150]

The concrete organizational results of the Nuremberg rally represented a confirmation of the decisions at Munich and Weimar and a strengthening of the Gauleiter's position as administrative division chief. The organizational framework and the personnel cadres of the party had stood the pragmatic test of political success. Hitler

147. For the first time SA members and political leaders (as well as Hitler) appeared in brown shirts. The only difference between the uniform of the civilian and paramilitary members was the button on the cap — metal for the SA, leather for the party. *VB*, 23 July 1929.

148. Hitler prepared himself for this physical ordeal by a lengthy vacation before the congress. See Krebs, *Tendenzen*, pp. 133–34.

149. *VB*, 12 Sept. 1928, has a list of the special sessions and their results.

150. The phrase "aus höherer Parteiräson" was obviously intended to parallel the German *Staatsräson*, i.e., reason of state. The Uschla regulations are in RL, *Richtlinien für die Untersuchungs- und Schlichtungsausschüsse der Nationalsozialistischen Deutschen Arbeiterpartei* (Munich, 1929), HA, roll 56, folder 1375.

appointed a new Gauleiter for Düsseldorf,[151] but all others remained
at their posts. In fact, they were by now familiar with their functions and so unquestioningly obedient to Hitler, both as person and
as embodied in the Reichsleitung, that the party's leader could
increasingly withdraw from any active involvement in the day-to-
day administration. After the congress he even felt secure enough
to relinquish his personal control of the Munich party organization.
In October the Munich local was raised to the status of a Gau,
headed by Adolf Wagner.[152] The sections in turn became locals. The
appointment of Wagner underlines again the overwhelming power
of the Hitler myth-person: Wagner was a man who had led the
advocates of a pro-worker wing in the party, yet once this attitude
had been specifically prohibited by Hitler, he served the myth-
person well in what Hitler only recently regarded as the most sensitive
Gauleiter post.

Hitler's most remarkable and significant achievement was the establishment of an organizational framework and a homogeneous functionary corps that stood ready at the end of 1929 to ingest an influx of
members and voters which exceeded all realistic expectations of even
the most optimistic prognosticator. Hitler had succeeded in staffing his
party with cadre personnel who were both by education and social background conditioned to welcome the party's further transformation and
growth as a middle-class party. Moreover, the party cadres all but
duplicated the status divisions of German middle-class society. The
number of university graduates (or at least "attendants") and the
prestige of pre-NSDAP occupations increased significantly in the upper
ranks of the party bureaucracy. In effect, far from leveling the social
divisions of Germany under the Kaiser, the NSDAP perpetuated
them among its party militants. Tables 6a and 6b illustrate the social
and educational composition of the party functionary corps at the end
of 1929.

The establishment of a functionary corps oriented toward middle-
class values made possible the party's new propaganda and organi-

151. For the Düsseldorf appointment see VB, 25 Sept. 1929; and Karl Florian
to RL, 1 Oct. 1929, NA, T-580, roll 19, folder 199b. In addition, Karl Kaufmann,
formerly Gauleiter in the Ruhr, had taken over Hamburg on May 1. Kaufmann to
Hitler, 24 June 1929, in Jochmann, Nationalsozialismus, p. 280.

152. VB, 23 Oct. 1929.

TABLE 6a

Education

Vertical Level of Leadership Position	Years of Formal Schooling			Number of Functionaries Covered
	8 (Volks- schule)	12 (Oberschule or Gymnasium)	Univ.	
Reichsleitung		6	5	11
Gauleiters	5	12	11	28
District Leaders	13	10	9	32
Local Leaders	37	14	9	60
n	55	42	34	131

TABLE 6b

Occupation

Vertical Level of Leadership Position	Laborer	Artisan	White-collar Worker	Farmer	Teacher	Lower Civil Servant	Independent Businessman	Upper Civil Servant	Professional	Officer	Number of Functionaries included
Reichsleitung		1	1	1				2	2	4	11
Gauleiters	2		9	1	8		1	4	2	1	28
District Leaders	1	5	9	2	3	3		5	4		32
Local Leaders	5	12	20	3	4	6	2	4	4		60
n	8	18	39	7	15	9	3	15	12	5	131

Source: Polizeidirektion Berlin, "Gliederung der NSDAP in Gaue, Untergaue, und Bezirke" (Oct. 1929), Hauptarchiv der NSDAP, roll 70, folder 1510.

(Note: the totals do not represent the entire cadre force of the party, but only those members for whom the information listed could be obtained.)

zational assault upon non-agrarian segments of the middle class. In retrospect it is clear that the campaign was inaugurated at the Nuremberg congress.[153] The image which the party presented at Nuremberg was directed particularly at two significant groups in

153. For example, the special sessions devoted to the discussion of the party's approach to occupational groups all decided to expand the NSDAP's system of party-affiliated front organizations. See *VB*, 12 Sept. 1929.

Germany, the Wehrverbände and the business community. Hitler had scheduled the congress deliberately to coincide with the fifteenth anniversary of the outbreak of World War I, and in the ceremonies and speeches he and other leaders portrayed the party as continuing the tradition of 1914. At the congress Hitler personally courted prominent Wehrverbände and business leaders. Both Düsterberg, the second in command of the Stahlhelm, and Count v.d. Goltz, head of the Union of Völkisch Associations (Vereinigte Völkische Verbände, VVV), were honored guests at the rally, and Goltz later repaid the kindness with a highly laudatory article in the *VB*.[154] The business community was less prominently represented, but Emil Kirdorf made up in praise (and later money) what he lacked in representation.[155]

Always a political realist, Hitler unhesitatingly seized every opportunity to enhance the party's standing among the middle classes. Late in the summer, shortly after the Nuremberg rally, the Stahlhelm and the German National People's Party sponsored a national initiative action against Germany's acceptance of the Young Plan, the system of reparations payments worked out by the Allies and the German government. Without consulting the leadership corps, Hitler committed the party's organization to cooperate in the referendum effort.[156] There was little favorable sentiment among the party's militants for this alliance of the NSDAP and the party of Junkers and industrialists. Nevertheless, Hitler had no difficulty engaging his Gauleiters and other functionaries overnight in a political effort to which many of them were wholeheartedly opposed.[157] Nor was there a mass exodus of the older, more left-wing members when Hitler, the erstwhile champion of anti-capitalism, appeared side by side with Alfred Hugenberg, the head of the DNVP and Germany's leading press lord and capitalist.[158] This is all the more remarkable

154. *VB*, 4/5 Aug. 1929; Goltz, "Die Tage von Nürnberg," *VB*, 15/16 Aug. 1929.

155. Kirdorf to Hitler [Aug. 1929], *VB*, 27 Aug. 1929.

156. Uhse, *Söldner*, p. 182.

157. Lohse's reaction to Hitler's coup may be regarded as typical: "He [Hitler] must have his reasons. . . . We have yet to hear what he has to say — got to wait — do nothing foolish." *Ibid.*, p. 216.

158. The *VB*, 25 Oct. 1929, described Hugenberg and Hitler as the "two most hated nationalists in Germany." How "arrived" the party had by this time become may be indicated by the fact that at the rally Hitler, in SA uniform, stood next to Admiral Tirpitz.

since Hitler throughout the campaign kept very tight control over the behavior of the functionary corps and specifically regulated the limits of their actions. The NSDAP cooperated in staging the referendum, but it kept its organizational independence at all times. The Reichsleitung prohibited all party officials from joining interparty planning committees on a permanent basis, though consultations were allowed from time to time.[159]

As a revolt against the Allied reparations the initiative and the referendum that followed were futile gestures, but such cooperative ventures did much to restore the NSDAP to a position of political respectability not only among middle-class voters, but also among the paramilitary groups. Increasingly, leaders and members of the far-right Wehrverbände abandoned their apolitical stand and joined the NSDAP.[160] Financially, too, the party benefited. Despite all efforts beforehand, the party again faced a sizable debt after the congress had adjourned. Hitler and other leaders turned to the business community. Shedding the last vestiges of its socialist past,[161] the party boldly appealed for business support.[162] Some of the appeals fell on deaf ears,[163] but it seems clear that for the first time since 1923 the NSDAP successfully obtained large-scale support from the more substantial and well-to-do portions of the middle class.[164]

159. RL, Org.-Abt. (Strasser) to all GL (strictly confidential), 12 Aug. 1929, NA, T-580, roll 24, folder 206; and Hitler to all Gauleiters, district leaders, and leaders of larger locals [Aug. 1929], HA, roll 10, folder 203.

160. Paetel, *Versuchung*, p. 54. For the conversion of a prominent Stahlhelm member and general see *VB*, 15/16 Sept. 1929.

161. See "Hausbesitzer! Die N.S.D.A.P. ist nicht eigentumsfeindlich," *VB*, 7 Dec. 1929.

162. See Krebs, *Tendenzen*, pp. 174–75; and GL Württemberg to several business firms [Nov. 1929]. The latter document was published in the Communist paper *Neue Zeitung*, 13 Nov. 1929.

163. See Krebs, *Tendenzen*, pp. 174–75, for a description of Hess' fruitless trip to Hamburg.

164. The terms of a new discretionary fund were obviously designed to appeal to investors: at least RM 10.00 had to be contributed, and the amount would be repaid with interest after January 1, 1931. RL, "Rundschreiben an sämtliche Ortsgruppen der NSDAP," 15 Oct. 1929, HA, roll 56, folder 1375. The affluence of the party may be illustrated by the income figures for the local Schwabing in Munich: its income for the first ten months of 1929 was RM 388.89; in the last months it took in RM 803.90. See Hilble, "Kassabericht der . . . Ortsgruppe Schwabing . . . pro 1929," 31 Dec. 1929, HA, roll 2A, folder 224.

Toward the end of the year it became increasingly evident that the NSDAP was the primary beneficiary of the rapid politicization of the German middle class — both rural and urban. In late 1929 the depression was beginning to effect all segments of German society. To be sure, the party did not receive the support of the production-line workers already unemployed. These turned in their desperation to the KPD, not to the far right. As yet, the classes that turned to the Nazi Party still had their employment and status positions. They turned to the NSDAP because they feared the future. In its initial stage, the depression produced fear among the middle classes — fear of economic hardship, fear of loss of social status — which led to hopelessness, despair, and finally willingness to support any party that combined familiar appeals to traditional values with promises of immediate relief.[165]

To a considerable extent the party was an almost unconscious beneficiary of the great fear. The party's leaders had not grasped the importance of the stock market crash in October 1929,[166] and it had absolutely no positive programs to institute. Indeed, Hitler's appeal on the eve of the communal election of 1929 merely reiterated the party's well-worn thesis that communal problems could be solved only after the party had obtained national power.[167] Nevertheless, National Socialist rallies were not only well attended, but their middle-class audiences exhibited a fanatic enthusiasm that had not been there in 1927 and 1928. Moreover, the party's membership continued to rise sharply in all parts of Germany.[168] On the other hand, Hitler reacted quickly and decisively once he appreciated the political significance of the economic crash in Germany. The importance of the 1928–1929 organizational reforms now became evident. The NSDAP had a structural framework

165. William S. Allen, *The Nazi Seizure of Power: The Experience of a Single German Town, 1930–1935* (Chicago, 1965), p. 24.

166. The *VB* never even mentioned it.

167. PD Mü, "Bericht über die . . . Wählerversammlung der [NSDAP] am 29. November 1929," HA, roll 88, folder 1842.

168. In mid-October Schwarz expected the party to reach 160,000 members "in a few weeks." See Schwarz to Kube, 17 Oct. 1929, HA, roll 53, folder 1240. On the general mass enthusiasm and membership rise, see also PD Mü, "Auszug aus Lagebericht München," 17 Dec. 1929, HA, roll 70, folder 1510; PD Mü, "Notiz," 14 Jan. 1930, HA, roll 24A, folder 1758; and the PND reports for November and December, HA, roll 88, folder 1841.

that was able to receive a large influx of members without major alterations. Consequently the primary organizational result of the bandwagon effect was the expansion of the party's front organizations. The NSDAP was particularly interested in enlarging its occupational associations. Thus it expanded the National Socialist Lawyers' Guild.[169] Even the NSBO obtained a new lease on life. Once its leaders had accepted the Reichsleitung's dictum that the NSBO would never become a prototype for party-affiliated unions, the NSDAP's leadership actually encouraged the NSBO as a useful receptacle for the numerous salaried white-collar workers who were driven to the party by the deteriorating economic situation in late 1929.[170]

It was very unfortunate for the future of parliamentary democracy in Germany that the nationwide communal and provincial elections were scheduled for December 1929, that is, at a time when the fear syndrome had already penetrated into large sections of the urban as well as the rural middle classes. To the NSDAP the local elections were the baptism of fire for the reorganization of 1928. As before, the party's campaign was highly centralized, but during this election the orders of the central leadership were transmitted quickly through channels and executed in even the smallest hamlet. Gregor Strasser functioned as national campaign director and for the first time he worked exclusively through the Gauleiters, who were in complete charge of the campaign effort in their geographic areas. The Gauleiters confirmed local candidates, subject only to Hitler's personal review.[171] Even so, both the size of the vote and its social origins exceeded the party's most optimistic expectations.[172]

The party had used its highly centralized organizational struc-

169. Beginning in January 1930, the *VB* carried a biweekly, full-page supplement "The Struggle for a German Judicial System." See *VB*, 10 Jan. 1930. For a listing of the party's front groups before the fall, see PD Mü, "Zusammenstellung der NSDAP nach dem Stande vom 20.8.1929," HA, roll 70, folder 1510.

170. Hans-Gerd Schumann, *Nationalsozialismus und Gewerkschaftsbewegung* (Hanover, 1958), pp. 34–35.

171. PD Mü, "Auszug aus Lagebericht München N/Nr. 86," 13 Nov. 1929, HA, roll 88, folder 1842; and RL to Bzl Niederrhein/Bergisch-Land, 21 June 1930, NA, T-580, roll 19, folder 199B. (The document refers to an earlier directive.)

172. Adolf Hitler to . . ., 2 Feb. 1930, in Fritz Dickmann, "Die Regierungsbildung in Thüringen als Modell der Machtergreifung," *Vierteljahrshefte für Zeitgeschichte*, XIV (Oct. 1966), 461.

ture to convert the national campaign into what was in effect a propaganda concentration in two areas, Thuringia and Bavaria, since these
promised to yield the best results.[173] However, while the Nazis
retained and even increased their rural support, their greatest relative gain came from the large cities of Germany. Thus, the Berlin
returns showed an almost 400 percent increase over 1928 (39,052
or 1.5 percent as compared to 132,097 or 5.7 percent in 1929).[174]
These figures were both gratifying and unexpected by the Reichsleitung, but the Nazis also realized that they did not constitute a
belated triumph of the urban plan. Far from it, the NSDAP received
almost no support in the traditional working-class sections of the
large cities. In Berlin, for example, no National Socialist candidate
was elected from any of the traditional proletarian strongholds such
as Wedding, Prenzlauer Berg, Friedrichshain, Neukölln, Treptow,
Köpenick, Lichtenberg, Weissensee, and Pankow.[175] On the contrary,
the Nazi ballots were part of the fear vote among groups that were
still not directly affected by the depression. The Reichsleitung realized
this immediately and set out to exploit its surprising success both
financially and organizationally. Names were collected for a special
"S[sympathizer]" file of well-to-do individuals and firms who could
be counted upon to support the party financially.[176] Also the party
raised its membership dues and charged each member RM 2.00
toward the purchase of a new party office building[177] — indications
that the membership was economically not desperate at this time.

The acquisition of the new party headquarters in Munich, the
Brown House, was the most dramatic symbol of the party's bureaucratic and organizational expansion.[178] As a result of the rapid influx
of members, the party's functionary corps was growing rapidly at

173. GL Ostmark, "Gaubefehl des Gaus Ostmark," 18 Nov. 1929, HA, roll 10,
folder 203.

174. Johann K. von Engelbrechten and Hans Volz, *Wir wandern durch das nationalsozialistische Berlin* (Munich, 1937), p. 12.

175. *Ibid.*, p. 13.

176. Oehme and Caro, *Kommt*, p. 22; and George W. F. Hallgarten, *Hitler,
Reichswehr und Industrie* (Frankfurt, 1962), p. 96.

177. *VB*, 25/26 May 1930.

178. According to Anton Lingg, *Die Verwaltung der Nationalsozialistischen
Deutschen Arbeiterpartei* (2d ed.; Munich, 1940), p. 58, Schwarz had suggested
the purchase of the Barlow Palais to Hitler in the spring of 1930.

all levels of the vertical structure. By mid-1930, salaries for party functionaries were a major item in the party's budget: of a total of RM 392,000 in expenditures for 1929, RM 88,000 (22.4 percent) was spent on salaries, a figure that was even slightly higher than the expenses for propaganda (RM 87,000).[179] Hitler actively encouraged the expansion. As before, he paid detailed attention to the office equipment, and he showed himself visibly pleased when a Gau office possessed the latest in filing cabinets and office management techniques.[180]

The physical and personnel expansion of the Gau offices and the Reichsleitung does not seem to have presented any major problems, but the party was less successful in staffing its lower-echelon offices as rapidly as the membership increase demanded. This seems to have been less true of the rural areas, where the party had already created an in-depth organizational structure which merely needed to be expanded by the creation of new districts and some additional staff personnel in the new offices.[181] The party had made less of an effort, however, to saturate the middle-class urban areas organizationally after it abandoned the urban plan. To remedy this past failing it now adopted a scheme to saturate the urban areas as effectively as the country regions. This was the so-called Muchow Plan, named for its originator, then the organizational leader of the Berlin Gau. The scheme provided for a series of vertical subdivisions within an urban local, ranging from a section (perhaps ten to twenty city blocks) to a cell (which might consist of as few as five members). The Muchow Plan had two obvious advantages. It made the integration of a new member into the organizational life of the NSDAP a relatively smooth process by preserving the personal contacts between low-echelon leaders and followers even in an urban context. At the same time the plan enabled the party to preserve among its membership a high percentage of militants, which became the indispensable prerequisite for the propagandistic saturation of the urban

179. These are Schwarz's figures as reported to the 1930 membership meeting held in May. See PD Mü, "N/No. 91," 23 May 1930, HA, roll 24A, folder 1758.

180. Hans Zeverus Ziegler, "Ein Besuch beim Berliner Gau," *Führerbriefe*, II (July 1930), HA, roll 5, folder 133.

181. Staatspolizei Württemberg, "W. 13" (secret), 24 April 1930, HA, roll 58, folder 1403.

areas during the next national election campaign.[182] This last consideration was by no means insignificant, since the Reichsleitung expected Reichstag elections by the fall of 1930.[183] Consequently, it pressed for the utmost specialization of labor at the section and local levels (in effect, making semi-functionaries of a large part of the membership).[184] Indeed, the Reichsleitung was even willing to lift its prohibition on double membership (membership in the party and in another far-right organization) in isolated cases if this was the only possible means of obtaining suitable local leaders.[185]

Almost overnight, the local elections of 1929 had brought the NSDAP to national political prominence, and filling positions in its staff structure was not the only problem that arose as a result. There was a sudden membership spurt in some of the affiliates as well, and this increase had to be organizationally absorbed.[186] More important was the sudden proliferation of Nazi legislators in the city and county councils.[187] The party had won its victories without any meaningful positive program, and it had few experienced communal officials in its ranks. In itself the lack of positive suggestions for curing Germany's ills was no particular worry to Hitler, but at the beginning of 1930 this lack created a vacuum which might harbor potentially dangerous organizational consequences. Faced with concrete communal problems, the Nazi legislators and officials needed specific guidelines to interpret more precisely what was meant by supporting Adolf Hitler. The absence of such directives might result in a proliferation of programmatic studies or simply politically awkward legislation in some localities.

The short-term solution to the problem of programmatic and

182. In February 1930 Hitler issued a new and more detailed directive on propaganda drafting and distribution to the party organization. See *VB*, 12 Feb. 1930.

183. "W. 8," 7 May 1930, HA, roll 58, folder 1403.

184. GL Berlin, *Führerbriefe*, II (July 1930), HA, roll 5, folder 133.

185. Strasser to Loeper, 8 Jan. 1930, NA, T-580, roll 23, folder 204 (Elbe-Havelgau).

186. HJ membership, for example, rose rapidly in the spring of 1930. See Carl Rachor (apparently HJ leader in Wiesbaden in 1936), "Der Weg der Jugend des Nassauer Landes in den Kampfjahren 1925–1931," (MS 1936), HA, roll 19, folder 363.

187. Thus, the NSDAP held an absolute majority in the city council of the Bavarian city of Koburg.

legislative coordination was simply to put the Gauleiters in charge of communicating instructions to the representatives-elect in their Gaus.[188] However, since the Gauleiters were no more authorized to make programmatic decisions than the local legislators themselves, this was hardly a permanent answer. Instead, Hitler assigned the coordinating functions to a separate division of the Reich Organization Leadership, the *Reichsorganisationsleitung II*. The office itself had been established at the Nuremberg congress, but it had no real significance until 1930 when it became obvious that the party needed both more detailed programmatic statements and a means of attracting or training officials who could administer *Fachministeria* (technical ministries) instead of merely cadre organizations.[189] The Reichsorganisationsleitung II was headed by Konstantin Hierl, a retired colonel, associate of Epp and Strasser,[190] and author of a plan for a national voluntary labor service. His relationship to Hitler was similar to that of Buch: he too regarded Hitler as the political leader of Germany selected by destiny itself.[191] Since Hitler had no real interest in either ideas or proposals for concrete solutions to Germany's social and economic problems, Hierl's office never became anything approaching a brain trust or kitchen cabinet, but it did produce some propagandistically very effective policy statements. The first of these was the party's official statement on the agricultural question. This was the work of Walther Darré, a pseudointellectual and writer on agricultural affairs, who had become head of Section V (agriculture) of the Reichsorganisationsleitung II shortly before. Like most Nazi programmatic statements, it was a combination of romanticized wishful thinking, calculated appeal to material interest, and status-oriented promises: a declaration that the farmers were the real nobility of Germany was followed by promises of massive tax relief,[192] once the Nazis came to power.

188. See *VB*, 29 Nov. and 10 Dec. 1929.

189. The left wing in the party had realized much earlier that if the NSDAP should ever attain national power, it had no leader really qualified to lead a functional ministry. See Heinz to B. v. Salomon, 19 July 1929, HA, roll 13A, folder 1349.

190. Konstantin Hierl, *Im Dienst für Deutschland* (Heidelberg, 1954), p. 63.

191. Hierl, "Wie ich zu Hitler kam," in *Ausgewählte Schriften und Reden* (Munich, 1941), I, p. 97.

192. The statement, signed by Adolf Hitler, was published in the *VB*, 7 March 1930.

The importance of the agricultural program was obviously not its content, but the public-relations image which it produced for the NSDAP as the party that had recognized both the nobility and the economic problems of the farmer.[193] This was equally true of the tenure of the first National Socialist minister in Germany. It will be recalled that in the communal elections the NSDAP concentrated its campaign efforts on Bavaria and Thuringia. In the latter state the Nazis held the balance of power in the state legislature (which had also been elected in December), and as a result of the vote Hitler demanded that a National Socialist become a member of a right-of-center coalition cabinet. He proposed Frick, one of the least popular of the party's leaders and a "dried-up fountain pen," as minister of interior and education.[194] The coalition partners, particularly the DVP (Deutsche Volkspartei), objected, but Hitler who personally handled the negotiations, pressured the DVP leaders into yielding by appealing behind the scenes to their financial backers.[195]

Despite these triumphs the NSDAP found itself in a somewhat ambiguous situation as the summer of 1930 approached. The flow of members continued unabated, but with it came a correspondingly large number of pure opportunists who were not really totally engaged in the Hitler myth-person when they filled out their membership applications.[196] Thus it is significant that at the end of 1929 in only six of the twenty-five Gaus did 50 percent or more of the party's membership pay their compulsory dues to the SA insurance scheme. Only one Gau reached a figure of 70 percent, and in five Gaus less than 40 percent of the members subscribed. For seven Gaus the figures were so low that the Reichsleitung refused to make them public.[197] In addition, the party was experiencing the traditional difficulties of a political group that hopes to obtain revolutionary aims with legal or at least pseudolegal means. Hitler had apparently hoped

193. Heberle, *Landbevölkerung*, p. 163.
194. Frick was almost the only party leader with any governmental administrative experience. Thus the *VB* began a biographical series "Kämpfer des kommenden Reiches," on Aug. 8, 1930 with a description of Frick's career, but the series also ended with him. On Frick's personality see Krebs, *Tendenzen*, pp. 205–07. The quote is from Uhse, *Söldner*, p. 270.
195. Hitler to . . ., 2 Feb. 1930, in Dickmann, "Regierungsbildung," pp. 461–62.
196. See the complaints about this in GL Berlin, *Führerbriefe*, II (July 1930), HA, roll 5, folder 133.
197. See the listing in *VB*, 20 Dec. 1929.

to form a national coalition government with the DNVP under Hugenberg in the spring, but the DNVP's vote against Hugenberg, a move that surprised Hitler and made him "furious (*wütend*),"[198] destroyed that hope. To add to his difficulties, the Bavarian government in early June prohibited uniformed demonstrations. Hitler countered by ordering a concentration of all propaganda on the Bavarian action for the next eight months, only to find the Prussian government issuing a similar prohibition a week later.[199] It is not surprising that a feeling of helplessness and even despondency permeated the party leadership during the early part of the summer.[200]

The NSDAP was relieved of the necessity of critically evaluating the effectiveness of its organizational and propagandistic structure by the short-sighted action of the Brüning government in calling for a Reichstag election in September. Heinrich Brüning, a leading member of the Center Party, had become Reich chancellor at the end of March. Although he had the support of Hindenburg and faced no danger of a vote of no confidence from the Reichstag, he insisted on dissolving the legislature, in order to increase his legislative majority. The decision was a massive political blunder.[201] At once, the NSDAP shook off its lethargy; gone were the days of despair. The massive organization moved quickly to mobilize the voting masses and saturate the cities and rural areas with National Socialist propaganda. This time the Nazis were particularly anxious to win the vote of the disengaged, ostensibly apolitical voter in Germany. Hitler keynoted the NSDAP's appeal as the "preservation and securing of the bases of our Christian–German culture, the nationalization of the people and the defense of federalism." The NSDAP pictured itself not as a party, but as the hope of the middle classes in their struggle against Marxism.[202]

198. Buch to Johannes Bierbach, 21 April 1930, HA, roll 56, folder 1375. See also Hitler's article, "Prinzip und Taktik," *VB*, 9 April 1930.

199. *VB*, 7 and 13 June 1930.

200. PD Mü, "[Auszug aus] Münchener Lagebericht Nr. 92," 9 July 1930, HA, roll 70, folder 1510. The *VB* articles in July are also noticeably less permeated by the expectation that national power would soon be within the NSDAP's grasp.

201. See Karl-Dietrich Bracher, *Die Auflösung der Weimarer Republik* (3d ed.; Villingen, Schwarzw., 1955), pp. 345 and 368, for the reasons which led Brüning to take this step.

202. *VB*, 25 June, 19 July, and 10 Sept. 1930. See also G. M., "Soziologie der Sachsenwahlen," *Tat*, XXII (Aug. 1930), 385; and *F. Z.*, 24 Mar. 1930.

The Reichstag election campaign of 1930 contained within it both the greatest challenge and the most satisfying rewards for the Nazi Party's functionary corps. The rewards came primarily in the form of the prestige and monetary benefits that came with a Reichstag deputy's seat. Virtually all of the party's national candidates, both on the general Reich list and on the individual district lists were members of the NSDAP's functionary corps. Moreover, Hitler was clearly determined to provide the Reichsleitung executives and the Gauleiters with the prestige of a Reichstag seat as Table 7 shows. The upper echelons of the functionary corps had indeed come a long way since the days of Bamberg.

TABLE 7

Level of Office	Relative Numerical Place Positions								Candidates Listed on both Districts and Reich Ballots	Candidates not Attached to a Specific Locale
	On District Ballots						On Reich Ballots			
	1	2	3	4	5	6	1st–10th	11th–15th		
Reichsleitung							2	2	6	
Gauleiter	10	6	1						4	6
District Leader		3	1	3					1	3
Local Leader				1	2					1
No Specific Office									3	

SOURCE: *Völkischer Beobachter* (Summer issues, 1930).

On the other hand, the executives of the Reichsleitung had personally to earn their legislative rewards. The election campaign of 1930 gave the Reichsleitung and Gauleiters their most challenging opportunity yet to show their ability to function as romanticized bureaucrats. After a national planning conference on July 27,[203] a tireless Hitler (he delivered at least twenty major speeches between August 3 and September 13), over a hundred Reich speakers,[204] and countless local luminaries blanketed Germany with an endless

203. *VB*, 29 July 1930.
204. RL, Reichspropaganda-Abteilung, "Rednerverzeichnis der [NSDAP] . . . Nach dem Stande vom 1. März 1930," HA, roll 24A, folder 1758.

series of rallies. The overall direction of the entire effort remained centralized in Munich. The Reichsleitung made final decisions on matters ranging from the determination of priority concentrations to the size of posters. This did not mean, however, that the Gauleiter was an unimportant link in the propaganda chain. On the contrary, as divisional campaign manager he was responsible for the most effective use of the human and material resources which Munich assigned to him. The Gauleiter reached no political decisions, but the very magnitude of the Nazi campaign effort forced him to institute complex divisions of labor in his area and thus prove his ability to administer a sizable staff of subordinates under conditions of extreme pressure.[205] The election of 1930 was the most decisive test for the organizational reforms of 1928–29.

205. For an example of the administration of a Gau election campaign see GL Gross-Berlin, "Propaganda Rundschreiben Nr. 16," 5 Aug. 1930, HA, roll 70, folder 1529.

Illusions and Dilemmas

The Reichstag elections of 1930 provided striking statistical evidence of the NSDAP's successful efforts to disengage large numbers of politically articulate Germans from the pluralist values of Weimar. The NSDAP became a major political force in Republican politics because it had persuaded some 6.4 million Germans that it represented an alternative to the Republic. Initially, the size of the vote was as much a surprise to the party as it was a shock to its opponents. Loyal party members had "expected fifty, perhaps hoped for seventy [seats]."[1] Instead, the overflow audience at election central in Munich could cheer 107 delegates to the Reichstag, and, sometime after midnight, Hitler appeared in person. Unlike 1928, he was pleased with his party's showing.[2]

The victory was impressive. The NSDAP registered spectacular gains in all districts, and increases of 90 percent over the (admittedly dismal) showing of 1928 were not uncommon.[3] However, its best showings were among the farmers and middle-class (especially lower-middle-class) voters in the rural and Protestant areas north

1. Hermann Gmelin, letter of 1 Sept. 1930 [sic; the date is incorrect] in "Kampfjahre eines Kreisleiters — Briefe, 1930–33" (MS, ca. 1937) (cited hereafter as "Briefe"), HA, roll 5A, folder 514.

2. VB, 16 Sept. 1930.

3. In Berlin, for example, hardly a National Socialist stronghold, the percentage of the NSDAP's vote rose from 1.6 (1928) to 14.6. See Vorwärts, 18 Sept. 1930. In "Thalburg," a Hanoverian county seat the party vote increased astronomically from 123 in 1928 to 213 in 1929 and 1,742 in 1930. See William S. Allen, The Nazi Seizure of Power: The Experience of a Single German Town, 1930–1935 (Chicago, 1965), pp. 24 and 34.

of the Main line.[4] Relatively less impressive, though still formidable, were the results in the Catholic areas and in the working class districts of major industrial cities. Thus, the NSDAP's percentage of the total vote in three typical precincts in Berlin shows the following: in Wedding, mainly a working-class district, the NSDAP polled 8.9 percent of the vote; in Steglitz, a middle-class district, 25.8 percent of the vote; and in Zehlendorf, middle- to upper-class, 17.7 percent of the vote.[5]

The election results shocked the pluralistic parties out of the world of political illusions in which they had conducted their election campaigns. The SPD had pronounced the NSDAP politically dead and largely ignored it during the campaign.[6] The bourgeois parties, on the other hand, all but accepted the NSDAP's definition of the SPD and the KPD and concentrated their attacks against "Marxism."[7] Few of the supporters of Weimar understood that for many Germans the fundamental political issue in 1930 was the pluralistic system of politics itself, not substantive issues within the system. The NSDAP benefited from a disintegrative process in Weimar politics that was evident even in the local elections of 1929. In the face of threatened socioeconomic chaos, the German middle classes clung even more desperately to the emotional and political values of nationalism. And no party matched the NSDAP's demagogic chauvinism.[8]

The victory also demonstrated the political effectiveness of the party's vertical organization, and the NSDAP showed justifiable pride not only in the "thirty-seven perfectly operating organizational ma-

4. James K. Pollock, "An Areal Study of the German Electorate, 1930–1933," *American Political Science Review*, XXXVII (Feb. 1944), 90; and Werner Stephan, "Zur Soziologie der Nationalsozialistischen Deutschen Arbeiterpartei," *Zeitschrift für Politik*, XX (March 1931), 794–95.

5. *Ibid.*, p. 797.

6. Wilhelm Keil, *Erlebnisse eines Sozialdemokraten* (Stuttgart, 1948), II p. 395.

7. In the state of Brunswick, the Bourgeois Unity Slate *(Bürgerliche Einheitsliste)* conducted its campaign almost exclusively against the SPD, while the NSDAP directed its attacks against the middle parties. See Ernst-August Roloff, *Bürgertum und Nationalsozialismus 1930–1933: Braunschweigs Weg ins Dritte Reich* (Hanover, 1961), pp. 23 and 25.

8. Stephan, "Zur Soziologie," p. 796, notes that nationalistic appeals were a greater factor in the party's electoral success than actual economic hardship. See also Allen, *Seizure,* pp. 28 and 40.

chines, the thirty-seven Gaus,"[9] but in the other components of the Muchow Plan as well. Literally thousands of cell leaders and cell fore-men *(Zellenobleute)* worked tirelessly to integrate each member into the framework of the totalitarian society.[10] The election results also revealed, however, that while a well-functioning vertical organization could propel the NSDAP to political prominence, it alone was not suffi-cient to give the party control of Germany.

Until now the bulk of the NSDAP's membership and support came from individuals who had become completely disengaged from the values of Weimar. Once politically and emotionally adrift, they went through the steps of the party's propaganda and organizational spiral and, as participants in the vertical structure, became reengaged in the values of the National Socialist myth. In 1930, an entirely different type of individual cast his (or her) ballot for the NSDAP. He voted for Hitler not because he was desperate, but because he expected the NSDAP to provide a better material life for him.[11] Vast numbers of NSDAP voters in 1930 were against Weimar, but they were also calculating enough not to follow-up their votes auto-matically with a membership application.[12] Since the party's political impact depended directly upon the number of members subject to Hitler's personal and institutional will, the NSDAP after September had to find organizational means to turn these sympathizers and voters into dedicated followers.

As yet the party was ill prepared for its new task. Its immediate assets were tremendous prestige and a greatly augmented force of propagandists and organizers who proudly carried an *M.d.R.* or *M.d.L.* (member of the Reichstag or Landtag) behind their names. But even the 107 new Reichstag deputies were in some ways an anachronistic group: they were relatively young (average age forty-

9. Gau Oberfranken, "Rundschreiben Nr. 31," 31 Dec. 1930, NA, T-580, roll 19, folder 199 (Gau Oberfranken). See also *VB*, 15 Oct. 1930.

10. A "cell foreman" headed 5 party members. See Staatspolizei Württemberg, "W. 18," 15 Oct. 1930, HA, roll 58, folder 1403.

11. Sociologically, the main source of the NSDAP's urban votes had been white-collar workers under 40 who feared the effects of the depression on their jobs and status positions. Stephan, "Zur Soziologie," p. 800.

12. In "Thalburg" the party had 40 members, but 1,000 fellow travelers. Allen, *Seizure*, p. 72.

six),[13] and overwhelmingly belonged to the middle classes, but virtually all held a position in the party bureaucracy. Hence they were clearly part of the older, more desperate, and less calculating membership, which reduced their usefulness for the organizational needs of the present.[14]

The integration of the calculating sympathizers was also made more difficult by the party's failure to obtain any position of real governmental power either in the Reich or in the states as a result of the elections. Hitler saw a quick solution to the problem in a coalition with the Brüning government. Supported by what the *VB* called "the rise of the people,"[15] the NSDAP's leader offered Brüning a coalition government with the NSDAP, provided that the party could hold at least three ministerial portfolios.[16] To Hitler's visible disappointment, Brüning refused to invite the NSDAP into the government.[17] The dream of immediate power was over. (Hitler and other party leaders did hold talks with a variety of political figures and organizations throughout the fall of 1930).[18]

The sudden entrance into the inner councils of politics was immediately reflected in the party's membership and financial status. The very fact that other political groups took the NSDAP seriously for the first time since 1923 led to a bandwagon effect and rapid increases in the membership rolls. Even without specific organizational measures, special clerks had to work a 6-to-11 P.M. shift to

13. See Heinrich Geiger, "Streifzug im verjüngten Reichstag," *Tat,* XXII (Jan. 1931), 812.

14. It is symptomatic, however, that the most successful organizer of the new wave, Darré, was not elected to the Reichstag in 1930. See also Karl-Dietrich Bracher, *Die Auflösung der Weimarer Republik* (3d ed.; Villingen, Schwarzw., 1955), pp. 373-74 n32.

15. *VB,* 16 Sept. 1930.

16. Hermann Pünder, *Politik in der Reichskanzlei,* ed. Thilo Vogelsang (Stuttgart, 1961), entry for 20 Sept. 1930, p. 62; and Kunrat von Hammerstein, "Schleicher, Hammerstein und die Machtübernahme 1933," *Frankfurter Hefte,* XI (Jan. 1956), 15.

17. Albert Krebs, *Tendenzen und Gestalten der NSDAP* (Stuttgart, 1959), p. 141.

18. On these various contacts see Bracher, *Auflösung,* pp. 424 and 425 n67; Hjalmar Schacht, *Abrechnung mit Hitler* (Hamburg, 1948), p. 6; Theodor Düsterberg, *Der Stahlhelm und Hitler* (Wolfenbüttel, 1949), p. 36; Krebs, *Tendenzen,* p. 33; and Pünder, *Politik,* entry for 5 Oct. 1930, p. 64.

process the applications that poured into national headquarters.[19] The flow of application fees and the simultaneous sudden influx of business advertising revenue for the *VB* and other party newspapers put the NSDAP on a solid financial footing and almost overnight wiped out its often-staggering debts.[20]

The Reichsleitung was less pleased by the high mobility factor that accompanied the impressive gains in the membership figures. A sizable portion, but by no means all, of the new members were "emotionally attracted"[21] to the party, filled out an application blank, and perhaps paid dues for one or two months, only to lose interest when the NSDAP could not present them with an immediate positive solution to their social and economic problems. This procedure was a financial asset for the party (the RM 2.00 application fee was not returned), but such members were obviously not really integrated into the totalitarian mind-set. In addition, the party's sudden popularity brought on the dangers of "clubbiness" again. While previously the small band of NSDAP members had been tempted to cut themselves off socially as well as politically from the larger society in which they lived, the large number of sympathizers and "on-again off-again" members might transform the NSDAP organization into little more than another desirable political and social "in-group" in the towns and villages of Germany. This danger was particularly acute if the local or Gau administrators were impressed by their sudden social prominence and did little to discourage members from dropping in and out of the party.[22]

The round of negotiations with major political forces had other unpleasant side effects. The talks revealed in all its glaring naked-

19. "Kontrollbuch des Sekretariats Hitler, 1.X.30–2.III.31" (ms), HA, roll 2A, folder 235. This is a daily register of persons coming to and leaving the Brown House.

20. See Krebs, *Tendenzen*, p. 86, for an account of the fortunes of the Hamburg party press at this time.

21. Wolfgang Schäfer, *NSDAP* (Hanover, 1956), pp. 17-18.

22. The head of the NSDAP faction in Bremen, a merchant and Siamese consul in Bremen, joined the party only after he had been placed on the slate of candidates. See Herbert Schwarzwälder, *Die Machtergreifung der NSDAP — Bremen 1933* (Bremen, 1960), p. 30. Such incidents were apparently not isolated. In August 1931, the RL prohibited the practice of "temporarily dropping-out." See NSDAP, Reichsorganisationsleiter, *Verordnungsblatt der Reichsleitung der NSDAP* (cited hereafter as *VOBl*) (No. 5; 19 Aug. 1931), p. 13.

ness the essential negativism of the NSDAP's program. What some sympathetic observers had regarded as the party's outer layer of demagogic baggage turned out to be its only positive contribution on most substantive issues.[23] In addition, the sudden prominence necessitated a flurry of decisions at all levels of the party which severely strained the always excessively centralized decision-making process[24] and quickly produced situations in which various official party spokesmen worked at obvious cross-purposes.[25] The need to show positive stands on current issues also led to some bizarre programmatic contradictions. While the Berlin party organization vigorously supported a metal workers' strike, high party officials in Saxony expressed the NSDAP's opposition to strikes.[26]

The absence of positive programs became particularly embarrassing when the new Reichstag met. At first it was all very impressive: 107 deputies clad in identical brown shirts marched into the chamber, answered with resounding "Here! Heil Hitler!" to the roll call of members (which the Communists countered with "Red Front Heil!"), but it soon became apparent that in order to hold the allegiance of its various voter groups, the National Socialist faction would have to make some positive contribution to the work of the Reichstag.[27] This was especially true when the Reichstag amended its rules of order to exclude demagogic resolutions proposing irresponsible benefits to all social groups.[28] The NSDAP decision to boycott

23. Krebs, *Tendenzen*, p. 151. There was no sudden change in the party's propaganda approach. A speech which Hitler gave before a select audience of Hamburg businessmen in December 1930 "barely touched on the immediate problems facing us." See "Bericht über Hitlers zweite Rede im Nationalclub von 1919," 1 Dec. 1930, in Werner Jochmann, ed., *Nationalsozialismus und Revolution* (Frankfurt, 1963), p. 309.

24. Kube to RL, 23 Dec. 1930, NA, T-580, roll 23, folder 205; and *Vorwärts,* 27 June 1930.

25. While Gauleiter Loeper fought against the influence of a certain politician, Göring concluded agreements with him by authority of Hitler. Loeper to Strasser, 10 Nov. 1930, NA, T- 580, roll 23, folder 204.

26. GL Gross-Berlin, Sektion Prenzlauer Berg, *Mitteilungsblatt* (No. 22; Nov. 1930), HA, roll 19, folder 362; Otto-Ernst Schüddekopf, *Linke Leute von Rechts* (Stuttgart, 1960), p. 377; and Walter Oehme and Kurt Caro, *Kommt "Das Dritte Reich"* (Berlin, 1930), p. 48.

27. Krebs, *Tendenzen*, p. 150.

28. The amended rules provided that any bill which altered the budgetary balance would have to be accompanied by a proposal to offset the imbalance through new sources of revenue. Bracher, *Auflösung*, p. 387.

the Reichstag rather than accept the new rules was hardly a positive contribution.[29] The same was true of some futile efforts to topple a number of state governments through votes of no confidence and plans to stage a rump national parliament in Weimar.[30]

At the end of the year the NSDAP was both realistic and visionary. On the one hand, Hitler assured some of his negotiating partners on the right that he would control the Reich and Prussian government by February 1931.[31] At the same time he was making some badly needed personnel appointments,[32] and his 1931 New Year's Proclamation publicly recognized the necessity of organizationally digesting the sympathizers of September. This, said Hitler, was to be the party's task in 1931.[33]

Since so much in the NSDAP depended upon the public image of Adolf Hitler himself, it was only natural that the process of integrating the sympathizers would begin with the creation of a Hitler image that conformed to the values of the status-conscious middle classes. The party did not abandon its claim of speaking for all social groups in Germany,[34] but when Hitler converted himself into the scion "of a family of Austrian financial civil servants" who had "dedicated himself [to the study] of the building discipline (*Baufach*) in Vienna,"[35] a major shift in emphasis was apparent. Other signs reinforced the conclusion. To impress the anxious right with the NSDAP's respectability,[36] Hitler never tired of affirming publicly and privately

29. *VB*, 22 Nov. 1930. On the other hand, the decision by the DNVP and the bulk of the Landvolk party to follow the NSDAP's boycott demonstrated the party's new position of leadership among the parties of the right.

30. Bracher, *Auflösung*, p. 388.

31. Seldte and Düsterberg to Hitler, 11 Dec. 1932, in Düsterberg, *Stahlhelm*, p. 32.

32. Hitler negotiated with Röhm to take over leadership of the SA after Pfeffer's resignation in September (see below, p. 211), and Göring was evolving at least informally into the party's coordinating official for legislative affairs. See RL to GL Danzig, 25 Oct. 1930, NA, T-580, roll 20, folder 200.

33. *VB*, 1/2 Jan. 1931. See also GL Schlesien, "Gaupropagandarundschreiben 5/30," 18 Dec. 1930, NA, T-580, roll 25, folder 207.

34. The NSDAP still delighted in scheduling rallies in which "Prince August Wilhelm of Prussia" and "Locksmith Franz Dreher" spoke from the same platform. See *VB*, 1 May 1931.

35. Hitler's autobiographical entry in the 1931 edition of the *Reichshandbuch der Deutschen Gesellschaft*, quoted in Walter Görlitz and Herbert A. Quint, *Adolf Hitler* (Stuttgart, 1952), p. 298.

36. Thilo Vogelsang, *Reichswehr, Staat und NSDAP* (Stuttgart, 1962), p. 91.

the legality of the party's aims and tactics.[37] The new national headquarters, the Brown House, was a former mansion located a stone's
throw from Munich's most elegant section. It had been acquired at
considerable financial sacrifice for the party,[38] but it too certainly
added to the NSDAP's image of respectability and solidarity.

Late in 1930 the NSDAP also set out to prove that it had already
worked out some positive programs. The propagandists reminded
the party's sympathizers that in 1930 the NSDAP had produced
notable policy declarations on agricultural policy, private property,
the civil service, and the question of church and state, though they
neglected to point out that none of these statements addressed themselves to the immediate and vital issues of the day.[39] The party's
pseudo-intellectual organ, the *NS-Monatshefte*, began to print theoretical articles on various economic and social problems, and the NSDAP
even announced that it had an official foreign policy line: it was
for England and against Russia.[40]

The entire process of image-building was, of course, only a prelude to and not a substitute for actually organizing the National
Socialist voters. That could only be accomplished if the NSDAP
established organizational forms that met two criteria. To begin
with, they had to do more than "denounce red and black political
bosses";[41] that is, they had to stand for a program of positive benefits for the various interest groups. At the same time, the sympathizers
had to be convinced that the realization of these economic and social

---

37. Germany, Reichsgericht, 4. Strafsenat, "[Urteil] In der Strafsache gegen
... Scheringer ... Ludin ... Wendt, 12 J. 10/1930 - XII H 41/30" (MS), HA,
roll 24A, folder 1758, p. 36; and Groener to Alarich von Gleich, 26 April 1931,
quoted in Reginald H. Phelps, "Aus den Groener Dokumenten," *Deutsche Rundschau*, LXXVI (Dec. 1950), 1015.

38. On 8 Dec. 1930, Goebbels transferred RM 4,452.00 in regular dues and RM
5,259.00 in special contributions for the Brown House. See Goebbels to Schwarz,
8 Dec. 1930, NA, T-580, roll 19, folder 199a. Hitler noted that from the profits of
his rallies between RM 3,000.00 and RM 5,000.00 had to be transferred to the
Brown House account. Adolf Hitler, "Das Braune Haus," *VB*, 21 Feb. 1931.

39. GL Gross-Berlin, Propaganda-Abteilung, "Propaganda Rundschreiben Nr.
19," 6 Dec. 1930, NA, T-580, roll 19, folder 199.

40. Röhm, "Denkschrift ... für Zwecke aktiver Information im Auslande,"
22 April 1931, Vogelsang, *Reichswehr*, doc. 10, p. 424.

41. Darré to Landwirtschaftliche Gaufachberaters (LGF), 27 Nov. 1930, HA,
roll 46, folder 951.

benefits could come only after the NSDAP had achieved political power.[42] One possible organizational form to combine the party's political aims with the socioeconomic goals of the sympathizers might be a duplicate set of pluralist interest groups, that is, a National Socialist Association of Pharmacists, a National Socialist League of Munich Coal Dealers, etc.[43] This course had some obvious advantages: the new organizations would have a clearly defined relationship to the party, and presumably they would be readily welcomed by dissatisfied elements in the established groups. But they had even greater disadvantages. For some time at least, they would probably remain small and powerless organizations. The German middle classes thought of their interest groups as apolitical organizations, so that to join an interest group affiliated with the NSDAP would involve a major political decision which these inherently conservative elements would be reluctant to take. If, on the other hand, the new affiliates grew overwhelmingly large, they might at some future date be in a position to dominate party policy, as the SPD-affiliated unions clearly influenced party policy at this time. The second method involved a form of what later came to be known as *Gleichschaltung*. Instead of establishing parallel interest groups, the NSDAP would attempt to undermine the influence of the non-National Socialist leadership in existing interest groups, replace the leading personnel by National Socialists, and thus subject the organization, while still intact, to Hitler's decisions.[44] Basically, the process of Gleichschaltung involved a massive, centralized corps of staff officials placed at all levels of the party's vertical organization who

42. *Ibid.*, 20 Nov. 1930.
43. The latter organization actually existed for a brief time.
44. The distinction between the two methods was well expressed in the different treatment accorded the NS-Association of Physicians and the Reich Association of NS-Chiropractors. The former received official approval when it described itself as "a part of the agitation organization *(Kampforganisation)* of the NSDAP, not an economic association," but the latter was denounced because it represented primarily the economic interests of its members. See "Satzungen des Nationalsozialistischen "Ärtztebundes e.V." [ca. 1930], HA, roll 89, folder 1868; and *VB*, 2 Apr. 1931. A very candid post-1933 description of the *Gleichschaltung* method as used in agricultural associations is in Eugen Schmahl and Wilhelm Seipel, *Entwicklung der völkischen Bewegung* (Giessen, 1933), p. 149. See also *VB*, 6 Nov. 1931.

developed plans (at the top) and carried on propaganda (at all levels) designed to appeal to a specific social or economic group. The aim was quite simply to persuade a sufficient number of members of an established interest group to politicize their desires and elect National Socialists to positions of control in the group. In general, the party chose the Gleichschaltung method to associate economic interest groups, while creating or reactivating separate affiliates to identify the party and the social interests of its sympathizers.

The NSDAP's most successful Gleichschaltung campaign was its effort to control the German farmers through their major interest group, the *Landbund*. This organization had always been politically conservative, usually following the DNVP line. By late 1930, many farmers, however, were dissatisfied with this affiliation and a substantial number of Landbund members had cast their votes for the NSDAP in September.[45] In following up this initial victory, the party established the Office for Agriculture (*agrarpolitischer Apparat,* a.A.), a system of party officials distributed all over Germany headed by Walther Darré. The officials were experts on agricultural policy and agitation methods among the rural population. Their sole task was to further the party's control of the Landbund from within.[46] In November and December Darré saturated Germany's farm areas with his officials; by the end of November every Gau had an agricultural expert (*Landwirtschaftlicher Gaufachberater,* LGF) and Darré could register his first political successes: in late November, the farmers of Ostpriegnitz (Silesia) had recalled the non-NSDAP board of governors of the district Landbund organization, and Darré confidently expected that the new board would be controlled by the NSDAP.[47]

Next to the farmers, the artisans and small shopkeepers were probably the economic group most directly affected by the psychological and material consequences of the depression. Many of these small businessmen, squeezed by the competition of department stores on one side and big labor's attacks on the patron ideal on the other,

45. Gerhard Stoltenberg, *Politische Strömungen im Schleswig-Holsteinischen Landvolk* (Düsseldorf, 1962), p. 158.

46. Darré to all LGF, 18 Nov. 1930, and 16 Dec. 1930, HA, roll 46, folder 951.

47. Darré, "Rundschreiben" to all LGF, 22 Dec. 1930, *ibid.*

demanded governmental curbs on chain stores and a return to the *Zunftzwang* (compulsory guild membership).[48] The NSDAP's propaganda version of the *Ständestaat* (corporate state, à la Mussolini), a romanticized pseudomedieval economy, seemed to answer the complaints of small businessmen,[49] and the party attempted to take over the artisan's guilds and businessmen's associations. The Militant Association of Retailers (*Kampfbund des gewerblichen Mittelstandes*) had the same functions as the a.A., but it was far less successful. Partly because it lacked a skilled organizer like Darré and partly because no one national organization like the Landbund was dominant in this field, the Kampfbund made only sporadic inroads into the economic middle-class interest groups during 1931.

Potentially the most serious threat to the survival of the Republic itself was the NSDAP's effort to control the German civil-service interest groups. The life of the Republic had been saved at least once by the loyalty of its civil servants (during the Kapp Putsch), and in 1931 this group had many legitimate grievances against the government. In the form of a series of salary cuts it had to bear the major consequences of the government's rigid deflation policy. Formally, the Republic had protected itself by making civil-service status incompatible with membership in the NSDAP or KPD, but it was doubtful if the law would be sufficient against disintegration from within. The party's civil service department fought vigorously to repeal the prohibition against NSDAP members in the civil service, while simultaneously organizing clandestine groups of party members in the civil-service interest groups to bore from within. An informal Association of National Socialist Police Officers and reports of sympathizers in the ranks of the Reichswehr in Chemnitz testified to the success of the disintegration process in this area as well.[50]

48. A. R. L. Gurland, Otto Kirchheimer, and Franz Neumann, *The Fate of Small Business in Nazi Germany* (Washington, 1943), pp. 41 and 44.

49. The party consistently presented itself as an organized embodiment of the estate ideal. For example, the *VB,* 1 Oct. 1930, grouped the 107 Reichstag deputies into such occupational categories as: agricultural estate, productive estate, teaching estate, and military estate.

50. Bzl. Chemnitz (the present Karl-Marx-Stadt) to Hierl, 15 Jan. 1931, HA, roll 78, folder 1578. Röhm also reestablished his contacts with Schleicher at the beginning of 1931. See Vogelsang, *Reichswehr,* p. 117 n439.

The Nationalsozialistische Betriebszellenorganisation (NSBO) had the difficult task of infiltrating and controlling the German labor unions. The party would have preferred to have used an already *gleichgeschaltete* union as a battering ram, but its efforts in 1928 to take over the Association of German Nationalist Office Employees (*Deutschnationaler Handlungsgehilfenverband*, DHV) failed, while the NSBO movement began spontaneously in Berlin.[51] Goebbels recognized it as an official party organization for the Berlin Gau, but Hitler was reluctant to accord it a Reich status until the Strasser crisis of July 1930 and the elections had revealed the need to organize the small but vociferous group of working-class sympathizers in the party.[52] At the beginning of 1931, the Reichsleitung established a Reich Department for Industrial Cells (*Reichsbetriebszellenabteilung*, RBA)[53] with Reinhold Muchow, one of the party's "subjectively honest socialists,"[54] as national organizer. Like the a.A., the RBA's original purpose was solely to conduct propaganda among the membership of the established unions. The propaganda effort was to be directed by an elaborate staff organization. Beginning with the RBA itself, each Gau would have an NSBO staff official and by the spring of 1931 the NSBO hoped to have at least one cell in every factory.[55]

As an organizational device to take over control of the German labor unions, the NSBO was singularly ineffective. Unlike the Landbund, the unions were both economic and political organiza-

51. Krebs, *Tendenzen,* p. 70; and Hans-Gerd Schumann, *Nationalsozialismus und Gewerkschaftsbewegung* (Hanover, 1958), p. 35.

52. For the Strasser crisis, see below, p. 210; Schumann, *Nationalsozialismus,* p. 36. Schumann writes that the NSDAP's September votes included some 15%-20% "workers," but it is probably more correct to say "union-organized blue and white collar employees"—with the latter category no doubt supplying the bulk of the vote.

53. *VB*, 30 Jan. 1931. Even so, the NSBO remained something of an organizational stepchild: it still received no subsidy from the Reich treasurer of the NSDAP. See Schumann, *Nationalsozialismus,* p. 37.

54. This is Martin Broszat's characterization of Reinhold Muchow, the NSBO's national organizer. See Martin Broszat, "Die Anfänge der Berliner NSDAP 1926/27," *Vierteljahrshefte für Zeitgeschichte,* VIII (Jan. 1960), 87. For Muchow's own views, see his *Nationalsozialismus und freie Gewerkschaften* (Munich, 1930).

55. Reinhold Muchow, *Organisation der Nationalsozialistischen Betriebszellen* (Munich, 1930); and GL Baden, Prop.-Abt., "Rundschreiben Nr. 1," 15 Dec. 1930, NA, T-580, roll 19, folder 199.

tions, and they quickly adopted defensive measures to combat the National Socialist infiltration efforts: the unions simply expelled any member who attempted to maintain a formal allegiance both to the union and the NSDAP.[56] (The party tolerated and encouraged dual memberships.) On the other hand, the NSBO did attract some members of the free unions,[57] so that the defensive measures forced the NSBO either to abandon these converts or to enlarge the scope of its activities in order to provide the benefits of union membership. The NSBO decided on the latter course, and in time they became rivals — albeit very ineffective rivals — of the Marxist and Christian unions. In effect, the NSBO was one instance in which the Darré formula had failed.

The NSDAP was far more successful in efforts to create appealing social affiliates. The party realized that many of its sympathizers and voters were profoundly concerned not only about their own social status in an age of socioeconomic uncertainty, but also about that of their children. Many of the NSDAP's September voters belonged to the generation that had still known the stability of the Wilhelminian era, but had also experienced the disasters of 1918 and 1923. The specter of unemployment and status-decline for their children was therefore a very real one. Here the NSDAP had already reactivated the Hitler Youth as an organization championing stability and middle-class ethical values. Its political purpose was both to attract the youths themselves and start them on their road to full party membership and totalitarianization;[58] and equally important, the HJ was a device to impress their already voting parents with the party's concern for the future generation of Germany.[59]

The HJ was not unprepared for its new role. Although it had begun as a recruiting agency for the SA, the organization changed

56. See the various expulsion notices which the NSBO organ *Arbeitertum* bitterly published throughout 1931.

57. Schumann, *Nationalsozialismus*, p. 39. This is also confirmed by the biographical sketches of local and provincial NSBO leaders printed in *Arbeitertum*. See, for example, the sketches of Jakob Meyer and Stefan Kroyer, *Arbeitertum*, I (1 and 15 Feb. 1932), 11 and 16 respectively.

58. Kurt Gruber (at the time head of the HJ), "Finanzierung der Hitler-Jugend," n.d. [beg. of 1931], HA, roll 18, folder 339.

59. HJ, GL Brandenburg, "Richtlinien für den Aufbau einer HJ-Ortsgruppe," 17 Sept. 1931, HA, roll 19, folder 362.

its character considerably in 1929 and 1930 and entered the mainstream of the German völkisch youth movement.[60] After the September elections, the HJ organization expanded rapidly. The national
office was enlarged, and the HJ's leader, Kurt Gruber, traveled extensively throughout Germany to establish and fill salaried Gau-staff
positions.[61]

The HJ's effectiveness can be measured both in terms of its own
growing membership and in its ability to digest other, already established youth groups into its organizational framework. Thus, the
German Young People (*Deutsches Jungvolk*, DJV), a völkisch group
that organized boys as young as ten years, agreed to merge into the
HJ in March 1931, so that the HJ now had a membership age span
from ten to eighteen years.[62] The NSDAP attempted to channel a
considerable portion of middle-class members of the younger generation beyond that age limit into the NSDStB (National Socialist
Association of German Students), another already established affiliate
organization that had been growing rapidly in influence and members even before the September elections.[63] The fear of belonging to
an academic proletariat after graduation had driven many students
to support the NSDStB, so that by mid-1930, it was the most influential member of the national union of German student groups,
the German Student Diet.[64] The September elections and the growing effect of the depression accelerated this development. The party's
emphasis on middle-class respectability and the pseudointellectual

60. The HJ joined such groups as the Geusen, Freischar Schill, Artamanen, etc.,
for a national congress of völkisch youth groups held in Weimar during the spring
of 1930. The rally was attended by such party leaders as Schirach, Frick, Rosenberg,
Goebbels, and Darré. See Hermann Bolm, *Hitler-Jugend in einem Jahrzent* (Brunswick, 1938), pp. 119–20.

61. *VB*, 30 Oct. 1930 and 3 Mar. 1931; and Bolm, *Hitler-Jugend*, pp. 138 and
141. At the same time such HJ-related organizations as the NS-Pupil Association
(i.e., upper-grade elementary and high school students) began their organizational
growth. See the documents in HA, roll 18, folder 344.

62. See Reichsleitung-HJ, Abt. Organisation, "Anweisung Nr. 3," 15 March 1931,
HA, roll 89, folder 1849.

63. Since the minimum age limit for party membership was 18, success in attracting students to the NSDStB would presumably be directly reflected in increased
party membership as well.

64. Wolfgang Zorn, "Die politische Entwicklung des deutschen Studententums
1919–1931," in Kurt Stephenson, *et al.*, eds., *Darstellungen und Quellen der deutschen Einheitsbewegung im 19. und 20. Jahrhundert*, V (Heidelberg, 1965), p. 303.

discussion of positive ideas surprised and attracted new student members.[65]

At the beginning of 1931, then, a massive effort to undermine and eventually conquer most of the economically, socially, or politically influential pluralist associations in German society was in progress. On paper, the day could almost be predicted when the NSDAP's octopus of organizations would succeed in destroying the viability of the German body social and politic. In practice the matter was somewhat more complicated. With the success of the party's affiliates, the same heterogeneity and conflicts of interest within German society which made it vulnerable to the NSDAP's disintegrative aims were transferred to the party itself. In short, rapid proliferation of various affiliated organizations representing mutually antagonistic interest groups brought with it the danger of diluting the totalitarian aspects of the movement.[66] The party did limit the scope of conflict within the NSDAP by consistently prohibiting "mere" economic interest groups, but even so the official encouragement to present positive ideas soon led to sharp divisions among and even within the affiliates.

The most bitter exchanges resulted from the entrenched and, in view of the economic crisis, increasingly narrow views of labor and management. The economic department of the Reichsleitung gave semi-official sanction to a pamphlet which the NSBO's publication attacked in the most severe terms.[67] Even Darré's organization was not free from such programmatic conflicts. The first national con-

65. Cf. Albert Speer's (who was 26 in 1931) statement that the "event which led me to him [Hitler]" was the pleasant surprise when a Hitler speech at the College of Engineering in Berlin which Speer had expected to be a "bombastic harangue [*Polterrede*]" turned out to be a "reasoned lecture." Albert Speer, "Die Bürde werde ich nicht mehr los—Spiegel Gespräch," *Spiegel*, XX (7 Nov. 1966), 48. To further the party's effort to control the German student organizations, Hitler personally attended the National Student Convention in the fall of 1930. See *VB*, 1 Nov. 1930.

66. This danger was clearly recognized by Buch, head of the Reich Uschla. See *VOBl* (No. 1; 1 June 1931), p. 3.

67. Erich Koch, "Sind wir Faschisten! Ein paar notwendige Bemerkungen," *Arbeitertum*, I (1 July 1931), 7. The pamphlet was Hans Reupke's, *Der National-sozialismus und die Wirtschaft* (Berlin, 1931). The furor within the party against this particular publication grew so intense that the *VB* was forced to announce that this was not the official party view and that the author had only joined the party on Dec. 1, 1930. See *VB*, 11 March 1931.

ference of the agricultural experts in Weimar at the beginning of the year faced the explosive issue of reconciling the interests of independent farmers and landless farm labor.[68]

The expansion of the affiliate organizations was also costing a great deal of money. The NSDAP was a far wealthier organization after September, but the expense of staffing the rapidly growing bureaucracies in the affiliates and the propaganda costs to spread their influence were nevertheless enormous.[69] This was particularly true at the local level. The locals were asked to bear the brunt of the propaganda costs[70] while still continuing to support the bureaucratic buildup of staff positions at the Gau and Reich level.[71] Since the entire effort to expand the party's influence depended in large part on the tireless enthusiasm of the locals, the NSDAP clearly needed to insure that the organizational and financial burdens imposed at this level did not become too heavy.

The most important device to bridge the antagonism within the party and to fire the enthusiasm of the locals was the person–institution of Adolf Hitler. His role of unchanging myth despite his changing personal decisions remained an inspiration to the totalized members and became the instrument which blunted and dissolved all antagonisms in the party. "Hitler is the unchallenged, sole leader of the NSDAP,"[72] wrote Gregor Strasser, whom contemporaries usually cast in the role of rival. Strasser's description fit. Hitler's own image and stature grew in direct proportion to the growth of the membership and affiliated organizations. His role as all-seeing organizer and decision-maker was symbolized by his office in the Brown House, a room which he seldom entered but which served his organizational image well. It was a large room, tastefully decorated in reddish-

68. See Johann Dorner, *Bauernstand und Nationalsozialismus* (Munich, 1930); and Friedrich Hildebrandt, *Nationalsozialismus und Landwirtschaft* (Munich, 1930). This issue was potentially dangerous particularly since Darré clearly favored the farmers, while Hildebrandt, the champion of farm labor, was the Gauleiter of Mecklenburg.

69. See, for example, Gruber, "Finanzierung . . . ," HA, roll 18, folder 339.

70. Allen, *Seizure,* pp. 74–75.

71. Reichsschatzmeister, "Rundschreiben an alle GL," 15 Dec. 1930, in *Rundschreiben des Reichsschatzmeisters, 26. Juli 1926–31. Dez. 1934* (cited hereafter as *Rdschr.*) (Munich, 1935), n.p.

72. *VB,* 22/23 Nov. 1931.

brown, with ceiling-high windows overlooking the Königsplatz. On the walls were three paintings of a man who was himself both image and personal model for Hitler: Frederick the Great. "Nothing happens in this movement, except what I wish" read the caption under an official portrait of Hitler seated at his desk.[73] This was not quite true in an absolute sense; rather, Hitler's total control was permanently potential: he assigned spheres of administrative power to his subordinates with the expressed limitation that he could personally interfere in the party's administration at any time, simply by reserving a decision to himself, or even reversing one that had already been reached.[74] If he had reserved a decision to himself, the matter rested until he expressed his views; nothing could be done before, and all efforts to speed up the decision were futile.[75] Similarly, Hitler was roused to furious anger when a subordinate appeared to deny that Hitler's right to such personal interference was not absolute.[76] The primary means of coordination and control in the NSDAP's increasingly complex organizational structure was an ever-tighter fusion of Hitler the person with Hitler the movement and Hitler the godlike agent of history.[77]

Actually, Hitler's control institutionalized itself more and more in a proliferation of new staff positions in Munich. He, as flesh and blood, was seldom there. He was out among the people, personally winning mass support for himself and funds for the party.[78] He then led his supporters to the institutionalized Hitler in Munich,

73. Heinrich Hoffmann and Baldur von Schirach, *Hitler wie ihn keiner kennt* (Berlin, 1932), p. 79. This book of photographs was issued during the presidential campaign of 1932. The description of Hitler's office is based on the photograph in Anton Drexler, *Das Braune Haus* (Munich, 1939), p. 25.

74. See GL Brandenburg to RL, 3 Oct. 1930, NA, T-580, roll 23, folder 205.

75. Görlitz and Quint, *Hitler*, p. 304.

76. Krebs, *Tendenzen*, pp. 155–56.

77. See the description of the prayer scene during the SA-crisis in Berlin (see below, p. 212), in PD Berlin to PD Mü, 16 Sept. 1930, HA, roll 73, folder 1551. It is also interesting to note in this connection that at a closed party meeting in July 1930, Hitler quite consciously compared the NSDAP's system of administration to that of the Catholic Church, and himself to the Pope. See Krebs, *Tendenzen*, p. 138.

78. See the account of the division of the profits from a Hitler rally among the SA units of Bavaria in Gausturm München-Oberbayern, SA-Brigade I, "Abrechnung," 14 March 1931, HA, roll 90, folder 1869. The net profits were RM 3,577.00.

and controlled them through the departments in the Reichsleitung and the Gauleiters in the provinces. In fact, Hitler's personal control of both the party itself and the affiliate structures was for the most part nothing but the administration of the men whom he put in charge of the various divisions. Even when his personal attention was requested, it was usually Hess who spoke, not Hitler. Hess was almost literally Hitler's alter ego during this time. He kept office hours that corresponded to Hitler's own insomniac habits, and when a Gauleiter called for instruction on a political decision, it was often Hess, not Hitler, to whom the decision was referred.[79]

To control the expanding affiliate organization, Hitler merely added more derivative agents. Men like Darré enjoyed the same relationship to Hitler as the Gauleiters; like them, each new department head at the Reichsleitung had complete control of his sphere of power — except when Hitler chose to deprive him temporarily or permanently of that status. Nor had the system of rewards and punishment changed. Hitler still refused to grant his presence to towns that had not delivered a substantial NSDAP vote,[80] and he rewarded Darré with a speech at the Office for Agriculture's February meeting, while he withheld his personal appearance from the NSBO until November. Also, self-institutionalization by other officials in the hierarchy remained a form of political service to Hitler and the party.[81]

In addition to the factor of his growing myth-person status, Hitler coordinated and controlled the party's far-flung operations by centralizing its decision-making processes as much as possible and by continuing to separate organizationally the members of the functionary corps from the membership at large.[82] By far the most important means of central control remained the office of Reich treasurer. Schwarz's intricate control and auditing system kept pace with the

79. See "Kontrollbuch," entry for 5 Feb. 1931 and the various entries noting Hess' time of departure from the Brown House between 11 P.M. and midnight, HA, roll 2A, folder 235.

80. GL Ostmark, "Gaubefehl 4 des Gaues Ostmark," 5 March 1931, NA, T-580, roll 23, folder 205.

81. See Goebbels' editorial in *Angriff*, 29 Nov. 1931, quoted in *Wetterleuchten— Aufsätze aus der Kampfzeit* (hereafter cited as *Wetterleuchten*), ed. Georg-Wilhelm Müller (Munich, 1939), p. 245.

82. The section Reichsleitung continued to expand its membership. In April 1931, the business manager and district leaders of the NSDStB were transferred from their locals to the elite section. *VB*, 18 Apr. 1931.

growth of the party's affiliated organizations.[83] Hitler's trust in Schwarz was undiminished; as far as can be ascertained, he never interfered in Schwarz's operations.[84] As a result, the treasurer's office extended its financial control over additional areas of the party's activities. In 1930 and 1931, it gained complete control of two important business ventures of the party, the party supply operations (formerly the SA quartermaster service) and the SA insurance system, which was renamed National Socialist Aid Fund *(NS-Hilfskasse).*[85] Schwarz also increased his control over Gau and local finances by establishing the office of Reich auditor. Three of his officials traveled throughout Germany with full powers to conduct surprise audits of the books of party and SA organizations. If they found grave irregularities, Schwarz was empowered to administer the financial affairs of the unit (including a Gau if necessary) directly.[86]

The central control of other routine policy decisions rested in the offices of the party's two organizational leaders, Gregor Strasser and Konstantin Hierl. Presumably Strasser (and perhaps Hitler) intended that he should control the administration of the vertical structure of the party itself, while Hierl, who was a close friend of Strasser's,[87] would coordinate the activities of the affiliate organizations. For a variety of reasons this plan failed. Strasser suffered a very serious skiing accident at the beginning of the year and was unable to work for two months.[88] Consequently he could not support Hierl in his quest to subordinate the affiliate chiefs. In addition

83. In December 1930, for example, he decreed that all official travel by any executive at the Reichsleitung had to be approved by his office at least three days prior to departure. See Reichsschatzmeister, "Bekanntgabe," 5 Dec. 1930, *Rdschr.*

84. There was no real reason to do so. Schwarz was an excellent administrator. Contemporary observers continued to be impressed by the "intricately developed" system of self-financing in the NSDAP, i.e., its independence of outside revenue sources for its day-to-day operations. See Oehme and Caro, *Kommt,* p. 91.

85. Reichsschatzmeister, "Rundschreiben" to all GL, 18 March 1931, in *Rdschr.;* and Anton Lingg, *Die Verwaltung der Nationalsozialistischen Deutschen Arbeiterpartei* (2d ed., Munich, 1940), p. 305. The Aid Fund was administered by Martin Bormann, who thus moved from the SA's administrative hierarchy to that of the party proper.

86. Reichsschatzmeister, "Rundschreiben" to all GL, 5 Dec. 1930, *Rdschr; VB,* 18/19 Jan. 1931.

87. Krebs, *Tendenzen,* p. 190; and Konstantin Hierl, *Im Dienst für Deutschland* (Heidelberg, 1954), p. 64.

88. Paul Schulz, "Bei Gregor Strasser," *VB,* 23 Jan. 1931.

Hierl had no real basis for imposing his authority on the affiliated organizations, since his own relationship to Hitler was no different from that of the other department heads at the Reichsleitung. Consequently the affiliated organizations quickly developed centralized bureaucracies of their own, headed by administrators who felt themselves to be agents of Hitler and who were accountable to no one but Hitler.[89] The party as a whole thus became a series of administratively and functionally autonomous feudal fiefs with their own vertical organizations arranged around the core of the vertical administration of the party proper.

This system lacked any real method of coordination among the various organizations attempting to channel the middle-class sympathizer into the party, but it had two obvious advantages: it prevented power blocs among the affiliates and it helped to isolate crises within the particular segment of the party in which they began.[90] There was also at least one grave disadvantage: the total public image presented by the various affiliates remained disunified and even contradictory. Since this would be politically counterproductive, Hitler created a new control office with a full vertical staff organization to insure that the totality of the public (not the internal administrative activities) image presented by the various organizations corresponded to the NSDAP's overall policy lines at any particular time. This was the Reich Propaganda Leadership (*Reichspropagandaleitung;* RPL), headed by Joseph Goebbels. There had been efforts to coordinate the party's propaganda activities on a national scale before, but not until 1931 did Goebbels obtain permission to establish staff positions at all levels of the party's organization.[91] At the Reich level, the RPL had both informational and control functions. It issued a monthly circular to its Gau executives de-

89. Hitler at least informally supported their claims by issuing orders directly to them rather than through Hierl. See Hitler's instructions to Schlemm, *VB,* 23 Jan. 1931.

90. Cf. the statement of the Berlin HJ leader during the SA crisis of September 1930: "The differences between the SA and the party in Berlin are of no interest to the HJ. The Berlin HJ remains as a united organization subject to my orders!! Basic principle . . . unchangeable loyalty to Adolf Hitler." HJ leader of Berlin, Brandenburg, and Ostmark to the subleaders in Berlin, 1 Sept. 1930, HA, roll 19, folder 362.

91. On the buildup of the staff organization see GL Brandenburg, "Gau-Propaganda Rundschreiben Nr. 2" [beg. of 1931], NA, T-580, roll 23, folder 205.

scribing, or rather interpreting, the political events of the past month and predicting major trends in the coming month. The circular was edited rather shrewdly to give the reader a sense of being on the inside of the political scene, particularly in its section dealing with the future plans of the party's political opponents. Actually, the lower staff officials merely received back an edited version of what they had earlier reported to the RPL. One of the major functions of the RPL's staff organization was to send complete statistical and descriptive reports on the propaganda activities of both the party and its opponents to Munich regularly. Originally compiled by each local propaganda leader, the material was reworked and synthesized at the various levels of the organization, so that only the Gau reports actually reached Goebbels.[92] The Reich Propaganda Leader in turn cast the raw data in the Gau reports into an often sarcastic but stylistically effective interpretation of Germany's present and future and sent them back to the Gaus.[93] The state offices then issued excerpts of the reports to the districts and even smaller excerpts went to the locals. Each month, then, the entire party propaganda apparatus received a unified political line from the RPL.

Goebbels had a more direct influence on the party's image through his actual control and appointment functions. The RPL had exclusive control over the appointment of Reich speakers.[94] Goebbels alone determined the subject of the various propaganda campaigns which formed the core of the NSDAP's propaganda activities. Once a campaign was determined, each level of the party's organization carried it through on the provincial or local level — even when the

92. Nevertheless, the RPL considered the local reports particularly important for its work. See GL Oberfranken, "1. Januar Rundschreiben der Gaupropaganda-leitung," 21 Jan. 1931, NA, T-580, roll 19, folder 199. For an example of a Gau report see GPL (i.e., Gaupropagandaleitung) Schleswig-Holstein to RPL, "Tätig-keitsbericht für Monat Januar 1931," 4 Feb. 1931, NA, T-580, roll 25, folder 207.

93. For examples of the national reports see the documents in HA, roll 54, folder 1290. In addition to Goebbels' information letters, Fritz Reinhardt, now head of the "Reichspropagandaleitung II," issued various statistical materials (votes on various bills in the Reichstag, etc.) to party speakers. See *VB*, 11 Feb. 1931.

94. This led to numerous complaints and a bitter paper war with some of the Gauleiters. See Kube to RL, 23 Dec. 1930, NA, T-580, roll 23, folder 205, for a Gauleiter's complaints about the RPL. The RPL also specified speaker's fees for the Reich speakers. See enclosure to "Gaubefehl 3 des Gaues Ostmark," 11 Jan. 1931, *ibid.*

national theme had little local relevance.[95] Some of Goebbels' powers foreshadowed his role as German press czar after 1933. His office issued instructions to the rapidly growing party press[96] not only on the general editorial policy to be followed, but also detailed orders on which German political figures could be attacked by the party press at particular times.[97]

The expansion of the affiliates and control offices like the RPL brought with it a corresponding growth of the Gau staff organizations, which in turn affected the position and function of the Gauleiter. The Gauleiter had entered the new era strengthened by the successes of September, and very few geographic or personnel changes followed in the wake of the triumph. The only major geographic changes occurred in western Germany. The Reichsleitung raised Düsseldorf and Essen to the status of Gaus, and divided Westphalia and Rhineland into two Gaus: Westphalia-North and Westphalia-South in the case of the former, Cologne-Aachen and Koblenz-Trier in the case of the latter. These were actually very logical changes, since the new Gaus corresponded to the electoral districts in these areas. The changes did not involve major personnel shifts; all of the new Gauleiters either had been Gauleiters previously or were prominent district leaders singled out for rapid promotion.[98] There was a notable shift of Gau seats in the party during the spring of

95. In late December the RPL decided on a national campaign against "Red Miscarriages of Justice" (see GL Gross-Berlin, Propaganda-Abteilung, "Ausserordentliches Propaganda Rundschreiben Nr. 20," 18 Dec. 1930, NA, T-580, roll 23, folder 205), and during the first Sunday in 1931 the locals held mass protest rallies. On the lack of success of such a campaign in a local area see Allen, *Seizure*, p. 43.

96. The NSDAP owned 46 newspapers in September 1930; a year later this number had grown to 72. In addition to the RPL's control over the paper's contents, the Eher publishing firm sought, whenever possible, to control the economic aspects of the provincial press as well. See Amann to Bouhler, 3 Feb. 1931, NA, T-580, roll 24, folder 206.

97. Staatspolizei Württemberg, "W. 22," 11 Dec. 1930, HA, roll 58, folder 1403.

98. The new Gauleiters of Düsseldorf and Essen, Friedrich Florian and Josef Terboven, were formerly district leaders of the same territory. Gustav Simon (Koblenz-Trier) and Helmut Meyer (Westphalia-North) were the only district leaders who had received a prominent place on the 1930 Reichstag candidate list. Grohé, the new Gauleiter of Cologne-Aachen, had been deputy Gauleiter under Ley. The only major dismissals were Emil Holtz in Brandenburg, Hinkler in Halle-Merseburg, and Weinreich in Hessen. For the complete list of new Gauleiters, see NSDAP, *NS-Jahrbuch 1931* (Munich, 1930), pp. 136–38.

1931; but this, too, was merely a reflection of the political success: it was only natural that a politically powerful organization should maintain its headquarters in the largest city of the Gau.

Nevertheless there were significant power shifts within the Gaus, but these were the result of the party's growth as a whole and the expansion of the affiliated organizations with proliferation of staff positions at the Gau level.[99] The Gauleiter personally had to oversee a mushrooming network of locals in his Gau.[100] All traces of local autonomy had vanished by now; the Gauleiter absolutely controlled the appointment of local and district leaders; and, once they were appointed, he accorded them the same derivative agent status that Adolf Hitler had bestowed upon him.[101] The locals' purpose and function was almost purely propagandistic and financial. They translated the party's centrally determined public image into an unending series of local rallies addressed to members of the various social and economic groups whose support and membership applications the party hoped to attract.[102] Equally important was their function as the receiving ends of the membership and money funnels. In effect, their organizational *raison d'être* was purely derivative; the locals existed only to serve the higher echelons of the party, not themselves.[103] On the whole, the locals were content to carry out the steady flow of orders that poured from the various offices above them. Despite numerous complaints, particularly about the expensive propaganda materials that had to be bought and the high mem-

99. The Gau organization of Baden at the end of 1930 consisted of the following offices: organization, propaganda, NSBO, treasurer, business manager, intelligence (evaluating the activities of political opponents), communal affairs, disabled veterans affairs, employment office, legal aid, tax consultant, social insurance advisor, union advisor, advisor on labor law, Gau librarian, finance committee, auditor, Uschla, office of the Landtag faction, and business manager of the Gau press. See Wagner to Strasser, "Organisation der Gauleitung Baden," 30 Dec. 1930, HA, roll 19, folder 199.

100. Schäfer, *NSDAP*, p. 19, reports a percentage increase in the number of locals of about 100% from a numerical base of 4964 in 1930.

101. GL Ostmark, "Gaubefehl 3 des Gaues Ostmark," 11 Jan. 1931, NA, T-580, roll 23, folder 205; and Kube to Kasche, 21 Nov. 1930, HA, roll 10, folder 206.

102. GL Oberfranken, "Rundschreiben Nr. 31," 31 Dec. 1930, NA, T-580, roll 19, folder 199.

103. GL Ostmark, "Gaubefehl 4 des Gaues Ostmark," 5 March 1931, NA, T-580, roll 23, folder 205; and GL Oberfranken, "Rundschreiben Nr. 31," 31 Dec. 1930, NA, T-580, roll 19, folder 199.

bership application fees,[104] the locals did their best to collect dues, attract new members, and further totalize ones already won over.[105]

The relations between the individual Gauleiter and his staff at the Gau office were often less satisfactory after the September triumphs. Since the growth of the affiliates was one test of organizational-political success for the Gauleiters,[106] they had to establish these organizations as rapidly as possible. At the same time the control and coordination of the far-flung party activities became increasingly difficult and time-consuming.[107] Though theoretically in charge of all executives at the Gau level, the Gauleiter's task was particularly difficult since both he and the heads of the affiliate organizations in Munich had the same relationship to Hitler. The head of an affiliate organization in the Gau thus owed a dual allegiance to two derivative agents: to the Gauleiter as Hitler's agent for that particular geographic area of Germany and to his superior in Munich as Hitler's agent for a specific area of party activity.[108]

The resulting difficulties and frictions soon led many of the Gauleiters to wonder if the expansion of their bureaucracies was not a mixed blessing. True, they now headed a vastly larger staff of subordinates, and the Reichsleitung did permit (actually ordered) them to institute some measures to tighten disciplinary control over their staffs. The executives of each Gauleitung now constituted their own party local, the section Gauleitung, headed by the Gauleiter. As totalized members of the NSDAP, the provincial executives served

104. GL Ostpreussen, "Monatliches Rundschreiben der Gaupropaganda-Leitung," 29 Dec. 1930, NA, T-580, roll 24, folder 206; and Gau München-Oberbayern, Bzl. Mühldorf, "Protokoll über die . . . am 19.10.30 in Mühldorf stattgefundene Besprechung der Ortsgruppenführer und Zellenleiter," n.d., HA, roll 8, folder 176.

105. See, for example, the documents in HA, roll 8, folder 176; and GL Gross-Berlin, Sektion Prenzlauer Berg, *Mitteilungsblatt* (No. 22, Nov. 1930), HA, roll 19, folder 362.

106. The *VB,* 1 Oct. 1930, noted that Hessen-Nassau-Nord showed better election results than Hessen-Nassau-Süd because the former had been more intensively worked over.

107. All of the Gauleiters were salaried executives now. Even the wealthier ones who had served without pay before had to resign because they did not have the time to run the complex Gau offices. This was the reason for the resignation of Corswant in Pomerania. See Hitler's "Anordnung," 1 April 1931, and Corswant to Hitler, 4 March 1931, NA, T-580, roll 24, folder 206. See also the reasons for Reinhardt's resignation as Gauleiter of Oberbayern in *VB,* 7 Nov. 1930.

108. For the pressures and counterpressures on a Gau propaganda leader see GL Schleswig-Holstein Prop.-Abt. to all district leaders, local leaders, and Gau speakers, 15 Jan. 1931, NA, T-580, roll 25, folder 207.

as direct subordinates of the Gauleiter.[109] The Gauleiter also had a full arsenal of bureaucratic powers; for example, all correspondence between the affiliate staffs and their superiors at the Reichsleitung had to be channeled through his office.[110] The various powers could not, however, prevent an erosion of the Gauleiter's prestige and power in the party. A major difficulty was the Gauleiters' administrative subordination to Bouhler or Strasser. Although the latter were in theory only an institutionalized Hitler, they were in an organizational-administrative sense the equal of the affiliate chiefs at the Reich level. As a result officials like Darré and Goebbels often acted as though the Gauleiter were administratively subordinate to all of the division heads in Munich, not merely to Bouhler and Strasser.[111] This feeling in turn communicated itself to the chief affiliate officials at the Gau level (who were the direct subordinates of their division superiors at the Reichsleitung) so that they began to treat the Gauleiters as equals and associates rather than as superiors. An equally serious problem was the sociopolitical gulf that separated many of the old Gauleiters from the new wave of technocrats that flooded into the affiliate staffs and threatened to inundate the older stock of party officials.[112] There was an understandable jealousy of the *Septemberlinge*,[113] whose careers in the affiliated organizations starved for staff officials seemed to advance with amazing rapidity.[114]

109. See GL Magdeburg-Anhalt to RL, Organisations-Abteilung I, 31 March 1931, NA, T-580, roll 23, folder 204. It will be recalled that the establishment of such sections had been specifically prohibited in 1926. See above, p. 124.

110. See Adolf Wagner (GL of München-Oberbayern) to heads of the departments at the RL, 23 Nov. 1931, NA, T-580, roll 24, folder 206. See also *VB*, 10 Jan. 1931.

111. As usual, the sharpest complaints came from Kube, who demanded that the RPL cease threatening Gauleiters. See Kube to [RPL?], NA, T-580, roll 23, folder 205.

112. On the differences in social origins of the "propagandists" and "administrators" see Daniel Lerner, *et al.*, "The Nazi Elite," in *World Revolutionary Elites*, ed. Harold D. Lasswell and Daniel Lerner (Cambridge, Mass., 1965), p. 201.

113. See Franz Petri, "Die Geschichte der SA in Cottbus N.[ieder] L.[ausitz]" (typescript, 1936), HA, roll 6, folder149. *Septemberlinge* is a play on the German word *Pfefferlinge*, a popular type of mushroom.

114. On the staff needs of the affiliates see GL Ostmark, "Gaubefehl 11 des Gaus Ostmark," 2 Sept. 1931, NA, T-580, roll 23, folder 205. The following may serve as an example of the career opportunities in the affiliates. Hermann Gmelin had apparently been local leader in Landsberg for some years (he visited Hitler in prison in 1924) and still occupied this post in August 1930. By late September, however, he had become district leader of the a.A. See his letters in "Briefe," dated Aug. 1930, 1 Sept. 1930, and 23 Sept. 1930.

As so often before, the Gauleiters grumbled and complained, but the SA acted. The SA, for the most part, had never wholeheartedly supported the rural-nationalist plan, and some units staged joint rallies with the Communists and planned campaigns to win over the KDP members well into 1929 and 1930.[115] Yet on its brawny fists and strong legs rested the success of the party's campaign to capture the middle classes. The SA men had to glue posters, make follow-up visits to prospective members, and, above all, guard the unending series of rallies.[116] It was therefore understandable that SA units in some areas of Germany broke out in open rebellion against the civilian leadership.

The most serious instances of open defiance took place in Berlin, a Gau whose SA had always had a strong tradition of violence and a large number of proletarian members. In July 1930 Otto Strasser publicly broke with Hitler and the NSDAP. This was by no means an SA revolt — unlike his brother, Otto Strasser was not a popular figure in the party and he had no organizational ability — but Strasser did articulate many of the SA's complaints about the party's policies. He advocated the opening to the left, an alliance with Russia, and an opposition to all legislative and electoral activities.[117] In addition, Strasser's ideas (though not necessarily his decision to break with Hitler) had the support of some major figures in the party, including two Gauleiters.[118] In the final showdown, however, no major leader

115. Arno Scholz, *Nullvier—ein Jahrgang zwischen den Fronten* (Berlin, 1962), pp. 126–27, describes a rally in Berlin (1929) in which both Goebbels and Heinz Neumann spoke and the SA and the RFB served jointly as ushers. See also "Appell der SA, Sturm 3 . . . am 17.1.30,: PND Nr. 687," n.d., HA, roll 73, folder 1552. *Vorwärts*, 2 Sept. 1930, also commented on the large number of people at an SA rally in Berlin who were familiar figures at RFB rallies.

116. See Allen, *Seizure*, pp. 73–74, for the use which a small local made of the SA.

117. Otto Strasser, *Aufbau des Deutschen Sozialismus* (2d ed.; Prague, 1936), Appendix "Anlass der Trennung."

118. Karl O. Paetel, *Versuchung oder Chance* (Göttingen, 1965), p. 211, writes that Reventlow, Koch, and Hildebrandt all promised Strasser that they would join his revolt against the NSDAP. The crisis was most severe in Mecklenburg. Here Hildebrandt had asked for a six months leave of absence in May 1930 (*VB*, 4/5 May 1930), and the Gauleiter pro tem had some difficulty clearing his name in July. See Albrecht (GL pro tem of Mecklenburg) to RL, 12 July 1930, NA, T-580, roll 23, folder 205.

followed Strasser's rebellion. Hitler expelled him from the NSDAP, and there were no major repercussions.

On the other hand, once outside the party, Strasser conducted a bitter and vigorous campaign against the party's middle-class emphases, and it is quite possible that his activities had a catalytic effect on the outbreak of open mutiny in the Berlin SA units which followed Pfeffer's resignation as Osaf. There is no evidence of actual cooperation between Pfeffer and Strasser, but Pfeffer, too, became increasingly dissatisfied with Hitler's leadership in the summer of 1930. Hitler obviously wanted to curb the SA's organizational autonomy even further,[119] while Pfeffer demanded some safe Reichstag seats to enable SA leaders to travel more freely, carrying the Osaf's writ into all corners of the Reich. It was on this last issue that Pfeffer and Hitler came to the final parting of the ways. Hitler either refused to allow SA leaders to become members of the Reichstag, or else turned down Pfeffer's demand that he, Pfeffer, should control the votes of the SA deputies.[120] In either case, Pfeffer finally withdrew his request and even lamely attempted to explain why the failure to have SA members in the Reichstag was best for the organization.[121] For Hitler the matter seems to have ended there, but Pfeffer felt the SA had a right to expect "other visible and materially [that is, financially] noticeable [proof] that the SA was benefitting [from the successes of the party]."[122] He did not specify what proof he had in mind, but it appears that in addition to wanting more money, he demanded more freedom to disintegrate the Reichswehr and to train the SA as the core of the new German mass army.[123] Since Hitler was particularly unwilling to em-

119. PD Mü., "Münch. Lagebericht Nr. 92 v. 9.7.30 [excerpt]," n.d., HA, roll 70, folder 1510.

120. Buch claimed the latter version was true. See Buch to Pfeffer, 13 Sept. 1930, HA, roll 56, folder 1374. The letter bears the marginalia "not sent."

121. Osaf, "SAF und Mandat" (strictly confidential), 2 Aug. 1930 in Jochmann, *Nationalsozialismus*, pp. 306–07. See also Heinrich Bennecke, *Hitler und die SA* (Munich, 1962), pp. 147–48.

122. Pfeffer to all SAF to Brigadeführer (incl.) (confidential), 29 Aug. 1930, HA, roll 73, folder 1549.

123. These charges are contained in the letter by Buch to Pfeffer, 13 Sept. 1930, HA, roll 56, folder 1374. See also Osaf-Stellvertreter Süd, "SABE (Anleitung für die Winterarbeit)," Nov. 1930, HA, roll 73, folder 1549. Corroboration of Buch's charges regarding the Reichswehr can be found in "Niederschrift des Landgerichtdirektor a.D. Hugo Braune, 1955," in Vogelsang, *Reichswehr,* doc. 7, p. 417.

bark on a campaign of subversion against the Reichswehr, Pfeffer had no choice but to resign his position.[124]

Pfeffer's demands and his impending resignation had serious repercussions in Berlin. In late August (before Pfeffer had actually resigned), the SA leader in Berlin and east Germany, Walter Stennes, asked Goebbels for more financial support for the SA. The Berlin Gauleiter refused, and the SA went on strike; that is, it refused to protect the party's rallies.[125] Since this in effect paralyzed the NSDAP's election campaign in Berlin, Hitler rushed to the capital to confront his rebellious SA men personally. As so often before, the personal appearance of the myth-person quickly brought the mutineers back into the fold. His arrival in the *Kriegervereinshaus* (veterans' club house) was greeted "with a noise volume that was unusual even for National Socialist rallies." In his actual speech he said little about the SA's grievances, because he did not have to: he knew that a tremendous ovation would follow his announcement that as of September 1, he personally would be the new Osaf.[126] After this declaration, substantive questions could wait until after the election, when Schwarz issued new directives to ease the SA's financial situation.[127]

Despite his dramatic announcement, Hitler had neither the time nor the inclination to lead both the party and the SA personally. Instead, he left the SA virtually without effective leadership under the caretaker administration of Otto Wagener, who kept the post of chief of staff which he had occupied under Pfeffer since early 1930.[128] The focus of day-to-day authority in the SA shifted from the Osaf to the Osaf-deputies, whose power Hitler did not curb despite the pleas of the Gauleiters.[129]

124. Pfeffer to all SAF . . . . In his letter the Osaf asked his subordinates not to follow his example, so as not to disrupt the NSDAP's election campaign.

125. PD Berlin to PD Mü, 16 Sept. 1930, HA, roll 73, folder 1551.

126. PD Berlin to PD Mü, 19 Sept. 1930, *ibid.*

127. Hitler authorized more money for the SA in early September, but Schwarz did not issue the necessary administrative directive until October. As a result "several" Gauleiters still refused to give additional funds to the SA units in late November. See Schwarz to all GL, 10 Oct. and 5 Dec. 1930, in *Rdschr.*

128. PD Mü, Ref. VI/d, "Vormerkung," 10 March 1930. Wagener was born in 1888 and was a "political unknown" at the time of his appointment as chief of staff.

129. Bennecke, *Hitler*, pp. 142 and 152–53. He did, however, curb their public displays of authority. Hitler prohibited an SA demonstration for units from all of eastern Germany which Stennes had planned for late September. See *VB*, 27 Sept. 1930.

By the end of the year, an uneasy quiet had settled over the SA.[130] The basic grievances of many SA men remained, but Hitler had in the meantime filled the leadership vacuum at the top. At the end of November, he called a staff conference to announce his choice for a new chief of staff: Ernst Röhm. Röhm offered a number of advantages for Hitler.[131] He was hardly an unknown quantity in the party. The former captain had a reputation as an able staff officer; he had led the SA in the Putsch and had kept in touch with the party after his return from Bolivia in 1928. The *VB* commented approvingly on his political appearances, and his memoirs appeared under the imprint of the party publishing house. Equally important, Röhm's relations with the Reichswehr were excellent. After his return from South America he had quickly reestablished his contacts with General Schleicher,[132] so that his appointment as chief of staff would be considered by the Reichswehr as a gesture of conciliation.

Hitler apparently had offered Röhm the post of chief of staff immediately after Pfeffer's resignation, but Röhm was less than eager to accept, so that the formal announcement was delayed until the beginning of the new year.[133] Röhm agreed with Hitler (at least at this time) that the SA should not attempt to be a proto-army, but he apparently hesitated to accept the position as *de facto* head of the SA in view of the substantially reduced powers of the post. Both the Quartermaster Service and the Aid Fund[134] were now firmly under the jurisdiction of Schwarz. The Gau SA leaders had to submit expense accounts to the Gauleiters.[135] The SS membership was

130. Ullrich (Inspector-General of the SA), "B.B. Nr. 152/30," 26 Nov. 1930, HA, roll 72, folder 1545.

131. "Führerbesprechung der SA am 29. und 30. 11.30 in München, PND Nr. 717," HA, roll 73, folder 1552. Hitler obviously did not consider the personal problems that Röhm's appointment raised for many party leaders: Röhm's homosexuality was well known by this time, and Strasser in the letter quoted above significantly noted that he welcomed Röhm's appointment for professional *(sachliche)* reasons, i.e., not for personal reasons.

132. Vogelsang, *Reichswehr*, p. 117 n439; Bennecke, *Hitler*, p. 159.

133. *VB*, 1/2 Jan. 1931.

134. The Aid Fund now involved only Bormann's offices in Munich and the local Aid Fund treasurer. The SA had no administrative functions whatever. See Bormann to all Ortsgruppenleiter and Stützpunktleiter, 10 Nov. 1930, HA, roll 8, folder 176.

135. Since this directive led to considerable friction between some Gauleiters and their SA leaders, it was later amended to have the SA leaders report to Röhm, and Schwarz then audited Röhm's books. See Reichsschatzmeister to all GL, 24 Feb. 1932 in *Rdschr.*

augmented at the expense of the SA,[136] and the Uschla now handled
SA cases as well as those of the party.[137] On the other hand, Hitler
was willing to give Röhm a great deal of autonomy to structure the
SA internally as he saw fit, and it was this presumably which led
Röhm to accept command of what was at the beginning of the
year a force of some sixty thousand men.

Röhm's plans centered on a far-reaching internal centralization
and militarization of the SA,[138] but he had no ambitions to interfere
in the political decision-making process of the party, nor was he
anxious to create a public image of the SA, other than as the party's
disciplined marching unit.[139] Once appointed he named many of
his old associates from 1923[140] to staff positions in Munich and began
to restore the authority of the center. He broke up some of the massive power concentrations in the states,[141] though primarily he used
the office of SA Inspector General to subordinate the SA to his own
direction. The Inspector General, von Ullrich, another retired officer,
and his staff traveled constantly, reporting on the morale, equipment,
and degree of obedience to Röhm's directives among the SA units.[142]

Röhm also made determined efforts to ease the tensions that continued to exist between the SA and the party organization. Many
of his measures were almost purely image-oriented. To stimulate
feelings of loyalty between party and SA, the party functionaries
were encouraged to enroll in new SA reserve units; Röhm also
bestowed a number of titles of high rank on leading executives
at the Reichsleitung.[143] Nevertheless, the perennial problems of

136. Osaf, "SA-Befehl Nr. 1 (Gleichzeitig für SS) . . . ." 16 Jan. 1931, HA, roll
73, folder 1549.

137. Bouhler to GL Brandenburg, 3 Jan. 1931, NA, T-580, roll 23, folder 205.
Stennes was particularly unhappy about this decision. See Stennes to Röhm, 28
Feb. 1931. HA, roll 17, folder 325.

138. He dropped Pfeffer's intricate abbreviation system and renamed some of
the SA's units.

139. Röhm prohibited SA leaders from serving simultaneously as party speakers.
See Osaf, "SA Befehl 5," 27 Feb. 1931, HA, roll 16, folder 306.

140. Bennecke, *Hitler*, p. 160.

141. Osaf, "Betriff: Gliederung der SA," 25 Jan. 1931, HA, roll 16, folder 306.

142. Osaf, "Betr.: Generalinspektion I Nr. 118/31," 10 Feb. 1931, HA, roll 89,
folder 1849.

143. Johann K. von Engelbrechten, *Eine braune Armee entsteht* (Munich, 1937),
p. 158; and the list of titles and recipients in HA, roll 73, folder 1549.

money,[144] administrative independence, and programmatic emphases remained. Indeed, the old issues were now joined by complaints about Röhm's homosexuality from some of the party functionaries[145] and increased grumbles about the SS' elite status in the ranks of the SA. Hitler's admonition to the SA and SS to conduct a "noble rivalry" among themselves fell on deaf ears, particularly since the SS had cultivated its own image as loyal praetorians (in contrast to the SA) during the Pfeffer crisis.[146]

Underlying all the substantive issues and personal rivalries was a fundamental disagreement over the future of the NSDAP. For the political leadership, the effort to indoctrinate the middle classes brought the party a major step closer to power; major elements in the SA were convinced that it was a step in the wrong direction,[147] and that if only for this reason the SA should control the future of Germany.[148] Despite the low morale in some units[149] and some actual mutinies on the local level, the SA's complaints did not become dangerous to Hitler and the party's political leadership until they

144. The money problem had theoretically been settled by a circular of Schwarz to all GL, 10 Oct. 1930, in *Rdschr.*, but it is indicative of the mutual mistrust between SA and party that the SA received the right in early January 1931 to have a representative physically present when the profits from rallies were counted. See GL Ostmark, "Gaubefehl 1 des Gaues Ostmark," 7 Jan. 1931, NA, T-580, roll 23, folder 205. See also Schwarz to all GL, 21 Feb. 1931 in *Rdschr.*

145. This brought forth Hitler's famous defense that the NSDAP was "not a school to educate daughters of the upper classes." See Osaf, "Erlass Nr. 1," 3 Feb. 1931, HA, roll 73, folder 1549.

146. PD Mü, "Appell der SS-Standarte München-Oberbayern am 11.3.31 . . . PND Nr. 727," and "Besprechung der SS-Führer der NSDAP am 8.12.30 . . . PND Nr. 718," n.d., HA, roll 73, folder 1547.

147. Cf. the statement of a later district attorney in Hamburg who was close to the SA in 1931: "no one at that time [May 1931] expected the national revolution to be bloodless." See Oberstaatsanwalt Renter to Justizrat Keim, 28 Nov. 1933, HA, roll B, folder 80.

148. Cf. a statement in the 3 Jan. 1931 issue of the *Schlesischer Beobachter*: "The future? It rests in the fists of the SA." HA, roll 24A, folder 1759.

149. There can be no doubt that the political street warfare was becoming increasingly bitter in 1931 (Engelbrechten, *Braune Armee*, pp. 147 ff.) and that the SA quite literally paid with its blood so that the martyr image of the party as a whole could be maintained. On suggested measures to make "dying for the movement virtually desirable," see Heines to Röhm, 9 Feb. 1931, HA, roll 77, folder 1565. Röhm in turn formalized most of these suggestions in his "Verordnung I Nr. 255/31," 20 Feb. 1931, *ibid.*

were championed by the one major power factor still left from the Pfeffer era, the Osaf deputies. These officials, handpicked by Pfeffer, surrounded by large staffs with territorial jurisdictions extending over several Gaus, grew increasingly dissatisfied with the NSDAP's policies and Röhm's unwillingness to oppose them.[150]

The feelings of mutual bitterness between party and SA leaders had always been particularly pronounced in the east,[151] and in the spring of 1931 the conflict of Hitler's myth with the older nation-myth aggravated them considerably. The eastern provinces were the areas of Germany most exposed to potential Polish attacks, and the SA units there had always participated in Reichswehr training courses designed to prepare them for use in repelling a Polish invasion if necessary. Walter Stennes, the Osaf Deputy East, approved of the cooperation, presumably both for patriotic reasons and because it gave the SA an opportunity to enlarge its contacts with the Reichswehr. Hitler, on the other hand, prohibited this form of Reichswehr–SA cooperation for narrow political reasons. He felt a successful Polish attack would automatically increase the National Socialist representation in the Reichstag by eighty or one hundred deputies.[152] In view of this open clash of nationalism and Hitler's own myth, it comes as no surprise to find that relations between the party and the SA leadership in the east were near the breaking point at the beginning of March.[153]

The Polish issue was actually only one manifestation of a widening rift between Stennes and Hitler. In the whole controversy, Hitler's blatant equation of his own political advantage and Germany's national future is clearly apparent, but it is somewhat more difficult to reconstruct Stennes' wider aims. He finally came to favor a thoroughly militarized, completely autonomous and largely non-political SA,[154] but his break with Hitler was not an easy decision.

150. The dissatisfaction was widespread. As late as January 1931 the Osaf Deputies Middle, South, and West had showed the antiparty attitude of Osaf Deputy East. See Vogelsang, *Reichswehr,* p. 120.

151. For Kube's assessment of Stennes in 1928 see Kube to Kasche, 19 Oct. 1928, HA, roll 9, folder 200.

152. Vogelsang, *Reichswehr,* pp. 118 and 118 n441. Stennes clearly disagreed with Pfeffer on the issue of Reichswehr–SA relations, and this may have been the major reason why, in spite of his support for the Berlin rebels, he was not dismissed along with Pfeffer.

153. See Fobke to Ullrich, 3 March 1931, HA, roll 44, folder 900.

154. Stennes established a leadership school for his command in late 1930. The

He and his staff seem to have proceeded by stages from generalized complaints to specific attacks on the Reichsleitung and certain political leaders, until, in the end, they disengaged themselves from the Hitler myth by consciously drawing a distinction between Hitler the person and National Socialism as a political program.[155]

The Stennes rebellion was a long-gathering storm cloud, though it burst with dramatic suddenness. On March 28, the Brüning government issued an emergency decree to curb the excesses of political warfare in Germany. Essentially, it provided that all political rallies had to be approved by the police twenty four hours before they were to take place. Hitler immediately ordered all party officials and agencies to obey the letter of the law. Simultaneously Göring addressed a mass rally in Berlin appealing to the SA to trust in Hitler and to Hindenburg to dismiss Brüning and form a National Socialist government.[156] Stennes refused to trust Hitler. He denounced both the Brüning decree and Hitler's decision to obey it. Then he and his staff met to plan the next move, if as expected, Hitler expelled Stennes for insubordination.[157]

When the expulsion notice arrived, Stennes promptly retaliated by dismissing the political leadership in Berlin and placing both party and SA under his own control.[158] But Stennes' triumph was short-lived. While virtually all members of his own staff supported his

curriculum consisted almost entirely of SA-oriented subjects (e.g., command language, channels of authority, military drill) with very little "political education." See "Auszug aus den Mitteilungen Nr. 23 vom 1.12.30 des Polizeipräsidiums Berlin," HA, roll 73, folder 1551.

155. On the progress of Stennes' rebellion see Stennes to Röhm, 28 Feb. 1931, HA, roll 17, folder 325; Conti (at this time head of the SA medical corps in the east) to Osaf, 8 Sept. 1930, *ibid.*; and Adolf Hitler, "Hitlers Abrechnung mit den Rebellen," *VB*, 4 Apr. 1931.

156. *VB*, 30 Mar. and 1 Apr. 1931.

157. Stennes' staff conference took place from midnight to 3 A.M. on the morning of April 1. His expulsion was expected to arrive about noon on the same day. See SS-Oberführer Ost to Röhm, 1 April 1931, HA, roll 17, folder 325. Throughout the crisis the SS once again demonstrated its unfailing loyalty to Hitler.

158. [Stennes' group], "National-Sozialisten Berlins!" *ibid.* Goebbels seems to have repeated his coup at Bamberg: he feigned sympathy with Stennes' aims, encouraged Stennes to make some anti-Hitler remarks, and then rushed to Weimar to report these to Hitler. Krebs, *Tendenzen*, p. 166–67. It is significant that only after he broke completely with Hitler did Stennes advocate the actual subordination of the political wing of his movement to the military side. See NS-Kampfbewegung Deutschlands, Reichsführung (Stennes' new organization after he had been expelled from the NSDAP), "Organisationsbefehl Nr. 1," n.d., HA, roll 17, folder 325.

moves and there were flickering sympathy protests in other SA units as well, Stennes had no success in disengaging any significant number of SA members from the Hitler myth-person.[159] In large part, his failure may have been due to Hitler's particularly lavish use of his myth-image in combatting Stennes' revolt. When it came, Hitler's reaction was swift and total; he convinced himself that Stennes was a paid agent of the negative set factor in his mythical version of reality[160] and immediately put his own person in the center of the controversy. He described his relationship to the SA and SS in pseudomystical terms: "I am the SA and the SS and you [the members] are members of the SA and SS as I am within you in the SA and SS."[161] Hitler separated himself from the institutions of the party completely in the first days after the revolt. All SA leaders were required to submit loyalty declarations to Hitler personally,[162] and Hitler's VB article justifying his actions contained his name or "I" 133 times.[163]

The personalized Hitler made way very soon for the institutionalized Hitler who conducted a purge of the SA organization in the east. The operation was headed by Göring (significantly, Röhm did not conduct the purge), who received the temporary title of Higher Political Commissar East (Politischer Kommissar Oberost) but the actual work was done by the political organization. All SA members were temporarily stripped of their SA membership and treated simply as party members. As such, using the Uschla system, they could be

159. Conti later described himself as the only one among Stennes' staff who opposed Stennes' aims. See Conti to Loeper, 14 June 1932. HA, roll 29, folder 546. See also "Aufruf an die Hamburger SA!" 25 April 1931, Jochmann, Nationalsozialismus, p. 340; Kremser (SA-Oberführer in Silesia) to all Standartenführer, Sturmbannführer, und Sturmführer, 2 April 1931, HA, roll 77, folder 1565; and Görlitz and Quint, Hitler, p. 312.

160. In 1932, Stennes sued Hitler and other party officials for libel after the Angriff had printed a story charging Stennes with operating as a police spy in the NSDAP. Hitler testified under oath that "I could only come to the conclusion that if anyone opposed me or my movement, he must have been a paid agent." See "Der Prozess Hitler–Stennes," Bayerischer Kurier, 18 Jan. 1932.

161. Hitler's Order of the Day as quoted in Münchener Post, 11/12 Apr. 1931.

162. VB, 4 Apr. 1931. "Mountains of loyalty telegrams," reported the VB, 5/6/7 Apr. 1931.

163. Hitler, "Hitlers Abrechnung," VB, 4 Apr. 1931. The figure of 133 "Adolf Hitlers" was counted by F.Z., 9 Apr. 1931.

expelled from the party by any political leader (from local on up, though the expulsion had to be confirmed through channels by Göring and Hitler.[164]

The SA suffered most directly in the east, but the organization as a whole also paid a heavy price for Stennes' actions. Schwarz apparently decreed substantial cuts in the SA budget.[165] In addition, the SA could not accept new members after July 1, while the SS engaged in an almost frantic drive for members.[166] The most severe restriction, however, was Röhm's inability to control the appointment of SA leaders. Hitler created a new office at the Reichsleitung, that of the personnel manager of the party, and named to head it Wilhelm Loeper, the Gauleiter of Halle-Merseburg and an early and bitter enemy of Stennes.[167] Loeper was given full powers to recommend (that is, screen) all appointments for Gauleiter, deputy Gauleiter, and state SA leader.[168] Thus, the major effect of the purge was less quantitative than qualitative: very few SA members were expelled from the party, and most of the SA leaders were confirmed in their positions, but there is no doubt that the political leadership and particularly the Gauleiters (and Loeper represented this group) gained significantly in power and prestige.[169] At least for the moment, the long-standing war between SA and party had a clear victor.[170]

Despite its swift collapse, the Stennes revolt sent a major shock wave through the NSDAP. The Reichsleitung apparently realized that

164. Kube to district leaders in Gau Ostmark, 9 April 1931, HA, roll 53, folder 1240; and Politischer Kommissar Oberost, "Anordnung III," 17 April 1931, HA, roll 17, folder 325.

165. NSDAP, SA, *Verordnungsblatt*, I (20 April 1931); and Osaf, "Stabsbefehl" and "Verfügung," 9 June 1931, HA, roll 16, folder 306.

166. SA-Gruf West-Nord-West, "Besondere Anordnungen," 30 May 1931, HA, roll 73, folder 1549; and Reichsführer-SS, "SS-Befehl-D-Nr. 34," 20 June 1931; and SA-Gauführer Ostland to Osaf, 31 Aug. 1931, HA, roll 72, folder 1545.

167. See Loeper to RL, 26 Sept. 1930, NA, T-580, roll 23, folder 204.

168. For additional discussion of the function of the personnel office, see below, p. 267.

169. See GL Ostmark, "Gaubefehl 5 des Gaues Ostmark," 7 April 1931, NA, T-580, roll 23, folder 205; and Hitler's instructions to Goebbels, *VB*, 3 Apr. 1931.

170. Hitler's emphasis on his personal, as distinct from his institutional, image in the party ended as abruptly as it had begun. In early June Hess announced that sending letters to Hitler marked "personal" was futile: all of Hitler's letters were opened by his secretariat, i.e., Hess. See *VOBl* (No. 1; 1 June 1931), p. 1.

the crisis in Berlin had an implication for the party as a whole. The party, through its affiliate organizations, had been moving too rapidly. In the hope of a swift rise to power, the NSDAP had been ingesting members and sympathizers without safeguarding the movement's organizational cohesion. By April it was clear, however, that the Weimar Republic was not yet in its death throes, while the NSDAP under the impact of the Stennes crisis discovered additional, though less explosive, weak spots within its organization. The women's auxiliary bordered on organizational chaos; the Gauleiter of Swabia wanted to consolidate his organization and eliminate "driftwood" from his membership.[171] In short, during the summer months the NSDAP needed to "breathe deeply," as Goebbels put it, before setting out to conquer again.[172]

The period of consolidation began with a Gauleiter conference in late April. The party's leaders apparently discussed internal integration measures on a broad front from new members to editorial policies of the provincial press, though the SA problem clearly dominated the discussions.[173] Unlike the settlements after previous SA crises, the Reichsleitung did not attempt to deal with the SA alone, but integrated the SA issue into a broad spectrum of reforms. The focal point of the program of consolidation was the local party organization, that is, the level at which the theoretical divisions of labor at the top were only rudimentarily reflected and where the institutional functions between various party wings automatically became personal animosities. To eliminate a major cause of SA complaints — the failure of local leaders to enroll all party members in the Aid Fund — Bormann and Schwarz began a massive campaign of appeals persuading local leaders to pressure their members into enrolling. The Reichsleitung applied emphasis to its appeals by holding local leaders personally responsible for injuries an SA man might suffer through the bureaucratic negligence of the leader.[174] At the

171. Conti to Goebbels, 3 June 1931, NA, T-580, roll 34, folder 230; and GL Schwaben, "Rundschreiben Nr. 7 des Gauleiters," 25 June 1931, NA, T-580, roll 26, folder 209.

172. Goebbels all but admitted the party's abstinence from agitation in the summer of 1931 in his *Angriff* editorials of 1 May and 1 Sept. 1931, in *Wetterleuchten*, pp. 139–40 and 197–98.

173. No detailed report of the meeting seems to have survived. This account is based on the *VB* reports of 24 and 29 April 1931.

174. *VOBl* (No. 2; 15 June 1931), pp. 1 and 5.

same time the Reichsleitung attempted to integrate the affiliate and membership activities at the local level after it realized that the locals had lagged far behind the rapid buildup of staff structure at the Gau level.[175] Local newssheets appeared, and the local leaders strengthened their subdivisions to insure that "there exists no party member who does not in some way work for the party." [176]

While the Reichsleitung encouraged the locals to develop a means of heightening the sense of solidarity among their members, it also removed the last vestiges of their right to make political decisions. Until now, the local leader had always attached his recommendation to new membership applications before sending them to the Gau, but in the future the locals were merely to forward them; only the Gau could make a political judgment.[177] Finally, to define the locals' sphere of activity still further, the Reichsleitung began to issue a biweekly gazette, the *Verordnungsblatt* and a new set of very detailed regulations *(Dienstanweisung)* covering all facets of the locals' reportorial, financial, and propagandistic duties.[178] While the new *Dienstanweisung* was an essentially permanent set of bureaucratic instructions, the *Verordnungsblatt* met the needs of the moment. Issued biweekly, the publication combined the directives and instructions issued by the various segments of the Reichsleitung into a compendium of guidelines for the lower party organizations. Together the two publications signaled the culmination of a series of developments which progressively removed any political decision-making powers from the locals and reduced them to the status of Gau field offices, free to devote all of their time to integrating sympathizers, totalizing the party membership, and collecting money.

What vestiges of political significance the locals lost were largely transferred to the districts. During the period of consolidation the districts developed into the lowest party echelon that had a fully developed staff system. The locals merely executed the orders received from above, but the districts also planned and coordinated

175. For an exception to this rule see Goebbels' praise of GL Röver in Oldenburg, *Angriff*, 7 May 1931, in *Wetterleuchten*, p. 148.

176. The first issue of the local newssheet in Thalburg appeared in August. See Allen, *Seizure*, p. 66. On the development of local subdivisions see Sektion Braunsfelde (Stettin) to all Zellenobleute, 21 July 1931, HA, roll 44, folder 900.

177. *VOBl* (No. 1; 1 June 1931), p. 2.

178. RL, *Dienstanweisung für Ortsgruppen und Stützpunkte der NSDAP* (Munich, 1931).

the efforts of the various locals in their geographic areas.[179] By July, much of the work of establishing staff positions in the districts had been completed, and districts throughout Germany staged regional congresses to inaugurate the district staff officials into their work.[180]

Until the end of the summer, the Reichsleitung bypassed the Gaus in its efforts to consolidate the party, and jumped instead, so to speak, from the districts to the Reich level. At this highest echelon of the party's structure, the focal point of the reforms was the SA. In the immediate aftermath of the Stennes revolt, Röhm had already demolished what was left of Pfeffer's organizational structure. He abolished the position of Osaf deputy and established smaller regional commands, though these, too, extended over more than one Gau. Röhm also centralized the administrative machinery of the SA, and prohibited direct access to Hitler, except through the office of the chief of staff.[181] And, as was to be expected, Hitler and Röhm expanded the authority and clarified the functions of the SA's Inspector General.[182]

All of these were essentially short-term measures to deal with the immediate consequences of the Stennes crisis. The party's greatest hope for a long-term solution to the problem of insubordination among the leaders and alienation among the SA in general was the Reich Leadership School (*Reichsführerschule*, RFS). The plan of training SA leaders militarily and indoctrinating them politically was not new; Stennes had established one for his jurisdictional region in late 1930, and Röhm had already appointed a director of the RFS in February of 1931.[183] What was new was merely the accelerated pace of the school's actual establishment[184] and the content and

179. "Bericht über die Tagung der Ortsgruppenführer des Bezirks Grenzmark . . . am 7. Juni 1931," HA, roll 10, folder 213.

180. See, for example, Erich Berger, "So haben wir im Gau Hessen gekämpft," *VB*, 26 Jan. 1932; and *VB*, 11 July 1931.

181. Vogelsang, *Reichswehr*, p. 229. The breakup of the Osaf deputy regions had been suggested (at least as far as Berlin was concerned) by Paul Schulz, the man in charge of purging the Berlin SA. See "Bericht zum Schreiben des Stabschefs vom 15.4.31 betreff Unterstellung Gausturm Berlin," 16 May 1931, HA, roll 77, folder 1565; and Osaf, Stabschef, "Verfügung," 10 Aug. 1931, HA, roll 16, folder 306.

182. Osaf, "Betreff: Generalinspektion Ia Nr. 1790/31," 21 April 1931," HA, roll 77, folder 1565.

183. Röhm to Kühme, 9. Feb. 1931, HA, roll 72, folder 1545.

184. The first session was June 1, but the school's new building was not completed and the sessions were held in a converted restaurant.

emphasis of the curriculum. The costs of retraining the SA were borne by the Gaus (who passed part of it on to the locals) — the price, so to speak, for a quiescent and cooperative SA.[185]

Hitler hoped that eventually every SA leader above the rank of *Sturmführer* (an SA *Sturm* corresponded more or less to a district in the political hierarchy) could take the three-week intensive training course[186] and thereby "be closer to his Führer, a distinction which will set him apart from thousands of his comrades." [187] The first group to be so distinguished (the enrollment for each course was eighty) came from the areas of Germany most likely to have been infected by the Stennes fever, that is, the northern and central regions bordering on the territory of the former Osaf Deputy East. (Matters in the east itself were presumably still too unsettled to permit enrollment from these areas.) It is unfortunately not possible to determine how many of the trainees owed their position to the recent personnel turnover, but they certainly represented the new image among SA officers. They were young political soldiers between twenty and thirty years of age, so that few could have served in the war. Socially, almost all "belonged without a doubt to the better classes," as the police report put it.[188] Outwardly, at least, they were a cross section of the party's own *Septemberlinge*.

The curriculum of the training courses put a heavy emphasis on political indoctrination instead of military drill. Hitler personally spoke for six hours on such topics as "The Nature of Leadership," and "The Need for Organization." The courses were also heavily interlaced with pseudoacademic lectures on "German History from a Racial Standpoint" and explanations of the affiliates' various aims and their relationship to the party and the SA. Subjects of primary interest to the SA alone occupied far less time on the schedule. (39 hours of "ideological instruction" compared to 12 hours for

185. "Hitler's Abrechnung mit den Rebellen," *VB*, 4 Apr. 1931; Reichsschatzmeister, "Rundschreiben" to all GL, 15 May 1931, in *Rdschr.*; and GL Ostmark, "Gaubefehl 7 des Gaues Ostmark," 13 March 1931, NA, T-580, roll 23, folder 205.

186. PD Mü, "Auszug aus L.[agebericht] Nr. 105 23.10.31," n.d., HA, roll 72, folder 1545.

187. Kühme, "Zweck und Aufgaben der Reichsführerschule," April 1931, *ibid.*; and Osaf, "Betriff: SA Führer-Vorschulen: Verfügung," 29 Oct. 1931, HA, roll 16, folder 306.

188. PD Mü, Referat VI/N, "Betr.: Reichsführerschule der NSDAP," 15 June 1931, HA, roll 73, folder 1548. See also the attendance list in the same folder.

"organizational" subjects.) Within the time allotted, however, the
school endeavored to touch on all aspects of SA activities, from a
discussion of the SA's finances and practical advice on handling
rallies to a futuristic talk by Röhm on "The Political Situation and
the Functions of the SA in the Third Reich."[189]

Daily life for the SA leaders at the RFS took place in an atmosphere which combined the forms of military and pseudouniversity
life. Though the participants wore uniforms at all times, saluted
every superior, and marched in formation to all functions, the party
was actually more interested in their psychological than in their
military and physical conditioning. Thus the courses began not with
lectures on party organization, but with talks on German history
since 1918 and the Jewish attempts to subvert German architecture.
Similarly, even the trainees' recreational activities continued the indoctrination program: the movies shown were chauvinistic war films.
Röhm did not appear until the sixth day of the three-week course,
and then only to greet the assembled leaders and speak briefly on
the need for the Führerprinzip in the SA. Hitler came three days
later, but this time only to greet each trainee personally and to pose
for a group photograph with them. His *pièces de résistance* among
the lectures came at the end of the course. Hitler filled two morn-
ings with two-hour talks about "The Virtues of a Leader" and "Socialism," while Gregor Strasser, a day later, labored for an hour and a
half over "The Organization of the NSDAP," tracing the party organizational structure back to medieval guild models. On the final two
days Hitler again held lengthy talks about the party's future policies
in the Third Reich and gave a hopeful interpretation of the party's
chances for early seizure of power. Thereafter came the inevitable
handshake for all trainees, the singing of the Horst-Wessel-Song,
and the SA leader was ready to return to the "front!"[190]

The intended aim of the school experience was clearly a renewed
infusion of the myth-person into the SA leaders, and in this the
party seems to have succeeded. There were no major revolts among

189. [RFS], "Erläuterungen zum Stundenplan der RFS für den 6. Lehrgang
1931," n.d., *ibid.*

190. This account is based upon the very interesting "Tagebuch—Reichsführerschule der NSDAP . . ." [Sept. 1931], *ibid.* The diary was apparently kept by a
staff member at the school.

the SA until 1934, although Hitler's optimistic prediction for a seizure of power was about a year early. The RFS was considerably less successful in changing the attitude of SA leaders on some party policies and in eliminating the rivalry between SA and SS. Himmler's lecture at the RFS on the role of the SS in the party was an unmitigated disaster. The "discussion" that followed his talk consisted almost entirely of accusations against the SS and "was not at all successful in clearing the air; if anything it aggravated the friction." Similarly, the SA trainees were obviously disappointed that the curriculum did not include more outright military training. Aside from meeting Hitler, their highest enthusiasm developed over a discussion of the stores of illegal arms hidden in the various Gaus.[191]

The link between the SA's and the party's consolidation at the Reich level was the personnel office, an institution which produced less equivocal results. Although its original purpose had been to aid in the purges of Stennes sympathizers in the ranks of the SA and party, Hitler quickly assigned additional powers to the office, so that by June Loeper not only recommended the appointment and dismissal of the four most important Gau officials (Gauleiter, deputy Gauleiter, business manager, and treasurer), but was also compiling a collection of personnel files that included all party functionaries from the district level on up.[192] Loeper was an ideal choice to be in charge of this unprecedented accumulation of potential power. Like Buch, Loeper was a simple soldier who, once convinced of Hitler's historical role, obeyed him as he would have obeyed a military superior — without question and without regard for his own personal inclinations.[193]

By the end of the summer, the period of consolidation drew to

191. *Ibid.*, pp. 1, 9–10, and 13. See also Kühme, "Erfahrungsbericht der RFS zum 3. Lehrgang 1931 vom 9. bis 30. 8. 1931," 15 Sept. 1931, HA, roll 73, folder 1548.

192. *VB,* 7/8 June 1931. Some of the Gaus were reluctant to submit to this new control measure, and Loeper had to publicly admonish them for their negligence. See *VOBl* (No. 3; 15 July 1931), p. 8. There is an example of a district leader's (and Gau staff official) personal questionnaire in HA, roll 29, folder 546.

193. Loeper, who died in 1935, was on active duty in 1923 and served as an instructor at the Reichswehr pioneer school in Munich. Apparently he was a convert to Hitler's teaching even then. See Hans Henningsen, *Unser Hauptmann Loeper* (Magdeburg, 1936).

a close. Although morale difficulties remained in the SA, Röhm was hopeful that they would decrease in the future.[194] The Reichsleitung was now in firm control of the locals, and its own internal bureaucratic divisions had a clearly apparent rationale. At the end of August, the Reichsleitung was divided into four main units; Hitler, the departmental chiefs (Reich Organization Leader I and II, Reich Propaganda Leader, etc.), the bureau chiefs (the heads of the major economic affiliates), and the "experts" (*Sachbearbeiter*) whose field of activity was not yet suitable for a separate affiliate organization.[195] At least on paper, the NSDAP had weathered the crisis and could resume its attack on the social and political system of Weimar.

The NSDAP's political offensive had largely marked time during the summer months, often with serious consequences for the militancy of the organization. Particularly at the Gau level, the party was losing much of its driving force. Without orders for specific agitation campaigns the Gau staffs devoted much of their energy to integrating the party organization into the state social and economic establishment, that is, engaging in business ventures, allowing outside interests to use the party name, etc.[196]

Not all of the work was internally oriented, of course. More specifically, affiliates whose activities contributed to the reintegration of the SA continued to expand their organizations during the summer lull. The growth of the agricultural apparatus continued unabated. The rebelling groups in the SA had been urban units, and the Reichsleitung hoped to dilute the SA's urban membership with an infusion of "healthy material" from the rural areas. The a.A. with its tentacles in all farming areas was an ideal partner for the SA's recruitment program.[197] The Reichsleitung assigned the "cultural" bureau a major role in the re-education of the SA, so that the Gaus were ordered to establish Gau offices of the "Bureau for Race and

194. Osaf, Generalinspektör [sic], "Bericht über Stimmung in der S.A. B.B. Nr. 384/31," 22 July 1931 and Röhm's marginalia on this report dated 30 July 1931, HA, roll 72, folder 1545.

195. *VOBl* (No. 6; 31 Aug. 1931), p. 16.

196. *Ibid.*, p. 15; and Bzl. Oschatz-Grimme [Leipzig], "Bezirksrundschreiben Nr. 6/31," 30 Aug. 1931, NA, T-580, roll 25, folder 207.

197. See Röhm, "Verfügung," 25 June 1931, HA, roll 16, folder 306; and Wilhelm Stegmann to Röhm [report on the August meeting of LGF], 12 Aug. 1931, HA, roll 89, folder 1868. The SS also concentrated its recruiting efforts in the rural areas. Reichsführer-SS, "SS-Befehl-C-Nr. 38," 12 Aug. 1931, *ibid.*

Culture," while the SA leaders in turn were directed to keep in close touch with these offices.[198] The connection between the Hitler Youth's continued expansion and the SA crises was more direct. Until the summer of 1931 the HJ was organizationally little more than a subdivision of the SA. HJ leaders served on the staffs of the respective SA leaders and had no direct power of authority over the subordinate HJ officials: the HJ administered its own day-to-day activities but all real decision-making power rested in the hands of the SA leaders. Under the impact of the Stennes revolt, the HJ gained increasing organizational autonomy. The HJ Superior Leaders (*Oberführer*), corresponding to the Osaf deputies, were immediately dismissed and their territories broken up. A massive purge eliminated most of the old leadership in Berlin.[199] The HJ also established its own Reichsleitung in Munich, changed its uniform to make it less of a copy of the SA uniform, and expanded into areas of youth activities that held no interest for the SA, notably the *Jungvolk* (ten to fourteen years) and the League of German Girls (*Bund Deutscher Mädel*). At the end of the summer, the HJ Gau leader was a fully autonomous staff member of the Gau leadership, comparable on the organizational chart to the agricultural expert.[200]

A meeting of all Gauleiters and major SA leaders in mid-September signaled the end of the reorganization period. Hitler now turned his attention to the Gauleiters and simultaneously strengthened and weakened their positions. The Gaus were subjected to a full auditing review in the fall,[201] but even more important, he announced the establishment of a Reich Inspector.[202] The new appoint-

198. *VOBl* (No. 1; 1 June 1931), p. 3; and Osaf, Stabschef, "Verfügung," 31 Aug. 1931, HA, roll 16, folder 306.

199. HJ–Reichsleitung, Abteilung 1b, "Anweisung Nr. 6," 21 May 1931, HA, roll 19, folder 364; and HJ, Gebiet Gross-Berlin, "Bericht über den Stand der Organisation der Berliner Hitlerjugend," 12 Jan. 1932, *ibid.*, folder 362.

200. HJ–Reichsleitung, "Anweisung Nr. 1," and "Anweisung Nr. 8," *Kommandobrücke*, I (20 July 1931), HA, roll 18, folder 342.

201. GL Ostmark, "Gaubefehl 12 des Gaus Ostmark," 18 Sept. 1931, NA, T-580, roll 23, folder 205.

202. Admittedly, there is no proof of an actual announcement. However, in view of the extreme importance of this meeting (only Gauleiters—none of their staffs— were permitted to attend) and the public announcement of the Reich Inspector's appointment in October, it seems reasonable to assume that Hitler used this platform to preview his plans.

ment was Robert Ley, Gauleiter of the Rhineland, and an unswerving supporter of all of Hitler's policies. He was also an enthusiastic advocate of the opening to the right and an important contact man to industrial and business leaders.[203] Ley was an ideal choice for Hitler but he seems to have been less popular with the Gauleiters and with Strasser, who remained his direct superior. As a result, Hitler not only delayed a specific enumeration of Ley's functions until the end of the year, but assigned far less comprehensive powers to Ley than he had to either Loeper or von Ullrich. For example, Ley was empowered to make inspection visits to the Gaus, but his travels had to be announced beforehand and approved by Strasser.

At the same time, Hitler reconfirmed the Gauleiters' agent status[204] and gave them permission both to push forward the thrust of the affiliates and, when necessary, to purge unwanted elements from their organizations.[205] The immediate consequences were major purges in some Gaus,[206] and, more generally, a rapid development of the Gau and district functionary corps. Large-scale Gau congresses in October assembled hundreds of new party executives (one thousand in Saxony) to hear lectures on their future work. Several Gaus also opened training institutes to inaugurate the recent appointees into their duties.[207]

The affiliates took immediate advantage of the decision to resume the NSDAP's forward thrust. The new HJ Reich leader, Baldur von Schirach, now combined the HJ, the NSDStB, and the National Social-

203. Schumann, *Nationalsozialismus*, p. 44; *VOBl* (No. 10; 31 Oct. 1931), p. 22.

204. Cf. Hitler's statement on the occasion of Sauckel's birthday: "The movement is today so united that the Gauleiters and political leaders instinctively make the right decisions." *VB*, 31 Oct. 1931. For Sauckel's own instinctive response to such praise see Sauckel to Hitler, 29 Dec. 1931, NA, T-81, roll 116, frames 136976–78. This document is a combination report on the organization in Thuringia and song of praise to Hitler.

205. There is indirect evidence for this conclusion in Goebbels' *Angriff* editorial, "Septemberlinge," 2 Nov. 1931, in *Wetterleuchten*, p. 214. See also Buch's letter to a local leader and the evidence of tightening in the Uschla organization in *VOBl* (No. 8 and 10; 30 Sept. and 31 Oct. 1931), pp. 19–20 and 23–24 resp.

206. Simon noted that 8% of the membership in Koblenz-Trier ("all lazy, rotten, useless") had been purged. *VB*, 3 Dec. 1931.

207. Reports on the Gau congress of Saxony-Essen and Ostmark are in *VB*, 5 Nov. 1931, 25 Oct. 1931, and NA, T-580, roll 25, folder 205 resp. On the school see *Angriff*, 29 Aug. 1931, in *Wetterleuchten*, p. 194; and *VB*, (Münchener Beobachter), 25 Sept. 1931.

ist Union of German Students (*Nationalsozialistischer Schülerbund,* NSSB) under his direction. He began his tenure of office by removing the party's youth organization even more from the direct influence of the SA and by restructuring the units of the HJ Reichsleitung in line with the party's division of labor into planning and propaganda units.[208] The NSBO was visibly reactivated. It moved its national headquarters to Munich at the beginning of September and held a training session for its functionaries from all parts of Germany in early November: like the RFS, the curriculum combined practical training (in this case, information on such topics as labor law) with heavily slanted ideological indoctrination (through lectures on such subjects as the history of the German worker and the NSDAP's internal organization as the model for the future Third Reich).[209]

The NSDAP also found time to settle some of the less pressing problems left over from the spring. The Order of German Women (*Deutscher Frauenorden,* DFO) was an anachronism in 1931. Originally a separate völkisch organization, the DFO became in time something of a corps of nurses for the SA, but its internal difficulties and feminist militancy ran counter to the party's new image. In October the DFO dissolved itself. Its members now formed women's auxiliaries (*Frauenschaften*) in every local, but the new units had neither organizational status nor dues. They existed solely to prepare women for their role in the Third Reich. The DFO's former national chairman became an advisor *(Referent)* in the Reichsleitung.[210]

The most important new affiliate organization was the Bureau of Disabled Veterans' Affairs.[211] Like its predecessors, the new affiliate combined propaganda with some positive functions. The party's staff of veterans advisors had both long- and short-term functions. While its Reich level functionaries worked out draft plans to demonstrate

208. Gruber resigned at the end of October, presumably because he was too closely identified with the HJ's old relationship to the SA. See Röhm to Gruber, 29 Oct. 1931, HA, roll 29, folder 555. On Schirach's reorganization see HJ–Reichsleitung, "Reichsrundschreiben 1/31," 23 Nov. 1931, HA, roll 18, folder 339.

209. RBA, "Schulungskurs der NSBO, 2, bis 7. November 1931," 15 Oct. 1931, HA, roll 89, folder 1867. The NSBO also created an inspector system corresponding to that of the party. See Schumann, *Nationalsozialismus,* p. 37.

210. *VOBl* (No. 3; 13 July 1931), p. 7; and *VB*, 3 Oct. 1931.

211. *VOBl* (No. 12; 30 Nov. 1931), p. 29. The Bureau of Disabled Veterans had apparently been established in September 1930, but remained organizationally dormant until the late fall.

the party's concern for the financial plight of the veterans, its local staff officials performed such positive tasks as providing aid in filling out forms. The Bureau's overall political aim was to inject the NSDAP's political influence into the major German disabled veterans' association, the Reich Association for Disabled Veterans.[212]

The Reichsleitung realized, of course, that renewed activism of the affiliates would bring back some of the old centrifugal influences, but it attempted to preclude any major crisis by greatly expanding the control functions of the Reich Organizational Leadership II. Not only did every document that was to be made public have to bear Hierl's countersignature, but the entire office was streamlined and clear channels of communication established. By the end of the year Hierl headed seven major subdivisions, some of which (for example, the a.A. and the Department for Race and Culture) were subdivided into as many as six bureaus. A clerical staff of fifteen kept busy typing plans for the NSDAP's "take-over of governmental authority."[213]

Although the NSDAP had grown rapidly in membership despite the summer reorganization,[214] it was really as far from actual political power in September as it had been at the beginning of the year. German society was still intact, but, so too, was the NSDAP. And in the fall it was ready to move into the mainstream of power politics again.[215] Reinhardt's speaker-training courses had already been revised to include greater emphasis on the work of the affiliates. With the coming of August, the school offered a steady series of intensive two-week training courses to enlarge the team of party agitators.[216]

The speakers were vitally needed as the party renewed its cam-

212. *VOBl* (No. 11; 16 Nov. 1931), p. 26.
213. "Organisationsabteilung II (Nach dem Stand vom 24. Oktober 1931)," HA, roll 90, folder 1869. For Hierl's directives regarding interoffice memoranda and paper work see Hierl, "Regelung des Dienstes innerhalb der Organisationsabteilung II" [ca. late 1931], HA, roll 72, folder 1545. The quote is from "Regelung . . . ."
214. In July, for example, the party launched another major effort to undermine the independence of the Landbund from within, this time in Schleswig-Holstein. Heberle, *Landbevölkerung*, p. 164.
215. The new thrust was undoubtedly delayed at least briefly by the suicide of Hitler's niece, Geli Raubal, on September 17. For several days Hitler simply withdrew from public life. Görlitz and Quint, *Hitler*, pp. 323–24; and Heinrich Hoffmann, *Hitler was my Friend*, tr. R. H. Stevens (London, 1955), pp. 153–58.
216. "Plan des mündlichen Lehrganges der Reichspropagandaleitung II vom 17. bis einschliesslich 31. August 1931 in Herrsching," HA, roll 70, folder 1529.

paign of propaganda saturation with rallies centered on the interests of the affiliates.[217] The a.A. coupled publication of its weekly *Landpost* with a further expansion of its staff, so that every local representative of the Farmers' Association (Landbund) had an NSDAP counterpart ready to take over the Association's function in the area.[218] The NSBO's main effort in the fall was the so-called *"Hib-Aktion"* (Operation Forward into the Factories!), which was apparently Goebbels' personal invention to expand the network of NSBO cells. The campaign began in September, and Goebbels hoped to win twelve thousand new members by the end of the year.[219] The HJ emphasized its apolitical, nationalist image (its Jungvolk units did not even carry swastika flags), but its functionaries, too, were not allowed to forget the political object of their work. The apolitical image was a facade to lure the uncommitted; once organized in any party group, no member was allowed to cooperate with those still on the outside.[220]

The party's public agitation effort had an ambivalent relationship to the internal planning which took place in the various staff offices. At times the planning resulted in new substantive draft proposals which could be translated into propaganda slogans; on other occasions, the propagandistic effort hid more conspiratorial blueprints that emerged from secret sessions. Toward the end of the year, the NSDAP accelerated the pace of the planning activities. With the steadily deteriorating economic situation, the party clearly hoped for an early collapse of the Republic. In preparation for its inheritance, Hitler created an Economic Council to "advise" the party on eco-

217. For October, 2,963 rallies had been registered with the Reichspropagandaleitung. See [RPL], "Zahl der für den Monat Oktober [1931] gemeldeten Versammlungen der Gaue," n.d., HA, roll 54, folder 1290.

218. GL München-Oberbayern, Abt. Landwirtschaft to Landwirtschaftliche Bezirksfachberater, 27 July 1931; and "Anweisung für die Tätigkeit der LVL [Landwirtschaftliche Vertrauensleute]," n.d., HA, roll B, folder 1868.

219. "Hinein in die Betriebe," *Angriff*, 29 Aug. 1931, in *Wetterleuchten*, p. 195. Somewhat earlier the HJ had begun a campaign to organize apprentices and this effort was continued during the "Hib-Aktion." See HJ–Reichsleitung, "Verfügung N. 2," *Kommandobrücke*, I (20 July 1931), HA, roll 18, folder 342; and Arthur Axmann (in 1940 Schirach's successor as Reich Youth Leader), "Bericht über die Berufsschulzellenorganisation (B.S.O.)," 14 Jan. 1932, HA, roll 19, folder 362.

220. *VB*, 18 Dec. 1931. Hitler's anger was brought on by the unwillingness of some members of the NSDStB to support the specific National Socialist policy line in all instances.

nomic policies; Hierl drafted bills for a compulsory labor service; and the Organizational Leadership II created new departments for technical, legal, and domestic (*innenpolitische*) policies.[221]

Although Hitler was seldom actively involved in drawing up the various plans for the party's actions after the seizure of power, the activities of the Reichsleitung obviously had at least his passive approval. The matter is less clear in the case of planning activities by the lower echelons. It is true, of course, that the seizure of power would have to be translated into decrees by the lower party organizations to be locally effective, and it is apparent that some Gau plans were drawn up in consultation with the Reichsleitung departments.[222] On the other hand, such planning activities were often indistinguishable from an actual conspiracy to seize power, and Hitler was understandably fearful for the NSDAP's none-too-secure image of legality. His fears were by no means groundless. In September, members of the Gauleitung of Hessen (led by Dr. Werner Best, the head of the Gau's legal department) met at a farmstead, the Boxheimer Hof, and drafted a series of decrees to be issued as emergency laws when the NSDAP came to power. The decrees provided a very frightening blueprint of local totalitarian control with an abundance of death penalties for a wide variety of small and large infractions.[223] The degree of coordination between the Reichsleitung and Best's efforts is difficult to establish. The Hessen officials certainly consulted Munich on some aspects of the draft legislation,[224] though it does not appear that the Reichsleitung knew of the full extent of Best's plans.

The Hessen documents were intended as secret, internal-party working papers, but they became public with the defection (from the NSDAP) of the district leader of Offenbach, the district in which

221. *VOBl* (No. 11; 16 Nov. 1931), p. 26; Schulz (at this time head of the Labor Service Department) to Röhm, 21 Nov. 1931; and Hierl's draft law, 23 Nov. 1931, HA, roll 72, folder 1545.

222. See Gmelin's letter of 22 Dec. 1931 in "Briefe"; and Dr. Wagener (head of the RL's economic department), "NSDAP," 28 Jan. 1932, HA, roll 77, folder 1565.

223. During the Third Reich, Best became a high official in the Reich Ministry of Interior and later Reich Plenipotentiary in Denmark. For the contents of the decrees see *Vorwärts*, 26 Nov. 1931; for the actual drafting process, Bracher, *Auflösung*, p. 431.

224. *B.T.* (M.A.), 21 April 1932. Best himself was not expelled for his illegal planning activities.

the Boxheimer Hof was located. Hitler's reaction was swift and furious. While Göring assured the Reich Minister of Interior that the Reichsleitung had known nothing about the plans, Hitler prohibited all further planning in the Gaus.[225] Hitler's anger was born of two reasons. The Boxheimer documents were an indication of the mood of frustration and restlessness for power which enveloped the party at this time and which Hitler was as yet powerless to fulfill. In addition, the Boxheimer papers with their clear revelation of the party's totalitarian ambitions repelled the rightist parties with whom Hitler was negotiating joint plans to topple the Weimar government.

Such negotiations became increasingly vital, since the NSDAP found it frustratingly difficult to translate the electoral victories of September into actual positions of power, either in the Reich or in the states. The situation had looked so promising at first: a large number of Gauleiters sat in the Reichstag and the state legislatures, the DNVP had supported the NSDAP's boycott of the Reichstag, and the party all but controlled the government of Thuringia.[226] In May, the NSDAP won an overwhelming election victory in Oldenburg — and the party clearly expected the trend to continue.[227] But then came the reverses. Frick received a vote of no confidence in Thuringia; the bank crisis of July did not result in the fall of the Brüning government as the party had expected.[228] Finally, the failure of the Stahlhelm-sponsored recall petition for the Prussian legislature and the Stennes revolt must have convinced even the most optimistic party leaders that the party was still a long way from power.[229]

At the September conference, Hitler informed the SA leaders (and presumably the Gauleiters) of a new tactic. The SA territorial jurisdictions would be reorganized to enable the units to support the local police in case of a Communist uprising. (In all other con-

225. *B.T.* (A.A.), 27 Nov. 1931; and Osaf, "Betr. Parteidisziplin, Nr. 7525/31," 9 Dec. 1931, HA, roll 16, folder 306. He also decreed a longer probationary period for members of other parties who wanted to join the NSDAP. The district leader of Offenbach had originally left the SPD.

226. See *NS-Jahrbuch 1931*, pp. 157 ff; and Hitler's proud telegram to Frick on the occasion of his first anniversary in office, *VB*, 25/26 Jan. 1931.

227. Goebbels prophesied the future drammatically as: "*Leitmotiv* and Prelude: Oldenburg; Act One: Prussia; Act Two: Reich," in his *Angriff* editorial of 19 May 1931, in *Wetterleuchten*, p. 156.

228. Krebs, *Tendenzen*, p. 151.

229. Goebbels, "Die Bilanz," *Angriff*, 11 Aug. 1931, in *Wetterleuchten*, pp. 188–90.

flicts, the SA and party would remain neutral.)[230] A short time later, Röhm lifted the prohibition on the participation of SA units in the Reichswehr's training courses and succeeded in convincing Schleicher that the SA had purely legal aims.[231]

These various measures were, of course, a continuation in the administrative and military spheres of the party's overall effort to destroy the fabric of German society from within. In the meantime, the NSDAP had also eagerly joined in another coalition government, this time in Brunswick. Although, as in Thuringia, the party had to import its minister from outside the state, the NSDAP insisted long before the name of the minister was announced that the party wanted to control the ministry of interior, that is, the police power of the state. After the resignation of the first appointee, Anton Franzen,[232] the coalition was continued with an even more outspoken and partisan National Socialist. Dietrich Klagges, a teacher who had been dismissed from the Prussian civil service for his political offenses, immediately plunged Brunswick into constant political controversy. He attempted to dismiss non-National Socialist professors, harrassed the political activities of other parties, and made the state a haven for SA men fleeing from justice in other parts of Germany. In short, Klagges' activities were a vivid demonstration that for a committed NSDAP member the interests of the party and the state were identical.[233]

230. See PD Berlin to Prussian Minister of the Interior, 5 Oct. 1931, NA, T-580, roll 19, folder 199; and PD Mü, "Auszug aus L. Nr. 105 v. 23.10.31," HA, roll 72, folder 1545.

231. Osaf, Stabschef to SA-Gruppe Hochland, 24 Nov. 1931, HA, roll 72, folder 1545; Sturmbann VI (Liegnitz), "Vierteljahresbericht an die Gruppe Schlesien," 5 Jan. 1932, *ibid.;* see Schleicher to Röhm, 4 Nov. 1931. A facsimile reprint is in Carl Severing, *Mein Lebensweg* (Cologne, 1950), II, between pp. 320 and 321. Hitler's first meeting with the East Prussian commanders Blomberg and Reichenau and his 4 hour meeting with Hammerstein also fall into this period. See Görlitz and Quint, *Hitler,* p. 319; and Hammerstein, "Schleicher," p. 17.

232. Franzen was a prominent party leader in Schleswig-Holstein, though he proved to be too "mythologized": against Hitler's wishes he resigned rather than enforce an anti-NSDAP Reich decree as Brunswick Minister of Interior. Hitler, by the way, handled the crisis in his usual dilatory manner: he refused to answer Franzen's request for instructions for weeks and then simply denounced his actions. Roloff, *Bürgertum,* pp. 53–56.

233. On Klagges' tenure as minister see *ibid.,* pp. 79 ff. See also the National Socialist program for Hessen "[This] . . . governmental program for Hessen is the program for the German people. He who opposes this program, is an enemy of the nation." *VB,* 12 Dec. 1931.

On the other hand, it was precisely this inability to separate the myth from the party that doomed to failure yet another attempt to unite the anti-Republican right. The major nationalist political parties and Wehrverbände had agreed to stage a demonstration in Harzburg (Brunswick) in mid-October to denounce the Brüning government. It was to be an impressive gathering, but actually the meeting demonstrated not unity, but lack of agreement. For the non-totalitarian groups the purpose of Harzburg was to demonstrate the power of the right, to discuss plans for a nationalist coalition after Brüning's fall, and to agree on a candidate for the Reich presidential election in 1932.[234] The NSDAP had far more parochial aims. Hitler wanted the combined forces of the right to issue a call for a new Reichstag elections, though he also expected that in itself the union at Harzburg would persuade Hindenburg (with whom he had his first meeting a day before Harzburg) to yield governmental power into his hands.[235] When this did not occur, Hitler lost interest in the meeting and pointedly insulted his partners by refusing to attend a joint dinner or to stay to review any but the SA's parade.[236]

Perhaps to demonstrate how little the party needed the support of other groups in its rise to power, Hitler staged a mammoth SA demonstration in the city of Brunswick itself a week later. The meeting had been planned before Harzburg (partially to replace the party's national congress which had not been held for two

234. Stahlhelm, "Führerbrief," 31 Dec. 1931, quoted in Düsterberg, *Stahlhelm,* p. 16; and Hugenberg to Hitler, 20 March and 17 April 1932, quoted in *B.T.* (M.A.), 20 Apr. 1932, Hugenberg, in particular, was interested in the presidential elections. Bracher, *Auflösung,* p. 412. On the NSDAP's role in the elections see below, pp. 241–50.

235. *VB,* 10 Oct. 1931. The *VB* also evoked the impression that the Harzburg meeting was in essence the realization of the party-sponsored proposal for a rump parliament. *VB,* 8 Oct. 1931. On Hitler's disappointment over his meeting with Hindenburg, see Vogelsang, *Reichswehr,* p. 135.

236. The *VB,* 13 Oct. 1931, printed Hitler's manifesto to the meeting, but its report underlined the importance of the Hitler–Hindenburg meeting and minimized the significance of the Harzburg union itself. It should be noted that the enforced unity protestations of the far-right leaders in no way increased the day-to-day cooperation of their organizations. On the contrary, the SA continued to recruit Stahlhelm members into its ranks and physically broke up Stahlhelm meetings whenever peaceful recruiting proved ineffective. See Osaf, Stabschef to Gruppen-führer Schlesien, 22 Jan. 1932, HA, roll 77, folder 1565; and Stahlhelm Bundes-führer to Hitler, 11 Dec. 1931, quoted in Düsterberg, *Stahlhelm,* p. 32.

years),[237] but only under the impact of his failure there did Hitler decide to enlarge its scope so that 100,000 SA members assembled in the city.[238] The meeting made a powerful impression, particularly on the middle-class inhabitants of Brunswick. A six-hour parade, exemplary discipline during the parade (terrorist acts were only permitted afterwards), and virtual control of the city by the SA all provided a foretaste of the new era.[239] For the party militant, Brunswick was a far more pleasing picture than Harzburg: "Harzburg was a tactical, partial aim; Brunswick the proclamation of the unchangeable final goal. At the end [of the road] lies Brunswick, not Harzburg."[240]

Stimulated by the success of Brunswick, the NSDAP leaders were ebullient and confident at the end of the year; even Hitler talked about the "last hour of the march."[241] There were some sound political reasons for this sense of imminent success. The pluralist forces in Weimar Germany were tired, and the steadily deepening depression made all efforts to stem the radical tide seem futile.[242] The NSDAP in turn was a prime beneficiary of the radical tide: its membership increased 53,000 in November alone. The Gau executive committees were major bureaucratic edifices now, and propagandists carried the party's message into every German village and hamlet.[243]

No doubt the figures were impressive, but they derived at least

237. Engelbrechten, *Braune Armee*, p. 186. Plans to stage a national congress in 1931 were dropped sometime after late April, presumably both for financial and tactical reasons in view of the needed internal reorganization of the NSDAP. For preliminary plans on the congress see GL Sachsen, Propaganda-Abt., "Rundschreiben Nr. 12/31," 28 April 1931, NA, T-580, roll 25, folder 207.

238. On October 12, Röhm permitted the use of the travel funds originally intended for the national congress to pay for the transportation of SA men to and from Brunswick. See Stabschef to SA Gruppen, 12 Oct. 1931, HA, roll 16, folder 306.

239. Roloff, *Bürgertum*, pp. 74–75.

240. *Angriff*, 21 Oct. 1931, in *Wetterleuchten*, p. 212.

241. Hitler, "Tagesbefehl an die SA und SS," 1 Dec. 1931, *VB*, 3 Dec. 1931; Reichsführer-SS to Organisationsleitung II, 18 Nov. 1931, HA, roll 77, folder 1565; and Otto Dietrich, *Zwölf Jahre mit Hitler* (Munich, 1955), p. 35.

242. Bracher, *Auflösung*, p. 396.

243. *VB*, 13/14 Dec. 1931; and PD Nü-Fü, "Lagebericht No. 196/II," 24 Oct. 1931, HA, roll 24A, folder 1759. E. Berger, "So haben wir im Gau Hessen gekämpft," *VB*, 27 Jan. 1932, reported that while Hessen staged 99 public rallies in January of the year, the Gau organized 500 in December.

part of their stature from the simple fact that the NSDAP (and particularly the affiliates) were not very significant organizations before 1931. The HJ, for example, even at the end of 1931 had organized only 5.1 percent of those youths of the age group eligible to join. Only two Gaus (South Hanover-Brunswick and Schleswig-Holstein) had risen above the 10 percent mark, while six were beneath 2.5 percent. In addition, several Gaus actually showed a decline in membership in the last months of the year.[244] And the HJ was not an isolated case. The NSBO membership increase was spectacular — from 4,131 in January to 39,000 in December[245] — but even the latter figure was a rather pitiful showing for a highly industrialized nation like Germany.

Finally, the NSDAP had greatly benefited from the bandwagon effect of politics, but there were signs that the forward momentum was slackening. The circulation of the *Angriff* (Goebbels' newspaper) was actually declining in the last quarter of 1931, even though the north and east of Germany (rather than the south) were becoming more and more the focal point of the party's strength.[246] The decreasing forward momentum also expressed itself in a growing self-centeredness among some of the party's organizations. The search for material rewards and status symbols began to cause considerable concern among the party's leadership.[247]

None of these factors, of course, was an actual threat to either the party leadership or to the unity of the party; they were, rather, manifestations of a sense of impatience and frustration that permeated the NSDAP at the end of the year. The party had made very signifi-

244. Reichsleitung–HJ, "Reichsrundschreiben 1/32," 5 Feb. 1932, appendix 3 and 5, HA, roll 89, folder 1849. In absolute terms, the HJ had 1000 members in all of Berlin in January 1932. See Walter Lacquer, *Young Germany* (London, 1962), p. 193 n4.

245. Schumann, *Nationalsozialismus,* p. 37.

246. Eher Verlag, Zweigstelle Berlin to NSDAP Hauptarchiv, 23 April 1936, HA, roll 47, folder 968; and Schäfer, *NSDAP,* p. 19. This geographic shift continued throughout 1932.

247. The main status symbol for the Gaus was a newspaper. Buch, in a lecture held at the RFS at the end of 1931, noted that the self-centeredness of the various party organizations proved "how deep the Jew has eaten into [the fiber] of the German people." See Buch, "Ehre und Recht," HA, roll 89, folder 1849. A printed version of the talk was distributed to all Uschlas in the party. See *VOBl* (No. 17; 15 Feb. 1932), p. 42.

cant political gains, but it had not achieved power. It was clear that the battle for governmental control in Germany would continue in 1932, but Hitler faced a major choice of tactics: should he continue to emphasize the process of undermining the German sociopolitical fabric, or throw the party's human and financial resources into some major battles that could propel the party to power overnight? The battles were certainly available in 1932. Germany had to elect new state legislatures in Prussia and Bavaria and, above all, a new Reich president.

Hope, Frustration, and Triumph

The NSDAP's leaders and members welcomed the new year in the confident expectation that before long 1932 would become the Year I in the era of National Socialist power in Germany. The party's membership probably stood around 450,000, and the SA claimed an increase of 100,000 between December and February.[1] The party militants were more firmly integrated into the organizational framework than before. Röhm had achieved the "miracle" of regaining and maintaining control of his rapidly growing unit,[2] while in the party proper Buch, Schwarz, and Strasser all extended the control functions of their respective offices. The Uschla disappeared as a vestige of local autonomy, and Buch all but encouraged political leaders to use the Uschla system as a permanent purging device.[3] Schwarz established a uniform accounting system for all Gaus (even the bookkeeping journals were supplied by the Reichsleitung), a control measure that became increasingly necessary as the party's full-time staff exceeded one thou-

---

1. For the SA see *VB*, 13/14 Dec. 1931; and PD Mü, "Auszug aus dem Morgenrapport des Ref. VI/N," 9 March 1932, HA, roll 73, folder 1549. The party membership figure is an educated guess. The NSDAP had 129,563 members on September 14, 1930, and 719,446 at the end of January 1933, so that 450,000 seems a reasonable figure for the beginning of 1932. See Reichsorganisationsleiter, "Statistische Erhebungen," (Munich, 1935), sheet 31, HA, roll 3A, folder 239.

2. Joseph Goebbels, *Vom Kaiserhof zur Reichskanzlei* (cited hereafter as *Vom Kaiserhof*) (Munich, 1934), entry for 9 Feb. 1932, p. 93.

3. See *VOBl.* (No. 15; 15 Jan. 1932), p. 37. For a complaint against a Gauleiter's personal use of the Uschla see Hans Angemann (Mühlheim a.R.) to Strasser, 23 June 1932, HA, roll 9, folder 549.

sand in almost every Gau.[4] Finally, the NSDAP had virtually no financial problems.[5]

There was a close connection between the party's membership, its large body of staff officials, and its financial security. In 1931 the NSDAP had infiltrated the German agricultural interest groups; the first half of 1932 marked the party's successful inroads into the world of finance and industry. The campaign was not new. In the summer of 1931, Hitler decided to "work on" the business community,[6] using the same methods which Darré had successfully pioneered in the case of the Landbund. He appointed as press chief Otto Dietrich, a journalist with good family and professional connections to the industrial leaders in the Ruhr. He also asked Wilhelm Keppler, another party member with good business connections, to form a circle of business advisors for the party. Hitler left the choice of members to Keppler, though he did insist that the party's star economic defender in the fall of 1931, Hjalmar Schacht, be included.[7] Early in the new year, Hitler put the campaign in the public limelight with a speech before the members of the Düsseldorf Industrial Club. His initial reception was not overwhelmingly enthusiastic, but "after only an hour's speaking time," the audience had been largely won over by Hitler's blend of chauvinism and vague generalizations.[8] The immediate consequences of the Düsseldorf speech, and of several others in the same area soon afterwards,[9] were financial and political rewards: the industrialists made considerable sums available to the party,[10] and, equally impor-

---

4. Reichsschatzmeister to all GL, "Rundschreiben," 15 Dec. 1931, in *Rdschr.* Even a relatively small Gau like Oberfranken employed 1300 persons in January.

5. Goebbels, *Vom Kaiserhof*, entry for 5 Jan. 1932, p. 18.

6. Otto Dietrich, *Mit Hitler in die Macht* (Munich, 1934), p. 45.

7. "Cross-Examination of Keppler . . . 18 Aug. 1947," in United States, Military Government in Germany, *Trial of War Criminals Before the Nuremberg Military Tribunals: Case 5: U.S. vs. Flick* (cited hereafter as *Flick Trial*) (Washington, 1952), VI, p. 289.

8. For contrasting reports on the impression of the speech on the listeners, see Otto Dietrich, *Zwölf Jahre mit Hitler* (Munich, 1955), pp. 46–49; and Louis P. Lochner, *Tycoons and Tyrants* (Chicago, 1954), pp. 79–90. The full text of the speech can be found in Max Domarus, ed., *Hitler, Reden und Proklamationen 1932–1945*, I (Munich, 1965), pp. 68–90.

9. George W. F. Hallgarten, "Adolf Hitler and German Heavy Industry," *Journal of Economic History*, XII (Summer 1952), 229; and Dietrich, *Zwölf Jahre*, p. 49.

10. On the actual sums made available to the party in 1932 see Konrad Heiden, *Adolf Hitler*, I (Zurich, 1936), p. 293; and George W. F. Hallgarten, *Hitler, Reichswehr und Industrie* (Frankfurt, 1962), p. 94; and Klaus Drobisch, "Flick und die Nazis," *Zeitschrift für Geschichtswissenschaft*, XIV (No. 3; 1966), 379–80.

tant, for many of the Ruhr business leaders, the NSDAP became a politically respectable alternative to the DVP.[11]

The successful business campaign paralelled the party's continuing efforts in other fields. The national organization of the Landbund was all but *gleichgeschaltet;* there remained only local pockets of resistance to a National Socialist take-over. National white-collar unions had to resist efforts to infiltrate their local and provincial organizations. More and more youth organizations affiliated themselves with the HJ.[12] Himmler's SS conducted a particularly vigorous propaganda campaign among younger police officers.[13] In fact, the party had succeeded in planting high-ranking agents among the police both in Berlin and Bavaria, so that the police forces in both of Germany's largest states were no longer fully reliable supporters of the Republic.[14] Thus for many party members the Gauleiter of Oldenburg, Carl Röver, was merely expressing an obvious expectation when he announced that by April Hitler would control the government of Germany.[15]

Actually, Röver's prophecy was not unrealistic, but it was not quite complete either. He did not mention that while the NSDAP might get to power by April, it was highly unlikely that the party would control the Reich in May if Hitler did not achieve his goal by April. Time, in other words, was not on the National Socialists' side; on the contrary, many of the party's problems could be overlooked for the moment, but not ignored in the long run. The NSDAP still had no substantive plans for governmental action, a lack that made itself increasingly felt as the NSDAP moved into government positions in

11. Since other NSDAP leaders carried the business campaign into additional areas of Germany, the immediate political danger was often the disintegration of local DVP party organizations. See Brandes (chairman of the provincial organization of the Deutsche Volkspartei in Brunswick) to Dingeldey (the national chairman), 22 March 1932, quoted in Ernst-August Roloff, *Bürgertum und National-sozialismus 1930–1933: Braunschweigs Weg ins Dritte Reich* (Hanover, 1961), p. 106.

12. Deutschnationaler Handlungsgehilfenverband to its subdivisions, 29 Feb. 1932, in Werner Jochmann, ed., *Nationalsozialismus und Revolution* (Frankfurt, 1963), pp. 360–61; and Harry Pross, *Jugend, Eros, und Politik* (Berne, 1964), pp. 400–01.

13. Reichsführer-SS to Nationalsozialistische Parteikorrespondenz, 9 March 1932, HA, roll 77, folder 1565.

14. Johann K. von Engelbrechten, *Eine braune Armee entsteht* (Munich, 1937), p. 217; *B.T.* (M.A.), 11 March 1932; and Carl Severing, *Mein Lebensweg*, II (Cologne, 1950), p. 330.

15. Herbert Schwarzwälder, *Die Machtergreifung der NSDAP—Bremen 1933* (Bremen, 1960), pp. 10–11.

some of the states.[16] There remained sharp differences in mood between some of the locals eager for action and the more sober approach
of the national leadership, anxious to preserve the party image of respectability.[17] Needless to say, further delays in getting to power
would increase this emotional difference. Above all, however, there
was the growing realization that sometime in the near future the
sponge would be full;[18] the party and its affiliates had very nearly exhausted their membership potential. The HJ was already discovering
that its components propagandized each other. Even pure demagogy
had its effective limitations: Kube introduced a resolution in the Prussian Landtag demanding that the government distribute free firewood
to the poor, only to find that Darré, representing the woodcutters and
foresters, wanted higher prices for wood.[19] The continuing depression,
too, was not an absolutely positive factor. While the NSDAP might
gain the support of most of the middle classes, increased misery among
the industrial workers increased the strength of the Communist Party.[20]
Moreover, while the NSDAP was often the first choice of the disengaged middle classes, the long delay in getting to power had strengthened a rival integrative system: in southern Germany the political
and emotional power of Catholicism became an effective barrier to
the party's progress in 1932.[21]

Time might be the party's enemy, but in early 1932 the NSDAP
was confident that a massive series of electoral victories would put the
party in control of Germany before its popularity began to wane.
There was no doubt about the party's vote-getting power at the be-

16. Albert Krebs, *Tendenzen und Gestalten der NSDAP* (Stuttgart, 1959), p.
149. See *B.T.* (A.A.), 15 Jan. 1932, for a description of National Socialist policies
in the state governments.

17. On radicalism among some of the locals, see the documents in HA, roll 33A,
folder 1786; for pleas for restraint from the top, see *VOBl* (No. 17; 15 Feb. 1932),
p. 43.

18. The limitations of the NSDAP's vote-getting power had been drawn theoretically with great accuracy as early as 1931. See Werner Stephan, "Grenzen des
nationalsozialistischen Vormarsches," *Zeitschrift für Politik*, XXI (Dec. 1931),
571–78.

19. Möller (of the NSSB, Gauverband Nord) to Renteln (head of the NSSB),
27 Jan. 1932, HA, roll 18, folder 340; and Abteilung Landwirtschaft, Unterabteil-
ung Forstwirtschaft, "Rundschreiben Nr. 3," 16 Feb. 1932, HA, roll B, folder 1868.

20. H. R. Knickerbocker, "Eine Nacht in Wedding," *B.T.* (M.A.), 31 Jan. 1932,
conveys a good picture of the atmosphere of economic hardship and political radicalism among the urban proletariat.

21. *B.T.* (M.A.), 10 Jan. and 20 Feb. 1932.

ginning of 1932. That year opened with provincial elections in Lippe, and the NSDAP registered impressive gains over its 1930 showing. (See Table 8.)

TABLE 8

| | Votes | |
Party	Jan. 1932	Sept. 1930
NSDAP	25,357	20,388
DNVP	8,114	7,487
SPD	22,651	20,150
KPD	9,533	6,045
Middle Parties	17,156	27,597

SOURCE: *Völkischer Beobachter,* Jan. 12, 1932.

The elections in Lippe were merely a sampling of what was to come. Though the government could attempt to prevent new Reichstag elections (the present legislature could legally sit until 1934), it could not avoid elections for a new Reich president, nor for the state legislatures of Germany's largest states, Prussia and Bavaria. If the NSDAP could win these, "[our] simultaneous take-over of power in the Reich and in Prussia is for us an accomplished fact."[22]

The party's confidence was also measurably bolstered by the knowledge that Hindenburg and the Brüning government were not only anxious to avoid a presidential contest, but were eager to include the NSDAP in the Reich government as well. Neither Hindenburg, Schleicher, nor Brüning really looked upon the NSDAP and Hitler as the menace to German sociopolitical life that they were.[23] On the con-

22. The quotation is from a speech by Kube in Breslau. Quoted in *VB,* 11 Feb. 1932.

23. For attitudes toward the NSDAP among the Republic's leaders, see "Vortragsnotiz aus der Wehrmachtsabteilung des RWM," 29 Aug. 1932 in Thilo Vogelsang, *Reichswehr, Staat und NSDAP* (Stuttgart, 1962), doc. 35, p. 480. Reginald H. Phelps, "Aus den Groener-Dokumenten," *Deutsche Rundschau,* LXXVII (Jan. 1951), pp. 19–21, and "Niederschrift des Staatssekretärs Dr. Meissner über eine Besprechung des Reichspräsidenten mit dem Staatspräsidenten," 12 June 1932, in Walther Hubatsch, ed., *Hindenburg und der Staat* (Göttingen, 1966), p. 335; and Theodor Eschenburg, "Die Rolle der Persönlichkeit in der Krise der Weimarer Republik: Hindenburg, Brüning, Groener, Schleicher," in Eschenburg, *Die improvisierte Demokratie* (Munich, 1963), pp. 252–53.

trary, rightist elements in Germany all wanted to involve the NSDAP in the responsibilities of governing Germany, although none, to be sure, wanted to give the party and Hitler dictatorial control over the fate of the nation.[24] That was the crucial difference: Hindenburg and the authoritarian leaders of Germany wanted a meaningful coalition with the NSDAP, Hitler wanted absolute power.

For a time early in the year it appeared that the two sides would be able to arrive at a mutually agreeable solution. The first major electoral contest of the year was the Reich presidential election; Hindenburg's term of office expired in May. In view of his age, the president was understandably reluctant to run again, though he also knew that his name alone was a symbol of political stability for millions of Germans. Hitler was equally eager not to test his myth against Hindenburg's name. Consequently, when Brüning proposed an extension of Hindenburg's term of office by a vote of the Reichstag, Hitler was not at all unreceptive.[25] After considerable hesitation, however, he named a high price. The NSDAP would vote for the government's proposal only if Hindenburg dismissed Brüning, dissolved the Reichstag, and scheduled new elections.[26] Since the NSDAP expected massive gains in the new Reichstag, Hitler might still get to power in a very short time and yet not risk a defeat to the prestige of Hindenburg's name. Hindenburg, however, refused to dismiss Brüning, and Hitler withdrew his proposal to extend Hindenburg's term without an electoral conflict.[27]

As long as the basic issue was the dismissal of Brüning, Hitler acted as the spokesman of the united anti-Republican right, but once Hin-

24. This included the anti-Republican right. Hugenberg claimed that in Harzburg the basis for negotiations had always been that Hitler would claim neither the presidency nor the Reich chancellorship. See Karl-Dietrich Bracher, *Die Auflösung der Weimarer Republik* (3d ed.; Villingen, Schwarzw., 1955), p. 663 n43.

25. Hermann Pünder, *Politik in der Reichskanzlei*, ed. Thilo Vogelsang (Stuttgart, 1961), entry for 7 Jan. 1932, p. 111.

26. Goebbels, *Vom Kaiserhof*, entry for 7 Jan. 1932, pp. 19–20; *B.T.* (A.A.), 8 Jan. 1932; Groener to Gleich, 24 Jan. 1932, in Phelps, "Aus," p. 1018; and Otto Meissner, *Staatssekretär unter Ebert-Hindenburg-Hitler* (3d ed.; Hamburg, 1950), p. 216. The party's official version of the negotiations is "Die parteiamtliche Darstellung der Vorgänge in Berlin," *VB*, 14 Jan. 1932.

27. On January 12, Frick gave a "clear no" to speculations that the NSDAP would permit Hindenburg's reelection by popular acclamation. See *B.T.* (A.A.), 13 Jan. 1932.

denburg's refusal rendered this goal illusionary, the united front quickly dissolved. The next immediate problem was the search for a rightist candidate to oppose Hindenburg, and on this issue the NSDAP and its Harzburg partners could find little basis for agreement. Hugenberg had hopes of finding a monarchist, while Hitler made it clear that he expected his partners to support whomever the NSDAP chose — probably Hitler himself.[28] Hitler's unwillingness to agree to a compromise led eventually to a multiplicity of candidates on the right, with the DNVP and the Stahlhelm supporting Düsterberg.[29]

Hitler himself was very reluctant to announce his candidacy, though with a series of negative decisions he had precluded any candidacy but his own for the party. By early February the presidential election had become the battle of Armageddon for most party members and, logically, only Hitler could lead the forces of right in such a contest.[30] Nevertheless, the outcome of the battle was most uncertain; indeed, Strasser told Hitler quite bluntly that he could not win against Hindenburg.[31] As a result, Hitler toyed with the idea of Epp or Frick as the party's candidate, but eventually dismissed it as completely unrealistic. At the end of January the choice had been narrowed to Hitler or Frick. The Reichsleitung called a Gauleiter meeting on February 3 to announce the NSDAP's candidate, only to send the state leaders away disappointed. Hitler still had not reached his decision.[32]

28. Hugenberg realized Hitler's ambitions in a conversation with Göring during the night of 11-12 January 1932. See Roloff, *Bürgertum,* p. 102. In its negotiations with the Stahlhelm the party demanded that "the Stahlhelm follow the NSDAP's orders during the campaign." See *Stahlhelm* (official biweekly organ of the Stahlhelm), 6 March 1932.

29. "Parole Düsterberg," *Stahlhelm,* 28 Feb. 1932; and Theodor Düsterberg, *Der Stahlhelm und Hitler* (Wolfenbüttel, 1949), p. 34.

30. On 17 February 1932, the *VB* labeled Hindenburg "the shield bearer of the red-black catastrophe front." Goebbels, in his strictly confidential "Denkschrift der R.P.L. zur Reichspräsidentenwahl—1. Wahlgang 13. März 1932?" [sic] (cited hereafter as "RPL Denkschrift") (Munich, 4 Feb. 1932), p. 1, HA, roll 30, folder 565, speaks of "the final dispute with the . . . system." A circular of the Dresden local to its subdivision put the issue even more crudely: "The next weeks will either see us as masters (*Herren*) of Germany, or Germany will perish." Ortsgruppenleitung Dresden to all sections, 16 Feb. 1932, HA, roll 24A, folder 1759.

31. Krebs, *Tendenzen,* p. 182.

32. *B.T.* (A.A.), 30 Jan. 1932; and Goebbels, *Vom Kaiserhof,* entry for 4 Feb. 1932, p. 38.

Behind the scenes at the Reichsleitung a fierce battle raged among Hitler's closest advisors. None of them sought (or would even think) to preempt a decision that only Hitler could make, but since the decision to run or not to run involved far-reaching consequences for the distribution of power centers within the party's organizational structure as well, it is understandable that the key subleaders fought vigorously to influence Hitler's decision. It was clear by now that the NSDAP would have to nominate a presidential candidate. It was equally obvious, though no party leader seems to have expressed this thought aloud, that no candidate but Hitler had a realistic chance of defeating Hindenburg. Any other nominee would conduct a token campaign — not unlike Ludendorff's attempt in 1925. This meant that if Hitler did not run, the NSDAP's infiltration process (that is, the continuing attempt to organize and reengage sympathizers) would continue to share organizational priority with the presidential campaign. This would not be the case if Hitler ran. If he became the party's candidate all "organizational" work would have to cease while the party poured all of its material and human resources into the presidential campaign. Since the propaganda effort would be run and coordinated by Goebbels, the head of the RPL was the most enthusiastic advocate of Hitler's candidacy. It represented a very real opportunity to make himself the foremost among Hitler's agents at the Reichsleitung. Since the states' elections would follow almost immediately after the presidential election, Goebbels would continue to be the most important party leader next to Hitler, at least until May, when he hoped to occupy a ministerial position in the new National Socialist government.[33]

Göring and Röhm were Goebbels' most prominent supporters. Göring had no official power base within the party, so that his real rise was dependent upon the party's seizure of power. Röhm, on the other hand, needed visible proof that his SA's sacrifices were not in vain. On the side of the opposition stood Gregor Strasser. As head of the Organizational Leadership I he was committed to the continuation of the party's erosion effort. With Hitler as presidential candidate,

33. Goebbels was fully aware of these long-range possibilities. See "RPL Denkschrift," pp. 32–33. He also obviously enjoyed his privileged position with Hitler and his standing above the other Gauleiters. See *Vom Kaiserhof*, entries for 16 March and 11 April 1932, pp. 65 and 78.

not only would that effort be suspended but also Strasser would be temporarily subordinated to Goebbels. Strasser, unlike Goebbels, Röhm, and Göring, stressed the potential dangers of Hitler's candidacy. Since Hitler's victory was hardly a foregone conclusion, not running would avoid the inevitable sense of defeat and depression that would envelop the party if Hitler ran — and lost.

Goebbels knew that the presidential election campaign was his greatest opportunity, and he prepared his arguments carefully. Sometime toward the end of 1931 he wrote a confidential memorandum outlining the physical and political requirements for a successful campaign. It is a masterpiece of political data and prognostication. Thus Goebbels supplied statistical data on voting patterns (both of the NSDAP and other parties) and correlated geographic focal points of a campaign with the available halls for mass rallies. He even suggested basic campaign themes and effective slogans.[34] At the end of January, Goebbels launched a major trial balloon. On January 29, Hans Hinkel, editor of Goebbels' newspaper, *Angriff*, addressed a rally at the Berlin Sportpalast. During his speech he said that, "whom the NSDAP will nominate as its candidate . . . ," and here the SA, obviously on cue, interrupted him with cries of "Hitler!", while the rest of the audience stood for several minutes to demonstrate approval of the chant. After the ovation calmed down somewhat, Hinkel continued rather anticlimatically ". . . is not yet decided."[35] Three days later, Goebbels thought he had won Hitler over.[36] But the issue was not settled that easily. It is obvious from Goebbels' own diary entries that Hitler changed his mind several times between the beginning and the end of February, presumably as Goebbels' and Strasser's arguments appeared more convincing to him. Thus Goebbels again thought he had triumphed on the twelfth, but on the sixteenth Adolf Wagner, the Gauleiter of Bavaria, definitely said Hitler would not run. Three days later, Goebbels wrote that Hitler had decided to run, but on the after-

34. "RPL Denkschrift." The document bears the date of February 14, but since Hindenburg is not mentioned as the opposing candidate, it is clear that the memorandum was prepared considerably earlier. Moreover, Goebbels noted as early as February 4 that his entire campaign machinery was ready; he only needed to push the button. See *Vom Kaiserhof*, entry for 4 Feb. 1932, p. 38.

35. *B.T.* (A.A.), 30 Jan. 1932.

36. Goebbels, *Vom Kaiserhof*, entry for 2 Feb. 1932, pp. 36–37.

noon of the twenty-second Hitler himself said the NSDAP was in no particular hurry to nominate a candidate. Finally, Hitler gave Goebbels permission to announce his candidacy in Berlin on the evening of the twenty-second, though his uneasiness continued: as always in times of stress and uncertainty, he began to reminisce about his war experiences. Nevertheless, the die had been cast. Goebbels announced Adolf Hitler as a candidate for the office of Reich President on February 22 to an enthusiastic audience at the Sportpalast. But even then Hitler wavered again. Immediately after the announcement the Reichsleitung dispatched telegrams to all Gauleiters informing them that Goebbels had made the announcement without Hitler's permission.[37]

It was impractical, of course, to step down after the public announcement, and Hitler was finally in the race. He had delayed his decision to the last principally because he continued to hope that some unforeseen event — specifically Hindenburg's death[38] — would deliver him from the ordeal. Hindenburg remained physically and mentally alert so that the NSDAP's presidential campaign had to take place under very unfavorable political circumstances. The party was not, however, unprepared for this contingency. Under Goebbels' tactical direction,[39] it transformed itself into an organism that existed solely to elect Adolf Hitler as Reich President. Every affiliate and every party division put aside the slow work of undermining German society and concentrated solely on developing campaign appeals that were geographically or interest-group oriented.[40] Even the financial administration became less rigorous. Locals were permitted to retain

37. The meandering course of Hitler's decisions and counterdecisions can be traced in *ibid.*, entries for 12, 19, and 22 Feb. 1932, pp. 45, 48, and 49–50; Gmelin, letter of 22 Feb. 1932, in "Briefe"; *B.T.* (A.A.), 17 Feb. 1932; and Krebs, *Tendenzen*, p. 153.

38. *Ibid.*, pp. 137 and 152. Hitler's candidacy was preceded by the curious maneuverings which gave him a pseudo-appointment in the Brunswick civil service and automatically made him a German citizen. See the documents in HA, roll B, folders 5 and 6; and Rudolf Morsey, ed., "Hitler als braunschweigischer Regierungsrat," *Vierteljahrshefte für Zeitgeschichte*, VIII (Oct. 1960), 419–48.

39. Every party speaker's schedule after February 17 was controlled by Goebbels' office. See "RPL Denkschrift," pp. 4–5; GL München-Oberbayern, Propaganda, Abt. to all district leaders, 6 Feb. 1932, HA, roll 9, folder 192.

40. The change of emphasis is particularly noticeable in such organs as *Arbeitertum*. This paper, which ordinarily did not deal with current political issues, contained virtually nothing but articles on the presidential election after March 1.

members on the rolls even when they were seriously behind in their dues because the party feared that expelling them would mean losing their votes in the election.[41] The Uschla network ceased to function; the NSDAP simply prohibited intraparty disputes during the campaign and used the Uschla personnel for propaganda purposes.[42]

The Hitler–Goebbels strategy was a very simple saturation campaign linking Hitler's name with Germany's emotional and material desires: "For Liberty and Bread! We are voting for Adolf Hitler." [43] As the campaign wore on Hitler's personal image was increasingly magnified so that in the final days before the election the pages of the *VB* consisted almost entirely of Hitler's speeches and wide-lens shots of the masses that listened to Hitler. As an organizational feat the Reich presidential campaign was an immense accomplishment. Thousands of rallies blanketed Germany with propaganda designed to appeal to every socioeconomic group.[44] SA and SS gave long hours of service — as guards, terror crews, poster squads, or protective units for Hitler.[45] Only Hitler surpassed the boundless energy of his party workers. Tirelessly he flew[46] from rally to rally, and when March 13 came, he had visited many Gaus several times over. It is true that his speeches followed a set pattern and hardly presented a wealth of new solutions, but the physical energy required to keep up his pace was nevertheless remarkable.[47]

Despite the party's efforts Hitler did not win on March 13. He

41. Ogrl. Kraiburg to GL München-Oberbayern, 22 March 1932, HA, roll 8, folder 176.

42. Ogrl. Dresden to all sections, 16 Feb. 1932, HA, roll 24A, folder 1759.

43. Goebbels' *Angriff* editorial of 5 March 1932 in *Wetterleuchten—Aufsätze aus der Kampfzeit,* ed. Georg-Wilhelm Müller (Munich, 1939), p. 270.

44. On local efforts, see Kampmann to NSDAP Hauptarchiv, May 1938, HA, roll 47, folder 968 (for Berlin); and William S. Allen, *The Nazi Seizure of Power: The Experience of a Single German Town, 1930–1935* (Chicago, 1965), p. 88 (for Thalburg).

45. Otto Dietrich, *Mit Hitler in die Macht* (Munich, 1934), p. 67. Even in small towns at least 600 SS men had to be available to protect Hitler. See Reichsführer-SS, "Richtlinien für den Sicherheitsdienst der Versammlungen des Führers," n.d., HA, roll 89, folder 1849.

46. Goebbels, "RPL Denkschrift," does not propose use of an airplane for campaign purposes; this was apparently Hitler's own idea.

47. For Hitler's daily routine during the campaign see Dietrich, *Mit Hitler,* pp. 73–75.

made substantial gains among the middle-class voters and kept Hindenburg from receiving a majority of the vote, so that a runoff election would be necessary, but Hitler's overall vote was significantly lower than that of the President. As Hitler may have feared all along, in the contest of images between himself and Hindenburg, he lost. The party militants were shattered. The average party functionary had apparently convinced himself that Hitler would be president-elect on the morning of March 14. Instead, "the dream of power was temporarily over." [48] Some of the party leaders were less surprised. Strasser, for one, never expected Hitler to win, though he too campaigned vigorously. On the other hand, Goebbels, Röhm, and Himmler apparently had no real doubts about Hitler's victory. Goebbels in particular convinced several doubters at the Reichsleitung that their pessimism was unfounded, and Himmler, somewhat prematurely, had already issued instructions limiting the consumption of alcohol at SS victory parties.[49]

Despite the disappointing results Hitler decided immediately that he would be a candidate in the runoff election, and he set to work restoring the party's shattered morale. Six days after the election he and Goebbels met the Gauleiters and Reichstag deputies to dispel the cloud of defeatism that had settled over the party stalwarts.[50] A few days later he converted the party's corps of editors to renewed optimism as well. These sessions were memorable performances of the myth-person. At the editors' meeting the man who had spoken earlier of the defeat as the "Kunnersdorf of the movement," [51] strode ebulliently and confidently into the hall offering greetings of "Heil Franconia!" "Heil Ruhr!" to individual editors as he made his way to the podium. He relived the moments of triumph, the hundreds of thousands who came to hear him. The defeat was almost a non sequitur: this was the responsibility of failure within the NSDAP's organi-

48. Goebbels, *Vom Kaiserhof,* entries for 1, 3, and 13 March 1932, pp. 55, 56, and 62; and Staatspolizei Württemberg, "W. 3," 13 May 1932, HA, roll 58, folder 1405.

49. Bormann later accused Goebbels of having raised false hopes. See Bormann to Hess, 5 Oct. 1932, HA, roll 17, folder 319. For Himmler's alcohol decree, see Reichsführer-SS, "SS-Befehl -C- Nr. 3," 3 March 1932, HA, roll 89, folder 1849.

50. Goebbels, *Vom Kaiserhof,* entry for 19 March 1932, p. 68; *VB,* 22 Mar. 1932.

51. Walter Görlitz and Herbert A. Quint, *Adolf Hitler* (Stuttgart, 1952), p. 336.

zation particularly at the lower and middle echelons. At the end of the meeting the editors were convinced that whatever had happened before, the Reichsleitung had corrected the mechanical problem. None of the responsibility for the disaster remained attached to Hitler.[52]

Not all of the party leaders were satisfied that organizational changes alone were sufficient to put Hitler over the top in the runoff election. Hitler was also faced with a demand that he dismiss Röhm. Hierl, in particular, argued that the presence of a proven (though not confessed) homosexual at the head of the SA would repel many of the rightist voters whom Hitler needed to win over from Hindenburg.[53] Hitler categorically refused,[54] not so much because he was personally attached to Röhm, but because he realized the political dangers of tampering with the status quo in the SA. The SA had confidently expected Hitler's victory in the election, and Röhm had already issued instructions on countering the Communist coup which the NSDAP expected would break out after Hitler's victory. On the night of March 13th, the SA was mobilized in their meeting halls and awaited the call for action.[55] It never came, and the letdown took some time to digest. As late as April the civilian leadership had great fears that the SA might "go off prematurely *(vorprellen).*"[56] At the same time, the SA leaders, including Röhm, made no secret of their dislike of what they considered the cowardice of the civilian leadership. Röhm himself even went so far as to establish contacts with the Reichsbanner organization, apparently with vague plans in mind to establish a union of German paramilitary units against civilians in general.[57] Nothing came of this, but the combined weight of these various factors convinced Hitler that an SA crisis two weeks before the runoff election would be most inopportune.

The NSDAP's campaign strategy for the runoff election was essentially a repetition of earlier methods, though Goebbels instructed the

52. Krebs, *Tendenzen*, pp. 52–54.
53. Hierl to Hitler, 24 March 1932, HA, roll B, folder 1502.
54. See Hitler's declaration of 6 April 1932 in HA, roll 53, folder 1240.
55. The actual instructions for March 13 are in Osaf, Stabschef, "Befehl I Nr. 673/32," 2 March 1932, HA, roll 89, folder 1849. See also Vogelsang, *Reichswehr*, p. 162; and Allen, *Seizure*, p. 92.
56. Goebbels, *Vom Kaiserhof*, entry for 2 April 1932, p. 74.
57. Vogelsang, *Reichswehr*, p. 308.

party propagandists to concentrate their appeals on the middle-class voters who had cast their ballots for Hindenburg in the first election. The NSDAP largely ignored the labor and Catholic votes as hopeless causes. The locals again performed incredible feats of political mobilization, first ferreting out middle-class Hindenburg voters and then "working them over." [58] The positive emphasis on Hitler's own person in the campaign was raised, if possible, to even greater heights of pseudoreligious intensity. A provincial party paper quoted Hitler's statement "I believe that I am God's instrument to liberate Germany." The *VB* headlined "The National Socialist movement is the resurrection of the German nation," and filled its pages once again with pictures of Hitler and the adoring masses.[59]

Despite the almost religious fervor of the party workers and Hitler's own near-mystical image, Hitler lost again to Hindenburg. In the long run it was a Pyrrhic victory, and the NSDAP could take pride in gaining virtually all of the Düsterberg votes for Hitler, but at least for the present the NSDAP had lost its gamble to come to power quickly via the electoral route. This was also clear to the Reich government and immediately after the election it attempted to regain the political initiative. It dissolved the SA and SS as organizational entities and prohibited the display of their uniforms. (The decree also included the HJ as an organizational subordinate of the SA.) The measure was neither unexpected,[60] nor very effective,[61] but it did force the NSDAP to reevaluate its overall political strategy.

There remained, of course, the Landtag elections in Bavaria and Prussia in April, and both Goebbels and the *VB* shortly after the presi-

58. Goebbels to GL, 16 and 23 March 1932, HA, roll 16, folder 290.

59. Hitler expressed his conviction to Ley and Streicher. It appeared in *Rote Erde* and is quoted in Görlitz and Quint, *Hitler*, p. 338. Since Goebbels had discussed the campaign coverage with Amann, the *VB*'s articles were presumably a part of Goebbels' propaganda tactics. See *Vom Kaiserhof*, entry for 20 March 1932, p. 68.

60. The NSDAP's infiltration of the police was by now so complete that all party offices were warned at least one or two days before the order was issued. See PD Mü, "Bericht über die am Mittwoch den 13. April 1932 abends . . . statt-gefundene Wahlversammlung der NSDAP," n.d., HA, roll 89, folder 1846; Goebbels, *Vom Kaiserhof*, entry for 11 April 1932, p. 79.

61. In "Thalburg" the SA and SS even continued to wear their uniforms in public. Allen, *Seizure*, p. 107.

dential elections resolutely stated the party's determination to fight on.[62] The Landtag elections, however, were not the simple propaganda campaigns the two presidential elections had been. It was impossible to conduct the election campaigns without state candidate slates and this in turn reopened the Pandora's box of conflicting claims and demands of the various wings and affiliates in the party. Although the Gauleiters began compilation of their suggested lists as early as December, the struggle for positions was still not over in April.[63] Moreover, the juggling was not finished when the Gauleiters had finally compiled a suggested slate and sent it to Munich,[64] because these lists had to be correlated with the needs and aims of the Reichsleitung executives. Many intraparty feuds were not settled until Frick (as national election chairman), Loeper, and Strasser made categorical decisions which could be appealed only to Hitler.[65]

The final slates left a trail of dissatisfied party organizations and individuals in their wake. They also left unanswered the basic query whether the NSDAP would be any more successful in achieving political power through the states than the party had been in the Reich. To be sure, it could be predicted with reasonable certainty that the NSDAP would show sufficient gains in all of the German states to make itself a very desirable coalition partner after the elections, but Hitler's views on genuine coalitions were rather equivocal. He had deliberately refused to enter coalition governments in Bremen and Hamburg at the beginning of the year when there was still hope for the presidential route. On the other hand, after the defeat of March 13, he favored a coalition in Prussia if a National Socialist headed it.[66]

The way around Hitler's fear that the NSDAP might "wear . . .

62. Goebbels clearly hoped for success in Prussia while the Bavarians at the Reichsleitung had similar hopes for Bavaria. See Goebbels, *Vom Kaiserhof*, entries for 10 and 14 April 1932, pp. 78 and 80–81; and PD Mü, "Bericht über die am . . . 13. April 1932 . . . ," HA, roll 89, folder 1846. See also *VB*, 17/18 April and 8 May 1932.

63. Goebbels, *Vom Kaiserhof*, entry for 1 April 1932, p. 73.

64. For an example of a Gauleiter's slate see [Goebbels], "Vorschlag zur Kandidaten-Liste für den Preussischen Landtag," n.d., HA, roll 30, folder 573.

65. Jordan to Loeper, 21 Jan. 1932, *ibid.;* and GL Thüringen to Loeper, 26 Jan. 1932, *ibid.*

66. *B.T.* (A.A.), 10 Jan. 1932; and Kube to Göring, 21 March 1932, NA, T-580, roll 23, folder 205.

itself out"[67] in a series of coalition cabinets lay in clear National Socialist majorities at the polls. Despite valiant efforts, ingenious tactics (like car pools to transport Prussian voters vacationing in Bavaria to the nearest polling place in Prussia), and spectacular overall gains, the party was not able to dominate the legislature of any major German state. The NSDAP controlled or participated in the governments of Brunswick, Mecklenburg-Strelitz and Anhalt. Somewhat later in the year additional states' elections brought the party to power in Mecklenburg-Schwerin and Oldenburg. Yet, even taken together, these governmental positions were a very narrow bridgehead. Not one of these states was populous or an economically or politically important area of Germany. The NSDAP simply could not make enough gains in the urban areas to achieve a majority of the votes.[68] Above all, Prussia and Bavaria eluded the party's grasp and without them the states road was as impossible as the presidential route.

The strategy of massive electoral votes was a failure. Even Goebbels had fears by now that the party was "winning itself to death in the elections," though he still hoped that the NSDAP could gain unrestricted power in Germany through a frontal attack on the Center Party, the only major middle-class party still intact.[69] For the moment, however, Goebbels' plan was not in favor. After three massive but futile election campaigns and considerable financial debts, the NSDAP leadership and Hitler himself were in a mood to attempt a new strategy. Weighed down with debts,[70] dismayed by the organizational difficulties of digesting the pseudodissolution of the SA,[71] and just simply tired of election campaigns, the party's functionary corps could not maintain the propagandistic momentum of the spring. Equally important, the ill feeling between the old guard and the September-

---

67. *B.T.* (A.A.), 10 Jan. 1932.

68. See Goebbels' *Angriff* editorial, "Die absolute Mehrheit," 31 May 1932, in *Wetterleuchten*, pp. 302–03; and *F.Z.*, 21 June 1932.

69. Goebbels, *Vom Kaiserhof*, entry for 23 April 1932 [sic], p. 87; and his *Angriff* editorial, "Die nächste Aufgabe," 28 April 1932, *Wetterleuchten*, p. 286. See also Roloff, *Bürgertum*, p. 106.

70. The Oberpfalz Gau actually declared its legal bankruptcy. See *B.T.* (A.A.), 4 June 1932.

71. See Reichsschatzmeister, Reichsgeschäftsführer and Rechtsabteilung to all GL, 30 April 1932; and Reichsschatzmeister to all GL, 4 May 1932, in *Rundschreiben des Reichsschatzmeisters, 26. Juli 1926–31. Dez. 1934* (Munich, 1935).

linge had not abated,[72] and Hitler found it increasingly difficult to settle the various disputes during the short meetings which he scheduled with local and provincial officials during his travels. The emphasis on pure propaganda also diluted the control of the center over the activities of the affiliates, so that embarrassing institutional rivalries abounded. While the Office for Agriculture organized foresters, the NSBO in turn invaded the agricultural domain by establishing cells of farm workers.[73] The HJ was particularly active during this period of supposed organizational moratoria. It held a national leadership meeting in early April and decided on major reforms of its organizational structure. The formal separation of the HJ from the SA enabled Schirach to undertake even more elaborate organizational changes including the establishment of some separate Gau leadership schools.[74] In short, the long-term assignment of a priority position to pure propaganda had led to a weakening of the central control lines that in theory coordinated and united the various affiliates and wings of the NSDAP. The organizational life of the party needed revitalization,[75] if the amoeba-like aimlessness of its organizational development was to be halted and centrally redirected.

The NSDAP needed a period of relative decrease in its outward aggressiveness in order to devote some energies to its inner stabilization. Even Goebbels recognized that, after the failure of the Prussian elections, the NSDAP had no choice but to pose as a conciliatory political organization willing to consider serious negotiations with other political groups. And though "it made him puke *(es ist zum Kotzen)*" he promptly wrote an editorial in favor of legislative negotiation with other parties.[76]

72. See the complaints of a HJ leader in HA, roll 19, folder 364; and Terboven (GL Essen) to Hagemann, 22 Jan. 1932, HA, roll 29, folder 549.

73. See *VOBl* (No. 17; 15 Feb. 1932), p. 43; and "Organisationsplan für die 'Nationalsozialistischen Landzellen' der Betriebsgruppe Landwirtschaft der NSBO," n.d., HA, roll 8, folder 176.

74. On the HJ during this period see Hermann Bolm, *Hitlerjugend in einem Jahrzent* (Brunswick, 1938), pp. 183, 186–87, 191–94, and 203–04; *VB,* 17/18 April 1932; and Reichsleitung of the NS Youth Movement, "Rundschreiben 1/32" and "Rundschreiben 2/32," 25 and 29 April 1932, HA, roll B, folder 337.

75. Even Goebbels recognized this. See *Vom Kaiserhof,* entry for 29 April 1932, p. 89.

76. *Ibid.,* entry for 25 April 1932, p. 87.

The two most obviously suitable issues for negotiation were the government of Prussia and the fate of the SA. The former required a coalition with the Center Party[77] and good legislative behavior in general, the latter an approach to the Reich government or the men behind it. The party made both. While Strasser delivered a major conciliatory speech in the Reichstag (which had been previously approved by Hitler) on May 10,[78] Hitler, somewhat later, opened a round of talks with the grey eminence of the Reich government, General Schleicher.[79] Hitler met the general at the end of May on the estate of Walter Granzow (Mecklenburg), the new National Socialist prime minister-designate of Mecklenburg. The two apparently had no major difficulty in reaching a temporary but quite specific working agreement: the NSDAP would tolerate, or at least not directly attack, a Reich Cabinet of Schleicher's own choosing. In return Schleicher promised to use his influence with Hindenburg to effect Brüning's dismissal, schedule new Reichstag elections, and, above all, lift the prohibition of the SA and SS.[80]

The NSDAP's lengthy negotiations with prominent politicians and generals[81] provided a political armistice which permitted the NSDAP to regroup its forces and strengthen its organizational cohesion. There now began a period in the party's organizational history that may be

77. Cf. Göring's statement in early February that "[the NSDAP] will never negotiate with the Center Party as it is constituted today," *B.T.* (M.A.), 2 Feb. 1932.

78. For reports on the speech see *B.T.* (A.A.), 10 May 1932; *VB,* 12 May 1932. Goebbels noted that "Strasser is the most popular of all of us among our enemies. That's a bad sign *(Das spricht stark gegen ihn)."* Goebbels, *Vom Kaiserhof,* entry for 10 May 1932, p. 94.

79. This move caught some party leaders by complete surprise. Albert Krebs, now editor of the *Hamburger Tageblatt,* was ostensibly expelled for writing a sharp editorial against the right-wing General Schleicher. See Hitler to Krebs (by order of the Reich-Uschla), 20 May 1932, Jochmann, *Nationalsozialismus,* p. 383. Krebs replied that he had not been aware that relations between Hitler and Schleicher were so cordial. See Krebs to Strasser, 25 May 1932, *ibid.,* p. 389. Krebs' editorial is reprinted in *ibid.,* p. 386.

80. Vogelsang, *Reichswehr,* doc. 24, pp. 458–59. Goebbels records Hitler's triumph with the words, "The Führer beams with satisfaction." *Vom Kaiserhof,* entry for 4 June 1932, p. 106.

81. Particularly the negotiations over a Prussian coalition government were drawn-out affairs. It was not until June 22 that the Center Party and NSDAP agreed that they were unable to find a coalition formula. See the entries in *Vom Kaiserhof* between June 4 and June 22, pp. 107–115.

accurately termed the Strasser era. It was characterized by a de-emphasis of Goebbels' strategy of pure propaganda and a return to the party's earlier tactics of a more gradual undermining of Germany's socioeconomic values. The shift was by no means absolute. The party still fought vigorous election campaigns and denounced all pluralist forces, but in the Strasser period the organizational activities of the party became once again an integral part of its political goals. The Strasser reorganization also eased the continuing frictions between the NSDAP's regular functionary corps and the affiliate bureaucracies by subordinating the latter to the former, particularly at the Gau level.

Gregor Strasser's organizational reforms began with what in retrospect appears to have been a conscious pilot project, the reorganization of the party's women's auxiliary in April. As on previous occasions, the NSDAP set out on a major political and organizational tangent while a previous emphasis had not yet run its course. The party as a whole was still fully preoccupied with the runoff presidential elections, but Hitler had already recognized the failure of Goebbels' strategy: the reorganization of the Women's Auxiliary was a result of the "experiences of the last election. . . ." The actual reorganization strengthened the authority of the Gauleiters over the Frauenschaft's functionary corps and subordinated the entire organization to the party's Uschla system. In short, the Women's Auxiliary administratively and organizationally ceased to be an affiliate and become instead a subunit of the party's vertical organization. A month later, the civil servants' affiliate and the department for racial questions and culture suffered similar fates. The latter was renamed Department for Cultural Policy and its Gau officials became the direct subordinates of the Gauleiters. The civil servants' group became part of Strasser's own organizational office.[82] A final prefatory reform was the division of the Reich-Uschla into three chambers with varying geographic jurisdictions, a move that foreshadowed the later establishment of the party's dual Reich inspector system.[83]

These pilot projects were apparently successful, for in June Hitler

82. *VOBl* (No. 21; 15 April 1932), pp. 47–48. Kube to Konopath (head of the Department for Cultural Policy), 21 May 1932, HA, roll 53, folder 1240; and *VOBl* (No. 24; 31 May 1932), p. 52.

83. See, below, p. 273. The Uschla's reorganization went into effect June 1. See *VOBl* (No. 24; 31 May 1932), p. 52.

empowered Strasser to extend his reform proposals to additional areas of the party's organization, and from June to September 1932, the NSDAP was clearly dominated by the organizational and political strategy of Gregor Strasser. During this time Strasser was both administratively and in the public image the man next to Hitler.[84] His reorganization of the party involved all aspects of the party's political and organizational life and all of the NSDAP's functionaries. A larger number of offices became Strasser's direct subordinates, and those that remained administratively separate, like Schwarz's agencies, reorganized their jurisdictions to correspond to Strasser's guidelines.[85] Even Hitler became a part of the reorganization when he donned the new uniform for party functionaries that was introduced along with Strasser's administrative reforms.[86]

Strasser's reforms swept through the NSDAP as two sets of massive reorganization decrees in early June and August. Between them lay a period of consolidation in which the party was able to digest the first wave of reform measures. The reforms had both administrative and political aims. On the one hand, the reorganization was designed to tighten the administrative lines of control and communication that had fallen loose in the spring. At the same time Strasser hoped to structure the politico-organizational activities of the NSDAP in such a way that the party could participate in governmental coalitions without fear of "wearing itself out." Politically, Strasser hoped to achieve power in Germany by using the NSDAP as a microcosmic organization of such cohesion and organizational strength that it could within a relatively short time neutralize any political group that opposed it and thus take over the larger German societal macrocosm. Strasser's strategy was essentially that used by the Communist parties in Eastern Europe after World War II.[87] Thus the basic ingredients

84. See the ostentatious photo on page 1 of the *VB*, 1 July 1932. It is also significant that Kube formally proposed Strasser as prime minister of Prussia in Hitler's presence. See Kube to Strasser, 6 June 1932, HA, roll 29, folder 555.

85. On the reorganization of Schwarz's territorial staffs see *VOBl* (No. 26; 30 June 1932), p. 57.

86. Domarus, ed., *Hitler-Reden*, I, p. 114 and 114 n162. Hitler also reissued his earlier announcement that he, like all other members of the party, was subject to the decisions of the Reich-Uschla. See *VOBl* (No. 27; 15 July 1932), p. 60.

87. Hugh Seton-Watson, *The East European Revolution* (3d ed.; New York, 1956), pp. 167–71.

of the Strasser system were administrative standardization to improve bureaucratic efficiency and an elevation and incorporation of planning and theoretical studies into the overall political activities of the NSDAP.

The Strasser reforms were a radical departure only in their political strategy. The administrative side of the reforms was merely a restatement of the often-expressed Führerprinzip, though Hitler did permit Strasser to concentrate more administrative power than ever before in the hands of one official (that is, other than himself). The rationalization of the party's administrative structure involved basically a standardization of the duties and jurisdictions of the party's geographic and functional units. The NSDAP's geographic jurisdictions were restructured to eliminate undue variations in membership strength, while at the same time the larger units (districts and above) — in preparation for the party take-over of governmental control — received geographic boundaries that corresponded to the prevailing governmental jurisdictions. Functionally, Strasser standardized titles and functions in the NSDAP's bureaucracy so that a department head in the agricultural affiliate would perform exactly the same level and type of work as his counterpart in the NSBO. This also had the advantage of making the officials more readily interchangeable in case rapid expansion of an affiliate made this necessary. Such interchanges were also greatly facilitated by the most far-reaching of Strasser's measures to increase the efficiency of the party's administration: the elimination of the Reich Organizational Leadership II and the subordination of the affiliates' Reich offices to Strasser. Instead of the various semi-independent offices the affiliates now became Main Departments *(Hauptabteilungen)* of Strasser's Reich Organizational Department, and their heads were administratively subordinate to Strasser (Hitler still held the power of appointment). The reorganization also eliminated the ambiguity of the affiliates' relationship to the Gauleiters, in that the Gauleiters now had the same relationship to their staffs as Strasser did to the executives at the Reichsleitung.

Strasser was fully aware that his office alone could not effectively control the newly centralized administrative apparatus of the party and the affiliates. His solution here was to expand significantly the inspectorate system. Although the office of Reich inspector was established in 1931, the institution had remained of secondary importance during the campaigns of the spring. Strasser's reorganization, however, provided not only for two Reich inspectors — Schulz (Strasser's deputy) and Ley — but for a series of state inspectors *(Landesinspekteure)* as well, though the latter were not appointed until the second phase of the reorganization. The two Reich inspectors supervised geographic areas of very unequal political significance, with Schulz in charge of the populous northern, western and eastern areas, while Ley had to be content with the less important southern and Austrian regions.[88]

The reorganization concentrated unprecedented administrative and control functions in the hands of Gregor Strasser. For the first time in its history the NSDAP had what was at least on paper a completely rational administrative structure.[89] (See chart on page 261.) Nevertheless, Strasser's plans evoked mixed reactions among the NSDAP's leaders. For the moment, however, the bitter opposition of Goebbels[90] and some others was of no significance. Hitler fully supported Strasser,[91] so that the latter was able to dominate the two leadership conferences that met to discuss the first phase of the party's reorganization. The first of these met on June 8, 9, and 10 in Munich. A large part of the discussion ranged around the makeup of the candidate slates for the forthcoming Reichstag elections,[92] but Strasser also announced the reorganization schemes. A second meeting at the end of the month gave Strasser an opportunity to underline the importance of the reorganization: during the forthcoming election campaign the NSDAP would not neglect all organizational activities in favor of propaganda. The reorganization remained a major concern of the party's functionary corps.[93]

88. The entire series of reforms is in *VB*, 15 June 1932, and *VOBl* (No. 25; 17 June 1932), pp. 53–56.

89. The "professionalization" of the NSDAP's functionary corps had made rapid progress. By this time even district leaders were generally full-time salaried employees. See SA Untergruppenführer Ostholstein to Osaf, 24 Sept. 1932, NA, T-81, roll 1, frame 11567.

90. Privately Goebbels compared the scheme to a "potted palm. Fat and swollen but without internal strength." *Vom Kaiserhof*, entry for 9 June 1932, p. 109.

91. See his remarks to the functionary corps in Thuringia quoted in *VB*, 25 June 1932.

92. See, below, pp. 266–68; and *VB*, 10 June 1932.

93. *VB*, 30 June 1932. See also Goebbels, *Vom Kaiserhof*, entry for 27 June 1932, p. 119.

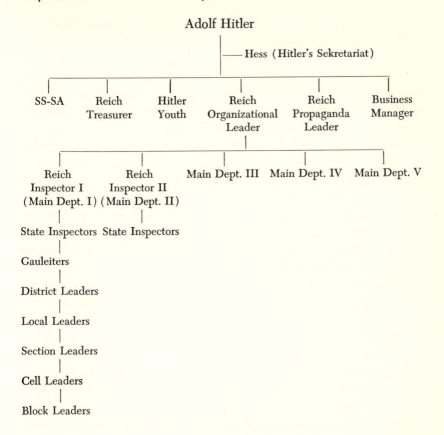

The NSDAP's social and paramilitary organizations were not focal points of Strasser's reorientation, and actually gained additional organizational autonomy as a result of his reforms. The Hitler Youth remained separate from the SA even after the military units were reestablished, and Schirach quickly assumed complete control of all youth activities in the party.[94] The office of the Reich Youth Leadership expanded rapidly with Schirach's new control functions: by July 12 separate de-

94. "Verfügung des Führers betr. Leitung der Nationalsozialistischen Jugendverbände," 13 May 1932, HA, roll 18, folder 337. On Schirach's control over the other party youth organizations see Krüger (Referent in Abt. IV of the HJ Reichsleitung), "Kameraden des N.[ational] S.[ozialistischen] S.[chülerbundes]," 27 June 1932, *ibid.*; Bundesführung Jungvolk, "Rundschreiben Nr. 1/32," 26 May 1932, HA, roll 19, folder 353; and Bund Deutscher Mädel, "Richtlinien," p. 2, *ibid.*

partments, headed by a chief of staff, reported to Schirach.[95] Like the
Hitler Youth, the SA and SS were not directly affected by Strasser's
reforms, though indirectly they too gained a greater amount of autonomy as the party's political offices attempted to ingest the newly
subordinated affiliates.[96] In addition, it is fair to say that the party
tried to appease the restlessness of the SA at least during the first part
of the Strasser era.[97]

The increasing efficiency and centralization of the party's administration made up only one side of Strasser's approach to gaining political
power for the NSDAP. Closely related to this aspect of the Strasser
reforms was his attempt to combine systematic planning activities[98]
with estate-based interest group structures into politicized microcosmic units of the new German society. For Strasser the party in the
Third Reich would not merely control societal life, but in fact would
be a model for societal life which needed merely to be expanded when
the NSDAP achieved political power.[99] Thus Strasser prohibited the
membership of artisans in the employee-estate organization — the
NSBO — and ordered that all officials of the Agricultural Apparatus
be practicing farmers.[100] It is almost as though the party as a political
elite unit would wither away progressively as the larger German society became politicized under the leadership of the National Socialists.
In a sense, Strasser's political strategy was a refinement of the party's
successful infiltration efforts in 1931. While previously the NSDAP's
primary goal had been to win the votes of those who were attracted
by the programs and promises of the affiliates, Strasser now recognized
that this strategy had reached the point of diminishing returns. Instead, he proposed to use the party's established strength to continue

95. On the Reichsleitung of the HJ see Reichsführer–HJ Stabsleiter, "Rundschreiben 5/32," 27 June 1932, HA, roll 18, folder 337; and "Gliederung der
Reichsjugendführung . . . ," 20 July 1932, HA, roll 46, folder 953.

96. SA Gruppenführer Ost to Osaf, 30 June 1932, HA, roll 29, folder 550.

97. See Göring's speech in Berlin on 15 July 1932 in *B.T.* (A.A.), 16 July 1932.
On the SA's image at this time see Goebbels, *Vom Kaiserhof*, entry for 26 June
1932, p. 119.

98. For Goebbels the Strasser era was the time of the "memoranda." *Vom
Kaiserhof*, entry for 13 Dec. 1932, p. 224.

99. For Strasser's never very clearly formulated ideas on these issues, see Krebs,
Tendenzen, p. 191.

100. *VOBl* (No. 27; 15 July 1932), pp. 61 and 62.

the process of taking over German society after the NSDAP had achieved positions of governmental power in a coalition with the non-totalitarian and organizationally weaker middle-class parties.

During the first phase of the reform era Strasser reconstructed the economic affiliates to underline their microcosmic character. When the first reform plans were announced in mid-June, the functional status of Main Departments III and IV remained unclear.[101] Main Departments I and II were the two Reich Inspectorates, while V was Darré's Office for Agriculture. The fourth unit became a thoroughly revamped Economic Department, and Strasser used III as a convenient catchall for offices that could not conveniently be fitted elsewhere, though he also announced that this would not be the final status of the third Main Department.[102] The general direction of Strasser's economic views were well known. Like Muchow and most of the NSBO's leaders, he was against liberalism and capitalism and favored a form of pseudomedieval socialism or, perhaps better, communalism. These doctrines were by no means unpopular either in the NSDAP or in German public opinion, and Strasser's Reichstag speech in May had received a generally favorable reception.[103] Strasser followed ideological pronouncements with a functional reorganization of the old Economic Department, now Main Department IV. In mid-June Walther Funk became Strasser's official advisor on all economic questions. Funk, who became Reich Economics Minister in 1938, had been editor of the conservative, business-oriented *Berliner Börsenzeitung*. But his economic views, at least at this time, resembled Strasser's and he joined the NSDAP and even met Hitler through Strasser.[104] A month later, Main Department IV was organizationally divided into six departments each with separate functional spheres from "economic policy" and "economic estates" to "press and propaganda."[105] Despite his support of Strasser's ascendancy in the NSDAP, Hitler was apparently reluctant to let the "left" wing of the party entirely dominate the

101. *VB*, 15 June 1932.

102. *VOBl* (No. 29; 15 Aug. 1932), p. 65.

103. On its reception by the "left" wing of the party see cover picture and comments on the speech in *Arbeitertum*, II (1 June 1932).

104. *VB*, 15 June 1932; and Funk's oral evidence, 3 May 1946, in *IMT*, XIII, pp. 79 and 82.

105. *VB*, 13 July 1932.

economic policy formulation of the party. Consequently, he did not allow the Reich Economic Council to be absorbed into Main Department IV. To be sure, its nominal chairman, Gottfried Feder, was a "left-winger," [106] but the Council's members were all businessmen and corporation executives, and the Council continued to report directly to Hitler, rather than to Strasser.[107]

Nevertheless, by mid-summer Gregor Strasser's reforms had enveloped virtually all of the NSDAP's administrative structure. This first phase of the reorganization came to an end when a new set of intraparty regulations went into effect on July 15, with a proviso that the new rules would be reviewed at the beginning of October, after their effectiveness had been tested in the day-to-day administrative life of the party.[108] The temporary halt in the reforms was also marked by the assignment of new office space and telephone connections for the executives in the Brown House. The telephone directories reveal not only the complete acceptance of Strasser's organizational scheme by the offices in the Reichsleitung (including Goebbels' Propaganda Office), but above all attest to the growth and pervasiveness of the Reich Organizational Office itself. At the end of July the Reich Organizational Leader headed a staff of ninety-five managerial and clerical employees, spread over fifty-four separate rooms in the Brown House. Strasser's organization was clearly the day-to-day nerve center of the NSDAP.[109]

Hitler, of course, had not accepted Strasser's reorganization scheme merely to enlarge the organizational leader's jurisdictional sphere. On the contrary, he approved it because Goebbels' approach to the seats of power had proved sterile. Strasser clearly had to produce results. Specifically and immediately, he had to obtain demonstrable benefits for the party from the Reich government in return for Hitler's agree-

106. Strasser and Feder were the two National Socialist leaders who wrote most frequently for the NSBO organ *Arbeitertum.*

107. *VOBl* (No. 28; 30 July 1932), p. 63. For the membership of the Council at this time see "Testimony of Baron von Schroeder," 28 July 1947, *Flick Trial,* p. 321. Actually, Hitler's control of the Council was more symbolic than real, since the body only met twice during all of 1932.

108. *VOBl* (No. 32; 30 Sept. 1932), p. 73.

109. Reichsorganisationsleiter, Adjudantur, "Gliederung der Reichsorganisationsabteilung" and "Alphabetische Liste des Personals der Reichsorganisationsabteilung," 20 July 1932, HA, roll 46, folder 953.

ment to the semi-armistice, and, perhaps equally important, organizationally he had to prepare the NSDAP for the Reichstag election at the end of July. Strasser accomplished both. The first fruit of the National Socialists' toleration of the Papen Cabinet (other than the lifting of the SA prohibition) was the elimination of the Social Democratic government in Prussia and the appointment of Papen as Reich Commissioner. To be sure, there is no demonstrable connection between the Strasser reform and Papen's "major step on the way to Hitler," [110] but the coup did occur during the Strasser era. Moreover, the NSDAP was convinced that Papen acted in response to its demands, and the party certainly benefited in a number of ways. The police were far more tolerant of party activities (and excesses) under the new regime,[111] and the SA experienced a measurable boost in morale: the storm troopers confidently expected that the new government would make use of their services.[112]

The Strasser reorganization had a more direct effect on the propaganda content and the makeup of the candidate slates for the Reichstag election. Strasser's enthusiasm for planning resulted in an official statement on economic policy which served as a guideline for all National Socialist propagandists during the campaign.[113] Additional theoretical statements on practical issues of the day followed,[114] and while the results were by no means always clear or sensible, at least the party's planning activities did yield a series of positive policy suggestions that served primarily to solidify interest-group support for the NSDAP and only secondarily as more demagogic polemics.

The first major administrative test of the June reforms came with the drafting of the party's candidate lists for the July elections. These

110. Waldemar Besson, *Württemberg und die deutsche Staatskrise, 1928–1933* (Stuttgart, 1959), p. 292.

111. *VB*, 22 July 1932; and Goebbels, *Vom Kaiserhof*, entries for 21 and 22 July 1932, p. 133. The Prussian coup had been rumored as early as June. See *F.Z.*, 8 June 1932.

112. Vogelsang, *Reichswehr*, p. 251.

113. *Wirtschaftliches Sofortprogramm der NSDAP* (Munich, 1932); and *F.Z.*, 13 July 1932.

114. Ottokar Lorenz (Referent of the Reichsleitung for social policy), *Die Beseitigung der Arbeitslosigkeit* (Berlin, 1932); and Alfred Pfaff (a member of the Reich Economic Council), *Der Wirtschaftsaufbau im Dritten Reich* (Munich, 1932).

were the first national legislative elections since the growth of the affiliates in 1931, and there was, understandably, massive competition among all of the party offices to assure safe seats for their representatives. In addition, the SA now competed for Reichstag deputy positions, and the NSDAP, in attempting to bolster its legislative strength through a series of election agreements with rightist splinter groups, allocated a certain number of seats to these groups. In short, even in 1932 the party had far more aspirants than safe seats, and a massive coordination and control effort was required if the final slate of candidates was to avoid both serious imbalances and deep-seated bitterness among those left out.

Hitler used the Gauleiter conference in early June to announce his basic criteria for the selection of candidates. He insisted that half of the safe seats in each district had to be allotted to the SA and SS. He wanted the functionaries of the Office for Agriculture to occupy prominent places, not least because the support of the farmers in northern and southern Germany was one of the major factors uniting the NSDAP in the two areas. He also wanted all of the members who had sat in the last Reichstag reelected, and, to prevent complaints about Septemberlinge, he insisted that no candidate for a safe seat should have a membership number higher than 300,000.[115]

The Gauleiters faced the unenviable task[116] of drawing up preliminary lists. Their labors were often accompanied by bitter complaints,[117] but in the end the proposed lists usually met Hitler's guidelines, as Table 9 (an example from the Brandenburg Gau) shows. In practice it was highly unlikely that the Gauleiters' proposals would be the final slate for that district. Compromising the feuds at the Gau level merely passed the first hurdle in the process of drawing up the

115. Since Hitler's remarks at the June meeting were not recorded, these guidelines must be reconstructed from a series of allusions to them by other party officials. See Brückner to Frick, 21 June 1932, HA, roll 29, folder 546; Jordan to Frick, 5 July 1932, *ibid.*, folder 547; Darré to Strasser, 13 June 1932, *ibid.*, folder 550; Frick to Bachem, 2 July 1932, *ibid.*, folder 555; and Grohé (GL Köln-Aachen) to Frick, 20 June 1932, *ibid.*, folder 548.

116. Goebbels, *Vom Kaiserhof*, entry for 5 June 1932, p. 107.

117. For examples of complaints see GL Halle-Merseburg to Strasser, 2 July 1932; and GL Halle-Merseburg, Gaugeschäftsführer to Hitler, 2 July 1932, HA, roll 29, folder 547; and GL Pommern, Gauobmann für Kriegsopferversorgung and KL Neustettin to RL, Abt. Kriegsopferversorgung, 8 July 1932, *ibid.*, folder 546.

TABLE 9

Name	Party Office	Membership Number
Schlange	Gauleiter	4,387
Graf Helldorf	SA-Gruppenführer	— [sic]
von Wangenheim	LGF (Agricultural expert)	77,217
Decker	Reichstag deputy	136,932
Hauke	SA-Standartenführer	112,828
Dieckmann	LGF (Agricultural expert)	85,970
Kannegiesser	District leader	292,173
Scheerer (1)	SA Sturmbannführer	199,788
Dassler	Gau Propaganda Leader	312,956 [sic]
Scheerer (2)	District leader	199,787

Source: "Wahlvorschlag des Gaues Brandenburg zur Reichstagswahl [Juli] 1932—Wahlkreis Potsdam I," n.d., Hauptarchiv der NSDAP, roll 29, folder no. 546.

final lists. Upon their arrival in Munich the lists had to undergo a series of reviews. It appears that Loeper checked the submitted names against the formal list of requirements, while Frick and Kube, the two Reich election leaders, had politically more significant tasks. They had to splice safe places into the lists not only for prominent executives of the Reichsleitung, but for well-known fellow-travelers of the party, and for candidates of groups with whom the NSDAP had concluded election agreements.[118]

The final decisions lay in the hands of Hitler and Strasser. As always, Hitler insisted that his right of absolute control be explicitly acknowledged by all party leaders,[119] but, aside from a nocturnal discussion with Schirach on candidates from the Hitler Youth,[120] Hitler did not actively intervene in the actual drawing-up of the slates. In practice, the final responsibility for the placement of all candidates

118. Loeper had compiled lists of potential candidates as early as January. See Brückner (GL Schlesien) to Organisationsleiter I, 7 June 1932, *ibid.* Willikens to Frick, 2 July 1932; and Frick to Willikens, 4 July 1932, *ibid.*, folder 555. On Frick's negotiations and agreements with other parties see the documents in *ibid.*, folder 551.

119. When an SA-Gruppenführer wrote that he had a right to expect a safe seat because of a promise from Röhm, Hitler wrote in the margin "Only I give promises! *(Zusagen gebe ich allein!)*." See SA-Gruppenführer Ost to Osaf, 30 June 1932, *ibid.*, folder 550.

120. Schirach to Röhm, 15 June 1932, HA, roll 19, folder 360.

except for those of the SS, SA, and HJ lay with Gregor Strasser. The June reforms enabled Strasser and the Gauleiters to speak with clear authority when dealing with the affiliate chiefs at their respective levels. With the explicit subordination of the Gau staff officials to the Gauleiters, the latter had a much more clearly defined authority to overrule their affiliate staffs. Appeals by the Gau affiliate officials to their superiors in Munich were also futile, since these were now Strasser's administrative subordinates. In addition, Strasser had the authority to overrule both Loeper and Frick, and his position in the party was now so prominent[121] that he even prevailed against officials, such as the Reich Youth Leader, who were not part of his jurisdiction.[122]

As a result, the final slate of candidates reflected Strasser's ideas on the party's approach to political power. The NSDAP candidates appeared to the voters as politicized representatives of the German estates; Strasser insisted that the final slates show a wide cross section of occupational groups, and that the candidates list their party position to demonstrate the NSDAP's microcosmic structure.[123] At the same time, the party preserved its image of a thoroughly political band of followers of Adolf Hitler. Once selected as candidates the party members took a personal oath of obedience to Hitler, since "it is necessary that they obey blindly. . . ."[124] The "Strasser list" was thus a group of totalized followers, broadly representative of the occupational and social groups in German society, but also single-mindedly devoted to absolute political goals.

Quite aside from facilitating the preparation of the party's slate of candidates, the Strasser plan also prepared the NSDAP politically for either of the two predictable outcomes of the Reichstag elections.

121. The *VB* described the triumvirate of party leaders under Hitler as follows: "Strasser . . . head of the political organization. Röhm, chief of staff of the SA, Göring . . . [the] political plenipotentiary . . . three of Hitler's comrades-in-arms." See *VB*, 10/11 July 1932.

122. See von Sybel (one of the fellow-traveling Landbund leaders) to Strasser, 15 June 1932, HA, roll 29, folder 546; and Strasser's marginalia in Reichsjugend-führer, deputy to [Strasser], 8 June 1932, *ibid.*, folder 550.

123. Thus, one candidate who had been giving his occupation as "white collar worker" in 1930 on Strasser's request now listed himself as "head of the Department Maritime Commerce (*Seefahrt*) of the Reich Organizational Leadership." See Thiele to Frick, 17 June 1932, *ibid.* See also GL Baden to Strasser, 11 June 1932, *ibid.*, folder 550.

124. Goebbels, *Vom Kaiserhof*, entry for 11 June 1932, p. 109.

No realistic observer of the German political scene could doubt that the NSDAP would make impressive gains in the elections, but it was doubtful if Hitler could unite a majority of the German voters behind him. He certainly tried. For a third time in five months his chartered plane took him from one hurried stop[125] to the next, into every corner of Germany. But again he failed. A comparison of the National Socialist vote in 1930 and 1932 in some key Gaus reveals the reasons. (See Table 10.)

TABLE 10

	NSDAP Vote			
Gau	Sept. 1930	Percent	July 1932	Percent
Ostpreussen	236,507	22.5	536,278	47.1
Berlin	158,257	12.8	281,531	24.6
Schleswig-Holstein	240,288	27.0	506,117	51.0
Sachsen	561,371	18.0	1,306,955	36.0
Westfalen-Nord	161,993	12.0	368,416	25.7
Westfalen-Süd	195,466	13.9	404,850	27.2
Köln-Aachen	169,510	14.5	249,086	20.2
Franken	281,118	20.5	589,865	39.8
München-Oberbayern	218,326	16.3	385,771	27.1
Württemberg	131,683	9.4	426,533	30.3
Hessen	284,996	20.8	645,394	43.6

SOURCE: *Statistisches Handbuch des Deutschen Reiches–1933* (Berlin, 1934), p. 524.
    Saxony still included more than one district. For an analysis of the results, see also Karl-Dietrich Bracher, *Die Auflösung der Weimarer Republik* (3d ed., Villingen, Schwarzwald, 1955), p. 609.

The results are not difficult to interpret. The NSDAP simply could not demand full governmental power under the legislative rules, and indeed the party's position in the southern and industrialized areas of Germany was far from secure. Strasser's political strategy had prepared the party for this contingency: the NSDAP could enter a coalition government and, after a time, achieve total power through the

125. For an "inside" description of Hitler's activities during his stops see Gmelin, letter of 8 July 1932 in "Briefe."

back door. A feeling that this would be the party's path to power was widespread among party officials, both before and after the elections.[126] Thus the SA before the elections confidently (and naïvely) offered its aid to the Reichswehr in suppressing the expected Communist putsch attempt, while after the voting some SA section leaders quite sincerely expected the Reichswehr to give them weapons to subdue the left "in accordance with the agreements made in Berlin." [127] There were also indications that Hitler never left this possibility out of the campaign. Despite the bitter National Socialist attacks on virtually all political figures in Germany, the party's propaganda left Schleicher completely unscathed and Hitler let it be known privately that he trusted the general.[128] Moreover, Hitler announced that after the seizure of power party officials would remain in their party posts even if they assumed governmental positions,[129] a measure that fit neatly into Strasser's notion of politicizing German society through the party microcosm. Thus, while no party militant disputed Hitler's absolute right to determine the future decisions of the NSDAP, few seem to have doubted that he would enter the NSDAP in a coalition government.

Schleicher, too, was prepared to grant Hitler a number of ministerial portfolios in a coalition government, so that he expressed no surprise at most of the demands which Hitler presented him on August 4: National Socialists were to hold the portfolios of chancellor and minister of the interior in the Reich and Prussia, and, in addition, ministers of education, agriculture, air, and justice in the Reich cabinet. Schleicher apparently felt the price was rather high,[130] but he

126. PD Mü, "Amtswaltersitzung des Bezirksvorstandes der NSDAP am 18.7.32, PND Nr. 784," HA, roll 88, folder 1838. The speaker, a member of Gauleiter Adolf Wagner's staff, was preparing the functionaries for a numerical disappointment on July 31. See also Lehmann to Dr. Stellrecht, 15 Sept. 1932, NA, T-81, roll 1, frames 11537–38.

127. On the SA–Reichswehr contacts during these weeks see Heinrich Bennecke, *Hitler und die SA* (Munich, 1962), p. 194; and Vogelsang, *Reichswehr*, docs. 31, 32, and 33, pp. 475–76, 476–77, and 478–79 resp. The quotation is from a letter by the SA leader in Württemberg to Röhm, 9 Aug. 1932, quoted in *ibid.*, p. 479.

128. Bracher, *Auflösung*, p. 608; and Hans Husmann (a personal friend of Papen's) to Papen, 24 June 1932, quoted in *ibid.*, p. 550 n118. The letter reports a conversation which Husmann had with Strasser.

129. Goebbels, *Vom Kaiserhof*, entry for 8 Aug. 1932, p. 140.

130. The Papen–Schleicher government had thought in terms of Hitler as vice-chancellor, Strasser as Reich and Prussian minister of the interior, and Frick as minister of education. See Pünder, *Politik*, entry for 18 Aug. 1932, p. 141.

agreed to these terms.[131] No doubt one major factor in his acquiescence was the knowledge that the NSDAP had an alternative to the Schleicher combination. Strasser and Göring (with Hitler's permission) were also exploring the possibility of forming a coalition government with the Center Party,[132] and the likelihood of such a legislative combination, which could have assumed office under the rules of the legislature with a majority of Reichstag votes, was by no means remote.

It was Hitler who destroyed all chances of realizing either scheme. On August 3, Schulz, Strasser's right-hand man, had informed Schleicher's office that Hitler insisted on personally assuming the post of Reich chancellor. Both Strasser and Göring had attempted to dissuade Hitler from presenting this demand to Hindenburg[133] but he had remained adamant. The Strasser plan was doomed. Its entire strategy had been based upon a covert National Socialist take-over of Germany, while Hitler's appointment as chancellor would mean an open demonstration that the NSDAP was in charge of the Reich government. And for precisely this reason, Hindenburg categorically refused to appoint Hitler chancellor unless he could command a Reichstag majority. Hitler, however, could not meet that prerequisite since the Center Party refused to enter a cabinet headed by him. The immediate result was a "severe personal defeat"[134] for Hitler. On August 13 he met formally with Hindenburg and demanded to head a government with decree powers. Hindenburg refused.[135] Immediately afterwards, the SA, which had literally been mobilized in preparation for the expected SA–Reichswehr cooperation in enforcing the first decrees of the new government, was furloughed for two weeks.[136]

There can be little doubt that Hitler personally sabotaged the Strasser plan, but it is considerably more puzzling why he felt compelled to do so. He clearly did not need to fear the rivalry of Strasser's

131. Vogelsang, *Reichswehr*, pp. 257–58; and Goebbels, *Vom Kaiserhof*, entries for 4 and 6 Aug. 1932, pp. 138–39.

132. Görlitz and Quint, *Hitler*, p. 347.

133. Vogelsang, *Reichswehr*, p. 256.

134. *Ibid.*, p. 265.

135. Meissner, "Aufzeichnung über die Besprechung des Herrn Reichspräsidenten mit Adolf Hitler—13 Aug. 1932," in Hubatsch, ed., *Hindenburg*, pp. 338–39.

136. Vogelsang, *Reichswehr*, pp. 262–63; and Engelbrechten, *Braune Armee*, p. 238. On the preparations and maneuvers of the SA in early August see also the article by the Stahlhelm leader von Stephani in the *Kreuzzeitung*, quoted in *B.T.* (M.A.), 19 Aug. 1932.

growing power. To be sure, Strasser would have become a cabinet minister while Hitler remained outside the government, but Strasser had never intended to usurp Hitler's position, and Hitler had demonstrated throughout 1931 and 1932 that he could control the party's Reichstag delegation very effectively from his hotel room without being a member of the Reichstag. It may be that Goebbels persuaded Hitler to demand the supreme position; his diary entries certainly applaud Hitler's eventual decision. Yet, perhaps the simplest explanation is the most likely: Strasser's strategy involved a time-lapse factor between the NSDAP's joining of a coalition and its eventual complete take-over of the society, and Hitler throughout 1932 was a very impatient man.[137]

In the meantime, however, his gamble had failed. The NSDAP's bid for power had been clearly, even ignominiously, rebuffed, and a deep depression settled over the movement. Goebbels cited the "laws of history" that would put power in Hitler's hands, and Röhm publicly called Hitler's refusal to accept Hindenburg's terms "soldierly," but in private he admitted that the SA's morale had been severely shaken.[138] Röhm met the crisis by reemphasizing military drill in the activities of the SA,[139] but this was at best a stopgap measure which would even become counterproductive if drill did not eventually lead to action by the party as a whole.

Ironically, the fiasco of August 13 inaugurated the second phase of Strasser's reorganization scheme. It is as though Hitler, shortly after his meeting with Hindenburg, realized his mistake and hastened to put the party back on the Strasser course. The party press resumed its accolades of Strasser; training manuals underscored the scope and importance of his offices.[140]

By this time relatively little could be added to the efficiency and

137. Cf. Hitler's statement to Krebs during the presidential campaign on the reasons for his running, "I don't have time to wait . . . . I can't lose a single year. I have got to get to power shortly to solve the gigantic problem during the time that remains for me. I have got to. I have got to." Krebs, *Tendenzen*, p. 137.

138. See Goebbels' *Angriff* editorial, "Die Macht an Hitler," 15 Aug. 1932, in *Wetterleuchten*, pp. 322–23; Röhm, "Der Entschluss eines Soldaten," *VB*, 17 Aug. 1932; and Goebbels, *Vom Kaiserhof*, entry for 13 Aug. 1932, p. 146.

139. Engelbrechten, *Braune Armee*, p. 243.

140. See, for example, *VB*, 7 Sept. 1932; and the description of the party organization in *Der Politische Soldat* (*Blatt für politische Schulung und Bildung der SA, Standarte 7* [*Berlin*]), 15 Sept. 1932, HA, roll 17, folder 311.

standardization side of the reforms. The bureaucratization of the party's activities had reached a saturation point, with explicit, standardized instructions regulating all activities of party officials from the proper titles to be used on communications to superior officials to the correct types of uniform buttons.[141] Strasser did, however, complete the buildup of the inspectorate system. The position of state inspector, which had been established on paper in June, now became fully operative. The ten state inspectors who took up their duties in mid-August were all long-time Gauleiters and seven of the ten had been associated with Strasser in the old Northwest Association of 1925. The position was a full-time office, and all of the appointees gave up their responsibilities as Gauleiters (but not their titles) when they became inspectors.[142] This last link in the inspectorate system was not particularly popular among the Gauleiters,[143] since the inspectors' authority included the right to supersede the writ of the individual Gauleiter if this became necessary. Unlike Ley, the state inspectors were free agents, able to carry out surprise inspections at any time of the day or night. In addition, they coordinated the work of the National Socialist Landtag delegations.[144]

Strasser strengthened the Reichsleitung's control of the Gauleiters,[145] but he also allowed the Gauleiters to increase their authority in their individual Gaus. The Reichsleitung confirmed the Gauleiters in their administrative spheres and extended this control to the functional aspects of the Gau activities.[146] Administratively the Gauleiters used their newly defined authority particularly to enforce the provision of the Strasser plan calling for the alignment of party districts with the

141. Reichsorganisationsleiter, "Anordnung Nr. 1" [sic], HA, roll 14, folder 265; and Wolfgang Schäfer, *NSDAP* (Hanover, 1956), p. 20.

142. *VOBl* (No. 30; 31 Aug. 1932), p. 67.

143. Hinrich Lohse (GL of Schleswig-Holstein), "Der Fall Strasser," n.d., (typescript MS in the possession of the Forschungsstelle für die Geschichte des Nationalsozialismus in Hamburg). Lohse was one of the new inspectors.

144. Reichsorganisationsleiter, "Anordnung Nr. 1," 19 Aug. 1932, HA, roll 14, folder 265; and Engelbert Huber, *Das ist Nationalsozialismus* (Stuttgart, 1933), p. 39.

145. Although appointed by Hitler, the state inspectors as an organizational device were apparently Strasser's own idea. Hitler later claimed that he had never really approved of the idea. See Lohse, "Der Fall Strasser," p. 27.

146. *VB*, 11 Aug. 1932; and *F.Z.*, 12 Nov. 1932.

governmental districts.[147] On the other hand, a Gauleiter's direct authority ended at the boundaries of his Gau. Goebbels could decree a boycott of all non-NSDAP papers for the party members of the Berlin Gau, but the Reichsleitung denied him the right to extend the measure to other Gaus.[148]

Thus, the Gauleiters became in their Gaus what Strasser was rapidly becoming at the Reich level: the chief executive of the party's activities, responsible both for future planning and day-to-day administration. The second phase of the Strasser reforms continued the transformation of the party into a politicized microcosm, but, while the earlier reforms had concentrated on the political organization of the NSDAP per se, the new decrees focused attention on the interrelation of the NSDAP's microcosmic organizational structures and their planning activities. In June Strasser had established Main Department III as an organizational haven for all those affiliates which did not yet fit the new microcosmic image of the party, that is, all the affiliates that could not be fit into the economic department (IV), the Agricultural Apparatus (V), or the NSBO (VI). In September, however, Main Department III was "organically subdivided." By raising several affiliates to the status of new Main Departments the party underscored its concern with the areas of German societal life which they represented: civil service (VII), women's auxiliary (VIII), and disabled veterans (IX). What remained of Main Department III became a vital component in Strasser's concept of the NSDAP's role as a politicized microcosm: "the scientific-theoretical *(wissenschaftliches)* laboratory of the party." This was the new general staff of the movement, the agency which had no other duties but to draft bills for use by National Socialist governmental organs. For the movement, the general staff had only departments for interior, communal, educational, and public health policies, but Strasser also planned offices for "scientific" planning on agricultural, economic, labor, and physical education policies.[149]

Simultaneously, Main Departments IV and VI experienced structural modifications which gave them even more the character of prototypes

147. Goebbels, *Vom Kaiserhof*, entry for 27 Aug. 1932, p. 151; and GL München-Oberbayern to all KL, Ogrl., and Stützpunktleiter, 10 Oct. 1932, HA, roll 9, folder 193; and *VB*, 8 Sept. 1932.

148. *B.T.* (M.A.), 29 Sept. 1932.

149. *VOBl* (No. 32; 30 Sept. 1932), p. 73.

for the National Socialist version of the corporate state. The offices on economic affairs were broadly separated into subdivisions dealing with those areas which in the Third Reich would be state-controlled facets of the economy (IVa) and those areas in which the private sector would remain predominant (IVb).[150] Even the Reich Economic Council was reorganized. Its members now represented various departments at the Reichsleitung as well as prominent business men: Funk and Feder became co-chairmen.[151] The Council continued to be the party's highest authority on economic matters, but since it had not met since May it was hardly an effective control organ. Nothing shows more clearly the strengthened position of Gregor Strasser than the fortunes of the party's perennial stepchild, the NSBO, in the second phase of the reorganization. The NSBO now became a fully-accepted member of the proto-estates at the Reichsleitung. It enlarged its staff positions at all levels, defined their duties more clearly, and — the surest sign of an "in-group" in the NSDAP — even received subsidies from the Reich treasurer.[152]

Equally significant was the systematic buildup of a National Socialist proto-government within the Gau organizations. It is true, of course, that this development had reached only very rudimentary stages in January 1933, but this was hardly Strasser's fault. On the contrary, the quasi-governmental offices of some Gaus had reached staggering proportions even in November. Main Department III of the Berlin Gau had a massive array of offices that concerned themselves with virtually every aspect of German governmental life — from constitutional matters to the administration of state forests. In addition, it is clear that at least in Berlin the party had successfully infiltrated the ranks of the regular civil service, so that the officials heading the various Gau offices which paralleled the governmental agencies were party officials actively politicizing their state agencies.[153]

The Strasser reorganization came to a formal conclusion in early

---

150. *Ibid.*, p. 74; and *VB*, 30/31 Oct. 1932.

151. *VOBl* (No. 32; 30 Sept. 1932), p. 72; and GL München-Oberbayern, Hauptabteilung VI, *Informationsdienst* (No. 1; 1 Dec. 1932), HA, roll 89, folder 1867.

152. Hauptabteilung VI, *Verfügungen der Hauptabteilung VI* (Munich, 31 July 1932); Hauptabteilung VI, "Arbeitsanweisung für den Ortsgruppen-Betriebswart," Sept. 1932, HA, roll 89, folder 1867; and Hans-Gerd Schumann, *Nationalsozialismus und Gewerkschaftsbewegung* (Hanover, 1958), p. 37.

153. GL Berlin, "Gliederung der Hauptabteilung III des Gaues Gross-Berlin—Stand 24. November 1932," n.d., NA, T-580, roll 19, folder 199.

fall with the reorganization of Main Department IV and the publication of a revised, permanent version of the *Dienstanweisung* issued provisionally in July.[154] The NSDAP now needed only to work and plan for the eventual take-over of German society. To be sure, under Strasser's strategy that event could not come overnight, but there certainly were signs that the party was making steady progress. As of July, the NSDAP was again receiving new members,[155] and the influx had not lessened since then. The politization of the German agricultural interest groups — particularly the Landbund, but others as well — was virtually complete. Officials of the chambers of agriculture openly proclaimed that they regarded themselves responsible only to Hitler and Strasser.[156] The National Socialists were also making rapid progress in other occupational interest groups. The artisans' associations, which had eluded them in 1931 now fell increasingly under the party's influence.[157] The same was true of professional groups: in October the National Socialist Association of Physicians staged its first national convention in Brunswick.[158] Even the NSBO contributed actively to the undermining of German societal cohesiveness Its official organ supported more strikes than earlier in the year, and, perhaps partially as a result, its membership increased rapidly during the latter part of 1932: membership in January 1932 was 43,793; in May 1932, 106,158; and by January 1933, almost 400,000.[159]

The NSDAP's successful politization of previously largely apolitical areas of German societal life was not confined to the functional and organizational areas under Strasser's direct control. Perhaps the most impressive public display of the party's political power outside the legislative halls was the Reich Youth Day *(Reichsjugendtag)*, held in

154. See Strasser's announcement dated 17 Sept. 1932 in *VB*, 30/31 Oct. 1932; and GL München-Oberbayern to all KL, Ogrl., und Stützpunktleiter, 10 Oct. 1932, HA, roll 90, folder 1869.

155. *VOBl* (No. 27; 15 July 1932), p. 60.

156. *VB*, 7 May 1932; and B.T. (M.A.), 2 Nov. and 13 Dec. 1932. The National Socialist take-over of the agricultural interest groups was so obvious that the Papen government attempted counter-measures "to drive the farmers away from the Nazis [sic]." See Pünder, *Politik,* entry for 8 Oct. 1932, p. 149.

157. Roloff, *Bürgertum,* pp. 111–12.

158. *F.Z.*, 6 Oct. 1932.

159. Gerhard Starcke, *NSBO und Deutsche Arbeitsfront* (Berlin, 1934), p. 40.

October in Potsdam. Almost 100,000 HJ members demonstrated their allegiance to Adolf Hitler thereby indirectly denouncing the government's attempt to depoliticize Germany's youth by establishing an official, all-inclusive youth organization.[160]

The party's success in subordinating pluralist interest groups in Germany paralleled equally significant increases in its formal and informal governmental power. In the fall the party controlled the governments of five German states: Anhalt, Oldenburg, Mecklenburg, Thuringia, and Brunswick. In addition, a large number of National Socialist mayors and communal officials held office throughout the Reich. Each official, at whatever level, looked upon his post as a political office. He assumed his duties, as the Gauleiter of Oldenburg said on his election as prime minister of the state, "by order of Adolf Hitler."[161] Once in office, the National Socialists proceeded to politicize all aspects of life within their control: they attempted to control theater repertoires, expelled the Bauhaus School of Design from Dessau (Anhalt), and above all staffed civil-service positions solely with candidates previously screened by the appropriate party functionaries.[162]

The political effect of the NSDAP's governmental positions was magnified, as Strasser had intended, not only because the incumbents continued to use their offices as instruments to extend the party's control in Germany, but also because all of their efforts were centrally correlated with the equally highly controlled activities of the various party and affiliate offices. As interest group members, as governmental officials, and as party functionaries, members of the NSDAP systematically destroyed German pluralist society because they no longer lived in that society, but saw themselves only as simultaneous destroyers of the old and builders of the new. A particularly flagrant example of the NSDAP's successful use of its organizational strength to destroy a Weimar institution was the party's infiltration of the Reich Committee for Youth Education *(Reichskuratorium für Jugendbildung)*. This group had been established by the Papen government to soften the political

160. On the planning and running of the Reich Youth Day, see the documents in HA, roll 19, folder 367. See also Görlitz and Quint, *Hitler,* p. 350; and Arno Klönne, *Hitlerjugend* (Hanover, 1956), p. 10.

161. *F.Z.,* 11 June 1932.

162. For various abuses of governmental positions by the NSDAP officials see *B.T.* (M.A.), 29 July and 22 Oct. 1932, and *B.T.* (A.A.), 23 Aug. 1932.

differences among rival youth groups by uniting them in physical fitness programs under the banner of German nationalism. Ostensibly, the plan was a resounding success; both the SPD and the NSDAP agreed to participate. Schleicher and the cabinet were pleased,[163] but only because they did not understand the dynamism of the National Socialist organization. The NSDAP participated but because of its superior organization and control its very participation meant that "now the plans are being drawn to suit us."[164]

The concept of a coalition government in both the Reich and Prussia continued to be an integral part of Strasser's strategy. The NSDAP's cooperation in a Reich or major state government was the governmental basis which alone would both guide and permit the party's planned expansion of its organization into positions of societal control. For this reason Strasser almost immediately after the fiasco of August 13 began a series of negotiations with a variety of German public figures. Hitler was aware of these talks and tolerated Strasser's approach.[165] On August 23 Strasser met with Brüning,[166] and by late summer he had also established valuable contacts with Schleicher and some union officials, particularly in the Association of German Nationalist Office Employees, a leading white-collar union which had earlier supported Brüning.[167] From Strasser's contacts it is not difficult to surmise the direction and aim of his coalition plans. He clearly envisioned a coalition between the left and moderate elements (all of whom were firmly opposed to Papen) of the Center Party and the NSDAP. Such a combination was a very real possibility in the fall of 1932. It was born of two considerations. Strasser realized that in the electoral campaigns of the spring, the NSDAP had reached the outer limits of its middle-class vote appeal and that the party needed to turn again to

163. Vogelsang, *Reichswehr*, p. 348.

164. Reichsleitung–HJ to Gebietsführer and Bannführer (a *Gebiet* and a *Bann* corresponded roughly to an SA *Gruppe* and a party Gau), 26 Aug. 1932, HA, roll B, folder 337.

165. Bracher, *Auflösung*, p. 622 n94.

166. *F.Z.*, 26 Aug. 1932.

167. Vogelsang, *Reichswehr*, p. 145; and Hans-Otto Meissner and Harry Wilde, *Die Machtergreifung* (Stuttgart, 1958), p. 98. Hitler himself was still relying on Schleicher as his entry into the seats of power. See Joachim von Ribbentrop, *Zwischen London und Moskau*, ed. Annelies v. Ribbentrop (Leoni am Starnberger See, 1954), p. 36, ed. note.

the non-Communist urban masses.[168] At least a portion of this urban potential was represented by the Center Party. A second factor was the willingness of some major elements in that party to trust the pseudo-socialist (but non-Marxist) image which Strasser had reintroduced into the party, coupled with a complete lack of understanding of either Strasser's motives or the nature of National Socialist totalitarianism. Thus it was by no means merely idle speculation and political optimism which led Strasser to predict as early as June that the National Socialists would be part of a Reich government in the fall. Significantly, however, he did not think that the NSDAP would be in complete control of the government at that time.[169]

The July Reichstag met for the first time at the end of August. Its first sessions revealed not only the triumph of Strasser's political strategy, but brought the specter of an NSDAP–Center Party coalition considerably closer. The National Socialist delegation exhibited exemplary behavior in the legislature. They listened in icy silence as the aged Communist Party stalwart, Clara Zetkin, stumbled through her opening speech, and they did not obstruct the election of the Reichstag's parliamentary officers. In return, the Center Party promptly voted for Hermann Göring as the first National Socialist president of the Reichstag. The Papen government, which had intended to dissolve the Reichstag as soon as it met[170] and expected the usual National Socialist and Communist obstructionist tactics to provide it with a formal reason, found itself outmaneuvered by a peaceful parliament.[171]

Not all party leaders welcomed the obvious success of Strasser's strategy. Hitler had a meeting with the opposition groups (led by Goebbels) on August 31,[172] but he was as yet unconvinced that the frontal attack concept which Goebbels favored was a workable alternative. In a full-scale review of the NSDAP's political methods three days later Strasser, backed by Frick and a number of Gauleiters, again won

168. This point is persuasively argued by Hellmuth Elbrechter, "Wider den Sozialismus in jeder Form?" *Tat*, XXIV (July 1932), 310–17. Elbrechter in turn had great influence on Strasser. See Schulz to Lehmann, 12 June 1933, HA, roll 56, folder 1375.

169. Bracher, *Auflösung*, p. 550 n118.

170. The *F.Z.* reported Papen's decision to dissolve the Reichstag on August 23 and upheld its story a day later despite an official denial by the government.

171. On the government's reaction see Vogelsang, *Reichswehr*, p. 272.

172. Goebbels, *Vom Kaiserhof*, entry for 31 Aug. 1932, p. 154.

Hitler's support over Goebbels' bitter opposition.[173] The following day Strasser reiterated his and the NSDAP's position in a speech obviously directed at the Center Party.[174] Finally, on September 6 the Reichstag worked and debated for a full day with the active and constructive participation of the NSDAP delegation.[175] Germany seemed to have experienced a miraculous return to political stability.

This session of the Reichstag was also Strasser's last triumph. Six days later the Strasser era in the party came to an abrupt end. At the beginning of the Reichstag session on September 12, the KPD asked for a vote on a motion of no confidence in the Papen government. Since such a motion was not on the agenda, the Communist resolution required unanimous consent. It was obvious that if the House were to grant the consent, the result would be an immediate dissolution of the Reichstag, since the Papen government would never be able to survive a vote of no confidence. Neither the DNVP, the Center Party, nor Strasser wanted the Reichstag dissolved. On the other hand, no one wanted to evoke the impression of supporting Papen. The NSDAP delegation, caught as much by surprise as the other parties, asked for a half-hour recess. During the delay the entire Strasser plan was reviewed again: Goebbels, Strasser, Göring, Frick all talked to Hitler who was directing his forces from the Kaiserhof. In the end Hitler ordered the delegation not to object to the Communist motion. There followed the tragicomic scene of Papen's attempt to dissolve the Reichstag, while Göring administered the vote that dismissed Papen, but this was an anticlimatic farce. Papen clearly had the decree powers to dissolve the Reichstag, and Hitler in effect had decided to risk the NSDAP's future in new national elections. Goebbels was jubilant.[176]

173. *Ibid.*, entry for 2 Sept. 1932, p. 155; and Meissner, *Staatssekretär*, p. 252. Goebbels' implication that Hitler opposed Strasser's ideas at this time must be discounted; Hitler would hardly have permitted the strategy to continue if he had disapproved of it.

174. Strasser gave the speech in Dresden, on the occasion of dedicating a "Gregor Strasser Rest Home" there. See *VB*, 6 Sept. 1932.

175. Vogelsang, *Reichswehr*, pp. 339–40.

176. For analyses of the crucial Reichstag session see Bracher, *Auflösung*, pp. 628–29; Vogelsang, *Reichswehr*, p. 279; and Heiden, *Hitler*, I, pp. 312–13. A good eyewitness account of the maneuvering among the National Socialists is in *B.T.* (M.A.), 13 Sept. 1932. For Goebbels' and Hitler's reactions see *Vom Kaiserhof*, entry for 8 and 12 Sept. 1932, pp. 162–63.

Hitler's decision destroyed the political foundation of Strasser's approach to power. It also reversed the equally personal judgment of Hitler ten days before to support Strasser's plan. The reasons for his sudden change of mind did not seem to lie in any specific event that had occurred in the intervening days. No major political event had, in fact, come about which might have changed the qualitative relationship of the drawbacks and advantages inherent in the Strasser plan. The major tactical advantage of the Strasser plan continued to be the probability that it would succeed in getting the NSDAP to power, and that it had already ushered in a period of administrative stability among the party functionaries after the constant series of electoral campaigns in the spring had left them "nervous."[177] On the other hand, time continued to be on the side of Strasser's political rivals.

Hitler liked least the temporal uncertainty of the Strasser plan, and each day that passed without a National Socialist minister in the government confirmed his fundamental suspicions that power could not be achieved through legislative negotiations. From this point of view his decision is less unpredictable. The Strasser plan was already controversial in early September and, while Hitler had backed Strasser previously, the KPD resolution provided him with another opportunity — several days later — to review his previous stand. He now voted against Strasser's strategy.

The liability of the "time factor" was for Hitler a valid political and personal objection to Strasser's approach. Not only was Hitler impatient to obtain the title of chancellor, but he sensed perhaps more clearly than Strasser that the period of waiting and good behavior did nothing to appease the drive for action in the SA. Already angered by the party's defeat in August, the SA's frustration erupted in numerous acts of terror and localized revolts against the political leadership.[178] The party's leadership attempted to maintain morale by glorifying the particularly heinous Potempa murders,[179] but such measures were clearly only stopgap devices. In September the SA's morale was gen-

177. Goebbels, *Vom Kaiserhof*, entry for 15 Oct. 1932, p. 180.
178. See, for example, *B.T.* (A.A.), 1 Sept. 1932.
179. This partywide support was organized by Strasser. Bennecke, *Hitler*, p. 200. In August 1932, a band of five storm troopers broke into the home of a Communist worker in Potempa (Silesia) and brutally murdered him while his wife stood by helplessly.

erally low even in areas with a large membership. The party's paramilitary groups had "full confidence in the Führer," but they were also "finally expecting substantial *(durchgreifende)* military actions."[180] The severe attacks by several party leaders on Röhm merely added fuel to the already inflamed passions of the SA. Buch, Schulz, and Bormann in particular (though it is difficult to imagine that Strasser did not agree with them) criticized Röhm for his homosexuality and attempted to persuade Hitler to dismiss him. Röhm in turn surrounded himself with a personal bodyguard and counterattacked by planting some articles against Schulz in the Socialist press.[181]

The SA was not the only group that developed increasing reservations about Strasser's tactics. The business community, which was by now supplying substantial sums to the NSDAP, also reexamined its relationship to the party. Through a spokesman who was a personal acquaintance of Strasser, the Ruhr coal magnates frankly admitted that the NSDAP's negotiations with the Center Party and the NSBO's militancy in strikes disturbed them.[182] There were no specific threats to withhold financial support, but presumably threats were unnecessary. Hitler knew that the party could not afford to lose the financial backing of the business community. The expansion of the functionary corps, particularly at the district level, had already forced Schwarz to raise party dues in September, despite the complaints of "several Gauleiters." [183] Finally there was a constant and very real danger that unless political power accompanied the bureaucratic buildup, the latter

180. SA, Untergruppe Ostholstein to Osaf, 24 Sept. 1932, NA, T-81, roll 1, frame 11565. This is one of a series of situation reports which Hitler requested from Röhm after September 12, but the findings obviously reflect problems of longer standing. The entire series of reports is on NA, T-81, roll 1, frames 11554–67. See also Bennecke, *Hitler*, p. 203, and Vogelsang, *Reichswehr*, p. 309.

181. The entire controversy is covered in *Flammenzeichen*, 5 Nov. 1932, HA, roll 81, folder 1608. For the establishment of Röhm's bodyguard see PD Mü, Referat VI/N, "Vormerkung," 17 Aug. 1932, HA, roll 73, folder 1551. Bormann's sharp letter to Hess (5 Oct. 1932), is in HA, roll 17, folder 319. For additional details see Vogelsang, *Reichswehr*, p. 309; and Friedrich Stampfer, *Erfahrungen und Erkenntnisse* (Cologne, 1957), p. 251.

182. See August Heinrichsbauer (at this time public relations counsel for the coal industry) to Strasser, 20 Sept. 1932, NA, T-81, roll 1, frames 11441–44. On Heinrichsbauer's later career in the Third Reich see Dietrich Orlow, *The Nazis in the Balkans* (Pittsburgh, Pa., 1968).

183. Reichsschatzmeister to all GL, 6 and 25 Sept. 1932, in *Rdschr.*

would become an end in itself, in time paralyzing the party's political aggressiveness.[184]

Hitler doubtlessly realized that all of these factors had an inherent cumulative effect which increased their weight as liability factors. Thus, faced with the slowness of Strasser's approach, the physical activism of the SA, and the danger of bureaucratic sclerosis in the party; Hitler decided to revitalize his followers by leading them once again into another electoral battle. Both he and his subleaders knew from the outset that this would be a very difficult campaign. A leadership conference shortly after the Reichstag dissolution could agree only on a basic strategy of opposing Papen (and "reaction" in general) and otherwise pursuing a thoroughly opportunistic course.[185] The specific ingredients of the NSDAP's fall platform were a curious continuation of Strasser's emphasis on positive plans coupled with blatant demogogic appeals. Hitler agreed with Strasser that the party had exhausted the reservoir of "ideologically-motivated" voters — those who voted NSDAP primarily for emotional and psychological reasons — and that the party would have to appeal to the electorate with positive plans. At the same time Hitler hoped to convict Papen of philosemitism in the eyes of middle-class voters by pointing to liberal press support of some of his measures.[186] Finally, he deliberately appealed to the monarchist vote with some veiled references to the restoration of the Hohenzollerns.[187]

This use of some of Strasser's tactics while rejecting his overall strategy was actually far more of a political gamble for Hitler than his earlier acceptance of the Strasser plan had been. Strasser himself was

184. Strasser to Landesinspekteure and GL, 15 Oct. 1932, HA, roll 14, folder 265. There were good reasons for the warning against overgrown staffs at the bottom. The personnel of the Gau offices in Berlin at this time numbered 150, and even some districts boasted two-story office complexes. See Goebbels, *Vom Kaiserhof*, entry for 17 Oct. 1932, p. 182; and *VB*, 24 Nov. 1932.

185. *VB*, 15 Sept. 1932. See also Hess' statement that "if necessary the NSDAP will ally itself with the devil himself" to get to power. Hess, "Bemerkungen zur Propaganda für den Reichstagswahlkampf," n.d. (Sept. 1932), NA, T-81, roll 1, frame 11430. This memorandum is apparently addressed to Goebbels and is in response to the Heinrichsbauer letter cited earlier.

186. *Ibid.*, frames 11430–31. Since Hess had never written on propaganda tactics before, it can be assumed that he was merely expressing Hitler's thoughts.

187. Görlitz and Quint, *Hitler*, p. 349; and Hallgarten, "Adolf Hitler," p. 239.

convinced that it could not succeed and that the NSDAP would suffer disastrous losses in the Reichstag elections.[188] He had valid statistical bases for his belief. A number of factors indicated that the NSDAP as a whole was really not prepared for a new electoral campaign. The party had not done well in recent local elections. (In the Reichstag election of 1932 the NSDAP had polled 1074 votes in Königsberg and 1074 in Gerdauen [East Prussia]. In the local election on October 9, 1932, the vote was 483 in Königsberg and 126 in Gerdauen.[189]) In some areas, subscriptions to party newspapers dropped off sharply, and there were even Gaus in which the number of resignations exceeded the applications for membership.[190] Above all, the party's finances were under severe strains. Many of the Gau organizations still had debts from the July elections, and it was understandably far more difficult to collect special campaign contributions for this fourth national campaign in a year.[191] (On the other hand, it was also true that continued adherence to the Strasser plan discouraged business contributions, so that financially Hitler could not escape the dilemma in either case.)

Strasser was not alone in his pessimistic appraisal of the party's election chances. Through his constant and regular contacts with the Gauleiters, who were after all his immediate administrative subordinates, Strasser learned that a number of the party's leaders in the states supported his basic strategy. Most of the support came from the populous northern Gaus, but at least one southern leader, Bürckel (Palatinate), also agreed with Strasser. Moreover, the leaders regarded the decision of September 12 as a temporary setback which did not permanently change the NSDAP's political course. They continued to further the implementation of the Strasser plan. Strasser reintroduced informal regional discussion among several Gauleiters and such talks

188. Goebbels, *Vom Kaiserhof*, entry for 4 Oct. 1932, p. 175.

189. *B.T.* (A.A.), 10 and 11 Oct. 1932.

190. See the letter of the publisher of *Der Nationalsozialist* (Thuringia) to Sauckel, NA, T-81, roll 116, frame 136729; *B.T.* (A.A.), 1 Nov. 1932; and *F.Z.*, 24 Dec. 1932.

191. Goebbels, *Vom Kaiserhof*, entry for 20 Sept. 1932, p. 167; Leni Kaufleitner (wife of an Ortsgruppenleiter) to KL Mühldorf (Oberbayern), 21 Sept. 1932, HA, roll 8, folder 176. The militant Association for German Culture had debts of RM 120,000 at this time. See Hugo Bruckmann to Rosenberg, 9 Nov. 1932, NA, T-454, roll 71, frame 1405.

continued at least until early fall. There is also evidence that several high-ranking officials at the Reich level, notably Buch and Frick, shared Strasser's pessimistic views on the outcome of new elections.[192]

None of these activities were directed against Hitler, nor did the Gauleiter meetings constitute anything like the beginning of a *fronde*. On the contrary, once Hitler had reached his decision, the party's leaders immediately rallied to the new campaign effort. A three-day leadership conference at the beginning of October signaled the transfer of authority from Strasser to Goebbels. Strasser presided over the meeting, but the agenda was dominated entirely by addresses of the party's propagandists — Goebbels, Amann, Dietrich.[193]

At least publicly, the NSDAP entered the campaign with undiminished confidence.[194] The party concentrated its attacks generally on the right and "reactionary cliques," and Goebbels caused something of a sensation, when, shortly before the election, the NSDAP in Berlin openly cooperated with the KPD in organizing and maintaining a wildcat strike among the Berlin transport workers. Even Strasser had never advocated such a drastic opening to the left. Actually, Goebbels acted more out of frustration than strategic considerations.[195] Five days before the vote he realized that the NSDAP would lose "a couple million votes," [196] and his dramatic move in Berlin was clearly designed to minimize the losses in his home Gau.

192. See Krebs, *Tendenzen*, pp. 192 and 199; Bracher, *Auflösung*, p. 682 n134; and the memorandum by Werner Jochmann, head of the Forschungsstelle Hamburg on a talk between himself and the former Gauleiter of Hamburg, Karl Kaufmann on 27 Jan. 1964 in the "NSDAP–NSAG" folder of the Forschungsstelle.

193. Strasser to departmental heads of the RL, 22 Sept. 1932, HA, roll 14, folder 265; Strasser, "Anordnung Nr. 9," n.d., NA, T-81, roll 1, frame 11554; and Strasser, Goebbels, Amann, "Tagesordnung," 20 Sept. 1932, *ibid.*, frames 11555–56.

194. The *VB* abounded with such headlines as "More people than ever want to hear our Führer," and "Papen's rule collapses under the attacks of Adolf Hitler." See *VB*, 28 Oct. and 3 Nov. 1932. Cf. also Dietrich's statement, "On November 6th the NSDAP will achieve its greatest and most impressive victory in the history of the movement." *VB*, 5 Nov. 1932.

195. For Goebbels' justification of the cooperation see *Vom Kaiserhof*, entry for 2 Nov. 1932, p. 191. Meissner and Wilde, *Machtergreifung*, pp. 17 and 267 n5, quote Amann on the financial effects. The *VB* deliberately de-emphasized the events in Berlin.

196. Goebbels, *Vom Kaiserhof*, entry for 1 Nov. 1932, p. 190.

His fears were fully justified. On November 6, the NSDAP suffered severe setbacks in all areas of Germany. The percentage of vote losses varied from region to region, but no Gau was able to maintain its July strength.[197] The November elections proved decisively that the strategy of massive electoral victories had reached a dead end.

The renewed failure to achieve power persuaded many less committed members to leave the party — quite often to join the KPD which had been the real victor in the fall election.[198] A severe depression seized those who remained; there are definite indications that the psychology of the small group of militant believers huddled in an alien world again permeated the movement.[199] Yet, paradoxically, in November 1932, the Strasser plan offered a more certain way out of the National Socialists' dilemma than ever before. The simultaneous cresting of the NSDAP's electoral wave and the impressive gains scored by the Communists both encouraged and frightened the middle-class parties into greater readiness to accept the NSDAP as a coalition partner. On the NSDAP side Strasser all but offered the Center Party a coalition shortly after the election.[200] Hitler, on the other hand, repeated his performance of August. Unwilling to accept Strasser's plan after the party's greatest electoral victory, he now refused to negotiate after a defeat.[201] On November 19, he again met Hindenburg. The Reich President encouraged Hitler to participate in a coalition government, but Hitler demanded decree powers for a cabinet headed by himself. Hindenburg, as he had in August, refused.[202] "Germany's Savior from the Red Flood" [203] again found the gates of power closed.

---

197. For a detailed analysis of the voting see Bracher, *Auflösung*, pp. 648–55.

198. PD Mü, "Amtswaltersitzung des Kreises West der NSDAP am 8.11.32 . . . PND Nr. 796," n.d., HA, roll 88, folder 1838.

199. See Goebbels' *Angriff* editorial of 7 Nov. 1932, in *Wetterleuchten* pp. 338–39; and PD Mü, "Appell des SS Sturmes 1/I/1 am 9.11.32 . . . PND Nr. 796," HA, roll 73, folder 1547.

200. "Taktik oder Angebot? Eine Erklärung Gregor Strassers," *F.Z.*, 16 Nov. 1932.

201. Goebbels, *Vom Kaiserhof*, entry for 8 Nov. 1932, p. 198, notes that "peace is concluded after a victory; after a defeat the war goes on."

202. Meissner, "Aufzeichnung über die Besprechung des Herrn Reichspräsidenten mit Herrn Adolf Hitler am Sonnabend, den 19. November 1932," in Hubatsch, ed., *Hindenburg*, p. 351.

203. *VB*, 20/21 Nov. 1932. This is a caption under a picture showing the arrival of Hitler, Strasser, and Frick in Berlin.

Hitler's refusal to settle for a partial victory after the November elections marks the beginning of Strasser's disillusionment with Hitler and the NSDAP. He no longer took any real part in the policy deliberations of the party's leadership. Thus, when Hitler, Papen, and Meissner exchanged a series of futile letters following Hitler's meeting with Hindenburg, Hess and Goebbels helped to draft Hitler's replies, but Strasser had no part in the deliberations.[204] The reason was quite simply that Strasser was increasingly convinced that Hitler's course of action could only lead to the party's disintegration.[205] The political developments of November and early December served only to increase his feelings of apathy and depression. The NSDAP clearly had no new positive ideas; its propaganda line was against the KPD, "otherwise splendid isolation." [206] Beneath the vacuum at the top, the party experienced a distinct revival of earlier centrifugal tendencies. In fact, the NSDAP suffered the beginning of an organizational crisis that continued until the seizure of power.[207] Without Strasser's firm administrative hand, the intricately complementary spheres of authority of the various offices became blurred and party officials had to be admonished to observe administrative channels.[208] Business practices also suffered, so that Schwarz issued a curt reminder that careless business management was a form of political failing.[209] Membership increases declined sharply (Brandenburg actually suffered a net decline during November), and reports of SA revolts appeared more frequently in the press.[210] The financial picture was "hopeless." The party labored under stag-

204. See the composing process of the Hitler to Meissner letter (24 Nov. 1932), in NA, T-81, roll 1, frames 11330–31; see also Goebbels, *Vom Kaiserhof*, entry for 20 Nov. 1932, p. 206; and Vogelsang, *Reichswehr*, p. 328.

205. Hitler, too, was aware of this danger. In fact, he attempted to blackmail Hindenburg with the threat that if he (Hitler) were not appointed chancellor, Germany's strongest anti-Communist bulwark would disintegrate. See Meissner, "Aufzeichnung . . ."

206. Goebbels, *Vom Kaiserhof*, entry for 15 Nov. 1932. p. 203. Goebbels uses the English phrase in his diary.

207. Bracher, *Auflösung*, pp. 644 and 656. See also Otto-Ernst Schüddekopf, *Linke Leute von Rechts* (Stuttgart, 1960), pp. 374–75.

208. *VOBl* (No. 36; 30 Nov. 1932), pp. 78–79.

209. Reichsschatzmeister to all GL, 2 Dec. 1932, in *Rdschr.*

210. *B.T.* (M.A.), 14 Dec. 1932; PD Mü, "Auszug aus dem Morgenrapport," 21 Jan. 1933, HA, roll 69, and folder 1508; and the press reports on SA troubles in HA, roll 73, folder 1550.

gering debts,[211] and at the end of the year only eleven of the Gaus had fulfilled their financial obligations to the Reichsleitung, while the others were at least three months in arrears. The locals in turn owed substantial sums to the Gaus.[212]

Politically, the NSDAP continued to lose its voter appeal. Each local or state election in November and December brought a new setback. Only eight days after the Reichstag elections, local contests in Saxony gave the results shown in Table 11.

TABLE 11

	NSDAP Vote	
City	*November 6*	*November 14*
Dresden	134,330	104,107
Leipzig	128,558	101,690
Plauen	33,720	26,840
Chemnitz	79,766	69,538

Source: *Berliner Tageblatt* (Abendausgabe), 16 Nov. 1932.

A month later local elections in Thuringia produced even more disastrous results, although several of the party's most prominent speakers (including Hitler) participated in the campaign. (See Table 12.) It is therefore not surprising that the NSDAP in late 1932 appeared even to sympathetic observers as a disintegrating giant.[213]

Both Schleicher and Hitler were aware of the crisis within the NSDAP, and in early December both decided to deal with it. Schleicher, who had just been appointed Reich chancellor, hoped to succeed where Papen had failed: in forming a coalition government with the party, specifically by "using the hunger [for power] of his [Hitler's] asso-

211. Goebbels, *Vom Kaiserhof*, entry for 11 Nov. 1932, p. 200; and Hallgarten, "Adolf Hitler," p. 232, cites a debt of RM 70–90 million.

212. Reichsschatzmeister to all GL, 27 Jan. 1933, in *Rdschr;* and *B.T.* (M.A.), 14 Dec. 1932. The latter is a report of remarks made on December 12 by the Gauleiter of Brandenburg.

213. See, for example, "Gespräch zwischen Dr. Keller und Dr. Bang auf dem Verbandstag des Alldeutschen Verbandes in Rudolstadt," n.d. (end of 1932), NA, T-81, roll 1, frame 11317.

TABLE 12

	NSDAP Vote	
Urban Areas	*November 6*	*December 3*
Weimar	11,003	7,122
Gera	16,577	13,809
Jena	8,420	6,459
Gotha	10,046	7,565
Eisenach	8,002	5,980
Apolda	6,389	4,430

	NSDAP Vote	
Rural Districts	*November 6*	*December 3*
Weimar	20,570	15,778
Meinigen	22,180	16,193
Hildburghausen	16,616	12,839
Schleiz	22,835	8,941
Greiz	14,322	10,997
Gera	17,735	12,769
Saalfeldt	14,739	10,645
Rudolfstadt	11,381	8,102
Armstadt	18,821	15,693
Sondershausen	16,313	11,352

SOURCE: *Berliner Tageblatt* (Abendausgabe), 5 Dec. 1932.

ciates against Hitler."[214] By this time Schleicher knew that a coalition could be arranged only against Hitler's wishes; the NSDAP's leader had made it clear that he would not permit any party member to join a cabinet that did not include him as chancellor. On the other hand, Schleicher also knew that not only Strasser and his supporters among the Gauleiters but Göring as well favored a coalition government and hoped to persuade Hitler to accept his temporary exclusion from the cabinet.[215] The pressure on Hitler to change his views was particularly great at this time, since the NSDAP could achieve a major power position if it was willing to use the Strasser plan: while Hitler felt depressed

214. Bracher, *Auflösung*, p. 671 n76.
215. *Ibid.*, pp. 669 and 671–72; and Vogelsang, *Reichswehr*, p. 323.

about his political prospects,[216] the Center Party was prepared to accept Strasser as Prime Minister of Prussia and thus usher in a National Socialist-controlled government in the largest German state.[217]

Schleicher asked Hitler to come to Berlin for a conference on December 1. Hitler, however, decided not to accept the invitation, but to go to Weimar instead to confer with the major leaders of the NSDAP on the coalition offer which Hitler knew Schleicher would hand him. Before the meeting, Strasser, Frick, and Feder, as well as most of the Gauleiters in the industrial areas, favored a coalition,[218] but at the meeting itself Hitler's firm opposition to the plan won over all but Strasser.[219] Schleicher dispatched his aide, Ott, to Weimar to change Hitler's mind with a firm offer of the vice-chancellorship for Hitler, and the posts of Prussian prime minister and minister of the interior for other party members, but Hitler remained adamant.[220]

Strasser had a conference with Schleicher on the following day, and apparently told the new chancellor that a substantial number of the party's leaders favored a coalition government. Schleicher mistakenly interpreted this to mean that Strasser could split the party, something which the Reich Organizational Leader had neither the power nor the intention of doing.[221] Unlike Schleicher, Strasser did not underestimate the power of Hitler's myth-person in the NSDAP.[222]

Strasser was thinking not of rebellion, but of one last effort to change Hitler's mind — with the undeniable evidence of the Thuringian fiasco in hand. Indeed, Hitler seemed to be less sure of his ground. Although he still denounced the "creeping willingness to compromise" [223] at the leadership conference on December 4 and 5, he also accepted Stras-

216. Görlitz and Quint, *Hitler*, p. 354.

217. *F.Z.*, 13 Dec. 1932. See also Kube to Jungbluth (one of the NSDAP's Reich speakers), 30 Nov. 1932, HA, roll 53, folder 1240.

218. Schulz to Lehmann, 12 June 1933, HA, roll 56, frame 1375. In the letter Schulz explains his actions during the later Strasser crisis. See also Meissner and Wilde, *Machtergreifung*, p. 135.

219. Goebbels, *Vom Kaiserhof*, entry for 1 Dec. 1932, p. 212.

220. Vogelsang, *Reichswehr*, pp. 330 and 341.

221. Otto Engelbrecht, "Bericht," 5 Jan. 1933, NA, T-81, roll 1, frame 11320. The report was requested by Martin Bormann, presumably as an aid in determining the political fate of Gottfried Feder. On the Strasser–Schleicher meeting, see also Meissner and Wilde, *Machtergreifung*, p. 135.

222. Vogelsang, *Reichswehr*, p. 323.

223. Goebbels, *Vom Kaiserhof*, entries for 4 and 5 Dec. 1932, pp. 215–16.

ser's proposal for a massive personal confrontation of Hitler and the anxious party functionaries in the early part of December. Between the beginning of the month and Christmas, Hitler, Strasser, and the various Reich and state inspectors planned to address the functionaries of the Gaus to reaffirm the bond between leader and militant followers.[224] Strasser apparently hoped these meetings would convince Hitler that his opposition to a coalition was politically unrealistic and financially disastrous.[225] Hitler, on the other hand, clearly hoped to use the meetings to strengthen the party's internal discipline[226] through the emotional response which his appearances always generated among the militant party members.

Strasser's hope was a forlorn one. The Thuringian election (in which the NSDAP lost 40 percent of its November strength) simply confirmed Hitler in his decision to refuse categorically all compromises. The same figures and Hitler's attitude convinced Strasser that only a coalition could prevent the NSDAP's disintegration, and that even the December meetings with Gau functionaries were unlikely to narrow the differences of opinion between himself and Hitler. Under these circumstances Strasser saw no future for himself in the NSDAP. On December 8 he sent Hitler a letter submitting his resignation as Reich Organizational Leader. Immediately afterwards, before Hitler had even received the note, he left Berlin for Munich. Strasser's resignation was both completely unexpected and an entirely personal decision. Even Paul Schulz, his closest associate, learned of it only half an hour before Strasser dispatched his letter.[227]

Strasser's break with Adolf Hitler was an act of personal resignation, not a call for revolt against the Hitlerian myth. The Reich Organizational Leader was still not free from what Karl Paetel has called his "paladin complex";[228] despite Schulz's urgings, he refused to hand Hit-

224. *VB*, 6 Dec. 1932. Hitler was scheduled to speak in Silesia, Saxony, Halle, Magdeburg, and Hamburg; Strasser in Koblenz, Frankfurt, Mainz, the Palatinate, the Ruhr, and Düsseldorf.

225. On the continuing financial difficulties of the Gaus see Goebbels, *Vom Kaiserhof*, entries for 10, 21, and 22 Dec. 1932, pp. 223, 227, and 228.

226. Shortly before, the Uschla had moved to expel members for such minor offenses as failure to vote in elections. See Schulz to Buch, 29 Nov. 1932, HA, roll 56, folder 1375.

227. Schulz to Lehmann, 12 June 1933, HA, roll 56, folder 1375.

228. Paetel, *Versuchung oder Chance* (Göttingen, 1965), p. 210.

ler his resignation in person.[229] In the final analysis he resigned not only because of his substantive differences with Hitler, but also because their differing views had enabled other agents of the myth — he named Goebbels, Röhm, Göring — increasingly to place themselves between Hitler and Strasser. Unlike Stennes, Strasser neither lost his belife in Hitler's myth, nor did he intend his resignation to be a signal for an open revolt of his many supporters. On the contrary, his letter specifically asked all other party officials to remain at their posts.[230]

Hitler was literally shocked into inactivity by the news. He met with the party's inspectors in the afternoon,[231] but announced no decisions to fill the administrative vacuum left by Strasser's resignation. He spent the evening at Goebbels' apartment; still he could not bring himself to acknowledge the reality of Strasser's leaving. As he had done when his niece died a year before, he merely paced the floor hour after hour. At 2 o'clock in the morning of December 9, Ley called to report a general feeling of unrest throughout the party. Hitler did not react. Not until some hours later had he mentally digested and categorized Strasser's unexpected step. As always, Adolf Hitler could not comprehend anything but complete subordination from his agents, nor anything but total animosity from his enemies. Strasser had stepped outside the membership of the positive set factor, but had not joined the opposition. (For example, he did not resign his party membership.) Hitler could not react to his resignation until he had successfully fit Strasser into the negative set factor. This he was able to do only when the Berlin morning papers appeared on December 9. Beginning with the *Tägliche Rundschau* (which had a spy in Hitler's entourage) the various newspapers reported the (officially still secret) resignation story. Moreover, since the liberal press generally wrote favorable comments on Strasser's steps, Hitler decided that Strasser had cooperated with the "Jewish newspapers." Strasser, by giving comfort to the enemy, became a part of the negative set factor. At that point Hitler "had per-

229. Schulz to Lehmann, 12 June 1933.

230. No copy of the Strasser letter has survived, but Lohse, "Der Fall Strasser," pp. 21–22 gives a good account of the contents. For contemporary accounts of the letter (which were remarkably accurate) see *F.Z.*, 11 Dec. 1932; and *Vossische Zeitung* (M.A.), 10 Dec. 1932; and *B.T.* (A.A.), 9 Dec. 1932.

231. Hence Lohse, the author of "Der Fall Strasser," was one of the first to know of his step.

sonally gotten over Strasser *(hat jetzt Strasser . . . persönlich überwunden)"* and "settled the account by utterly destroying [him] *(vernichtende Abrechnung)"* in front of the party leaders assembled in the Kaiserhof. (In the meantime the party leaders had moved back from Goebbels' flat to the hotel.) [232] Gregor Strasser had "stabbed him [Hitler] in the back five minutes before the final victory," he added as welling tears forced him to stop. [233]

Only after Hitler had fit Strasser's resignation into his personal view of reality was he able to deal with the organizational problems confronting the NSDAP. To give himself time to reorganize the party, Hitler gave Strasser a three-week leave of absence (this step had actually been suggested by Strasser), and then announced, following the precedent set after Pfeffer's resignation, that in the future he personally would be the party's organizational leader. He named Ley his chief of staff. [234] At the same time, he once again reactivated his personal myth to guide the party over this latest crisis. As loyalty declarations poured in from all parts of Germany, Hitler confirmed the "personal agent" status of the Gauleiters, and de-emphasized the inspectors' role as watchdogs of the states' leaders. [235] He also used the previously scheduled speaking engagements to renew the personal, emotional ties binding the functionary corps to himself and to "settle accounts" with Strasser. Between the tenth and eighteenth of December he spoke in Breslau, Dresden, Chemnitz, Leipzig, Halle, Magdeburg, and Hamburg — all cities whose Gauleiters had previously sympathized with Strasser's views. [236] In each successive address Strasser became a more integral part of the negative set factor. By early January he even denied that Strasser was an effective organizer. [237] The campaign was success-

232. Hitler's struggle to fit Strasser's action into his own mythical version of reality is easily traceable from Goebbels, *Vom Kaiserhof,* entries for 8 and 9 Dec. 1932, pp. 219–21.

233. *B.T.* (A.A.), 10 Dec. 1932; and Meissner and Wilde, *Machtergreifung,* pp. 142–43 and 287 n27. The authors' source for the weeping scene is Amann again.

234. *VB,* 10 Dec. 1932. The decision to take over Strasser's position personally must have been made on December 9. There is an undated draft decree to this effect in NA, T-81, roll 1, frame 11316; the *VB* carried the announcement in its issue of 11/12 Dec. 1932.

235. See Hitler's "Verfügung," 9 Dec. 1932, in NA, T-81, roll 1, frame 11355.

236. Domarus, ed., *Hitler–Reden,* pp. 166–67.

237. PD Mü, "Amtswaltertagung der NSBO am 5.2.33. . . . PND Nr. 803," n.d., HA, roll 89, folder 1867.

ful. The party's militants exorcised Gregor Strasser. Whatever his previous merits, the man who had still stood at Hitler's side in early December succumbed to the temptation of parliamentarism, while Hitler — a Christ-figure to some members — remained pure and untouched.[238]

Although Hitler now denied that Strasser had made any major contributions to the party's organizational structure, he also took considerable care to destroy the organizational edifice that Strasser had built. In two lengthy memoranda dated seven days after Strasser's resignation, Hitler attacked Strasser's concept that the party organizational functionaries should be in charge of both the propaganda and the planning activities of the party. Consequently Hitler decreed a thorough decentralization of Strasser's administrative empire. The organizational apparatus (now renamed *Politische Organisation,* PO) was reduced to purely administrative functions. Ley, as chief of staff of the PO was restricted to supervising the party's personnel office, the actual political organization, and intraparty training programs for the functionary corps.[239] Although his position on the party's organizational chart was analogous to that of Röhm, he had in fact far less power and authority. Hitler reemphasized that the special relationship between himself and the Gauleiters raised them to a position in the party second only to himself, and he authorized them as his agents to purge the party of all "rats, finks, and traitors *(Schweinehunde, Lumpen und Verräter)."*[240]

Hitler assigned the bulk of Strasser's former political control functions to Rudolf Hess, the man "most familiar with [Hitler's] basic ideas . . . and his intentions." [241] He headed a Political Central Commission (*Politische Zentralkommission,* PZK), which in turn was divided into three subdivisions responsible for coordinating the work of the National Socialist legislative groups in all states except Prussia and

---

238. See Gmelin's letter of 21 Dec. 1932, in "Briefe."

239. Adolf Hitler, "Denkschrift über die inneren Gründe für die Verfügungen zur Herstellung einer erhöhten Schlagkraft der Bewegung," 15 Dec. 1932, NA, T-81, roll 60, frames 69384-91. The decrees were originally drafted by Ley. See the drafts in Ley's handwriting in HA, roll 54, folder 1293. See also *VOBl* (No. 38; 31 Dec. 1932), p. 85. Simultaneously, Schwarz rescinded his organizational reforms of the Strasser era. See *VOBl* (No. 39; 15 Jan. 1933), p. 86.

240. Hitler, "Denkschrift . . . ." The quotation is from a speech by Brückner, the Gauleiter of Silesia. See *F.Z.,* 15 Dec. 1932.

241. *VB,* 18/19 Dec. 1932.

Bavaria (these reported directly to Hitler), for supervising the party press, and for determining the NSDAP's stand on economic matters. The inspectorate system ceased to exercise any major control functions. All of the state inspectors resumed their Gauleiter positions, were renamed commissioners, and exercised their inspector duties only from time to time at the specific request of Hitler or Ley.[242]

The third pillar of Strasser's interconnected administrative structure had been his control of the affiliates' activities. Hitler also decreed major changes in this area. He removed Main Departments VI, VII, VIII, and IX from the sole jurisdiction of the PO and placed them under the dual authority of the PO and the PZK. (Parts of Main Department III went as spoils to Goebbels' Propaganda Department and the Reich Legal Department).[243] Main Department V (the Office for Agriculture), again became an independent affiliate directly subordinate to Hitler's authority.[244] Main Department IV, which had been the primary source of the positive plans on which Strasser had intended to base the party's constructive image, all but ceased to exist. Hitler dissolved both the department and the Reich Economic Council and merely retained Funk and Feder as his personal economic advisors.[245]

The primary purpose of Hitler's realignment of administrative jurisdictions was clearly to destroy the concentration of power in the office of Reich Organizational Leader. The NSDAP again became a series of fragmented offices and interests, held together only by their loyalty to Hitler. Yet Hitler's reorganization measures had far-reaching policy implications as well. He destroyed every vestige of the emphasis on planning that had been the most important innovation among Strasser's reforms. For Hitler the purpose of the NSDAP was solely to achieve power for National Socialism in Germany; "scientific experiments" and

242. Hitler, "Verfügung 2," 15 Dec. 1932, HA, roll 54, folder 1293; and Ley, "Verfügung" (draft), 14 Dec. 1932, *ibid.*
243. Hitler, "Verfügung," 14 Dec. 1932, *ibid.*
244. Ley, "Anordnung Nr. 3," 6 Feb. 1933, HA, roll 14, folder 265. See also Darré, "Anordnung des Amtsleiters für Agrarpolitik—Anordnung Nr. 1/1933" (Jan. 1933), HA, roll 46, folder 953. Hitler promised the same status for the NSBO, but only after the January elections. See PD Mü, "Amtswaltertagung der [NSBO] Gau München-Oberbayern am 8. Januar 1933 . . . PND Nr. 799," n.d., HA, roll 89, folder 1867.
245. Hitler, "Verfügung 3," 15 Dec. 1932, HA, roll 54, folder 1293; and Görlitz and Quint, *Hitler*, p. 353.

preparations for its later governmental functions lay outside the scope of its activities. In effect, Hitler rejected Strasser's concept of the party as the microcosm of the new Reich. The NSDAP was a means to power, not a test laboratory for a new society in miniature.[246]

The fragmentation of the party's administrative structure and the limitation of its basic program undoubtedly suited Hitler's own personal inclinations and may well have been the most effective immediate answer to the December crisis, but it hardly solved the NSDAP's political dilemma. In fact, it may well be argued that in mid-December the party was farther from its goal of achieving power than at any time since September 1930. Since the NSDAP had obviously exhausted the supply of "ideological" voters, it needed positive proposals to attract votes — a political fact which Feder had the courage to tell Hitler even after Strasser had resigned.[247] But Hitler had abandoned Strasser's emphasis on "memoranda," and thereby cut off the major source of the party's positive programs. In addition, the removal of Strasser's integrative political strategy quickly led to renewed fragmentation of party programs. Thus some units of the SA promptly returned to activities which really interested them: combat sports, drill, field maneuvers, weaponry instruction. Political training rated last on the list.[248]

Hitler had weathered the immediate administrative difficulties presented by Strasser's leaving, but in doing so he had also reached a dead end politically. He had neither a strategy of his own — except to favor another Reichstag election — nor was he clear about Strasser's future intentions,[249] though he was aware of Schleicher's continued interest in Strasser. Hitler (and the NSDAP) were rescued from their dilemma by Franz von Papen. On December 16, Franz von Papen delivered a speech in the *Herrenclub* which could only be interpreted as an offer to Hitler to approach the Reich President through the ex-chancellor.[250] Three days later Wilhelm Keppler, a prominent National Socialist economic expert, wrote Hitler suggesting the later famous meeting

246. Hitler, "Denkschrift . . . ," 20 Dec. 1932, NA, T-81, roll 60, frame 69392.
247. Otto Engelbrecht, "Bericht," 5 Jan. 1933, NA, T-81, roll 1, frame 11321.
248. SA, Sturmbann I/2 (München-Land-West), "Verfügung," 16 Dec. 1932.

249. At least until January 9, 1933, Hitler had no knowledge of Strasser's real intentions. See Vogelsang, *Reichswehr*, pp. 352–53 and 357.

250. Theodor Eschenburg (who heard the speech in person)," Franz von Papen," in *Die improvisierte Demokratie* (Munich, 1963), p. 280.

with Papen at the house of the Cologne banker Baron von Schröder. Keppler left no doubt that Papen (and Schacht) originated the idea.[251] Papen came away from the meeting satisfied that Hitler would no longer insist on dictatorial powers, though Hitler still demanded to be chancellor. Hitler was equally pleased that Papen would now be his spokesman at the presidential palace.[252]

In the meantime, Strasser reentered the political arena. He did not return to Berlin until January 3, but earlier he resumed contacts with the NSDAP through Mutschmann, the Gauleiter of Saxony, and Schulz, but also kept in touch with Schleicher, and through the latter with Hindenburg. At least at this time Strasser had not given up all hope for a reconciliation with Hitler.[253] On the other hand, Hindenburg had indicated that he would welcome Strasser as vice-chancellor in a Schleicher cabinet. In fact, in early January Hindenburg had what he thought was a choice of National Socialist vice-chancellors: Strasser under Schleicher and Hitler under Papen. Papen, in reporting on his meeting with Hitler, gave the Reich President the impression that he, Papen, would head the Hitler–Papen combination.[254]

The decision between the two candidates was made by the voters of the minute German state, Lippe-Detmold, when they elected a new Landtag in mid-January.[255] Hitler needed an impressive victory both to convince Hindenburg and Papen that he was not negotiating from a position of weakness and to eliminate what remained of the "Strasser vermin *(Strasserschädlinge)*" in the party.[256] The NSDAP fought for the provincial election in Lippe as though it were a new Reichstag election. In the midst of adoring crowds Hitler regained some of his

251. Keppler to Hitler, 19 Dec. 1932, NA, T-81, roll 1, frame 11318. The letter is also reprinted in Vogelsang, *Reichswehr,* doc. 39, pp. 485–86.

252. On the reactions to the meeting on both sides see Meissner, *Staatssekretär,* pp. 254 and 261; Goebbels, *Vom Kaiserhof,* entry for 9 Jan. 1933, p. 238; and Dietrich, *Mit Hitler,* p. 170.

253. See Goebbels, *Vom Kaiserhof,* entry for 28 Dec. 1932, p. 230; and *F.Z.,* 30 Dec. 1932.

254. Meissner, *Staatssekretär,* p. 262. See also "Im Kampf um die Mehrheit—Kombinationen über Strasser als Vizekanzler," *B.T.* (A.A.), 14 Jan. 1933.

255. On January 10 Hitler broke off all further negotiations with Papen until after the election in Lippe-Detmold. Similarly, he instructed Göring to delay a meeting of the Reichstag until the vote was in. See Ribbentrop, *Zwischen,* p. 38; and *B.T.* (A.A.), 11 Jan. 1933.

256. Goebbels, *Vom Kaiserhof,* entry for 10 Jan. 1933, p. 238.

lost élan; top party leaders addressed village rallies. The gamble worked: the NSDAP won, not as impressively as in the July 1932 elections, but sufficiently to evoke the impression that the party was moving forward again.[257]

One day later (on January 16) Hitler addressed what was to be the last Gauleiter conference before the seizure of power and, in a sense, the last significant event of the party's organizational history before 1933 as well. Hitler spoke for three hours about Strasser. Secure and confident after the election in Lippe, he deeply moved the Gauleiters with a detailed account of Strasser's life-long treason against Hitler. "Delirious ovations *(rasende Ovationen)*" followed his remarks. For these agents of the Hitler myth Strasser ceased to be a case; the man who more than anyone besides Hitler had been responsible for the organizational strength of the party became a political nonentity. The NSDAP's functionary corps had no part in the two-week long backstage intrigues that brought Hitler to power on January 30, except that its blind devotion to Hitler obviously gave Hitler an impressive aura of strength that was not without effect on his negotiating partners.[258] Ironically, even on the eve of the Nazi take-over, the Strasser plan proved its effectiveness. On the morning of January 30 it proved unnecessary to alert SA units to assure Hitler's installation as chancellor because a pro-NSDAP Berlin police major had already drawn friendly police forces together and sealed off the Wilhelmstrasse quarter.[259]

257. Goebbels' *Angriff* editorial of 20 Jan. 1933 in *Wetterleuchten,* p. 359. See also *VB,* 16 Jan. 1933.

258. Thus it was Papen, not Hitler, who attempted to convince Düsterberg that a new government under Hitler was an "imperative *(zwingende)* necessity." See Düsterberg, *Stahlhelm,* p. 38. On the final negotiations and intrigues, see Bracher, *Auflösung,* pp. 708 ff.; Vogelsang, *Reichswehr,* pp. 389 ff.; Kunrat von Hammerstein, "Schleicher, Hammerstein und die Machtübernahme 1933," *Frankfurter Hefte,* XI (Jan. 1956), 165–66; and the relevant entries of Goebbels' *Vom Kaiserhof.*

259. Vogelsang, *Reichswehr,* p. 396.

*Conclusion**

The scene on the fateful morning of January 30 was not without irony; much of it was very reminiscent of the turbulent days in November 1923. Hitler had again entered into a partnership with the far-right conservatives. To be sure, his partners were no longer old-line Bavarian aristocrats, but the political views of Papen and Blomberg were not far different from those of Lossow and von Kahr. And yet the ten intervening years had created a profoundly different political situation: the power relationship of the two sides was literally reversed. In 1923 Hitler and the NSDAP had been content with a role as junior associate in the far-right conspiracy; ten years later Hitler imposed his personal will on the timid and powerless conservatives.[1] Thus it was only fitting that Hitler almost contemptuously left his new governmental colleagues shortly after the oath-taking ceremony to return to the Kaiserhof. He spent the remainder of the day not as Reich chancellor in cabinet sessions with his ministers, but as Führer of the NSDAP. He conferred with the party's leadership corps in the afternoon, and in the evening reviewed the seemingly endless parade of triumphant SA and SS units. January 30 was a triumphant day both for Hitler and for the party organization.

Adolf Hitler liked to boast that he "learned" very little after he

---

*Portions of this chapter have been given previously as a paper under the title "The System of Administration and Organization in the NSDAP" at the meeting of the Southern Historical Association in November 1967.

1. A good description of the last-minute maneuvers before Hitler took office is in Karl-Dietrich Bracher, *Die Auflösung der Weimarer Republik* (3d ed.; Villingen, Schwarzw., 1955), pp. 726 ff.

reached young adulthood; his life's philosophy was rigidly set by this time. This was undoubtedly true — to a large extent — of his basic political beliefs. Thus Hitler clearly engaged in the totalizing and reflexive myth when he entered political life in 1919, and he never wavered in this belief until his death. On the other hand, his views on political organization and strategy underwent profound changes in the years covered in this study. To be sure, the foundations of his later career as an effective organizer are recognizable even in 1919. Unlike most of his contemporaries on the far-right in Germany, he recognized quite early in his career that the relationship of propaganda and organization in a totalitarian party had to be sequential rather than parallel for maximum effectiveness. Propaganda and organization for Hitler were always successive steps of a spiral which progressively disengaged a politically articulate German from the pluralist values of the Weimar Republic and reengaged him in the values of the myth. Both propaganda and organization in a political party had rather specific, separate aims. The party's propaganda efforts were designed to complete the process of political disengagement and reengagement to the point at which the listener or reader of Nazi propaganda would be willing to fill out a party membership application. Once he became a member, his life was divided by the organizational setup of the party into a dual role: on the one hand he actively propagandized the NSDAP among those not yet won over; on the other hand, he had a passive function which consisted of becoming an obedient and reliable subordinate to the party's leadership.[2]

Hitler's views on the relationship of propaganda and organization in political life did not change after the unsuccessful putsch, but his relationship to the totalizing and reflexive myth did. After the putsch, Hitler consciously inserted his own person as the positive set factor in the myth. While he had previously regarded himself as part of the positive set factor, he now personalized the myth and created an image of himself in which he was both living person and historical force or set factor. The cornerstone of the party's propaganda and its organiza-

---

2. Hitler explained the relationship of propaganda and organization in *Mein Kampf* (Munich, 1938), p. 654. For a full discussion of the relationship, see also Hannah Arendt, *The Origins of Totalitarianism* (Cleveland, O., 1958), pp. 361 and 364.

tional principles after the putsch was Hitler's view of himself as a superhuman force, an agency of history destined to resurrect Germany's national greatness.[3] Those who followed him and subordinated themselves to his direction became derivative agents; his opponents became instruments of evil who were attempting to thwart the will of history. In this absolute dichotomy there was room for neither equivocacy, relativity, nor compromise. It was even impossible to be apolitical: Hitler recognized no apolitical human actions, and he had only contempt for those who sought to keep politics out of certain spheres of human activity. This in turn made him literally omnipotent, since he publicly proclaimed the infallibility of his political judgments.[4] For Hitler, all politically articulate Germans had no choice but eventually to subordinate themselves completely to him or to pursue a course of equally fanatic opposition. At a more programmatic level, Hitler also decided after the putsch to gain governmental power in Germany primarily with political rather than military means.

The effectiveness of Hitler's new propaganda image and his organizational and administrative authority clearly depended upon acceptance by the NSDAP's membership and particularly the functionary corps of the identity of Hitler, the flesh-and-blood person, and Hitler, the superhuman historical force. For most party members the recognition of this identity was a two-step rather than a simultaneous process. Their internalization of Hitler began with the formation of a personal relationship first to the flesh-and-blood Hitler, and the party's leader was well aware of this.[5] His foremost task in 1925, in fact, was to transfer his personal martyr image and prestige into institutional, permanent controls of the party organization. Hitler returned from prison at Landsberg as a personal hero of virtually all elements on the

3. Although Hitler's self-concept was unusually extensive, the idea of being a historical force was common to other totalitarian leaders as well. See Alex Inkeles, "The Totalitarian Society," in Carl J. Friedrich, ed., *Totalitarianism* (New York, 1964), pp. 88 ff.

4. Hitler to Artur Dinter, 25 July 1928, in Dinter, "Der Kampf um die Vollendung der Reformation—Mein Ausschluss aus der Nationalsozialistischen Deutschen Arbeiterpartei," *Geistchristentum*, I (Sept.–Oct., 1928), 353–56.

5. Even in well-functioning pluralist societies, the notion of personal fealty is an important unifying element in highly authoritarian and bureaucratized structures. See Morris Janowitz, *The Professional Soldier* (New York, 1960), p. 220.

far right, but this type of popularity was not far different from that of a free corps leader like Ehrhardt, or even a political failure like Ludendorff. Hitler wanted more than this; he demanded that those who joined the party, and even more so the members of the functionary corps, accept his person not only as personal leader, but also as program (or propaganda content), and as normative principle for the party's organizational and administrative activities.

Since the personal allegiance of the functionary corps to Hitler was the strongest bond between leader and subordinates in the party, it would appear that bureaucratizing or depersonalizing this relationship could only be done at the expense of weakening the personal bonds between Hitler and his administrative staff. Such was not the case. Hitler successfully bureaucratized the party organization by convincing his functionary corps that their own successful role as his derivative agents depended upon their ability to internalize the concept that obedience to the dry, unpopular executives with whom Hitler staffed central party headquarters was an integral part of service to Hitler the person. As a result of this identification, the personal relationship of leader and follower could be transformed into a highly bureaucratic organization with a strict centralization and hiearchy, and a very rigid flow of authority. This also explains why the success of a political subleader in the NSDAP was measured not only by such conventional standards as voting and membership statistics in the official's district, but also by applying other tests such as his willingness to depersonalize his relationship to Hitler by following to the letter all directives issued by the Munich executives.

Hitler had in fact squared the circle. As a later draft of *Rules of Procedure (Dienstanweisung)* noted: "[in the NSDAP] the relationship of leader and follower *(Gefolgschaftsverhältnis)* [may] replace and/or amend the usual administrative relationship of superior and subordinate."[6] The conditional words "may" and "and/or" were a definite part of the NSDAP's administrative and organizational system. Hitler reserved to himself the right to intervene in person in any depersonalized procedure at any time he chose. In practice the extent

6. NSDAP, Reichsorganisationsleiter (Fritz Mehnert, Paul Müller), "Geschäftsordnung der NSDAP" (typescript) (Munich, 1940?), p. 95. Although written during World War II, the authors refer to conditions in the Kampfzeit.

of bureaucratic authority in the party was very uncertain. On the one hand, Hitler would hide his personal will behind a shield of institutional subordinates, yet he retained the option of breaking through the shield and interfering personally in the administration of the party whenever he chose. Neither action was a deviation from the norm, since in accepting his appointment the Nazi organizer or bureaucrat also acknowledged the identity of Hitler's roles as person and principle.

Despite lofty allusions to historical models — the Germanic war lord and his retainers were a favorite — there is no doubt that Hitler demanded more total, absolute, and complete control of every facet of human activity from his functionary corps than had any political leader before him. His subordinates had to give up all personal autonomy and accept whatever derivative authority Hitler accorded them — at any specific instant. Clearly, very few politically articulate adults were prepared to become "will-less" to such an extent, and even this small group accepted the full extent of Hitler's self-definition only on the installment plan.

To be sure, Hitler's original group of subleaders in 1925 — most of whom continued to serve him throughout the Kampfzeit—were psychosocially predisposed to be followers of a strong personality. By and large, the members of the functionary corps in the years 1925 to 1930 were not political opportunists, but a group of men who could be collectively described as failures: academic proletarians, like Goebbels; unhappy lower echelon civil servants and teachers, like Streicher or Klagges; lower level white-collar workers who aspired both to dominate and to be dominated, like Lohse; and retired professional soldiers who were adrift in the civilian world, like Buch and Loeper. For these types the party with its uniforms and titles, its strictly hierarchical organization presented an artificial society which was a pleasing alternative to the relatively unstructured pluralist German society. Nevertheless, even this group was not prepared for the full extent of Hitler's self-definition. Throughout 1925 they accepted only begrudgingly the increasing depersonalization of the relationship between subleaders and central party headquarters, and, above all, they did not yet comprehend that Hitler defined himself as the party's sole program and organizational principle. The result was the famous meeting at Bamberg, at which Hitler confronted his subleaders with the painful choice of either accepting the totality of the Hitler claim or giving up their status as derivative agents, losing their personal relationship to Hitler, and in fact becoming by definition a part of the negative set factor. Confronted with this prospect, all of the major subleaders accepted the totality of Hitler's claim.

The Bamberg meeting both secured Hitler's unquestioned control over all aspects of the party's organization and propaganda activities and inaugurated a period of political impotence and organizational experimentation in the party. The NSDAP's functionary corps had fully accepted the positive content of Hitler's role, so that the lack of political power was not a serious liability for Hitler's internal control of the party's organizational activities. On the contrary, there was even a tendency — particularly among the lower-level functionaries — to use the NSDAP's political impotence to enhance the atmosphere of ingrained clubbiness, an atmosphere which at times left party activities virtually indistinguishable from the activities of other pseudo-political clubs.

There was no doubt, however, about the loyalty and flexibility of the functionary corps in these lean years. As Hitler intended, the organizational basis for the party's meteoric rise after 1930 was laid during these years.[7] Thus Hitler endorsed the urban plan in the period 1926 to 1928. This strategy focused the party's organizational and propagandistic activities in the populous urban areas of Germany. Its aim was to capture mass support in these economically vital areas so that Hitler, like Mussolini, could command governmental power by threatening to paralyze Germany's economic lifelines. The plan was a failure since the urban masses were unwilling to desert the SPD or KPD. Toward the end of 1927 Hitler decided that history demanded the institution of the rural-nationalist plan. This meant a de-emphasis on urban organizational activities and a corresponding drive to establish a Nazi local in every German village. The functionary corps made an "about-face," and it is a remarkable testimony to Hitler's authority in the NSDAP that much of the initial work under the rural plan was carried out with urban-oriented personnel.

7. Adolf Hitler to . . . , 2 Feb. 1930, in Fritz Dickmann, ed., "Die Regierungsbildung als Modell der Machtergreifung," *Vierteljahrshefte für Zeitgeschichte,* XIV (Oct. 1966), p. 463.

The functionary corps' acceptance of Hitler's self-definition enabled the party to weather the various changes in organizational priorities with neither major ideological debates nor administrative chaos, and by September 1930 a set of well-defined organizational principles had been established for the party: the party aimed at organizational saturation of all geographic areas of Germany, but concentrated on the urban and rural middle classes; the Führerprinzip governed the internal flow of authority; and above all the absolute authority of Hitler was unquestioned. These principles proved equal to the challenges that confronted the party after its spectacular victory in September 1930. The problem now was not to attract mass support, but to develop means of politicizing and integrating the large number of sympathizers who cast their ballots for the NSDAP. Hitler did so by creating new derivative agents. The leaders of the various economic and social interest group affiliates — from the Hitler Youth to the National Socialist Association of Munich Coal Dealers — enjoyed a personal and institutional relationship to Hitler which was essentially the same as that previously bestowed on the Gauleiters and Reichsleitung executives. The old guard resented the influx of the Septemberlinge, but having already accepted Hitler's self-definition, they not only remained in the party, but acquiesced in the reduction of their status. As a result, the rapid expansion of the party, far from diluting the authority of Hitler, in fact expanded his status so that he was personal leader and program and bureaucratic head for the administrative staff of the party's interest group affiliates as well.

To be sure, even these years were not without their crises. The Bamberg meeting forced the functionary corps to acknowledge the entirety of Hitler's political claim, but it did not completely settle the relationship between Hitler and the party's paramilitary wing, the SA. Before the putsch Hitler's claim of infallibility had not extended to military matters, and the post-1925 storm troopers' organization preserved much of this autonomous *esprit de corps*. By the end of 1930 the strategic concepts of Hitler and the SA leadership had grown far apart. Significant elements of the SA still proclaimed the need for revolution and paramilitary violence, while Hitler wanted to demote the SA to the status of poster squads and rally ushers. In September 1930, Franz von Pfeffer, the head of the storm troopers, resigned over these differences, and in the following spring the SA leadership in Berlin and eastern

Germany revolted against Hitler by publicly proclaiming that Hitler and National Socialism were not identical concepts. Hitler's reaction was swift, effective, and very realistic. He stripped the controversy of all ideological and institutional implications and defined it solely as a question of personal loyalty to himself. Those who revolted became a part of the negative set factor;[8] those who remained loyal were rewarded by Hitler's proclamation that henceforth he would lead the SA in person. In effect, Hitler extended the organizational principles established at Bamberg to the SA, and thereby enlarged again the definition of his role as myth-person in the NSDAP.

The Stennes crisis did not threaten the organizational cohesion of the party any more than the National Socialist Working Association had in 1925. Hitler's self-definition and the organizational principles that derived from it structured and ingested the thousands of Germans who flocked to the party after the effects of the depression became visible. By mid-1932 the organizational accomplishments of the NSDAP were impressive. The party which had been a laughable fringe group three years before had now effectively politicized (in the Hitlerian sense) perhaps one fifth of Germany's politically articulate population. Moreover, this rapid growth had been accomplished without sacrificing either the radicalism or the centralization of the party. The NSDAP remained a unitary political organization, all of whose internal and external decisions were ultimately made by one man. The interest-group affiliates were additional supports for the authority of the party leadership, not undermining influences as they tended to be in other mass parties, notably the SPD. In addition, the NSDAP, as a result of the special relationship of the organizational apparatus to Hitler, had successfully eluded the dilemma of oligarchy which beset other mass parties, again notably the SPD.

Nevertheless, despite the party's evident political power, the summer of 1932 also revealed the major limitation of the effectiveness of Hitler's organizational system. Some of the various affiliates clearly

---

8. In 1932, Stennes sued Hitler and other party officials for libel after the *Angriff* had printed a story charging Stennes with operating as a police spy in the NSDAP. During the trial Hitler testified that "I could only come to the conclusion that if anyone opposed me or my movement, he must have been a paid agent." See "Der Prozess Hitler–Stennes," *Bayerischer Kurier*, 18 Jan. 1932.

represented mutually antagonistic economic and social interests, and a disintegration into warring factions was prevented only as long as the members and particularly the functionaries continued in their belief that their parochial material and psychological goals could be fulfilled only after Hitler and the NSDAP had achieved political power. This in turn was interrelated with a time factor; that is, the likelihood of the party's rise to power had to be demonstrable. The year 1932, despite the statistical voting triumphs of the NSDAP, really brought a series of sharp setbacks: in four national elections the NSDAP's attempt to win political power through the ballot box was rebuffed four times. There was a real danger, as Goebbels recognized, that the party would "win itself to death."[9]

At the end of the year the NSDAP had reached a political impasse and indeed stood on the verge of disintegration. Hitler met this third and potentially most serious crisis in the history of the NSDAP by once again extending the powers of the myth-person in the NSDAP. At this time Hitler included in the definition of his historical role the right to destroy both the party and National Socialism as a set of political goals, rather than compromise even temporarily his demand for full governmental power.[10] Gregor Strasser refused to accept the definitional extension and resigned his position. Hitler reacted as he had a year earlier. He announced his personal take-over of the functionary corps and appealed for the personal loyalty of the administrative apparatus. In addition, though it was personally painful for him, he defined his longtime close associate, Gregor Strasser, as an agent of the negative set factor. The device worked again. Though several of the Gauleiters and Reichsleitung executives agreed with Strasser's analysis of the party's political situation, no other major functionary could bring himself to cut the ties of personal loyalty to Hitler. The party remained intact.

Although this last crisis occurred barely two months before Hitler became chancellor of Germany, it is incorrect to say that a causal rela-

9. Joseph Goebbels, *Vom Kaiserhof zur Reichskanzlei* (Munich, 1934), entry for 23 April 1932, p. 87.

10. For an interesting discussion of the proximity, in psychoanalytical terms, of Hitler's desires to build and to destroy, see Erik Ericson, *Young Man Luther* (New York, 1962), pp. 107–09.

tionship existed between each of Hitler's new claims to authority and the party's rise to political power. On the contrary, the experiences of 1932 showed that the very effectiveness of Hitler's organizational principles could become the party's political Achilles' heel. The rigidity of the flow of authority and the very stature of infallibility which had been material assets in maintaining the unity of the NSDAP in the period of rapid expansion, now limited, indeed abolished, Hitler's political mobility. Hitler's authority completely preserved organizational flexibility within the party, but it severely limited his options for maneuver in dealing with political groups outside the party. To be specific, despite the severe setbacks which the NSDAP suffered in election after election toward the end of the year, Hitler categorically refused to accept Strasser's advice to enter the party in a coalition government with the Center Party. And from his own point of view Hitler was quite correct: the inherent logic of his self-definition, upon which his authority within the party rested, precluded compromises. Hitler either fulfilled historical destiny, or he had misread the laws of history. The latter case was of course unthinkable — both for him and for his derivative agents.

Since political realities have a way of thwarting those who read the laws of history, the NSDAP at the end of 1932 was well on its way to the rubbish pile of history. Its demise was delayed, but that was principally the work of Papen and the German conservatives. A more balanced judgment on the political effectiveness of Hitler's organizational principles must indicate that by the end of 1932 they had become counterproductive. Hitler's principles enabled the party to hold together an extremely dedicated functionary corps in a climate unfavorable to the growth of totalitarian movements from 1925 to 1930 and they permitted the NSDAP to grow rapidly in size without a corresponding dilution of the center's authority after 1930, thus building a massive bloc of political power in a relatively short time. On the other hand, the system also trapped Hitler since he could not risk his internal party position by separating himself from the myth. In short, the NSDAP's organizational system could build a strong party consisting of very disparate elements, but it would have become increasingly less effective in keeping them together if governmental power and positions had continued to elude the party.

ABBREVIATIONS USED IN NOTES
GLOSSARY OF ORGANIZATIONS
BIBLIOGRAPHIC NOTE
INDEX

Abbreviations Used in Notes

A.A.	Abendausgabe
BA	Bundesarchiv
BAStA	Bayerisches Allgemeines Staatsarchiv
BDC	Berlin Document Center
BGStA	Bayerisches Geheimes Staatsarchiv
B.T.	*Berliner Tageblatt*
Bzl.	Bezirksleitung
Forschst. NS Hbg.	Forschungsstelle für die Geschichte des National-sozialismus in Hamburg
F.Z.	*Frankfurter Zeitung*
GL	Gauleitung
GPL	Gaupropagandaleitung
HA	Hauptarchiv der NSDAP
IfZ.	Institut für Zeitgeschichte, Munich
IMT	International Military Tribunal, *Trial of Major War Criminals* (Nuremberg, 1947–49)
KL	Kreisleitung
LGF	Landwirtschaftlicher Gaufachberater
M.A.	Morgenausgabe
NA	National Archives
Ogrl.	Ortsgruppenleitung
Okdo	Oberkommando
OPG	Oberstes Parteigericht
PD Mü	Polizeidirektion München
PD-Nü-Fü	Polizeidirektion Nürnberg-Fürth
PKC	Parteikanzlei Correspondenz
PND	Politischer Nachrichtendienst; a reporting and surveillance activity of the Munich Police Department
Rdschr.	*Rundschreiben des Reichsschatzmeisters, 26. Juli 1926–31. Dez 1934*
RFS	Reichsführerschule
R.Ko.In.	Reichskommissar für die Überwachung der Öffentlichen Ordnung

RL   Reichsleitung
RPL   Reichspropagandaleitung
Schu. Slg.   Schumacher Sammlung
VB   *Völkischer Beobachter*
VOBl   *Verordnungsblatt der Reichsleitung der NSDAP*

Glossary of Organizations

Agrarpolitischer Apparat	a.A.	Office for Agriculture; the group of Nazi Party officials dealing with agricultural matters
Bund Deutscher Mädel	BDM	League of German Girls; party youth affiliate for girls aged 14–18
Büro der Abgeordneten		Office of the (Nazi) Deputies (of the Prussian state legislature); legitimate cover for the illegal activities of the party in Berlin during its period of dissolution (1927–28)
Center Party		The leading Catholic political party in Weimar Germany
Deutsche Arbeiterpartei	DAP	German Workers' Party; the original name of the Nazi Party.
Deutscher Frauenorden		Order of German Women; name of the NS Frauenbund before it became a party affiliate
Deutsches Jungvolk	DJV	German Young People; party youth affiliate for boys aged 10–14
Deutschnationaler Handlungsgehilfen Verband	DHV	Association of German Nationalist Office Employees; right-wing white-collar union; not a Nazi affiliate
Deutsch-Nationale Volkspartei	DNVP	German Nationalist People's Party; the leading conservative party in Weimar Germany
Deutsch-Sozialistische Partei	DSP	German Socialist Party; anti-semitic party active in the early 1920's, merged with NSDAP in 1923
Deutsche Volkspartei	DVP	German People's Party; a middle-of-the-Road party during the Weimar Republic
Deutschvölkische Freiheitspartei	DVFP	German Völkisch Freedom Party; anti-semitic splinter group of the DNVP active in northern Germany until about 1929

313

Frauenschaften		Women's auxiliary; name of the NS-Frauenbund after the reorganization of the affiliate in 1932
Frontbann		Front Union; the most important of the illegal organizations of the old SA members still active after the 1923 Putsch
Grossdeutsche Volksgemeinschaft	GDVG	Greater German People's Community; an organization of the southern remnants of the NSDAP during the interregnum, 1924–26
Hitler-Jugend	HJ	Hitler Youth; Nazi Party affiliate for boys aged 14–18
Hundertschaften		Centuries; action squads used by both SA (until 1923) and German police
Kampfbund		Militant Association; association of Bavarian far-right groups for the purpose of planning the 1923 Putsch
Kampfbund des gewerblichen Mittelstandes		Militant Association of Retailers; Nazi front organization whose main purpose was to organize retailers' resentment against the rise of chain stores
Kampfbund für Deutsche Kultur		Militant Association for German Culture; Nazi front organization to combat Jewish influences in German cultural life
Kommunistische Partei Deutschlands	KPD	Communist Party of Germany
Landbund		Farmers Association; the leading German farmers' interest group
Landtag		Legislature of each German state
Landvolk		Rural People; a radical protest movement active among the farmers of northern Germany in the late 1920's
Landwirtschaftlicher Gaufachberater	LGF	Gau expert on agriculture; the Gau level official of the a.A.
Nationalsozialistische Arbeitsgemeinschaft	NSAG	National Socialist Working Association; loose, ad-hoc group of northern German Gauleiters active in 1925–26
Nationalsozialistische Betriebszellenorganisation	NSBO	Organization of National Socialist Industrial Cells; industrial propaganda units and proto-union wing of the NSDAP

Nationalsozialistische Deutsche Arbeiterpartei	NSDAP	National Socialist German Workers' Party
Nationalsozialistischer Deutscher Arbeiterverein	NSDAV	National Socialist German Workers' Association; the legal name of the NSDAP
Nationalsozialistischer Deutscher Studentenbund	NSDStB	National Socialist Student Association; Nazi front organization for university students
NS Frauenbund		National Socialist Women's Order; women's auxiliary of the NSDAP
NS-Frauenschaften		*See* Frauenschaften
Nationalsozialistische Freiheitspartei	NSFP	National Socialist Freedom Party; tactical union of remnants of the NSDAP and the DVFP in northern German, 1924–26
NS-Hilfskasse		National Socialist Aid Fund; party-owned accident insurance scheme
NS-Schülerbund	NSSB	National Socialist Union of German Students; party affiliate for high school students
Nationalsozialistischer Volksbund	NSVB	National Socialist People's Association; short-lived anti-Hitler splinter group in the NSDAP active in Munich in 1925
Oberster SA-Führer	Osaf	Highest SA leader; designation of the commander-in-chief of the SA
Politischer Arbeiterzirkel		Workers' Political Society; Executive Committee of the Deutsche Arbeiterpartei
Politische Organisation	PO	Political Organization; general term for the NSDAP's party administration after the Strasser crisis of 1932
Politische Zentralkommission	PZK	Political Central Commission; intra-party commission established as part of the reorganization in December 1932
Reichsbanner Schwarz-Rot-Gold		Reich Banner Black-Red-Gold; pro-Republican paramilitary organization dominated by the SPD
Reichsbetriebszellenabteilung	RBA	Reich Department for Industrial Cells; the Reichsleitung office charged with administering the NSBO

Reichskuratorium für Jugendbildung		Reich Committee for Youth Education; unsuccessful attempt by the Papen government to alleviate the youth unemployment problem by a massive program of structured athletics
Reichsleitung		Reich leadership; top-level bureaucratic decision-making entity of the NSDAP
Reichspropaganda-Leitung	RPL	Reich Propaganda Leadership; the Reichsleitung office charged with administering the Nazi Party's propaganda effort
Reichstag		German national legislature
Reichswehr		German armed forces during the Weimar Republic
Rotfrontkämpferbund	RFB	Red Front Association; paramilitary group of the KPD
Schutzstaffeln	SS	Protection Squads; elite bodyguard formations of the NSDAP established in 1927
Schutz- und Trutzbund		Protective and Offensive Association; Bavarian rightist organization in the early 1920's
Sozialdemokratische Partei Deutschlands	SPD	Social Democratic Party of Germany
Stahlhelm		"Steel Helmet"; the largest and most influential of the German veterans' organizations in the Weimar Republic
Sturmabteilungen	SA	Storm troopers; paramilitary units of the NSDAP
Tannenbergbund		(Battle of) Tannenberg Association; rightist organization headed by General Ludendorff, active from 1924–27
Untersuchungs- und Schlichtungsausschuss	Uschla	Originally an intraparty arbitration committee within the NSDAP, later expanded into a full-fledged system of intraparty courts
Vereinigte Völkische Verbände	VVV	Union of Völkisch Organizations; Reich union of rightist associations in Weimar Germany

Völkische *Kampfgewerkschaften*	VKG	Militant Völkisch Labor Unions; scheme for creating nationalist labor unions advocated primarily by Arno Chwatal
Völkischer Führerring *Thüringen*	VFTh	Völkisch Leadership Ring of Thuringia; ad-hoc group of far-right leaders (including Nazis) formed for the purpose of coordinating the campaigns of the far-right groups in the Thuringian state elections of 1927
Wehrverbände		General term for the various paramilitary groups active in the Weimar Republic
Wehrwolf		One of the more important non-Nazi paramilitary groups on the far right

Bibliographic Note

I. LITERATURE ON THE THEORY OF TOTALITARIANISM
   AND BIBLIOGRAPHIC AIDS

Every book on the Nazi Party reflects the author's general view of the nature of modern politics in general and totalitarianism's place within the structure of contemporary politics. The best treatment of modern politics is still Seymour Lipset's well-known *Political Man* (New York, 1960). Jacques Ellul, *The Technological Society*, tr. John Wilkinson (New York, 1964), is a curiously neglected book which makes some profound observations about the influence of technology on modern societal life. By far the most useful overall analysis of European political parties is Maurice Duverger, *Political Parties*, tr. Barbara and Robert North (New York, 1954). The best introduction to the concepts of totalitarianism itself — both left and right — is the composite volume edited by Carl J. Friedrich, *Totalitarianism* (Cambridge, Mass., 1954). Among the voluminous theoretical literature on fascist or rightist totalitarianism, Hannah Arendt, *The Origins of Totalitarianism* (Cleveland, 1958) is the most satisfactory treatment. Ernst Nolte, *Der Faschismus in seiner Epoche* (Munich, 1963); English edition, *The Three Faces of Fascism*, New York, 1966) suffers from an overemphasis on the intellectual and philosophical bases of the fascist mindset. The massive work by Carl J. Friedrich and Zbigniew K. Brzezinski, *Totalitarian Dictatorship and Autocracy* (2d ed.; Cambridge, Mass., 1965), is the most careful analysis of the structural characteristics of a totalitarian state or movement. Zevedei Barbu, *Democracy and Dictatorship* (New York, 1956); Joachim C. Fest, *Das Gesicht des Dritten Reiches* (Munich, 1964); and Hans Buchheim, *Totale Herrschaft — Wesen und Merkmale* (Munich, 1962; English edition, *Totalitarian Rule*, tr. Ruth Hein, Middletown, Conn., 1968) are interesting treatments particularly of the mass psychological motivations of totalitarian movements. Finally, Sigmund Neumann, *Permament Revolution* (New York, 1942) and C. W. Casinelli, "The Totalitarian Party," *Journal of Politics*, XXIV (Feb. 1962), 111–41, while interesting as angry *tours de force*, assign rather too much influence to the leader-figure in totalitarian movements.

319

The best compendium of Nazi publications continues to be Otto Neuberger, *Official Publications of Present-Day Germany* (Washington, 1942). (It lists pre-1933 material as well.) Erich Unger, *Das Schrifttum des Nationalsozialismus von 1919 bis zum 11. Januar 1934* (Berlin, 1934) is a well organized (by subject), though obviously censored, listing of Nazi publications that had appeared up to 1934. The best compendium of Nazi newspapers is the first volume (the only one published) of *Die statistische und geschichtliche Entwicklung der NS-Presse, 1926–1935* (Munich, 1936). The most useful postwar bibliographic aids on all aspects of Nazism are the various specialized catalogs that have been and continue to be published by the Wiener Library (now the Institute for Contemporary History) in London.

II. Unpublished Sources

The bulk of this book is based upon the *NSDAP-Hauptarchiv* collection of unpublished documents. This record group, a miscellaneous compendium of party, police, and private manuscripts assembled by the Nazi Party's historical section, has been microfilmed by the Hoover Institution at Stanford University on 141 reels of microfilm. A descriptive index to the collection, *A Guide to the NSDAP Hauptarchiv* (Stanford, Calif., 1965), has been compiled and edited by Grete Heinz. In addition to the Hauptarchiv microfilms, the *Captured German Documents* collection at the National Archives in Washington, D. C., contains much useful material, particularly for the period before 1923. Guides to this large collection, published by the National Archives, are also available.

Among German archival sources, the Bayerisches Allgemeines Staatsarchiv (BAStA) and the Bayerisches Geheimes Staatsarchiv (BGStA), both in Munich, are the most fruitful. The Bavarian Ministry of Interior, whose files are in the BAStA, received copies of all reports issued by the Reichskommissar für die Überwachung der Öffentlichen Ordnung, and the BGStA has custody of the reports issued by the very well-informed political affairs branch of the police department in Nuremberg-Fürth. The files of the Berlin Document Center are less useful for this period than for the party's development after 1933, but a great deal of valuable information, particularly on the Gauleiters, is available in the alphabetical files, while some of the Uschla records of the era are a gold mine of information about intraparty intrigues. The well-organized and readily accessible collection of the Forschungsstelle für die Geschichte des Nationalsozialismus in Hamburg is particularly important for the NSAG's rise and fall, but other aspects of the history of the party in Hamburg and northern Germany are also reflected in these documents.

III. Published Sources: Official Party Documentary Collections, Chronicles, Statistical Handbooks, Speeches, and Memoirs

This period of German history is rich in official and unofficial compilations of political statistics and documents. National election returns can be followed in the official *Statistisches Jahrbuch des Deutschen Reiches* (Berlin, 1919–1933), which should be supplemented by the excellent graphic presentations in Heinrich Striefler, *Deutsche Wahlen in Bildern und Zahlen* (Düsseldorf, 1946). Biographical information on the Nazis who were members of the Reichstag (albeit supplied by the members themselves) is listed in the official *Reichstags-Handbuch,* edited by the Bureau des Reichstag (Berlin, new edition after each national election). A postwar analysis and summary is in Max Schwarz, ed., *MdR — Biographisches Handbuch der Reichstage* (Hanover, 1965). Ernst H. Posse, *Die politischen Kampfbünde Deutschlands* (2d ed., Berlin, 1931) is a useful guide to the murky subject of paramilitary groups on the far right.

There are two documentary collections on the history of the NSDAP. One, published during the Nazi era by the official party publishing house, is Adolf Dresler and Fritz Maier-Hauptmann, eds., *Dokumente zur Zeitgeschichte* (Die Sammlung Rehse, No. 1) (Munich, 1938). The collection is heavily censored, but does print some interesting documents from the early period of the party's history. Werner Jochmann, ed., *Nationalsozialismus und Revolution* (Frankfurt, 1963) is far more useful. It is an extremely well-edited selection of material from the holdings of the Forschungsstelle covering the years 1919–1933. It is particularly helpful in studying the development of the NSDAP in northern Germany, but is by no means limited to this geographic area.

The best handbook on the chronological development of the party is Hans Volz, ed., *Daten der Geschichte der NSDAP* (10th ed.; Berlin, 1938). (The work was republished frequently, bringing it constantly up to date.) For Berlin a similar guide is Johann K. von Engelbrechten and Hans Volz, eds., *Wir wandern durch das nationalsozialistische Berlin* (Munich, 1937), and, for the SA, Engelbrechten, *Eine braune Armee entsteht: Die Geschichte der Berlin-Brandenburger SA* (Munich, 1937).

The relatively insignificant Nazi party program is available in Alfred Rosenberg, ed., *Wesen, Grundsätze und Ziele der NSDAP* (Munich, 1930). This edition is particularly useful because it contains the new policy statement on agriculture. Far more significant are the various regulations on interoffice relationships within the party issued by central headquarters. For the party cadres themselves, they are the *Dienstanweisung für Ortsgruppen und Stützpunkte der NSDAP* (2 editions; Munich, 1931 and 1932), and, after the 1932 Strasser crisis, the *Dienstvorschrift für die P.O. der NSDAP* (Munich, 1932). The various horizontal divisions of the Reichsleitung also issued regulations for their spheres of power. Among these are the Uschla's, *Richtlinien für die Untersuchungs- und Schlichtungsausschüsse der Nationalsozialistischen Deutschen Arbeiterpartei* (Munich, 1929); the Reichsschatzmeister's *Rundschreiben des Reichsschatzmeisters 26. Juli 1926–31. Dez. 1934* (Munich, 1935); and the SA's *Verordnungsblatt der Obersten SA-Führung* (first published 20 April 1931) and *Führerbefehle des Obersten SA-Führers* (first published ,1 July 1932). An interesting early series of guidelines on propaganda is the Propaganda-Abteilung's, *Propaganda* (Munich, 1927 or early 1928). After the fall of 1930, regulations for all party divisions except the paramilitary units were combined in the serial publication *Verordnungsblatt der Reichsleitung der NSDAP.*

Among the official party publications intended for a wider audience, the yearly publication edited by Philip Bouhler, *Nationalsozialitisches Jahrbuch* (Munich, 1927–1933), is the most important source of organizational and biographical information about the party. The decision to utilize its parliamentary activities for propagandistic purposes is reflected in the publications of Wilhelm Frick, *Die Nationalsozialisten im Reichstag, 1924–1928* (Munich, 1928) and the serial *Mitteilungsblatt der Nationalsozialisten in den Parlamenten und gemeindlichen Vertretungskörpern,* which first appeared in 1928. Among the official reports of the party congresses during this time, the unpublished "Reichsdelegierten-Kongress im Deutschen Nationaltheater . . . 4. Juli 1926" (Hauptarchiv, roll 21, folder 389), and the published account, Alfred Rosenberg and Wilhelm Weiss, eds., *Der Reichsparteitag der Nationalsozialistischen Deutschen Arbeiterpartei, Nürnberg 19./21. August 1927* (Munich, 1927), are the most significant.

Any compilation of published collections of speeches and articles of various Nazi leaders must begin with the monumental labor of love edited by Max Domarus, *Hitler, Reden und Proklamationen, 1932–1945* (2 vols.; Munich, 1965). This magnificently edited collection surpasses all other compilations for the time period it covers. For the years before 1932, the best source of Hitler's speeches remains the *Völkischer Beobachter* (see below), and, for unpublished addresses, the police reports. (Norman H. Baynes, ed., *The Speeches of Adolf Hitler 1932–August 1939* (2 vols.; London, 1942) which has just been reprinted (1968) is a helpful, but not always reliable English translation of the early speeches). Joseph Goebbels' *Wetterleuchten — Aufsätze aus der Kampfzeit,* ed. Georg-Wilhelm Müller (Munich, 1939), is an interesting collection of editorials from the official Berlin party newspaper, *Angriff.* Gregor Strasser published some of his early speeches in *Freiheit und Brot* (2 vols. in 1; Berlin, 1928), and Walter Darré did the same in *Erkenntnisse und Werden — Aufsätze aus der Zeit vor der Machtergreifung,* ed. Marie-Adelheid Prinzessin Reuss-zur-Lippe (2d ed.; Goslar, 1940).

The memoirs and diary literature by both Nazis and anti-Nazis active in the Weimar Republic is vast. The book, or better booklet, which in a sense started the entire movement is *Mein politisches Erwachen* (Munich, 1920), by Anton Drexler. Fascinating both as a personal memoir and as a political program is Ernst Röhm, *Die Geschichte eines Hochverräters* (2d ed.; Munich, 1928). Hitler's own autobiography, *Mein Kampf* (first volume published in 1925, second in 1927, both in Munich), is, despite its numerous shortcomings, still an important source of information about both Hitler himself and the pre–1923 organizational development of the party. An excellent analysis of the changes which Hitler made for the various editions is H. Hammer, "Die deutschen Ausgaben von *Mein Kampf,*" *Vierteljahrshefte für Zeitgeschichte,* IV (April 1956), 171 ff.

The post war memoirs covering the entire period are a very uneven mixture. Hans Frank, *Im Angesicht des Galgens* (Munich, 1953) suffers from the author's own masochistic tendencies at the time of writing, although it is useful for numerous behind-the-scenes details of these early years. Karl Wahl, *Es ist das deutsche Herz — Erlebnisse und Erkenntnisse eines ehemaligen Gauleiters* (Augsburg, 1954), and Konstantin Hierl, *Im Dienst für Deutschland* (Heidelberg, 1954) are frankly apologetic and largely useless. Albert Speer's still unpublished account promises to be a refreshing change. There is a slight sampling of his views in "Die Bürde werde ich nicht mehr los," *Spiegel,* XX (7 Nov. 1966), 48–62.

Among those of Hitler's personal entourage, both Ernst Hanfstaengl, *Unheard Witness* (Philadelphia, 1957), and Heinrich Hoffman, *Hitler was my Friend,* tr. R. H. Stevens (London, 1955), are good examples of autobiographical Monday-morning-quarterbacking. Both are highly unreliable and must be used with extreme caution. This is also true of Kurt G. W. Lüdecke, *I Knew Hitler* (New York, 1938).

Hitler's political enemies, both within and outside the party, have left far more satisfactory accounts. Wilhelm Hoegner, *Der Schwierige Aussenseiter* (Munich, 1959) is the autobiography of the man who chaired the Bavarian legislature's investigation of the Hitler Putsch, and who remained in the political limelight through the Weimar period. In Prussia, Carl Severing maintained pluralism almost to the very end. He published an account of his struggle in *Mein Lebensweg* (2 vols.; Cologne, 1950). Theodor Düsterberg, *Der Stahlhelm und Hitler* (Wolfenbüttel, 1949) is a slim volume attempting to exonerate the Stahlhelm from the stigma of association with Hitler's rise to power, but it reveals more about the naivete of the rightist leaders than about their supposedly valiant struggle against totalitarianism. On the other hand, Albert Krebs, *Tendenzen und Gestalten der NSDAP* (Stuttgart, 1959), the memoirs of the former Gauleiter of Hamburg who broke with Hitler in 1932, is an indispensable source of shrewd observations about the party's internal workings and its leading figures.

IV. Published Sources: Newspapers and Periodicals

Research on the history of the Nazi Party is greatly aided by the very lively press coverage which party activities received, both in its own press and later in the leading dailies of Germany. The NSDAP's own central organ, the *Völkischer Beobachter* (*VB*) (during the interregnum the GDVG published a *Völkischer Kurier*), is obviously the primary source for the changing party line. It is by no means the only interesting Nazi paper. To be sure, most of the official Gau organs are tedious copies of the *VB*, but Goebbels' *Angriff* quickly developed both its own format and, to some extent, a distinct editorial policy. This is also true of the Strasser paper *Der Nationale Sozialist* (which for a time appeared in several provincial editions) and Krebs' *Hamburger Tageblatt*.

Among the periodical literature, *Auf gut deutsch,* edited by Dietrich Eckart, is a violently anti-semitic publication which appeared before the DAP was even founded, but which apparently had considerable influence on Hitler's thinking. The rather short-lived *Nationalsozialistische Briefe* are important for the intraparty conflicts of 1925–26. On the other hand, Rosenberg's *Nationalsozialistische Monatshefte* are boring examples of pseudointellectualism. Of the various specialized periodicals that began to appear after 1930, the HJ's *NS-Jugendpressedienst,* the NSBO's *Arbeitertum,* and the aA's *NS-Landpost* should be mentioned. The party began its own regular press service with the publication of the *NS-Partei-Korrespondenz* in January 1932.

Among the anti-Nazi dailies, the *Berliner Tageblatt* and the *Frankfurter Zeitung* provided by far the best day-to-day coverage of political developments. Their reporters on more than one occasion scooped both the Nazi Party and the Weimar government. The periodical *Tat,* with an editorial policy that advocated an authoritarian democracy of some sort, is noteworthy from about 1930 to 1933 because its editor, Hans Zehrer, had close connections with the Strasser wing of the Nazi Party. Arthur Dinter's *Geistchristentum,* an unimportant journal as such, is nevertheless useful for Dinter's account of his struggle with Hitler, and for the exchange of letters which he printed.

V. Published Sources: Secondary Accounts Covering
   the Entire Period

A large number of scholars and participants have attempted to sketch something of the climate of politics during the Weimar era. Ernst von Salomon, *Der Fragebogen* (Hamburg, 1961), remains one of the more successful of these, precisely because of its rather flippant tone. Another participant, Theodor Eschenburg, in his collection of essays, *Die im-*

provisierte Demokratie (Munich, 1958), accomplishes the same with less flair but considerably more scholarly detachment. Emil J. Gumbel, *Verräter verfallen der Feme* (Berlin, 1929) and Sigmund Neumann, *Die politischen Parteien in Deutschland* (Berlin, 1932; reprinted as *Die Parteien der Weimarer Republik*, Stuttgart, 1965) are both shrewd and, on the whole, accurate contemporary accounts.

The problem of German national bolshevism has fascinated a number of postwar authors. Armin Mohler, *Die konservative Revolution in Deutschland 1918–1932* (Stuttgart, 1950) is marred by its almost exclusive concern with intellectual trends, but Karl O. Paetel, *Versuchung oder Chance — Zur Geschichte des deutschen Nationalbolschevismus* (Göttingen, 1965), and, above all, Otto-Ernst Schüddekopf, *Linke Leute von rechts* (Stuttgart, 1960), are outstanding monographs on the ideological and political merging of the German extreme left and right.

As the Nazi Party gained increasing prominence, its opponents attempted both to combat and to understand the Nazi phenomenon. Much of this output did not extend beyond cheap polemics, but a number of works still make worthwhile reading. Ernst Niekisch, *Hitler — ein deutsches Verhängnis* (Berlin, 1931; reprinted in *Politische Schriften*, Cologne, 1965) retains its prophetic quality. The first of Konrad Heiden's several books on the Nazis, *Geschichte des Nationalsozialismus* (Berlin, 1932) overemphasizes the differences between Hitler and Strasser, but given its documentary limitations, it remains a valuable narrative of the party's history. Two contributions by the young Turk wing of the SPD, Walter Oehme and Kurt Caro, *Kommt "Das Dritte Reich"* (Berlin, 1930) and Carlo Mierendorff, "Gesicht und Charakter der national-socialistischen Bewegung," *Gesellschaft*, VII (June 1930), 489–504, together with Hans Gerth's well-known "The Nazi Party: Its Leadership and Composition," *American Journal of Sociology*, XLV (Jan. 1940), 517–41 are still good analyses of the socioeconomic components of the NSDAP.

There is no full-scale postwar treatment of the party, though Wolfgang Schäfer, *NSDAP* (Hanover, 1956) provides at least an organizational and statistical base for such a study. Joseph Nyomarkay, *Charisma and Factionalism in the Nazi Party* (Minneapolis, 1967), a study of intraparty revolts, is part of an effort to develop a theory of functional conflicts in charismatic parties.

Among the Nazi leaders only Hitler has fared well from his biographers. The best biography is obviously that of Alan Bullock, *Hitler — A Study in Tyranny* (New York, 1964), though it should now be supplemented for the early part of Hitler's life by the excellent *Adolf Hitler, His Family Childhood and Youth* (Stanford, Calif., 1967), by Bradley F. Smith. Walter Görlitz and Herbert A. Quint, *Adolf Hitler* (Stuttgart, 1952) despite some tantalizing details, suffers from the almost total absence of footnotes or scholarly apparatus. Helmut Heiber, *Adolf Hitler* (Berlin, 1960) is similarly intended primarily for the popular market.

Many of the specialized activities within the party's overall drive to power have also been analyzed. Eugen Hadamovsky, *Propaganda und nationale Macht* (Oldenburg, 1933) is of interest primarily because it candidly expresses Goebbels' point of view during the 1932 conflict over tactics. Ernest K. Bramsted, *Goebbels and National Socialist Propaganda* (Lansing, Mich., 1965) is rather superficial and appears to have been overhastily written. This is even more true of Hamilton T. Burden, *The Nuremburg Party Rallies: 1923–1939* (New York, 1967), which, in addition, abounds with factual errors. The development of the Nazi Party's press trust is the subject of Oron J. Hale's masterful book, *The Captive Press in the Third Reich* (Princeton, N.J., 1964). Arno Klönne's, *Hitlerjugend* (Hanover, 1956) is comparable to Schäfer's work on the NSDAP. The party's drive to capture the farmers' vote, especially in Schleswig-Holstein, is analyzed exhaustively in Rudolf Heberle, *Landbevölkerung und Nationalsozialismus* (German edition, Stuttgart, 1963; original edition, *From Democracy to Nazism,* Baton Rouge, La., 1945). Heinrich Bennecke, *Hitler und die SA* (Munich, 1962) is unfortunately too much of an apologia (the author was a high-ranking SA leader) to be entirely satisfactory.

VI. PUBLISHED SOURCES: LITERATURE ON SPECIFIC TIME PERIODS
OF THE NAZI PARTY'S DEVELOPMENT

Since in the formative period, the party's history can hardly be separated from that of the Bavarian right, the best accounts of the time span from 1919 to 1923 are really accounts of Bavarian politics as a whole. Among these Georg Franz, "Munich: Birthplace and Center of the National Socialist German Workers' Party," *Journal of Modern History,* XXIX (Dec. 1957), 319–34, should be read first. The Putsch itself has received a brilliantly integrated treatment from Hanns Hubert Hofmann, *Der Hitlerputsch* (Munich, 1961) and, within a somewhat narrower thematic framework, George W. F. Hallgarten, *Hitler, Reichswehr und Industrie* (Frankfurt, 1962).

On the Nazis themselves, the periodical literature is far more satisfactory than the full-scale treatments. Reginald H. Phelps, "Anton Drexler, der Gründer der NSDAP," *Deutsche Rundschau,* LXXXVII (Dec. 1961), 1134–43, and Ernst Nolte, "Eine frühe Quelle zu Hitlers Antisemitismus," *Historische Zeitschrift,* CXCII (June 1961), 584–606, concern Bavarian far-right politics before Hitler's emergence as an important leader, while Ernst Deuerlein, "Hitler's Eintritt in die Politik und die Reichswehr," *Vierteljahrshefte für Zeitgeschichte,* VII (April 1959), 177–227, and Werner Jochmann, ed., *Im Kampf um die Macht – Hitlers Rede vor dem Hamburger Nationalklub von 1919* (Frankfurt, 1960) provide documentation on Hitler's early appearances as a public speaker, the first in Bavaria, the second in Hamburg. The two book-length treatments of the early period that have appeared are both highly unsatisfactory. Georg Franz-Willing (the Georg Franz referred to above) *Die Hitlerbewegung — Bd. 1: Der Ursprung 1919– 1922* (Hamburg, 1962) (the second volume has not yet appeared) is a narrative of the party's development which accepts all too many of the NSDAP's self-created myths and, in addition, uses the available Hauptarchiv material only in a very casual and unsystematic manner. Gerhard Maser, *Die Frühgeschichte der NSDAP* (Frankfurt, 1965) is a good example of how not to write history. It is an account that is almost wholly obsessed with such insignificant items as the spelling errors in documents, etc. It should be used only in conjunction with the excellent review article by A. V. N. Van Woerden, "De jonge Hitler en de 'oude' NSDAP," *Tijdschrift voor Geschiedenes*, LXXIX (Dec. 1966), 439–45.

The interregnum period in the party's history (1924–1926) has recently received a great deal of scholarly interest, but a number of documents from that period are available as well. Of particular interest is Friedrich Plümer's passionately anti-Hitler pamphlet, *Die Wahrheit über Hitler und seinen Kreis* (Munich, 1925). It should be supplemented by the recent publication of Strasser's draft constitution in Reinhard Kühnl, "Zur Programmatik der nationalsozialistischen Linken: Das Strasser Programm 1925/26," *Vierteljahrshefte für Zeitgeschichte*, XIV (July 1966), 317–33. For the development of the northern faction and the resulting conflict, Joseph Goebbels' *Das Tagebuch von Joseph Goebbels*, ed. Helmut Heiber (Stuttgart, 1964; English translation, Oliver Watson, *The Early Goebbels Diaries 1925–26*, New York, 1962) is indispensable. So is Bradley F. Smith's unpublished M.A. thesis "Hitler and the Strasser Challenge" (Univ. of Calif., 1957). In addition, a series of articles explores the "Bamberg crisis" in considerable depth: Joseph L. Nyomarkay, "Factionalism in the National Socialist German Workers' Party, 1925–1926," *Political Science Quarterly*, LXXX (March 1965), 22–47, is an earlier version of a chapter in the author's monograph referred to above. Jeremy Noakes, "Conflict and Development in the NSDAP, 1924–1927," *Journal of Contemporary History*, I (Oct. 1966), 3–36, is a somewhat less theoretical account of the same subject.

For the years 1926–1928, the party's stormy and controversial activities in Berlin have received the most satisfactory treatment. Goebbels himself wrote a fascinating (and, on the whole, reliable) account in *Kampf um Berlin* (11th ed.; Munich, 1937), and the later mayor of Berlin, Julius Lippert, left *Im Strom der Zeit* (Berlin, 1942). Hans-Georg Rahm, *Der Angriff, 1927–1930* is a Nazi analysis of Goebbels' newspaper in Berlin. Above all, however, the Nazi mood of these early years in the Reich capital can be seen in Martin Broszat, ed., "Die Anfänge der Berliner NSDAP, 1926/27," *Vierteljahrshefte für Zeitgeschichte*, VIII (Jan. 1960), 85–118.

Dinter's side of that controversy is available in the form of three articles, all by Dinter, "Religion und Nationalsozialismus," "Der Kampf um die Vollendung der Reformation — Mein Ausschluss aus der Nationalsozialistischen Deutschen Arbeiterpartei," and "Stahlhelm, Hitlerpartei und sittlich-religiöse Erneuerung," in *Geistchristtum*, I (July–Aug. 1928), 273–84, I (Sept.–Oct. 1928), 352–86, and II (1929), 331–42 respectively.

The important at least in retrospect controversy over foreign affairs in the party is reflected in Alfred Rosenberg, *Der Zukunftsweg der deutschen Aussenpolitik* (Munich, 1927) and in Hitler's (at the time unpublished) manuscript on foreign affairs, which has now been published in well-edited form by Gerhard L. Weinberg, *Hitlers Zweites Buch* (Stuttgart, 1961). A scholarly analysis of the entire subject is in Günter Schubert, *Die Anfänge nationalsozialistischer Aussenpolitik* (Cologne, 1963).

The bitter controversy over the NSDAP's turn to the right in 1928–1930 is reflected in a number of contemporary accounts. Bodo Uhse, *Söldner und Soldat* (Paris, 1935) is, despite its fictional format, an important source for developments within the party in these years. So is Hans Fallada [Rudolf Ditzen], *Bauern, Bonzen und Bomben* (Berlin, 1931), though Fallada was a somewhat better novelist and less accurate historian than Uhse. Both need to be used in conjunction with Gerhard Stoltenberg, *Politische Strömungen im Schleswig-Holsteinischen Landvolk, 1918–1933* (Düsseldorf, 1962) and Heberle's *Landbevölkerung und Nationalsozialismus.*

The question of financial contributions to the Nazi Party by business and industrial interests was first raised by Fritz Thyssen, *I Paid Hitler*, tr. Cesar Saerchinger (New York, 1941) and his account has, on the whole, been verified by George W. F. Hallgarten. Louis P. Lochner, *Tycoons and Tyrants* (Chicago, 1954) is a passionate but not very convincing defense of the German industrialists.

The Nazi left remained surprisingly vociferous, although their political role was clearly played out. Erich Rosikat, *Die Lehren der Maiwahlen 1928* (Breslau, 1928), comes to different conclusions than Hitler did. Rolf Boelcke, "Die Spaltung der Nationalsozialisten," *Tat*, XXII (Aug. 1930), 357–67, saw the split in the party, but not the political impotence of the left. The most famous, and equally ineffective, rebel against Hitler in this period, Otto Strasser, left his account of the controversy in *Ministersessel oder Revolution* (Berlin, 1930; republished with additional material in *Aufbau des deutschen Sozialismus*, 2d ed.; Prague, 1936). Herbert Blank, writing under the pseudonym of Weigand von Miltenberg, wrote a stinging indictment of Hitler in *Adolf Hitler — Wilhelm III* (Berlin, 1931). Finally, the only remaining institutional hope of the left, the NSBO, was ably defended (even after 1933) in Gerhard Starcke, *NSBO und Deutsche Arbeitsfront* (Berlin, 1934).

The September 1930 elections clearly marked the visible beginning of the fall of the Weimar Republic. The decaying process has been analyzed well for both the national level and in various regional studies. Karl-Dietrich Bracher, *Die Auflösung der Weimarer Republik* (3d ed.; Villingen, Schwarzwald, 1961) is a monumental work of scholarship that encompasses virtually all aspects of the disintegration of pluralism in Germany. Hermann Pünder's diary, *Politik in der Reichskanzlei — Aufzeichnungen aus den Jahren 1929–1932*, ed. Thilo Vogelsang (Stuttgart, 1961) offers the dramatic day-by-day reflections of the period by the permanent secretary of the Reich chancellor. Waldemar Besson, *Württemberg und die deutsche Staatskrise, 1928–1933* (Stuttgart, 1959) and Ernst-August Roloff, *Bürgertum und Nationalsozialismus 1930–1933: Braunschweigs Weg ins Dritte Reich* (Hanover, 1961) are important monographs on the defeat of democracy in two of the German states. Fritz Dickmann, "Die Regierungsbildung in Thüringen als Modell der Machtergreifung," *Vierteljahrshefte für Zeitgeschichte*, XIV (Oct. 1966), 454–64, provides an important document dealing with Frick's appointment as prime minister in Thuringia. Finally, William S. Allen, *The Nazi Seizure of Power: The Experience of a Single German Town, 1930–1935* (Chicago, 1965) documents the struggle in a local case study.

The literature on the Nazi Party's own massive appeal to various pluralist interest groups after 1930 is also abundant. The drive to capture the Landbund is reflected in such official party publications as Johann Dorner, *Bauernstand und Nationalsozialismus* (Munich, 1930) and Friedrich Hildebrandt, *Nationalsozialismus und Landwirtschaft* (Munich, 1930). (These two pamphlets are also interesting because they reflect the differences of opinion among the aA's officials.) Eugen Schmahl and Wilhelm Seipel, *Entwicklung der völkischen Bewegung* (Giessen, 1933) reveals surprisingly frank memoirs of two party officials in Hessen. The best postwar analysis is the recent article by Horst Gies, "NSDAP und landwirtschaftliche Organisationen in der Endphase der Weimarer Republik," *Vierteljahrshefte für Zeitgeschichte*, XV (Oct. 1967), 341–76.

Relations between the party and industrial circles during this time have recently been subjected to an analysis from an East German Marxist point of view in Klaus Drobisch, "Flick und die Nazis," *Zeitschrift für Geschichtswissenschaft*, XIV (1966, No. 3), 378–97. The increasingly political role of the Reichswehr is carefully analyzed and documented in Thilo Vogelsang, *Reichswehr, Staat und NSDAP* (Stuttgart, 1962). The best analysis of the NSBO's development is Hans-Gerd Schumann, *Nationalsozialismus und Gewerkschaftsbewegung* (Hanover, 1958), though two of the pamphlets by the NSBO's organizational leader, Reinhard Muchow, *Nationalsozialismus und freie Gewerkschaften* (Munich, 1930) and *Organisation der Nationalsozialistischen Betriebszellen* (Munich, 1930), still make interesting reading. Hermann Bolm, *Hitler-Jugend in einem Jahrzent — ein Glaubensweg der niedersächsischen Jugend* (Brunswick, 1938), despite its Nazi orientation, is good on the rapid rise of the HJ as a device to attract middle class support after 1930.

The events of the year 1932 which marked both the triumph of the party and the whimpering fall of the Republic, gave rise to a number of self-praising accounts by leading Nazis. The most important by far is Goebbels' published diary, *Vom Kaiserhof zur Reichskanzlei* (Munich, 1934), which, despite its violent anti-Strasser bias, is still an important source of information on intraparty discussion and developments. Otto Dietrich, *Mit Hitler in die Macht* (Munich, 1934) is interesting as an example of a deliberate attempt to create an extreme personality cult around Hitler and should be used in connection with the same author's somewhat more somber analysis in *Zwölf Jahre mit Hitler* (Munich, 1955). There are no comparable accounts from the Strasser side. The two biographies that have appeared, Michael Geismaier (pseudonym), *Gregor Strasser* (Leipzig, 1933) and Hans Diebow, *Gregor Strasser und der Nationalsozialismus* (Berlin, 1932/ 33), are both popular accounts that make no real attempt to analyze Strasser's personality or his ideas. Strasser's ideological (or perhaps better, strategic) position is presented in two *Tat* articles, one which he supposedly wrote himself (the piece is unsigned), "Der Ultimo ist das Schicksal," *Tat,* XXIV (April 1932), 60–68, and a second authored by Hellmuth Elbrechter, a close associate of his, "Wider den Sozialismus in jeder Form?" *Tat,* XXIV (July 1932), 310–17.

The backstage intrigues that finally brought Hitler to power despite the party's losses at the polls have been the subject of much analytical and apologetic writing. On the civilian side, Heinrich Brüning, "Ein Brief," *Deutsche Rundschau,* LXX (July 1947), 1–22, and Otto Meissner, *Staatssekretär unter Ebert-Hindenburg-Hitler* (3d ed.; Hamburg, 1950), are revealing accounts by two participants who never really understood the nature and danger of modern totalitarianism. This attitude is still not entirely laid to rest. Heinrich Bennecke, "Alternativen der Not: Schleicher, Bürgerkrieg oder Hitler," *Politische Studien,* XIV (July–Aug. 1963), 444–64 resurrects the myth of the Communist danger. A refreshing change is Hans Schlange-Schöningen's *Am Tage danach* (Hamburg, 1946), which reveals him to have been a conservative politician of considerably greater ability than either Brüning or Papen.

The military side of the drama has been well documented in Vogelsang and in excerpts from the papers of two major participants, von Hammerstein and Groener: Kunrat von Hammerstein, "Schleicher, Hammerstein und die Machtübernahme 1933," *Frankfurter Hefte,* XI (Jan., Feb., and March 1956), 11–18, 117–28, and 163–76 respectively; and Reginald H. Phelps, ed., "Aus den Groener Dokumenten," *Deutsche Rundschau,* LXXVI (Nov. and Dec. 1950), 915–22, 1013–22, and LXXVII (Jan. 1951), 19–31 respectively.

On the final negotiations involving Hilter, Strasser, Schleicher, and Oskar von Hindenburg, Joachim von Ribbentrop's apologia *Zwischen London und Moskau,* ed. Annelies von Ribbentrop (Leoni am Starnberger See, 1954) provides some interesting technical details, as does *Die Machtergreifung* (Stuttgart, 1958), by Hans-Otto Meissner and Harry Wilde (the latter book is particularly good on the Strasser side of the negotiations), although Bracher's *Die Auflösung der Weimarer Republik* and the almost encyclopedic *Das Ende der Parteien,* ed. Erich Matthias and Rudolf Morsey (Düsseldorf, 1960) are by far the most complete and accurate accounts of the intrigues in their entirety.

Two major books appeared too late to be considered in the research for this volume. Hans-Adolf Jacobsen's monumental *Nationalsozialistische Aussenpolitik* (Frankfurt a. M., 1968) includes an excellent chapter on Nazi ideas on foreign policy before 1933, and Hans-Christian Brandenburg, *Die Geschichte der HJ* (Cologne, 1968) is a very readable, overall history of the Hitler Youth.

Index